Working with Families

An Integrative Model by Level of Need

FIFTH EDITION

Allie C. Kilpatrick

Emeritus, University of Georgia

Thomas P. Holland

University of Georgia

PEARSON

Boston   New York   San Francisco

Mexico City   Montreal   Toronto   London   Madrid   Munich   Paris

Hong Kong   Singapore   Tokyo   Cape Town   Sydney

Senior Series Editor: *Patricia Quinlin*
Series Editorial Assistant: *Carly Czech*
Senior Marketing Manager: *Wendy Albert*
Production Editor: *Won McIntosh*
Editorial-Production Service: *Omegatype Typography, Inc.*
Manufacturing Buyer: *Debbie Rossi*
Electronic Composition: *Omegatype Typography, Inc.*
Cover Administrator: *Kristina Mose-Libon*

For related titles and support materials, visit our online catalog at www.pearsonhighered.com.

Between the time website information is gathered and then published, it is not unusual for some sites to have closed. Also, the transcription of URLs can result in typographical errors. The publisher would appreciate notification where these errors occur so that they may be corrected in subsequent editions.

Library of Congress Cataloging-in-Publication Data

Working with families : an integrative model by level of need / [edited by] Allie C. Kilpatrick, Thomas P. Holland.—5th ed.
    p. ; cm.
  Includes bibliographical references and indexes.
  ISBN-13: 978-0-205-67392-6
  ISBN-10: 0-205-67392-9
  1. Family psychotherapy. 2. Family social work. I. Kilpatrick, Allie C. II. Holland, Thomas P.
[DNLM: 1. Family Therapy—methods. 2. Family Relations. 3. Needs Assessment.
4. Social Work. 5. Socioeconomic Factors. WM 430.5.F2 W9255 2009]

  RC488.5.K55 2009
  616.89'156—dc22

                         2008036655

Printed in the United States of America
10 9 8 7 6 5 4 3 2   HAM   12 11 10 09

The fifth edition of this book
is lovingly dedicated to all the
students and practitioners who
are working diligently toward the
development of healthy, resilient,
ethical, and spiritually connected
families internationally.

Contents

10 *Family Systems Theory*   *170*
Joseph Walsh

PART V • *Fourth Level of Family Need: Family and Personal Growth*   *197*

11 *Narrative Family Interventions*   *199*
Nancy R. Williams

12 *Object Relations Family Interventions   224*
Allie C. Kilpatrick and Elizabeth O. Trawick

Foreword

As both a family practitioner and an educator for over 40 years, I have been aware of the need to formulate a theoretical base for family practice that explains family dynamics and provides clear guidelines for effective interventions. In this book, the goal of bringing together family levels of need and practice models is accomplished in a manner that is both comprehensive and easy to grasp.

For me, the most valuable material in this book relates to the use of the practitioner's self in the helping process, which has been expanded in this fifth edition. Clearly, as in all helping endeavors, the person of the practitioner and the quality of the helping relationship are vital factors for facilitating change. Murray Bowen, in my opinion, accurately addresses the essence of family practice in his insistence that practitioners can progress with a family only as far as they have progressed in their own family relationships. Linking the maturity level of the practitioner to the overall conditions of the problem context captures a powerful dynamic in the helping process.

In this fifth edition of *Working with Families,* Kilpatrick and Holland outline ways to approach the diversity of family dynamics, family need levels and lifestyles, and the many commonalities shared by all human aggregates throughout the life cycle. Major additions to the fourth edition were an Instructor's Manual, which included PowerPoint presentations, relevant Internet resources, and an Ethical Challenges section in each practice chapter. This fifth edition builds on these foundations and amplifies them. In this text, the emphasis on diversity and difference has not obscured the common human needs, capacities, and coping styles of people. Chapters dealing with various strategies to meet different levels of need are written by national and international experts in the field. Two entirely new chapters have been written for this edition by outstanding expert contributors.

Some of the most cogent and thought-provoking parts of *Working with Families* are to be found in the constant emphasis on family strengths and coping capacities. While the authors assert that no single theory is adequate to deal with all family needs or styles, the theories presented here all contain a basic strategy that focuses on levels of need rather than on levels of pathology.

The expanded attention to the domains of family spirituality and professional ethics is especially relevant for the present period of rapid cultural change. The importance of the spiritual dimension cuts across all levels of family need. For many families, the spiritual dimension is crucial for their moral and behavioral guidelines. How can family practitioners understand family needs if they are unaware of the specific moral underpinnings for a particular family?

Family spiritual considerations and professional ethics form a critical part of the ecology of the treatment process for each family with whom we work, and all chapters have been revised and edited to reflect current thinking and practice in these areas. The attention *Working with Families* gives to spiritual and ethical considerations deserves careful reading.

Finally, this book directs attention to the specific needs of each specific family and to the specific interventions needed to address the uniqueness of the family. The content of this book provides the basis for reflective consideration of the meaning of the spiritual and ethical dimensions for family work.

D. Ray Bardill
Professor Emeritus, School of Social Work
Florida State University
Past President, American Association for Marriage and Family Therapy

Preface

Working with Families: An Integrative Model by Level of Need was written especially for use as a text for students in social work, marriage and family therapy, counseling, psychology, and human service courses. Faculties in over 100 colleges and universities nationally and internationally are using this text in both undergraduate and graduate courses. There was even a Korean translation in 2008. This book is especially geared toward applications with families that are usually seen in social service and family agencies, ones that students would typically be working with in their internships and practicum experiences. However, it also addresses family needs at higher levels. Practitioners in the various disciplines have also found it to be useful in their practices.

The purpose of *Working with Families* is to fill the need in social work and family therapy literature for an appropriately relevant textbook on family interventions, addressing the needs of families that students and practitioners typically see. Previous texts have focused on overviews of different models of family therapy, emphasizing primarily one model, one special population, or one problem group. Some have been geared toward middle-class, private-practice clients. Most have presented the therapist as the expert within a family systems context.

What is needed is an integrative model for practice, one based on an assessment of the level of need in the family and the particular problems clients are facing within a wider ecological context. Once this assessment has been done, then different interventions can be selected that are appropriate for that family's particular level of need at that time, around their specific problem area. Our goal was to meet the need for such a selective approach.

When students are given a broad overview of all the different models of working with families, they often come away from the course not knowing which specific approach to use in which particular situation. On the other hand, when only one model is taught, students are tempted to use that model with every family, even when it may not be suitable. When the focus is on a special population or problem group, students have difficulty generalizing appropriately to other populations or problem groups. Many family therapy texts are geared toward middle-class, walking-wounded, private-practice clients. These are *not* the families that students or practitioners typically see in agency settings.

This book presents an integrative model to help students and practitioners make the fit between therapeutic style and family need. An overall ecosystems–social constructionism metatheory serves as the philosophical and theoretical base for working with families on four levels of family need. Examples of specific approaches to intervention that would be relevant to use on each level of family need are given.

Revisions to the Fifth Edition

This fifth edition of *Working with Families* has been revised and updated to reflect current content and methods. The revisions include the following:

- *An Instructor's Manual.* This was a major addition to the fourth edition. The Instructor's Manual is an aid to instructors and to the learning experiences of students. This manual includes PowerPoint presentations for each chapter. They have been revised for this fifth edition.
- *Relevant Internet Resources.* These sections have been updated for each chapter and provide more resources for study.
- *An Ethical Challenges section.* This section, new to the fourth edition, was included for each method-of-practice chapter so that instructors and students would give special thought to this important area of practice. New material has been added in this edition.
- *New chapters and new authors.* Two entirely new chapters with new authors are included in this edition. Chapter 5, on meeting basic needs in Level 1 neglectful families, has been rewritten by an internationally known expert in this field whose major life research has been in the area of neglectful families. He gives effective practice guidelines for working with these families. The concluding Chapter 13, on the family in the community with ecosystem implications, has also been completely rewritten to reflect present-day circumstances. These two new chapters are excellent additions to this edition.
- *Current thinking and practice.* Each chapter has been revised and edited to reflect current thinking and practice.

An increased student and client interest in spirituality has led us to emphasize this area of sensitive practice in a specific chapter, as well as in the various chapters devoted to practice. This added emphasis reflects the current state of knowledge, interest, and attention surrounding this subject area. A framework for spiritual assessment is given, and many practice guidelines have been added.

More material on the ethical implications of varying and diverse spiritual beliefs and practices is also included in this edition. The concepts of resilience and family strengths are emphasized as the base on which to build. Ethically informed practice is a current issue. For this reason, we have again included Internet resources that contain the NASW, AAMFT, and Counselors' codes of ethics. The seven ethics cases with commentaries from experts in the field, along with references to specific standards of the code of ethics relevant to that particular case, remain in the appendix to the text. The glossary has been expanded to include terms used in the new chapters.

Organization of the Text

Part One of *Working with Families* covers the theory base and contextual and practice concerns that are useful with families at any level of need. Chapter 1, by Kilpatrick, presents a framework of the four levels of needs of families. This framework serves as a priority-setting guide that enables students and practitioners to determine which methods approach one would use with a specific family. As such, the chapter is a beginning assessment tool grounded in the therapeutic assumption that interventions must start addressing the level of the most basic need before moving on to higher levels of needs and interventions. In Chapter 2, the theory that undergirds this integrative approach is discussed by Holland and Kilpatrick. The metatheories of ecosystems and social constructionism form the philosophical and theoretical foundations for the needs of families and for the methods used to meet these needs as presented in this book.

In Chapter 3, Kilpatrick, Hopps, and Gray discuss the importance of the helping relationship/therapeutic alliance and the contexts of client diversities that must be addressed on any level of need. The focus on ethnic-sensitive practice, multiculturalism, and cultural competence gives a global perspective to students and practitioners and requires the practitioner to think in terms of a multisystem, interactive, international approach. Whether practiced in the United States or elsewhere, this perspective on diversity is crucial as the world becomes one community. A cultural assessment grid is presented, and client diversity in terms of gender, power, poverty, and family structures is discussed. Updated census data and statistics on poverty thresholds, implications for the poor, and differing family structures are included. Although the focus is on diversity issues, the emphasis is on commonalities that unite people, rather than on differences that divide them.

In Chapter 4, Kilpatrick, Holland, and Becvar provide suggestions for creating a practice that is well informed relative to ethical decision making and sensitive to the role of spirituality in the lives of both practitioners and clients. Guides for ethical decision making are presented, relevant codes of ethics are discussed, and Internet resources are given. The discussion on spirituality has been greatly enlarged and emphasized in this fifth edition. The introduction has been completely rewritten, and a new definition for spirituality has been provided. A Framework for Spiritual Assessment is also included, which students and practitioners should find very helpful. Specific examples of spiritually oriented helping activities that students and practitioners can use with their clients are also presented. New material on ethical challenges, especially under spirituality, is given.

Parts Two through Five focus on interventions that are appropriate for families on each of the four levels of family need. Each chapter includes examples of interventions that would be relevant, but they are not the only ones that could be used on that level. With a shift in emphasis, some of the approaches could be used at more than one level of family need. Each chapter discusses how a specific approach could be applied to families that have needs on levels other than the one focused on in that chapter.

Each chapter in Parts Two through Five follows a similar format, addressing and containing the following subjects and features:

- Needs presented by the family
- Assessment, especially determining the level of need of the family
- Goals of the intervention
- Intervention approach used, including the basic tenets of the approach, application to a family, and specific interventions
- Evaluation or how the interventions are evaluated for effectiveness
- Application to families on other levels of need

- Ethical challenges
- Summary
- Discussion questions
- Internet Resources
- Suggested Readings
- References

Page numbers indicating where each of these subjects can be found in each chapter are given in the Outline of Approaches on page xxvi.

In Part Two, the first level of family need, which deals with basic survival issues, is addressed. The chapters in this part present two approaches to family practice that are appropriate for families on the first level of need. Chapter 5, by Gaudin, presents an intervention approach with neglectful families, which is designed to address basic needs in high-risk families with children. In Chapter 6, Greene and Kropf present the case management approach, which is a process for assisting families who have multiple service needs.

The second level of family need is presented in Part Three. This level is concerned with structure, limits, and safety. In Chapter 7, Aponte, internationally known as one of the founders and developers of structural family therapy, presents this systems-based model, which places a special focus on the internal organization of relationships within families. In Chapter 8, Horne and Sayger present the social learning family interventions approach to families. This approach deals with both internal and external, or environmental, factors that affect family needs and focuses on learning more effective social skills.

Part Four deals with the third level of family need, concerned with boundaries and control. Both chapters in this part present approaches to intervention. In Chapter 9, Koob discusses solution-focused interventions, one of the brief intervention approaches that are appropriate for families at this level of need. The emphasis on health and strengths makes it an especially useful model for families at this level of need. In Chapter 10, Walsh presents family systems theory, a widely utilized approach to family assessment and intervention. It provides a comprehensive conceptual framework for understanding how emotional ties within families of origin influence the lives of individuals and also examines multigenerational family processes and interventions.

Part Five addresses interventions at the fourth level of family need: family and personal growth. This higher level of need is represented by a focus on inner richness and quality of life. In Chapter 11, Williams discusses narrative family interventions. This approach emphasizes the meaning that families make of their experiences instead of the cause of the problem. It makes use of a collaborative, co-learning therapeutic relationship. The second approach, presented in Chapter 12 by Kilpatrick and Trawick, is object relations family interventions (ORFI). ORFI is a bridge between working with individuals and working with families and is essentially interactional in its intervention processes. It gives primacy to the need for a human relationship, even at birth.

In Part Six, the final chapter looks at the larger issues of the family in the community context. Chapter 13, by Vonk and Yoo, discusses the ecosystem implications of working with families at the macrosystem level, thus integrating the previous intervention approaches with the theoretical and philosophical foundations presented earlier.

Acknowledgments

Our great appreciation goes to all the contributors to this fifth edition. They are experts in their fields, and we are grateful for the time and energy they have given.

The reviewers of the previous editions made some very valuable suggestions that made the book more relevant, readable, and user friendly. These suggestions and ideas were helpful and have been incorporated into later editions.

Dr. Ray Bardill kindly agreed to write the foreword for this fifth edition. Many thanks go to him for taking time out of his busy schedule and also for his many contributions and insights, as well as the inspiration he has provided the senior author of this book, Allie Kilpatrick, in working with families. He has been a role model in having the courage to write and speak about spirituality when it was not popular to do so.

Thanks are due to the reviewers of this fifth edition: Joseph Anderson, California State University at Sacramento; Carolyn A. Bradley, Monmouth University; and Deborah J. Holt, Jackson State University. We are also grateful to Patricia Quinlin and the editorial staff of Allyn & Bacon. They have been most supportive and cooperative even while gently pushing to get this new edition into production. Their contributions have been helpful, timely, and professional. Thank you!

Allie would like to pay special tribute to her extended familiy. The four living generations of my sisters, brother, and countless cousins inspire my study and appreciation of families. My parents and grandparents, and those ancestors who came before left our generation with a vital spiritual heritage that has sustained, nurtured, and challenged us. For this, I will be eternally grateful and will endeavor to pass this spiritual heritage on to our beloved children, grandchildren, and future generations that they may also be sustained, nurtured, and challenged.

Tom would like to pay special tribute to his extended family also. My parents and parents-in-law have been important models, and my daughter and grandsons are sources of hope for the future.

Our families have been very patient and loving during this process, and they have contributed in unique ways to our ideas about families. To Charles and Myra, we send heartfelt notes of love and appreciation.

About the Authors

Allie C. Kilpatrick, M.S.W., M.C.E., Ph.D., is a professor emerita of the University of Georgia School of Social Work, where she taught for almost 25 years. She has published extensively in areas of family and social work practice and was instrumental in the development of the interdisciplinary certificate program in marriage and family therapy (MFT) at the University of Georgia, where she served as its coordinator. She has been a diplomate in clinical social work, member of the Academy of Certified Social Workers, and clinical member and approved supervisor for AAMFT. She is licensed in Georgia as a marriage and family therapist and is currently licensed as a clinical social worker. She is also an ordained minister and serves as chaplain for hospice.

Thomas P. Holland, Ph.D., is a professor and former director of the Institute for Nonprofit Organizations, University of Georgia. He also has been associate dean and chairman of the doctoral program at the Mandel School of Applied Social Sciences, Case Western Reserve University, Cleveland, Ohio. Dr. Holland has published extensively on management and governance of nonprofit organizations. He was recently recognized by the University of Georgia as Outstanding Teacher of the Year and by his school as Outstanding Scholar of the Year.

About the Contributors

Harry J. Aponte, MSW, LCSW, LMFT, is a family therapist known for his writings and workshops on the person of the therapist, spirituality in therapy, therapy with disadvantaged and culturally diverse families, and structural family therapy. Dr. Aponte was a staff member and teacher of family therapy at the Menninger Clinic, and director of the Philadelphia Child Guidance Center. Currently, he is clinical associate professor in the Couple & Family Therapy Program at Drexel University in Philadelphia. He has a private practice in Philadelphia and conducts training and workshops throughout the country. Dr. Aponte has published *Bread & Spirit* (W. W. Norton, 1994), a book that speaks to therapy with today's poor in the context of ethnicity, culture, and spirituality. He received a doctorate in humane letters from Drexel University and a doctorate for public service from the University of Maryland.

Dorothy S. Becvar, Ph.D., M.S.W., is a professor in the School of Social Work at Saint Louis University. A licensed marital and family therapist and a licensed clinical social worker, she is also president/CEO of The Haelan Centers®, a not-for-profit corporation dedicated to promoting growth and wholeness in body, mind, and spirit. Dorothy has published extensively and, in addition to many other textbooks, journal articles, and book chapters, she is the author of the books *Families that Flourish: Facilitating Resilience in Clinical Practice* (W. W. Norton, 2007); *In the Presence of Grief: Helping Family Members Resolve Death, Dying and Bereavement Issues* (Guilford Press, 2001); and *Soul Healing: A Spiritual Orientation in Counseling and Therapy* (Basic Books, 1997). Dorothy is also the current editor of *Contemporary Family Therapy: An International Journal.*

James M. Gaudin, Ph.D., is a professor emeritus from the University of Georgia, School of Social Work. He is a nationally known expert in the area of child welfare and child neglect. He has conducted three federally funded studies on child neglect and published his research extensively through numerous articles in refereed journals, books, and book chapters. He continues to be active in designing training and in research on the professional training of public child welfare workers.

Kareema J. Gray, M.S.W., A.B.D., is a Ph.D. doctoral candidate at the University of Georgia and a member of Phi Kappa Phi Honor Society. She is a research associate, teaches social work courses, and serves as a guest lecturer in the School of Social Work. Her practice experience has been with adoptions, adolescents in crisis (behavior disorders and substance abuse), and foster care/child protective services. She has several publications and professional presentations in this area.

Roberta Greene, M.S.W., Ph.D., is a professor and the Louis and Ann Wolens Centennial Chair in gerontology and social welfare at the School of Social Work, University of Texas–Austin. She previously was professor and dean at the Indiana University School of Social Work and has worked at the Council on Social Work Education and the National Association of Social Workers. Dr. Greene has numerous publications, including *Resiliency Theory: An Integrated Framework for Practice, Research, and Policy; Social Work with the Aged and Their Families;* and *Human Behavior Theory and Social Work Practice.*

June G. Hopps, Ph.D., is the Parham Professor of Family and Children's Studies, School of Social Work, University of Georgia. She is dean emerita of the Graduate School of Social Work, Boston College, and chair of the Board of Trustees, Spelman College. She is former editor-in-chief of the journal *Social Work* and associate editor-in-chief for the *Encyclopedia of Social Work,* Nineteenth Edition. She is the author of numerous publications on social policy and on practice with overwhelmed clients.

Arthur M. Horne, Ph.D., is a distinguished research professor at the University of Georgia and currently serves as dean of the College of Education. He has served as faculty member and director of the Counseling Psychology Program, and was a member of the Certificate Program in Marriage and Family Therapy at the University of Georgia for 18 years. He then became the director of the Education Policy and Evaluation Center. He is a fellow of the American Psychological Association and the Association for Specialists in Group Work. He has co-authored six books and co-edited eight, and has presented his research findings on reducing aggression and violence in children, families, and schools throughout the United States and internationally.

Jeffrey J. Koob, M.S.W., L.C.S.W., Ph.D., is an associate professor at California State University, Long Beach, Department of Social Work. He originally interned at the Brief Family Therapy Center in Milwaukee, Wisconsin, in 1985, when Steve de Shazer and Insoo Berg were developing Solution-Focused Brief Therapy (SFBT). His research, teaching, and service are directed toward the application of SFBT to different populations and treatment settings. He is also a talented singer and composer.

Nancy P. Kropf, M.S.W., Ph.D., is a professor and the director of the School of Social Work at Georgia State University. Her area of research and scholarship is late-life caregiving relationships, with the focus specifically on older adults as care providers. Dr. Kropf was a John A. Hartford Faculty Scholar (1999–2001) and is a fellow of the Gerontological Society of America. Dr. Kropf has over sixty peer-reviewed articles and book chapters in the social work and gerontology literatures.

Thomas V. Sager, Ph.D., is a professor and co-director of training in counseling psychology at the University of Memphis. He is a licensed psychologist, member of the Division of Family Psychology of the American Psychological Association, and member of the Executive Board of the Council of Counseling Psychology Training Programs. The focus of his research and clinical practice is prevention, early intervention, and family–school collaborative programs for behavior-disordered children and their families.

Elizabeth O. Trawick, M.D., is a psychoanalyst in private practice in Beverly Hills, California. She has been interested in object relations/Kleinian theory for many years and treats children, adults, and families using these formulations. Dr. Trawick is an assistant clinical professor of psychiatry at the University of California, Los Angeles, and a past president of the Los Angeles Psychoanalytic Society. She is a training and supervising analyst at the New Center of Psychoanalysis and the Psychoanalytic Center of California.

Betsy Vonk, M.S.W., Ph.D., L.C.S.W., is an associate professor of social work at the University of Georgia. She completed her M.S.W. in 1980, had a clinical fellowship at the Judge Baker Guidance Center in 1983, and received her Ph.D. in social work in 1996. She practiced clinical social work with children, adolescents, and young adults and their families for 16 years. Currently, her primary teaching area is clinical practice. The focus of her research is social work practice, particularly with transracial adoptive families.

Joseph Walsh, Ph.D., L.C.S.W., is an associate professor of social work at Virginia Commonweath University, where he teaches courses in clinical practice and human behavior. He has been a clinical practitioner in the field of mental heath since 1974, specializing in work with people who have mental illnesses and their families. He is the author of *Endings in Clinical Practice, Clinical Case Management with Persons Having Mental Illness: A Relationship-Based Perspective,* and *The Social Worker and Psychotropic Medication.*

Nancy R. Williams, Ph.D., is an associate professor of social work at the University of Georgia. Her doctorate is in marriage and family from Florida State University and she is licensed both as a clinical social worker and as a marriage and family therapist. She has over 25 years of direct practice experience in the mental health/human services field, working with individuals, groups, couples, and families. Her current research areas include resilience development in trauma survivors, conflict resolution skills development, and integrative psychoeducational groups for couples.

Sun Young Yoo, M.A., is a doctoral candidate at the University of Georgia School of Social Work. She received her master's degree in social welfare from Yonsei University and worked in the ELAND Welfare Foundation and the Research Institute for the Prevention of Child Abuse and Neglect in Seoul, Korea. Her research interests include immigrant families and children, abusing and neglecting families, childrearing practices, culturally competent practices, and innovation in nonprofit organizations.

TABLE 1 *Outline of Approaches*

Level of Need	I	I	II	II	II	III	III	IV
Authors	*Gaudin*	*Greene & Kropf*	*Aponte*	*Horne & Sayger*	*Koob*	*Walsh*	*Williams*	*Kilpatrick & Trawick*
Approach	*Interventions with Neglectful Families*	*Case Management*	*Structural Family Interventions*	*Social Learning Family Interventions*	*Solution-Focused Interventions*	*Family Systems Theory*	*Narrative Family Interventions*	*Object Relations Family Interventions*
Need(s)	76	96	117	129	149	171	200	225
Assessments	78	97	118	132	149	171	204	227
Goals	86	99	120	132	152	177	200	232
Intervention approach	87	100	120	134	150	177	205	232
Basic tenets	86	100	120	134	150	177	201	232
Application	87	103	120	135	154	179	205	232
Interventions	87	105	120	135	158	177	205	236
Evaluation	92	108	123	140	163	188	214	239
Other levels	91	109	124	141	165	190	215	240
Ethical challenges	92	109	124	141	166	190	216	241
Summary	92	110	125	141	166	191	216	241
Discussion questions	93	110	125	142	167	192	217	242
Internet resources	93	111	126	142	167	193	217	242
Suggested readings	93	111	126	143	167	193	218	242
References	94	111	127	143	167	194	219	243

Note: Numbers in the table body are page references.

Part I

Theory Base and Contextual Practice: Metatheories for Working with Families at Four Levels of Need

Working with families is so important that having a family focus is now a major priority for the helping professions. Yet existing approaches to this field tend to emphasize only one model for practice, assuming that it fits all types of family problems. The differences in types of family issues and problems are extensive, however. These differences indicate a need for multiple methods from which the family practitioner may select and apply an approach on the basis of how well it fits the needs and issues a specific family is currently facing.

This part begins with Kilpatrick's analysis of types, or levels, of family needs in Chapter 1. To start where the family is, it is essential that the practitioner first assess the family's needs. The theoretical framework of the ecosystems and social constructionism perspective utilized in this book is set forth in Chapter 2 by Holland and Kilpatrick. In Chapter 3, by Kilpatrick, Hopps, and Gray, the contexts of helping are explored, with a focus on the helping relationship/therapeutic alliance and on client diversity. Ethnic-sensitive practice, gender issues, powerlessness, poverty, and changing family structures are discussed. In Chapter 4, Kilpatrick, Holland, and Becvar deal with ethically informed and spiritually sensitive practice when working with families.

The chapters in this first part set the stage for those that follow. The specific approaches to working with families at various levels of need flow from this theoretical and philosophical base and build on it.

1

Levels of Family Need

Allie C. Kilpatrick, Ph.D.

Helping professionals work with families who have many different levels of need and who have a wide variety of circumstances, problems, and skills. The practitioner who uses only one model of assessment and intervention can be described by the saying "If the only tool you have is a hammer, everything looks like a nail." This practitioner requires the family situation to fit his or her model, even when there is no workable fit. Thus, the practitioner's need is met, rather than the clients'. This chapter describes four levels of family need and explores various methods of assessment and intervention that are relevant at each level.

In her 1945 social work classic, *Common Human Needs,* Charlotte Towle wrote about needs in relation to factors that affect human development. She contended that the following elements are essential if persons are to develop into maturity and be motivated toward social goals: (1) physical welfare, such as food, shelter, and health care; (2) opportunity for emotional and intellectual growth; (3) relationships with others; and (4) provision for spiritual needs. Towle pointed out that needs are relative to a person's age and life situation. Most human needs are typically met within a family structure or in relationship with others.

Abraham Maslow (1970) developed a hierarchy of needs that supports Towle's thinking and expands our understanding of human development. According to his hierarchy, a person must satisfy primary physiological needs before social needs can be considered. Maslow included five levels of need: (1) physical and life-sustaining needs, such as the need for food, water, air, warmth, sexual gratification, elimination of bodily wastes, and so on; (2) physical safety, or the need for protection from physical attack and disease; (3) love, or the need to be cherished, supported, and aided by others; (4) self-esteem, including the need to have a sense of personal worth and value and to respect and value one's self; and (5) self-actualization, or the need to be creative and productive and to attain worthwhile objectives. Practitioners must remember, however, that often a lower-level need cannot be satisfied without having a relationship with another person. For example, a young child's need for food must be met by an adult caretaker.

Building on these two formulations of needs, family problems encountered in helping situations may be seen as clustered around various levels of need based on the primary need at that time. These range from basic survival needs to concerns about the self-actualization and spiritual needs of family members. Weltner (1985, 1986) views functional levels of families' needs from the analogy of building a house, which draws our attention to the necessity of addressing the most basic level of needs before moving to higher levels. Figure 1.1 illustrates the four levels of family need that will be utilized in this book.

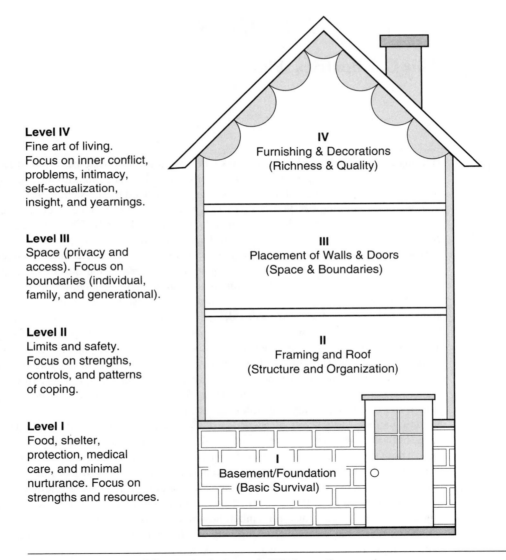

Level IV
Fine art of living. Focus on inner conflict, problems, intimacy, self-actualization, insight, and yearnings.

IV
Furnishing & Decorations
(Richness & Quality)

Level III
Space (privacy and access). Focus on boundaries (individual, family, and generational).

III
Placement of Walls & Doors
(Space & Boundaries)

Level II
Limits and safety. Focus on strengths, controls, and patterns of coping.

II
Framing and Roof
(Structure and Organization)

Level I
Food, shelter, protection, medical care, and minimal nurturance. Focus on strengths and resources.

I
Basement/Foundation
(Basic Survival)

FIGURE 1.1 *Levels of Family Needs: Issues and Relevant Interventions*
Source: Kilpatrick & Cleveland, 1993.

Level I

The most basic level of family need has to do with the requisites for survival and well-being. These include the family's needs for food, shelter, protection from danger, health care, and minimums of nurturance. Referring to Weltner's house analogy, Level I is the basement and refers to issues of life and death (see Figure 1.1).

Some families are unable to meet these needs because they experience a crisis, such as a job loss or major illness that leaves them destitute. Other families do not adequately meet these needs on an ongoing basis and are considered neglectful and underorganized. These families lack the leadership and control structure needed to meet their members' basic nurturing and protection needs. In other words, there is insufficient parenting capacity. According to the Beavers Family Competence Scale (Beavers, Hulgus, & Hampson, 1988), these families are leaderless; no one has enough power to structure interactions. Researchers found this situation to be more descriptive of neglectful families in lower-socioeconomic circumstances than of nonneglectful families in similar circumstances (Gaudin, Polansky, Kilpatrick, & Shilton, 1991).

Sometimes, families struggling with Level I problems show evidence that the parental coalition is weakened or undermined by a parent–child coalition; family closeness is amorphous and vague, with indistinct boundaries among members. Deprived of such basic resources as food, shelter, protection, education, clothing, transportation, and medical care, these families are rarely able to provide their members with the necessary emotional nurturance (Epstein, Bishop, & Baldwin, 1982). Examples of typical problem situations may include an overwhelmed single mother (as is the case in most neglectful families); the incapacitation or dysfunction of the strongest family member by illness, alcohol, or drugs; and natural or emotional catastrophes and pervasive life stresses that have depleted physical and emotional resources.

The practitioner working with these families must build on basic strengths and resiliences, as is true at all levels, and focus on resources. For Level I families, Weltner (1985) suggests that the intervention should center on mobilizing support for the ineffective executive or parental system. Intervention could begin with a survey of potential resources from the community, including church groups and extended family (genograms and ecomaps are helpful; see Hartman & Laird, 1983), and then assess and build on family resilience and strengths. Resilience, or the ability to withstand and rebound from crises and adversities, can be strengthened (see Chapter 5). Helping families to discover positive meanings in stress and distress is an important ingredient in strength-based interventions. Wolin and Wolin (1993), for example, highlight the "survivor's pride" (p. 8). This help could be offered to families demonstrating resilience in some area.

Other necessary measures in crises may include case management and referral to medical, income maintenance, and legal resources; protective services and family preservation programs; and hospitalization (see Chapter 6). Advocacy and guidance may be indicated, as well, depending on the situation. Guidance on the use of respite care, referral to substance abuse counseling, child development and child care information, and budget and time management may also be necessary. Often, an advocacy role with school, welfare, and correctional or juvenile justice systems is necessary. Table 1.1 illustrates some of the issues, relevant intervention strategies, and possible intervention techniques that could be applicable on this level.

TABLE 1.1   *Family Assessment and Intervention*

Level	Issue	Intervention Strategy	Intervention Technique

I	• Is executive capacity sufficient to manage all basic nurturant needs?
	• Is there food, shelter, protection, medical care, minimal nurturance?
	• Do the individual and family have resilience?
		• Focus on strengths, not problems.
		• Survey and mobilize available support to bolster executive capacity.
		• Build family resilience.
		• Promote positive response to stress.
			• Family preservation.
			• Case management.
			• Marshal more troops from:
			    Nuclear family.
			    Extended family.
			    Community.
			• Professional as convener, advocate, teacher, role model.

II	• Is there sufficient authority to provide minimal structure, limits, and safety?	• Focus on strengths.
		• Develop a coalition of those in charge against those needing control.
		• Increase clarity of expectation.
			• Develop parental coalitions.
			• Set limits.
			• Clear communication.
			• Social learning skills:
			    Written contracts.
			    Behavioral reinforcers.
			    Task assignments.

III	• Are there clear and appropriate boundaries?
	    Family.
	    Individual.
	    Generational.
		• Focus on problems.
		• Clarify the "ideal" family structure in conformity with ethnic or family expectations.
		• Have generational clarity.
			• Defend family and individual boundaries.
			• Balance triangles.
			• Rebuild alliances.
			• Develop generational boundaries.
			• Promote communication skills.

IV	• Are there problems of inner conflict or problems with intimacy? • Are family members self-actualizing?	• Focus on problems. • Clarify and resolve legacies and historical trauma. • Promote insight. • Focus on yearnings and spiritual needs.	• Narrative interventions. • Family sculpture. • Object relations interventions. • Resolution of three-generational issues. • Spiritual growth.

Source: Adapted from Weltner, 1985, p. 49.

The following brief case study is illustrative of a family with needs on Level I and the typical interventions that could be used. The case study demonstrates the mobilization of resources through case management skills and building on strengths to meet family needs.

Mrs. M came to the attention of Family Services after she called the hotline. She had not been feeling well for some time and had lost her job. After she was diagnosed with AIDS, which she contracted from her husband, he left her. She had no source of income and was being evicted from her apartment in the housing project. She had two daughters, ages two and four, and they were without food. Family Services was able to meet her immediate needs by helping with food and paying the rent. They then referred her to Family Support Services. The worker there, using case management skills, helped her to obtain treatment for AIDS.

After assessing her potential resources and strengths and receiving some encouragement from the worker, Mrs. M agreed to contact some family members to get help with the children. In the meantime, with education and support from the worker, she was able to provide more security, nurturing, and support for them. With Mrs. M's approval and cooperation, the worker helped to locate her husband. After counseling with his wife, Mr. M agreed to obtain medical treatment and to return home.

Level II

With Level II families, the basic needs of minimal safety, stability, and nurturance have been met, and maintaining authority and setting limits are the prominent issues. In the house analogy in Figure 1.1, Level II refers to the framing and roof of the house and represents the family's structure and organization. The parental system is unable to set and maintain sufficient limits for one or more family members, and this inability threatens the stability of the whole family system. This failure could involve either a lack of clear expectations or a lack of power to enforce expectations.

Other examples could include families where the children are out of control, with acting-out teenagers and parents who are involved in substance abuse or excessive gambling or otherwise failing to maintain key structures for the family. Marital conflict may appear to be out of control and threaten dissolution of the family unit. Violence in the family may be threatened, but members are not seen as needing immediate protection.

Again, intervention would begin with a survey of strengths, resiliences, and resources. To have the authority to deal with the situation and to offer sufficient hope, the practitioner must be in charge of structuring the sessions. Structural interventions enable the spouses to develop a coalition strong enough to demonstrate sufficient authority for the family to gain control of threatening or destructive behaviors (see Chapter 7).

Weltner (1986) points out that the focus of treatment in such situations must be to "develop a coalition of those in charge against those needing control" (p. 53). Family mapping of coalitions (Hartman & Laird, 1983; Minuchin, 1974) could be helpful with these families. Social learning and behavioral techniques with structural considerations may prove empowering to family members (see Chapter 8). Paquin and Bushorn (1991) show how behavioral techniques can help clarify the family's expectations for the behavior of each of its members and help them recognize their potential for modifying the behaviors of other family members.

The following case study is typical of Level II family needs. As in Level I, intervention would begin with a survey of strengths, resilience, and resources.

> Jose, age ten, was referred to the school social worker for disrupting the classroom, fighting with the other boys, and failing to do homework. His father was the head of household in this single-parent, Hispanic family. Jose's mother had died of cancer when he was seven. He had two older sisters in high school who were going through turbulent teenage years.
>
> After talking with Jose, his teachers, and then his father, the social worker began working with the teachers on some social learning and behavioral techniques to modify Jose's behavior in the classroom. Jose's father was unable to come to the school during the day because he could not get off work. The worker talked with him by phone in the evening and found that Jose was alone at home after school, with little or no supervision or structure from his sisters. Jose's father worked long hours and was so tired at night that he just wanted to sit and drink beer. The children usually ate junk food for dinner on their own.

The worker scheduled an appointment to see Jose's family together in the evening. The mother's sister, who lived nearby, also attended. After discussing the concerns they all had about the family, they agreed that the aunt would work with the girls to help them take more responsibility for supervising Jose and helping him with his homework. She would also help them to prepare more nourishing meals at night. The father agreed to spend more time with Jose, especially on weekends.

Family members related that they had all become more disorganized since the mother had died. Jose, in particular, had gradually become more aggressive and less interested in school. The worker suggested a referral to the mental health clinic so that Jose, as well as the rest of the family, could do their grief work concerning the mother's death. They all agreed to go. Within a few months, Jose's behavior and grades improved, and he was taking more interest in school.

Although a wide variety of techniques may be used, both Level I and Level II interventions are essentially structural (Weltner, 1985) and ecosystems oriented. The goal is to mobilize all of the resources available, to modify the organizational patterns of the family, and to increase and test the strength of the parental or executive system. It is important to remember that children such as Jose have a readiness to fall in line. They are often aware of how much their own and other family members' lives suffer as a result of their lack of discipline and control.

Level III

Level III focuses on space, with privacy and access as the issues. Using the house analogy in Figure 1.1, this level is concerned with the inner architecture. Although the foundation, walls, and roof are satisfactory, the arrangement of inner space, or the placement of walls and doors, is not.

Level III families are complicated, and they have a structure and style that is often perceived as working. They may draw on and express a three-generational legacy, not a set of inherited deficiencies (Weltner, 1985). As pointed out by Aponte (2003), Level I and II families usually are underorganized, lack family structure, and do not transmit adequate patterns of coping. By contrast, Level III and IV families have a rich mixture of coping mechanisms. Weltner (1985) describes these coping mechanisms as their characteristic defenses, the culture to which they are committed and that they attempt to pass on to and through their children.

If work with such families involves changing ingrained patterns, the practitioner can anticipate some struggle. Therefore, intervention techniques need to encompass and adapt to such struggle. The Beavers Interactional Competence Scale (Beavers et al., 1988) rates these families as having marked or moderate dominance. (Control is close to absolute, with little or no negotiation; dominance and submission are the rule.) Family members are isolated and distanced from one another.

A Level III intervention involves processes of reshaping the internal architecture of the family so everyone has appropriate space, access, and privacy. The intervention must challenge the existing family structure and confront the family's tendency to remain in current patterns of behavior. Examination of the communication and power structures around the presenting problem may be useful. The development of differentiation and individuation of family members from each other and the emotional system, flexibility, and clear generational boundaries are essential.

The following case study summarizes a case presented by Pippin and Callaway (1999) and is illustrative of the needs of families in Level III. Although a family systems approach is taken in this case, other Level III families' needs could be approached through solution-focused family interventions (see Chapter 9).

> Bill Sr. and Carmen have two children: Bill Jr., age 14, and Sonia, age 12. Bill Jr. has always been difficult to manage. At this time, he is sullen and negative at home, his school grades are low, and his parents fear that he is involved with alcohol and marijuana. Sonia seems to be a model child. Carmen is quiet and has an overinvolved relationship with her daughter, but appears to be bonded with Bill Jr. Bill Sr. is a successful surgeon. At home, he exerts absolute authoritarian control. Both parents describe their own parents' relationships as conflictual and their own relationship as conflictual.
>
> There are three significant intergenerational triangles. First, Bill Jr. and his mother are allied against his father. Next, Carmen and her mother have an overinvolved relationship, which is repeated in Carmen's relationship with her own daughter. The third significant triangle is that of Bill Sr., Carmen, and Bill Jr., which is the same as Bill Sr. had in his family of origin. The significance of these triangles is the degree of fusion. Members in this three-generational family are so deeply enmeshed that inevitable growth and change with age is viewed with terror.

The overarching goal of treatment with this Level III family is to realign the family system and establish boundaries. A second overall goal is to identify and ameliorate the sources of chronic anxiety within the family system that undermine individual growth and autonomy. The parental subsystem must be strengthened to become a supportive team in the management of the children (see Chapter 10).

Level IV

In Level IV families, basic needs are met, and structural boundaries are relatively clear and satisfactory. Presenting problems often focus on a desire for greater intimacy, a greater sense of self, or more autonomy. The concern of Level IV families is the fine art of living fully and growing toward actualization of each member's potential. In relation to the house analogy, this level of functioning represents decorations, pictures, rugs, and lamps. Here, the richness and quality of individual and family life becomes the focus of intervention. Although some of these issues may have been discussed at earlier levels, it is at Level IV that such issues as inner conflicts, intimacy, self-realization, insight, and spiritual yearnings become the primary focus and are explored in depth.

Genograms extending over three or four or more generations are useful at this level in showing transgenerational patterns. Family sculpting may also be used. A focus on narrative interventions and rewriting one's own story are especially applicable at this level of family functioning (see Chapter 11). Object relations family interventions may also be particularly helpful with these families, who desire insight into patterns and intergenerational functioning (see Chapter 12). Some families or individuals may want to focus on clarifying personal values, meanings, and spirituality, or they may wish to deal with existential issues. Helping professionals must be open to pursuing such issues, be comfortable in discussing them, and be able to assist family members in clarifying their values and discovering the transcendent aspects of their being without imposing personal conclusions on them. Referrals to church-related counseling centers may be indicated.

The following family situation may be a typical example of a Level IV family:

> A middle-class couple with several children entered treatment with the complaint by the wife of having vague feelings of depression and loneliness. She and her husband began to do extended family work with some emphasis on object relations. Working through some of their earlier relationships and projection processes and contacts with family made the wife feel more connected and less lonely. The couple was able to weather the terminal illness of the wife's mother in a relatively calm fashion, without the wife becoming too depressed during the grief-work period.
>
> The loss of the wife's mother motivated both members of the couple to focus more on inner awareness and spiritual growth. By building on the insights they had gained and having ongoing contact with extended family, both were able to rewrite their own life story to some degree.

Intervention Criteria

Once the primary current level of need has been assessed, then an opening for intervention must be determined. Does the practitioner start with the family, the couple, or an individual? Should the focus be on what people do, what they think and feel, or what has happened in the past? Does the practitioner assume health or pathology? Is the primary need for maintenance of functioning or problem resolution?

These questions are addressed by an intervention choice points grid developed by Pinsof (1991, 1995), as shown in Figure 1.2. The "Contexts" columns in the figure refer to the people who are involved in the problem maintenance structure. This could be the family (including the extended family and the community), the couple in the same generation (allowing for alternate lifestyles), or an individual. The "Orientations" items refer to three intervention choices:

1. The *behavioral/interactional choice* has to do with what people do—their actions and how to change them. It involves surface behavior and is visual. Social learning and strategic, functional, and structural techniques may be used here.

2. The *experiential choice* makes use of cognition, affect, communication, and interpersonal relationships—what people think and feel. It involves meaning and is auditory (listening). As with choice 1, the focus is on the here and now.

3. The *historical choice* is the third intervention. It adds the dimension of time and addresses what has happened in the past. Family-of-origin work and psychodynamic or psychoanalytic methods may be used.

This model assumes that the people involved are healthy and that the problem can be resolved at a direct behavioral level. Therefore, in choosing how to intervene, the practitioner's

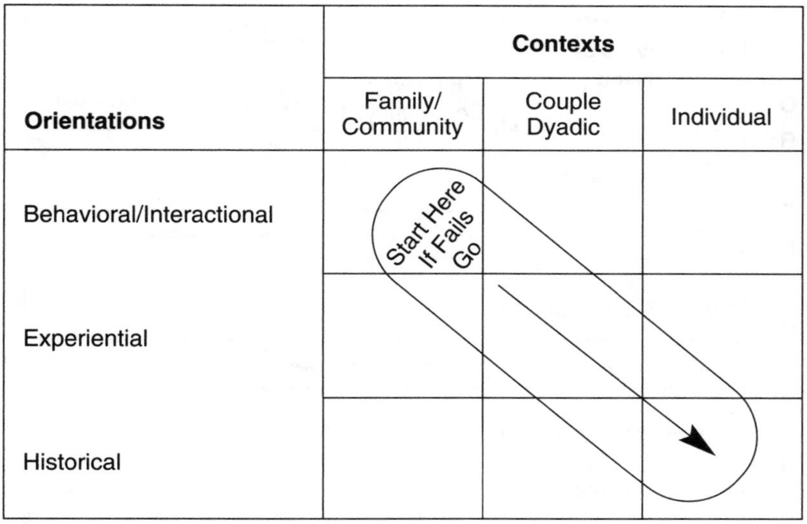

Orientations	Contexts		
	Family/ Community	Couple Dyadic	Individual
Behavioral/Interactional	Start Here If Fails Go		
Experiential			
Historical			

FIGURE 1.2 *Intervention Choice Points*

Source: Adapted from Pinsof, 1991, 1995.

decision points should progress from the upper left to lower right, as shown in Figure 1.2. In other words, the practitioner should begin with the context of the family and the behavioral orientation. If the approach in this cell does not work, he or she should proceed down the cells diagonally to working with the couple experientially. If this approach does not work, then the practitioner should go to the individual and work with historical material.

The progression is problem or failure driven in that if a more direct approach is not successful, the practitioner proceeds to another less direct approach. It is also circular in that the practitioner continues to deal with meaning and behavior and to link what he or she is doing with the presenting problem. There is an explicit contract between the practitioner and the family to address the problem, so there must be a link between the presenting problem and what the practitioner does. This helps to keep the practitioner honest.

The essence of the choice framework is that working with families is a process of discovery, a "peeling of the onion." Is the problem simple and superficial or deep and complex? The family is assumed to be healthy and to have a simple, superficial problem that can be addressed at the family unit level with behavioral interventions until it has been proven that the problem exists at deeper levels. Therefore, practice begins with simple, cost-effective interventions. The goal is to teach the family to learn from the practitioner how to solve problems for themselves. This process may involve internalizing the approach of the practitioner so the family can assume what he or she would say or do and thus work things out for themselves.

Once a family's basic survival needs have been met, this choice framework can provide a guide for work at the four levels of need within the house analogy. The three orientations of the Pinsof (1991, 1995) choice points grid are then applicable at the intersection of

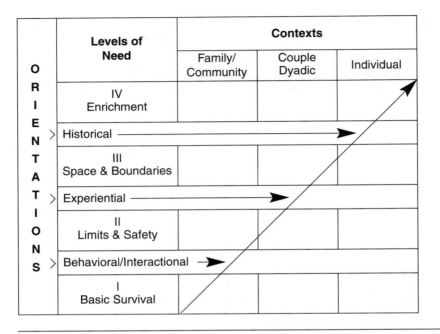

FIGURE 1.3   *Intervention Choice Points by Level of Need*

the levels of the family need, as shown in Figure 1.3. The overlay of these two grids provides a practical guide for choosing the most applicable treatment model and the individual, couple, or family focus based on the assessment of family need. One caveat must be mentioned: These guidelines provide a rough framework into which every family may not easily fit. A family may be characterized by several levels of need, as well as orientations. Professional judgment is required to decide the more relevant point of entry and intervention. The key question for the family practitioner is this: What specific therapeutic intervention produces specific change in specific families under specific conditions?

Summary

The needs and problems of families are quite varied. Given this, it is helpful to view a family through the lens of their particular level of need in order to assess strengths and resiliences and provide relevant interventions. Problems encountered in practice with families tend to cluster into four levels of need, from very basic to very high. Lower-level needs must be met before higher-level needs can be addressed. The four levels of family need range from basic survival to self-actualization.

An analogy of building a house can be used to illustrate the basic assumptions. In the first two levels, strengths are emphasized. On the higher two levels, problem areas are addressed directly. Working with these types of problems requires purposive selection from among methods of practice and application of appropriate interventions according to the situation and needs of the specific family. Intervention strategies and techniques must be matched with the issues on each level.

The four levels of family need are not discrete, however. Rather, they exist along a continuum and can rarely be categorized. Some characteristics are found in several levels. In the assessment process, the level that is most characteristic of the needs experienced by a particular family at that time must be assessed. In Levels III and IV, particularly, the most crucially felt need of a given family could vary between the two levels, depending on whether a specific problem or crisis must be addressed at that time or if the need is more toward growth.

Interventions that are particularly appropriate at a given level may also be used at some other levels, given certain conditions. An intervention choice point grid provides a guide that can be used in connection with the levels of need to decide the context and orientation for intervention. The application of specific methods of interventions with other levels of need is discussed in each chapter in Parts Two through Five, along with related caveats and ethical challenges.

Discussion Questions _____

1. Describe the four levels of family needs, and identify some intervention strategies and techniques that may be useful for each.

2. On which level would families involved with addiction issues likely be found, and where would be the most likely point for intervention?

3. What are some challenges or obstacles that would keep a family's basic needs at a low level? What are some strengths, skills, or actions that would raise a family's basic needs to a higher level?

4. In Weltner's house analogy, what do the "decorations" represent? At what level of need is a family concerned with these decorations? How would a therapist help them?

5. Formulate a case study to illustrate Level IV families.

6. Is determining the level of family need the responsibility of the clinician, or is it a joint effort involving the clients? What happens in the event of a disagreement on the level of need?

7. Apply all the concepts discussed in this chapter to the choice point grid (Figure 1.2), utilizing families you are working with or know.

8. Select an incident from your childhood. Identify and describe the level of need of your family at that time. Choose a point of intervention in terms of context and orientation, and explain the rationale for your choice.

Internet Resources _____

www.parenting.com
www.questia.com/library/psychology/relationships-and-the-family

Suggested Readings

Beavers, W. R., & Hampson, R. B. (1990). *Successful families.* New York: Norton.
> Family competence is viewed along a progressive continuum, such that families are seen as ranging from healthy functioning to severely dysfunctional. The approach focuses on assessment and intervention and stems from years of clinical, observational, and empirical work.

Minuchin, S., & Montalvo, B. (1967). Techniques for working with disorganized low socioeconomic families. *American Journal of Orthopsychiatry, 37,* 380–387.

Minuchin, S., Montalvo, B., Guerney, B. G., Rosman, B. L., & Schumer, F. (1967). *Families of the slums.* New York: Basic Books.
> These two works by Minuchin and associates focus on the structure and dynamics of poor and disorganized families and give specific techniques for working with them. The books are based on a study of families with more than one delinquent child and are especially helpful when working with Level I families.

Towle, C. (1945). *Common human needs.* Washington, DC: National Association of Social Workers.
> This book is one of the classics in social work. It discusses in great detail the human needs that are common to all people, and is one of the few books that urges providing for spiritual needs.

Weltner, J. S. (1986). A matchmaker's guide to family therapy. *Family Therapy Networker, 10*(2), 51–55.
> This is an easy-to-read summary of the levels of functioning, as seen by Weltner. It offers more detail than is given in this chapter for those who wish to explore the concept further.

References

Aponte, H. J. (2003). Structural family interventions. In A. Kilpatrick & T. Holland (Eds.), *Working with families: An integrative model by level of need* (3rd ed.). Boston: Allyn & Bacon.

Beavers, W. R., Hulgus, Y. F., & Hampson, R. B. (1988). *Beavers system model of family functioning: Family competence and family style evaluation manual.* Dallas: University of Texas Health Science Center.

Epstein, N. B., Bishop, D. S., & Baldwin, L. M. (1982). McMaster model of family functioning: A view of the normal family. In F. Walsh (Ed.), *Normal family processes.* New York: Guilford Press.

Gaudin, J., Polansky, N. A., Kilpatrick, A. C., & Shilton, P. (1991). *Structure and functioning in neglectful families.* Paper presented at the Ninth National Conference on Child Abuse and Neglect, Denver, CO.

Hartman, A., & Laird, J. (1983). *Family-centered social work practice.* New York: Free Press.

Kilpatrick, A., & Cleveland, P. (1993). Unpublished course material, University of Georgia School of Social Work.

Maslow, A. (1970). *Motivation and personality.* New York: Harper & Row.

Minuchin, S. (1974). *Families and family therapy.* Cambridge, MA: Harvard University Press.

Paquin, G. W., & Bushorn, R. J. (1991). Family treatment assessment for novices. *Families in Society: The Journal of Contemporary Human Services, 72*(6), 353–359.

Pinsof, W. (1991). An integrated approach to chronic marital conflict. *The Learning Edge Series* (Video). Washington, DC: American Association for Marriage and Family Therapy.

Pinsof, W. (1995). *Integrative problem centered therapy: A synthesis of biological, individual, and family therapies.* New York: Basic Books.

Pippin, J. A., & Callaway, J. (1999). Family systems interventions. In A. C. Kilpatrick & T. P. Holland, *Working with families: An integrative model by level of need.* Boston: Allyn & Bacon.

Towle, C. (1945). *Common human needs.* Washington, DC: National Association of Social Workers.

Weltner, J. S. (1985). Matchmaking: Choosing the appropriate therapy for families at various levels of pathology. In M. P. Mirkin & S. L. Koman (Eds.), *Handbook of adolescents and family therapy* (pp. 39–50). New York: Gardner Press.

Weltner, J. S. (1986). A matchmaker's guide to family therapy. *Family Therapy Networker, 10*(2), 51–55.

Wolin, S. J., & Wolin, S. (1993). *The resilient self.* New York: Villard Books.

2

An Ecological Systems–Social Constructionism Approach to Family Practice

Thomas P. Holland, Ph.D., and Allie C. Kilpatrick, Ph.D.

This chapter presents an overall framework within which the integrative model to family practice by level of need takes place. For family practice to be more applicable to the families served by helping professionals, we are adapting the comprehensive theories, or *metatheories,* of ecological systems and social constructionism for this framework. Each meta- or comprehensive theory offers a way of looking at the world, and each includes other methods (Breunlin, Schwartz, & Kune-Karrer, 1992; Payne, 1991). These metatheories, which diverge and converge, ultimately blend to form a firm foundation for an integrated approach to family practice.

Ecological Systems Perspective

The *ecological systems (ecosystems) perspective* is a framework for assessment and intervention. It has been a dominant theoretical approach for viewing human behavior in the social environment. The environment is all inclusive of micro- to macro-level systems and resources required for meeting family needs. The interface between people and their environment is seen as bidirectional and interactional, meaning that people affect the environment and, in turn, the environment affects people.

The focus for the practitioner is to assess and intervene in all relevant factors at all levels of systems. Doing so allows the practitioner to view situations holistically in assessment and intervention. It also stimulates the use of a broad repertoire of interventions that are suitable for the varying needs of particular family situations. Because the ecosystems approach can encompass any relevant treatment model, it can serve as a unifying perspective in family practice (Long & Holle, 1997; Meyer, 1988).

The Ecological View

The ecological perspective is based in the metaphor of biological organisms that live and adapt in a complex network of environmental forces. Von Bertalanffy (1968) believed that living organisms are organized wholes, not just the sum of their separate parts, and that they are essentially open systems, maintaining themselves with continuous inputs from and outputs to their environments.

The ecological perspective rests on an evolutionary, adaptive view of human beings in continuous transaction with their environment, with both the person and the environment continuously changing and accommodating each other (Brower, 1988). The key assumptions of an ecological perspective emphasize that people and environments are holistic and transactional. This approach makes clear the need to see people and their environments within their historic and cultural contexts, in relationship to one another, and as continually influencing one another, as described by Germain and Gitterman (1995).

Because ecologists were among the first systems thinkers, the ecological perspective is also systemic. Germain and Gitterman (1987) identify seven major concepts of the ecosystems perspective that are applicable to working with families:

1. Transactions are understood as continuous *reciprocal exchanges* in the person–environment system. Through these exchanges, each shapes, changes, or otherwise influences the other over time. People's needs and predicaments are viewed as outcomes of person–environment exchanges, not just as the products of personality or environment alone (except in those cases where a specific problem may be an outcome of environmental or societal processes alone).

2. *Life stress* can refer to either a positive or a negative person–environment relationship (Lazarus, 1980). Germain and Gitterman (1995) state that stress can be seen as positive when an environmental demand, process, or event is experienced as a challenge and therefore associated with positive feelings, a higher level of self-esteem, and the anticipation of mastery. Stress can be seen as negative when actual or perceived environmental demands, harms, losses, or conflicts (or the future threat of any of these) exceed the actual or perceived capacity for dealing with them. Germain and Gitterman also state that life stress and challenge express forms of person–environment relationships because they include both the external demand and the accompanying physiological or emotional stress at a subjective level.

3. The concept of *coping* refers to the special adaptations that are made in response to internal stress. Lazarus (1980) states that two major functions of coping are problem solving and managing negative feelings and that these are interdependent. Each of these coping adaptations needs personal, familial, and environmental resources and relationships. When coping efforts are working, the demand or threat that causes the stress may be reduced or eliminated, thus avoiding a crisis. If coping efforts are not successful, disruption in social functioning may result in various areas. Stress and coping are both transactional. Therefore, they help the practitioner to maintain a focus on both people and environments.

4. *Habitat* refers to the place where a person or family lives:

> In the case of human beings, the physical and social settings within a cultural context are the habitat. Physical settings such as dwellings, buildings, rural villages and urban layouts must support the social settings of family life, social

life, work life, religious life, and so on, in ways that fit with life styles, age, gender, and culture. Habitats that do not support the health and social functioning of individuals and families are likely to produce or to contribute to feelings of isolation, disorientation, and despair. Such stressful feelings may interfere further with the basic functions of family and community life. (Germain, 1985, p. 41)

Clearly, many impoverished communities around the world, both rural and urban, lack the resources of a habitat that supports healthy social functioning and overall human well-being.

5. A *niche* is perceived as the result of one's accommodation to the environment. It refers to the status that is occupied by a member of the community. Niches are defined differently in different societies and in different historical eras. In modern U.S. society, one aspect of a good niche is a set of rights, including the rights of equal opportunity to educational and economic resources. However, devalued personal or cultural characteristics—such as color, ethnicity, gender, age, affinity/sexual orientation, disability, poverty, and so on—force millions of people to occupy niches that are incongruent with human needs and well-being (Germain, 1985).

6. The concept of *relatedness,* based on attachment theory (Bowlby, 1973), incorporates ideas about emotional and social loneliness and isolation (Weiss, 1973). Many research studies demonstrate the important influences of supportive networks of relatives, friends, neighbors, work colleagues, and pets in helping people cope with painful life stresses (Cobb, 1976; Gaudin, 1993, 1999). This aspect of the ecological perspective suggests the entry points in social networks for professionals to help people work out adaptive social arrangements in family, group, community, and institutional life.

7. It is important to remember that *adaptations,* as used in the ecological perspective, are active, dynamic, and often creative processes. People and their environment create an ecosystem in which each shapes the other. Thus, people are not mere reactors to environmental forces. Sometimes, they change environments to allow themselves to meet their physical and psychological needs. An example is a recent sit-in at a major university by students with disabilities who were seeking better accessibility to buildings. Having achieved their goal, these individuals then had to adapt to the changes they induced. At other times, people change themselves to conform or adjust to environmental imperatives or to satisfy needs and reach goals (Germain & Gitterman, 1980, 1995).

The Family Systems View

Systems theory was developed to go beyond mechanistic biology to include the interfunctioning of parts that make up whole systems. It goes beyond static concepts to take account of the temporal quality of life and the omnipresence of change. Among the key assumptions of this theory that are particularly relevant to the *family systems view* are wholeness, feedback, equifinality, and circular causality (Watzlawick, Beavin, & Jackson, 1967):

1. Because systems behave as wholes, change in any one part will cause change in other parts and throughout the entire system. When this assumption of *wholeness* is applied to family systems, it means that a family is not simply a collection of individuals but a coherent composite whose components behave as an irreducible unit. Therefore, the behavior of each individual in the family is related to and dependent on the behavior of all the others. For this reason, improvements or regressions in one family member prompt repercussions, positive and negative, in other family members (Goldenberg & Goldenberg, 1991; Nichols & Schwartz, 1991; Watzlawick et al., 1967).

   2. Open systems are regulated by *feedback* loops, or inputs from family members and from the environment. These inputs are acted on and modified by the family system. Feedback can be either positive or negative. Negative feedback contributes to homeostasis by the process of self-regulation and plays an important role in maintaining the stability of relationships. It reduces the tendency toward deviation from the family norms. Positive feedback leads to change when it is used by the family system to amplify a pattern. For learning and growth to occur, families must incorporate positive feedback. All families together must use some degree of both forms of feedback to adapt while maintaining their equilibrium in the face of developmental and environmental stresses (Goldenberg & Goldenberg, 1991; Simon, Stierlin, & Wynne, 1985; Watzlawick et al., 1967).

   3. *Equifinality* means that the same result may be reached from different beginnings (Von Bertalanffy, 1968). In an open system, different initial conditions may lead to the same final result, and different outcomes may be produced from the same causes. The primary principle here is that, to understand families, it is more important to consider the ongoing organization of their interactions, not just the genesis or the product of these interactions (Simon et al., 1985; Watzlawick et al., 1967).

   4. *Circular causality* means that systems are constantly modified by recursive circular feedback from multiple sources within and outside the system. Events are related through a series of interacting loops or repeating cycles. In other words, there is no simple, linear cause and effect; events and behaviors interacting with one another over a period of time produce the effects (Nichols & Schwartz, 1991).

Applications to Family Practice

The use of the ecosystems metatheory in working with families supports adherence to certain principles that are consistent with this perspective:

   • This perspective requires professionals to carry out their practice according to the needs of a particular family, rather than view all family needs in terms of a single preferred treatment.

   • This perspective supports a variety of practice roles and tasks. It can serve as a basis for internal and external changes, legislative advocacy, policy and planning, program development, primary prevention activities, research, and administration.

   • The practitioner's attention must encompass three interdependent realms or contexts in which human growth, development, and social functioning take place. *Life transitions* encompass developmental changes, such as puberty, aging, role changes, loss, and crisis events faced by families. *Interpersonal processes* include patterns of relationship and communication in dyads, families, groups, social networks, communities or neighborhoods, and organizations. *Environmental properties* include the aspects of social and physical settings—their formal and informal resources and deficits—as they affect families (Germain & Gitterman, 1987). The use of genograms and ecomaps (Hartman & Laird, 1983; Mattaini, 1997) can facilitate the focus on these contents.

• The focus is on strengths, not deficits; on solutions, not problems; and on the potential for continued family and individual growth and needed social change.

• Assessment and intervention from an ecological systems perspective require knowledge of the diverse systems involved in interactions between people and their environments (Hefferman, Shuttlesworth, & Ambrosina, 1988). The four different levels of systems, shown in Figure 2.1, are helpful in the assessment process for a given problem situation:

1. The *microsystem* represents the individual in family and group settings that incorporate the day-to-day environment.
2. The *mesosystem* incorporates the interactions of individuals, families, and groups within the person's microsystem.
3. The *exosystem* represents the social structures, both formal and informal, that influence, delimit, or constrain what goes on there. It also includes community-level factors that affect how the person functions.
4. The *macrosystem* involves societal forces and subsumes cultural and societal values, attitudes, and beliefs that influence the micro- and exosystems.

The example of homelessness shown in Figure 2.1 illustrates the use of the figure in helping students learn the ecosystems model. First, look at the causes of homelessness, which may be apparent in several levels of systems. For example, mental illness, alcoholism, unemployment, and domestic violence may have precipitated the loss of income and housing. Any of these causes could be interrelated at micro-, meso-, exo-, or macrosystem levels. Services for homeless families must also be provided at several system levels. Individual/family counseling at the micro- and mesosystem levels is indicated in the emergency and transition levels. Resources at the exosystem level for temporary shelter and other transition services are needed. Changes in public attitudes and policy concerning employment opportunities, emergency responses, and causes of homelessness may take place at the macrosystem level.

The key assumptions in family systems theory of wholeness, feedback, equifinality, and circular causality are applied at the microsystem and mesosystem levels. The ecosystems perspectives of reciprocal exchanges, life stress, coping, habitat, niche, and relatedness are applicable at the exo- and macrosystem levels.

Consideration should be given to the interplay of influences on all four levels during the assessment and intervention processes with families. Recognizing this interplay helps in understanding the causes of a particular problem situation and also in the provision of services for such problems. Information concerning other problem areas can be used to fill in the blanks in the model to make the ecosystems theory more visible. Effective case management skills are important to applying this framework with some families.

By utilizing knowledge of all levels of the ecosystems perspective, the practitioner is better equipped to assess and provide services for families in accordance with the presenting problems and the family's current level of need. This application requires flexibility, creativity, and mobility outside the office and into the home and community.

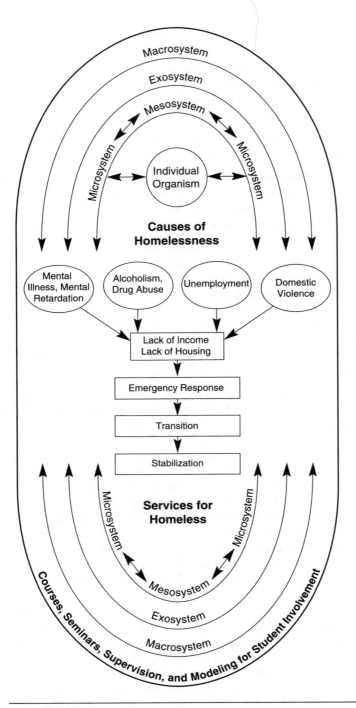

FIGURE 2.1 *An Ecosystems Model for Student Involvement with Homeless Families*
Source: From Cleveland & Kilpatrick, 1990.

A summary of how practitioners can implement this ecosystems perspective in their work is offered by Greene and Ephross (1999):

- View the person/family/environment as inseparable.
- See the family practitioner as an equal partner in the helping process.
- Examine transactions between the person/family/environment by assessing all levels of systems affecting adaptiveness.
- Assess life situations and transitions that induce high stress levels.
- Attempt to enhance a person/family's personal and interpersonal competence through positive relationships and life experiences.
- Seek interventions that extend the "goodness of fit" among the person/family and the environment at all system levels.
- Focus on mutually sought solutions and person/family empowerment. (p. 293)

Caveats in Using the Ecosystems Metatheory

Although ecosystems theory offers a wealth of ideas about families and family practice, the family practitioner must be aware of some possible pitfalls in its use. One issue is that this perspective may lead to a conservative stance of valuing the status quo and avoiding real change. Influences that upset the homeostasis of a system may be framed as problems or forms of deviance, leading to responses that assess them not on their own merits but in terms of reducing or limiting their threats to existing relational patterns. Conflict may be seen as a negative influence, disrupting systemic balance; conformity may be assumed to be good. The underlying concern of treatment can be on ways to reduce tensions in the system and return it to stability as soon as possible.

A second issue is that ecosystems theory emphasizes how people adapt to environmental structures that exercise social control. Existing circumstances tend to be accepted as givens, and the focus may become how to adjust participants within those limits, rather than to question the limits or valuing disruptions positively. Professionals may be in the role of experts in diagnosing sources of tension and in finding ways to enable participants to adapt in order to return to equilibrium. Thus, reducing tensions and reestablishing harmony may become goals of intervention. Successful adjustment of individuals within existing social norms may be assumed to be the highest good, and individuality, creativity, and autonomy become subordinate to the needs of the system.

Third, one may conclude that use of this metatheory requires many different interventive skills that practitioners must master to address the entire range of needs on all system levels. This conclusion, of course, is unrealistic. A metatheory provides a comprehensive theoretical framework within which the domain-specific theories and interventions are integrated and purposefully utilized to meet specific needs in a specific situation with specific persons. We support Wakefield's (1996) belief that ecosystems theory is not sufficient in itself and that practitioners should have skills in domain-specific interventions like those presented in this book. We disagree, however, with his contention that an ecosystems theory base is not clinically useful. Myriads of professionals have attested to the usefulness of the metatheory as presented here and supplemented by specific interventive methods to meet varying levels of need.

TABLE 2.1   *Key Principles of the Ecological Systems Perspective*

Ecological View
Transactions are continuous, reciprocal exchanges.
Life stresses are either positive or negative person–environment relationships.
Coping refers to problem solving and managing negative feelings.
Habitat is the physical and social setting within a cultural context.
Niche is the result of one's accommodation to the environment.
Relatedness involves supportive networks and attachments.

Systems View
Wholeness—Change in one part causes changes throughout system.
Feedback—Regulates system by inputs from family and environment.
Equifinality—There is more than one way to get to a final goal.
Circular causality—Not linear cause and effect, but interactions.

Practice Focus
Recognize diverse needs of families on varying levels.
Explore various practice roles involved in ecosystems dual focus.
Attend to life cycle transitions, interpersonal processes, and environmental settings.
Focus on strengths, not deficits; solutions, not problems.
Assess ecosystems at four levels: micro-, meso-, exo-, and macro-.

Pitfalls
Focusing on personal adaptations to the exclusion of social change.
Valuing homeostasis as the goal.
Making individuality, creativity, and autonomy subordinate to the system.

If family practitioners can avoid such pitfalls and heed these caveats, then ecosystems theory may be applied effectively to practice. The key points of this section on ecosystems theory are summarized in Table 2.1.

Social Constructionist Perspective

A more recent arrival on the family practice scene, the *social constructionist approach,* is based on the metaphor of literature. Human actions and relationships are seen in terms of organized efforts to create meaning out of personal experiences. These efforts are like composing narratives: stories that people write about themselves. Experiences of the objective and subjective realms are selectively arranged on the basis of assumed themes, which organize, structure, and bring meaning to the person or family (Berger & Luckmann, 1966; Hoffman, 1988, 1990; Sarbin, 1986; Von Glasersfeld, 1987).

Stories are crucial means that people in every culture use to create meaning and purpose in life. In all communities and families, stories appear in a variety of forms, including anecdotes, myths and fables, plays and movies, novels and poems, histories and biographies, case studies, and others. Much of people's development as social beings occurs through listening to and understanding narratives, the stories that people tell about their own and others' lives. Reminiscences by the elderly represent important efforts to articulate meaning in their lives, and encouraging such reflections has been recognized as an important component of practice with aged individuals. Stories constitute the basic structures all persons use to make sense of their lives, and hence, understanding narratives is fundamental to the practice of social work with families (Goldstein, 1988; Scott, 1989).

The social constructionism perspective on human behavior emphasizes the textual structure of everyday life, especially how people develop meaning in the diverse events of their day-to-day experience. Behavior is seen through the analogy of a story that a person is creating and telling about what he or she is doing and how such tasks and experiences are organized into a meaningful whole (Holland, 1991; O'Hanlon & Weiner-Davis, 1988). One's present, dominant story can be empowering, or it can undermine meaningful relationships and effective social functioning (Polkinghorne, 1988).

A fundamental assumption of social constructionism is that reality is constructed or generated by participants, rather than being objective, external, or given. People's efforts to make sense of inner and outer experience involve trying to formulate some coherence and meaning from streams of events (Ricoeur, 1981). To create this formulation, people draw on their culture's storehouse of themes and attributions, handed down by their relatives and community leaders. Persons interpret events and experiences on the basis of cultural patterns, preformulated clusters of meaning that serve to enable the person to make sense of perceptions. All of these constructed meanings depend for their existence on the minds of the persons carrying and using them. No one's beliefs or conclusions are more real than another's, and all participate in editing, revising, and continuing the stories of meaning that they share.

Such contexts of meaning take on a narrative form, linking past, present, and anticipated future and involving movement toward or away from goals. Or the form may emphasize blockage or no change (Gergen, 1982). Story patterns involving interrupted movement toward a desired goal, followed by an inescapable defeat, constitute the theme of tragedy, whereas patterns involving movement away from a desired goal, followed by unexpected success, constitute the romantic theme. Other themes in many cultures include the use of a journey as a metaphor for life experiences, eventual retribution for injustice, and struggles between light and darkness or hope and despair.

Another component of social constructionism is the assumption that themes and clusters of assumed reality (cultures) cannot be controlled from the outside. They are not amenable to reconstruction through objective or instrumental manipulation by any outside technical expert, because they are formulations of the participants themselves. Participants may observe their own patterns and explore alternatives for themselves, allowing them to understand their experiences in new ways and hence respond differently than in the past. All that an outsider can do is to reflect the themes in use and offer participants alternative themes for consideration in making meaning out of their experiences. Outsiders (including practitioners) can attempt to create a context that invites participants to pursue such observations, reflections, and developments for themselves, but they cannot directly change participants' themes or actions.

Applications to Family Practice

The social constructionist metatheory has extensive applicability for practice with families and for the role of the practitioner. In this chapter, the basic overarching principles that are consistent with this perspective are presented. (More specific methods and techniques are found in Chapters 9 and 11, where solution-focused and narrative family interventions are discussed.)

- It is assumed that all interpretations and meanings are created by the participants, so there is no outside, right standard by which to diagnose or modify. Because everyone, including the practitioner, is engaged in developing meaning to deal with experience, the helping relationship is essentially a process of joint work on the themes brought by the family and the practitioner. In this shared work, the relationship is between equals and is nonhierarchical, and the power or right to assert interpretations is equally shared (Gergen & McNamee, 1992; Simon et al., 1985; Whitaker & Bumberry, 1988).

- The practitioner respects the family's right to make use of its own themes and seeks to understand their origin and application. Together, the family and the practitioner explore the implications of the assumptions, directions, and anticipated ends of the family's dominant story.

- Practitioners can nurture the development of such supportive, rather than paternalistic, relationships with families by recognizing the importance of trying to understand what a particular person's experiences seem like from his or her own perspective and by attempting to appreciate life and its problems as they are construed in his or her subjective experience (Goldstein, 1988). What families often need is not so much expert advice, technical fixes, or precise data as a responsive listener who will try to make sense out of their experiences and provide overt, caring encouragement to resume their roles as the capable authors of their own stories (Gergen & McNamee, 1992). The social constructionism approach to family practice emphasizes the client's *strengths,* rather than pathology or deficits; emphasizes *exceptions,* or times when the problem was not present; and builds on those times when something the client tried *did* work effectively. The relationship between the family and practitioner is one of joint exploration and coauthorship, not a hierarchy in which one person provides solutions to the other's deficits (Link & Sullivan, 1989).

Caveats in Using the Social Constructionist Metatheory

Social constructionism has prompted a shift in the attention of family practitioners from actions to meanings, from expertise to collaboration, and from diagnosis of problems to mutual creation of solutions. However, the spread of interest in social constructionism should not be accepted as an unmixed blessing. Implications of its own story about how families and family interventions operate should be examined critically.

The first caveat regarding social constructionism is its assumption of relativism regarding all meanings. The theory holds that there is no single, correct reality and that meanings are strictly constructed by participants. If that is the case, then any interpretation would be as good as any other, from inclusive themes to destructive ones. The theory provides no explicit grounds for precluding various interpretations of experience, including illusions or sadism. Families trying to deny their pain would have a legitimate base for doing so with the maximum possible comfort, a condition about which the theory provides no evident guidance (Becvar & Becvar, 2009; Nichols & Schwartz, 1991). Although social constructionism does not necessarily lead to coauthorship of denials or destructive interpretations, nothing within the theory clearly precludes such possibilities.

A related problem with social constructionism is its inattention to the evident differences in power among family members and between families and communities. Dominant members of a family may impose their preferred interpretations on subordinate members, denying them the legitimacy of their own meanings and undermining their well-being. Likewise, community prejudice and discrimination may lead to the denial of basic resources and opportunities for some families, particularly those from minority groups, thus limiting their life chances and well-being regardless of the family's constructions or reconstructions. Again, nothing in social constructionism necessarily supports such abuses of power, but nothing in the theory draws explicit attention to them or provides explicit ways of dealing with them.

Underneath these problems lies a logical dilemma that confronts social constructionism: If there is no external reality, then that principle would preclude the assertion that the components of constructionism are true representations of anything, including its descriptions of how people deal with problems, develop meaning, undergo change, or do therapy (Held, 1990). In short, if people cannot know reality, then they cannot assert anything about it. Social constructionism cannot have it both ways.

Advocates of social constructionism would likely respond to such concerns by saying that all of people's perceptions of reality are incomplete. The theory is intended to be a metamodel for practice, rather than an assertion about ontological reality. Such a defense is hardly sufficient, however, because any theory would hasten to take refuge inside such permissiveness. So although social constructionism offers many useful ideas for family practice, it continues to face difficult challenges in its formulation and refinement. The concern for family practitioners is to emphasize the strengths of this metamodel and to avoid its pitfalls. The key points of this section on social constructionism are summarized in Table 2.2.

Comparing and Integrating the Metatheories

Both the ecosystems and social constructionism approaches to family practice are comprehensive theories, or metatheories, and both offer ways of looking at the world, particularly with regard to individual and social change (Payne, 1991). Each is inclusive in the sense that it accepts perspectives and methods drawn from other theories. We now look at a comparison of the two metatheories.

Both ecosystems and constructionism assume that a *family* is a group of persons involved in sustained, intimate interaction with one another. The interaction among these members becomes patterned or regularized on the basis of mutually shared expectations, meanings, and responses. Similarities or congruences among the meanings and expectations of members are the basis for stability and satisfaction, whereas incongruences lead to dissatisfaction and conflict. Creative explorations of alternative, more congruent shared meanings are the main concern of practice.

The two metatheories converge on a number of aspects and dimensions of family practice. The time focus of both is on the present and the anticipated future, rather than on the past. The context of each is the family as a group, not individuals. The goals emphasized by both perspectives involve enabling the family to identify and develop creative alternatives to unsatisfying patterns, rather than correcting past deficits. The role of the practitioner called for by both metatheories is to be a peer as much as possible in the process of mutual reflection and exploration of alternatives and change, not to be analytical, instructive, or

TABLE 2.2   *Key Principles of the Social Constructionist Perspective*

Stories and Personal Meaning
Stories transmit meaning.

Their creation formulates coherent sequences.

They shape one's identity.

They organize values and explain choices.

They are organized by plots and themes.

They involve choosing from alternative interpretations.

Family functioning depends on shared meanings.

Meanings cannot be controlled from outside.

Emphasis shifts from actions to meanings, from expertise to collaboration, from diagnosis of problems to mutual creation of solutions.

Practice Focus
Nonhierarchical relationship.

Shared explorations.

Offer new meanings and assumptions.

Bring families' themes and values to awareness.

Be coauthor of a living story with them.

Nurture supportive, not paternalistic, relationships.

Pitfalls
Seeing any interpretation as being as good as any other.

Inattention to power differences in family and community regarding interpretations.

Assuming that social constructionism has all the answers and that they are the best.

---

prescriptive. The style of intervention emphasized by each is exploratory, nondirective, less structured, and seeking exceptions to problems, not corrective, analytical, or educational.

Both metatheories interpret experience in symbolic or metaphorical terms, not as literal or as problems to be controlled. Their treatment of resistance is protective of the core meanings and relationships among family members; it does not function in terms of lack of motivation or dysfunction. The criteria for success of an intervention emphasized by both are mutual acceptability, satisfaction, and meaningfulness among family members, not logical, objective, or behavioral measures. The key similarities between these perspectives are summarized in Table 2.3.

The two metatheories diverge somewhat in their emphases within the treatment process. The ecosystems perspective focuses attention on breakdowns in family equilibrium needing negotiation to reestablish homeostasis or mutually satisfactory exchanges. Constructionism treats family issues in terms of breakdowns in shared meaning that need reconstruction into new and more satisfying shared meanings.

TABLE 2.3 *Convergences in Ecosystems and Constructionism*

Dimension	Comment
Time	Both are focused on the present and the anticipated future, rather than on the past.
Goals	Both seek to identify and develop creative alternatives, rather than to correct past deficits.
Style of intervention	Both are exploratory, nondirective, less structured, seek exceptions to problems; not corrective, analytical, or educational.
Context	Both focus on the family as a system, not on individuals.
Role of practitioner	A peer as much as possible in the process of mutual reflection and exploration of alternatives; not analytical, instructive, or prescriptive.
Interpretation of experience	Symbolic or metaphorical; not literal or in terms of problems to be controlled.
Understanding of resistance	Protective of the core meanings and relationships among members; not focused on lack of motivation or dysfunction.
Criteria for success	Mutual acceptability, satisfaction, and meaningfulness to participants; not logical, objective, or behavioral.

Both the ecosystems and social constructionism approaches to family practice provide broad perspectives on how to understand and deal with family issues. The ecosystems model focuses primarily on the transactions of the family within the larger social environment, whereas the social constructionist model emphasizes the meanings that families and their members formulate out of those streams of events.

Both approaches are based on specialized bodies of knowledge. The ecosystems theory emphasizes knowledge of the diverse transactions among people and their environments. Means of strengthening the effectiveness of those interactions are major concerns of practice. Social constructionism focuses on how people find meaning in the diverse experiences of their daily lives; treatment involves the development of meanings that are more empowering for families. The key divergences between these perspectives are summarized in Table 2.4.

Although neither approach is a complete practice model in itself, each has spawned a variety of specific methods and techniques for application in professional practice with families (Meyer, 1988; Rosen, 1988). For example, the life model of social work practice is rooted in ecosystems theory (Germain & Gitterman, 1980), as are the family-centered approach (Hartman & Laird, 1983) and the competence approach (Maluccio, 1981). The narrative approach to family practice (White & Epston, 1990) and the solution-focused approach (O'Hanlon & Weiner-Davis, 1988) are based on social constructionism. These and other practice models provide the specificity needed in working directly with families.

TABLE 2.4   *Comparisons in Ecosystems and Constructionism*

Criteria
1. *Explicit knowledge base:* How clear and extensive is the grounding of the approach in theory and research?
2. *Focus of attention:* How are family issues defined?
3. *Change process:* Does the approach explain how family change occurs?
4. *Guidelines for intervention:* Does the approach delineate actions of the practitioner?
5. *Values:* What values are emphasized?

Ecosystems	*Social Constructionism*
1. Moderate	Limited
2. Disruption of equilibrium	Meaninglessness
3. Negotiation of new homeostasis	Construction of new meanings
4. As expert	As coauthor
5. Harmony	Meaningfulness

Summary

The ecosystems–social constructionism approach to family practice is a combination of two metatheories that complement each other to form a broad theoretical base for family assessment and practice. This approach offers a way of looking at the world and particularly at personal and social change.

Each metatheory has specific strengths that inform family practice. However, each has limits, as well. The family practitioner should be aware of these limitations, as they have definite implications for practice. There are areas in which the two theories diverge that supplement each other and fill in particular gaps. There are more similarities that emerge as the theories are analyzed by specific dimensions. These convergences enable the practitioner to draw on the two metatheories in creating a meaningful approach to assessing and working with families.

The following sections of this book provide specific practice methods that can be used in working with families. Each is applied to one of the four levels of family need within the overall framework of the linked ecosystems–social constructionism approach.

Discussion Questions

1. Discuss the key assumptions of the ecological systems view and apply them to a family.

2. Select a presenting problem and design an intervention using the social constructionist perspective of human behavior.

3. Why is it important for practitioners to view a client system holistically?

4. How could the combined ecosystems–social constructionist approach be used with low-functioning clients? Does the use of social constructionist theory imply that clients must be verbally skilled?

5. Discuss how the two metatheories diverge in their emphasis within the treatment process and how the integration of these two metatheories could be helpful in working with families.

6. Discuss how the theories of social constructionism and ecosystems can be combined to address the problems of families in poverty.

7. Prepare a narrative about your life or an important episode in your life according to the concepts of the social constructionist approach.

8. What personal biases would limit your use of social constructionist theory in working with families?

Internet Resources

Family Systems

http://psychematters.com/family.htm
www.aamft.org
http://en.wikipedia.org/wiki/family_systems_therapy
www.addictionalternatives.com/philosophy/familysystems .htm

Social Constructionism

www.narrativeapproaches.com
www.narrativepsych.com

Suggested Readings

Coles, R. (1989). *The call of stories: Teaching and the moral imagination.* Boston: Houghton Mifflin.
  The training of child psychiatrists has been immensely enriched by the work of Robert Coles, whose volume leads the reader through his experiences working with the children in his practice as well as from the students in his classes. This book demonstrates the wide applicability of the narrative framework for practice and for education in the helping professions.

Greene, R. R. (1999). *Human behavior theory and social work practice* (2nd ed.). New York: Aldine de Gruyter.
  This book gives a good overview of the ecosystems perspective within a human behavior framework. Applications to practice are made.

Hoffman, L. (1990). Constructing realities: An art of lenses. *Family Process, 29*(1), 1–12.
  Social construction theory is used to move toward a more collaborative and unconcealed therapeutic stance. This theory plus a second-order view and sensitivity to gender issues are the three lenses used for constructing realities.

Polkinghorne, D. E. (1988). *Narrative knowing and the human sciences.* Albany: State University of New York Press.
  Using literary criticism, philosophy, history, and recent developments in the social sciences, this volume shows how to use research information organized by the narrative form—such information as clinical case histories, biographies, and personal stories. The relationships between narrative formats and classical empirical research designs are examined, and suggestions for studying human behavior from a narrative framework are set forth.

Sarup, M. (1989). *An introductory guide to poststructuralism and postmodernism.* Athens: University of Georgia Press.
  Three of the most influential figures in recent literary criticism—Jacques Lacan, Jacques Derrida, and Michel Foucault—have had extensive influence on the way people think about meaning in their experiences. This book traces the rise of narrative approaches to thought, radically opposed to the

Enlightenment tenets of progress and scientific truth, and explores some implications of this perspective for the future of human social life.

Wakefield, J. C. (1988). Psychotherapy, distributive justice, and social work, Parts 1 & 2. *Social Science Review, 62*(2,3), 187–210, 353–382.

Wakefield argues that social work's organizing value is minimal distributive justice, in which all people would have a minimally acceptable level of basic economic, social, and psychological goods. This concept seems to build on an ecosystems framework and then utilize varying methods and interventive skills for meeting specific levels of needs.

References

Becvar, D. S., & Becvar, R. J. (2009). *Family therapy: A systemic integration* (7th ed.). Boston: Allyn & Bacon.

Berger, P., & Luckmann, T. (1966). *The social construction of reality.* Garden City, NY: Doubleday.

Bowlby, J. (1973). Affectional bonds: Their nature and origin. In R. S. Weiss (Ed.), *Loneliness: The experience of emotional and social isolation* (pp. 38–52). Cambridge, MA: MIT Press.

Breunlin, D. C., Schwartz, R. C., & Kune-Karrer, B. M. (1992). *Metaframeworks: Transcending the models of family therapy.* San Francisco: Jossey-Bass.

Brower, A. M. (September 1988). Can the ecological model guide social work practice? *Social Service Review, 62*(3), 411–429.

Cleveland, P. H., & Kilpatrick, A. C. (1990). *Social work students' involvement with the homeless: An international model.* Paper presented at the International Congress of Schools of Social Work, Lima, Peru.

Cobb, S. (1976). Social support as a moderator of life stress. *Psychosomatic Medicine, 38*(5), 300–314.

Gaudin, J. M., Jr. (1993). *Child neglect: A guide for intervention.* Washington, DC: National Center on Child Abuse and Neglect.

Gaudin, J. M., Jr. (1999). Child neglect: Short-term and long-term outcomes. In H. Dubowitz (Ed.), *Neglected children: Research, practice, and policy* (pp. 89–108). Thousand Oaks, CA: Sage.

Gergen, K. J. (1982). *Toward transformation in social knowledge.* New York: Springer-Verlag.

Gergen, K. J., & McNamee, S. (1992). *Social constructionism in therapeutic process.* London: Sage.

Germain, C. B. (1985). The place of community within an ecological approach to social work practice. In S. H. Taylor & R. W. Roberts (Eds.), *Theories and practice of community social work* (pp. 30–55). New York: Columbia University Press.

Germain, C. B., & Gitterman, A. (1980). *The life model of social work practice.* New York: Columbia University Press.

Germain, C. B., & Gitterman, A. (1987). Ecological perspective. In A. Minahan et al. (Eds.), *Encyclopedia of social work* (18th ed., pp. 488–499). Silver Spring, MD: National Association of Social Workers.

Germain, C. B., & Gitterman, A. (1995). Ecological perspective. In R. L. Edwards (Ed.), *Encyclopedia of social work* (19th ed., pp. 816–824). Washington, DC: National Association of Social Workers.

Goldenberg, I., & Goldenberg, H. (1991). *Family therapy: An overview.* Monterey, CA: Brooks-Cole.

Goldstein, H. (1988). Humanistic alternatives to the limits of scientific knowledge. *Social Thought, 14*(1), 47–58.

Greene, R. R. (1999). *Human behavior theory and social work practice* (2nd ed.). New York: Aldine de Gruyter.

Hartman, A., & Laird, J. (1983). *Family centered social work practice.* New York: Free Press.

Hefferman, J., Shuttlesworth, G., & Ambrosina, R. (1988). A systems/ecological perspective. In *Social work and social welfare: An introduction.* St. Paul, MN: West.

Held, B. S. (1990). What's in a name: Some confusions and concerns about Constructivism. *Journal of Marital and Family Therapy, 16,* 179–186.

Hoffman, L. (1988). A constructivist position for family therapy. *Irish Journal of Psychology, 9,* 110–129.

Hoffman, L. (1990). Constructing realities: An art of lenses. *Family Process, 29*(1), 1–12.

Holland, T. P. (1991). Narrative, knowledge, and professional practice. *Social Thought, 17*(1), 32–40.

Lazarus, R. S. (1980). The stress and coping paradigm. In L. A. Bond & J. C. Rosen (Eds.), *Competence and coping during adulthood* (pp. 28–74). Hanover, NH: University Press of New England.

Link, R. J., & Sullivan, M. (1989). Vital connections: Using literature to illustrate social work issues. *Journal of Social Work Education, 25*(3), 192–230.

Long, D. D., & Holle, M. C. (1997). *Macro systems in the social environment.* Itasca, IL: Peacock.

Maluccio, A. N. (1981). *Promoting competence in clients.* New York: Free Press.

Mattaini, M. A. (1997). *Visual ecoscan for clinical practice.* Silver Spring, MD: NASW Press.

Meyer, C. H. (1988). The ecosystems perspective. In R. A. Dorfman (Ed.), *Paradigms of clinical social work.* New York: Brunner/Mazel.

Nichols, M. P., & Schwartz, R. C. (1991). *Family therapy: Concepts and methods* (2nd ed.). Boston: Allyn & Bacon.

O'Hanlon, W. H., & Weiner-Davis, M. (1988). *In search of solutions: A new direction in psychotherapy.* New York: Norton.

Payne, M. (1991). *Modern social work theory: A critical introduction.* Chicago: Lyceum.

Polkinghorne, D. E. (1988). *Narrative knowing and the human sciences.* Albany: State University of New York Press.

Ricoeur, P. (1981). *Hermeneutics and the human sciences.* Cambridge, UK: Cambridge University Press.

Rosen, H. (1988). The constructivist-developmental paradigm. In R. A. Dorfman (Ed.), *Paradigms of clinical social work* (pp. 317–355). New York: Brunner/Mazel.

Sarbin, T. R. (1986). *Narrative psychology: The storied nature of human conduct.* New York: Praeger.

Scott, D. (1989). Meaning construction and social work practice. *Social Service Review, 63*(1), 39–51.

Simon, F. B., Stierlin, H., & Wynne, L. (1985). *The language of family therapy.* New York: Family Process Press.

Von Bertalanffy, L. (1968). *General systems theory.* New York: Braziller.

Von Glasersfeld, E. (1987). The control of perception and the construction of reality. *Dialectica, 33,* 37–50.

Wakefield, J. C. (1996). Does social work need the ecosystems perspective? Parts 1 & 2. *Social Service Review, 70*(1,2), 1–32, 183–213.

Watzlawick, P., Beavin, J. H., & Jackson, D. D. (1967). *Pragmatics of human communication: A study of interactional patterns, pathologies and paradoxes.* New York: Norton.

Weiss, R. S. (Ed.). (1973). *Loneliness: The experience of emotional and social isolation.* Cambridge, MA: MIT Press.

Whitaker, C. A., & Bumberry, W. M. (1988). *Dancing with the family.* New York: Brunner/Mazel.

White, M., & Epston, D. (1990). *Narrative means to therapeutic ends.* New York: Norton.

3

Contexts of Helping: Commonalities and Human Diversities

Allie C. Kilpatrick, Ph.D., June G. Hopps, Ph.D., and Kareema J. Gray, M.S.W.

Four levels of family need applicable to assessing and working with families have been presented. Following the assessment of the primary level of need, intervention procedures are planned based on this information. The metatheories of ecological systems and social constructionism are utilized as comprehensive perspectives within which to undertake the assessment and interventions with each family.

Another important consideration in the context of family practice is the acknowledgement of both commonality and diversity. It is crucial that the family practitioner have knowledge, awareness, and skill in developing the necessary core and common conditions of the helping relationship or therapeutic alliance and in dealing with human diversity.

Practitioners share many more commonalities than differences with families. These commonalities can serve as the foundation for building the therapeutic alliance and also for exploring differences. Errors in professional judgment that should be avoided are the tendencies (1) to see differences or commonalties when they are *not* there and (2) not to see differences or commonalities when they *are* present. This chapter seeks to explore and balance these two concepts of commonality and difference.

The Helping Relationship/Therapeutic Alliance

Recent research indicates that the therapeutic relationship and personal ecosystems resources account for 60 percent of client system change, while the use of models and techniques generally affects the remaining influence on client system change (Duncan, Miller, & Sparks, 2004). The metatheories of ecosystems and social constructionism that provide the basis for the investigative approach to family practice emphasize the principles of respect, responsive listening, caring encouragement, nonhierarchical relationships, shared power, and equality of meanings as commonalities in working with families.

Closely related to these principles is the "I–Thou" relationship described by Buber (1958), in which there is an emphasis on what takes place between people—for our purposes, especially between the practitioner and the family. The goal is for each to relate to the other in a way that acknowledges the other's internal life, without any possibility of one being exploited by the other. The interaction is a dialogue. The focus or emphasis is on the interchange between them and the experience of mutual confirmation that can occur.

Historically, the concept of the helping relationship has permeated work with people since the early days of social casework and psychoanalysis. Biestek (1957) traced the development of this concept in social casework from Mary Richmond in 1899 through 1951. He then developed his legendary *seven principles of relationship,* which started with the client's needs expressed to the practitioner as the first direction of the interaction, the response of the caseworker to the client's needs as the second direction, and the client's awareness of the caseworker's responsiveness as the third direction. Based on the needs of the client, the seven principles were then articulated as individualization, purposeful expression of feelings, controlled emotional involvement, acceptance, nonjudgmental attitude, self-determination, and confidentiality. Biestek's conceptualization still holds currency, although it was published over fifty years ago (see Berlin, 2005; Brandell & Ringel, 2004; Gregory & Holloway, 2005; Larkin, 2003; Miehls & Moffatt, 2000; Palmer & Kaufman, 2003; Ruch, 2005).

We have adapted Biestek's (1957) formulation to include terms relating his concepts to working with families (see Table 3.1) and to incorporate awareness of the environment and the eighth principle of cultural competence. Further, we acknowledge that given changing demographics, practitioners for the future will need to reduce communication barriers and develop language skills, even becoming bilingual when essential for effective intervention.

These principles are relevant today and applicable to the family as the client system, although none is absolute. For example, the principle of confidentiality is limited by the rights of other individuals, the practitioner, the community, and society. Such behaviors as abuse are legally required to be reported and are never acceptable, regardless of claims of cultural acceptance.

The personal characteristics and behaviors displayed by practitioners are intrinsically related to the formulation of a working relationship. The research of Rogers, Gendlin, Kiesler, and Truax (1969) and Truax and Carkhuff (1967) presents evidence suggesting that the therapists' ability to function in three core emotional and interpersonal dimensions has a significant influence on effectiveness. These core characteristics are (1) *empathy,* the ability to accurately perceive what people are experiencing and to communicate that perception to them; (2) *respect,* positive regard and the indication of a deep and honest acceptance of the worth of persons apart from behaviors; and (3) *genuineness,* the ability to

TABLE 3.1 *Seven Principles in the Helping Relationship*

First Direction: The Need of the Family	*Second Direction: The Response of the Practitioner*	*Third Direction: The Awareness of the Client/Family*	*The Name of the Principle*
1. To be treated as individuals			1. Individualization
2. To express feelings			2. Purposeful expression of feelings
3. To get empathic responses to problems			3. Controlled emotional involvement
4. To be recognized as people of worth	The practitioner is sensitive to, understands, and appropriately responds to these needs.	The client/family is somehow aware of the practitioner's sensitivity, understanding, and response.	4. Acceptance
5. Not to be judged			5. Nonjudgmental attitude
6. To make own choices and decisions			6. Self-determination
7. To keep secrets about self and family			7. Confidentiality
8. To be aware of environmental context			8. Cultural competence

be honest with oneself and with others. Horvath (2000) agrees with this premise and supports the importance of the practitioner's relatedness to the client in the working alliance. An additional core condition of *warmth,* or treating people in a way that makes them feel safe, accepted, and understood, was added by Goldstein (1975), who observed that without warmth, the practitioner may be "technically correct but therapeutically impotent" (p. 31). These four core characteristics are necessary conditions for ensuring that no harm is done and for developing a therapeutic climate within which family work may be conducted.

Most family practitioners consider the relationship between the family and the practitioner to be an essential ingredient of the therapeutic process. However, little systematic attention has been given to examining the function of the therapeutic alliance in working with families. Minuchin (1974) has talked about the necessity for the therapist to "join" the family, and Davatz (1981) has emphasized the importance of "connecting" with family members.

Pinsof and Catherall (1986) state that the therapeutic alliance may be the primary mediating variable that determines the outcome of discrete interventions. They assert that adding the alliance concept to the theoretical base of family therapy illuminates and brings into focus a critical aspect of therapy that has existed in a theoretical twilight (p. 138). Pinsof (1994) builds on previous definitions to define the alliance, noting that it "consists of those aspects of the relationship between and within the therapist and patient systems that pertain to their capacity to mutually invest in and collaborate on the tasks and goals of therapy" (p. 7).

The major difference between this definition and preceding ones is that it tries to account for the social field in which the alliance occurs. There is an alliance between two systems, not just two people, regardless of the number of people directly involved in the sessions. The *client system* consists of all the human systems that are or may be involved in maintaining or resolving the presenting problem. The *therapist system* consists of all the people involved in treating the client system. In other words, the systems consist of all the people who can influence the change process.

In working with families, the therapeutic alliance exists on at least three levels: (1) the individual alliance with each family member; (2) the subsystem alliance with each of the multiperson subsystems such as parents and children; (3) and the whole family system (Pinsof, 1995; Pinsof & Catherall, 1986; also see Mandin, 2007). The alliance the practitioner has with one or two family members influences his or her alliance with other family members in a circular, reciprocal fashion. Therefore, no single alliance with a dyad or triad can be considered in isolation.

Horvath (2000) and Florsheim, Shotorbani, Guest-Warnick, Barratt, and Hwang (2000) suggest that studies over time have proven that the therapeutic alliance is an important element in the helping encounter, regardless of the theoretical perspective used in treatment. Research by Kivlighan and Shaughnessy (2000) confirms the importance of the overall strength of the therapeutic alliance. This study also supports the notion of an alliance rupture's being part of developing a successful working relationship with clients—"perhaps a general pattern of initial engagement followed by conflict and then reengagement characterizes successful treatment" (p. 370).

A significant contribution to understanding the therapeutic alliance has been the development of three systematically oriented scales to measure the alliance in individual, couples, and family work (Pinsof, 1994; Pinsof & Catherall, 1986). Each measures the content dimensions of tasks, goals, and bonds as they relate to the therapeutic alliance. None of this research, however, definitively addresses client diversity and its impact and influence on the therapeutic alliance.

Client Diversity

The United States is witnessing large-scale immigration, both legal and illegal, and this is reflected in the diversity found among clients and families. A practitioner may encounter differences in culture, ethnicity, race, social class, religion, regional identities, gender, age, disability, affinity, sexual orientation, and other factors that can significantly affect and define people's lives. Some of the differences that are most relevant to practice with families are addressed in the following sections about ethnic-sensitive practice, multiculturalism, and cultural democracy; gender justice; power and powerlessness; poverty; and family structure.

Ethnic-Sensitive Practice, Multiculturalism, and Cultural Democracy

The *ethnic-sensitive practice model,* which is based on an ethnocultural perspective, suggests that the core concepts of ethnicity, social class, and oppression are integrated within an organizing framework of intervention principles (Anderson, 2003). The model assumes that ethnic groups' cultural differences lead to unique realities for members that can be more clearly understood via knowledge of those differences (p. 44).

An important component is recognizing the oppression experienced by members of racial and ethnic groups and choosing relevant practice models for the family's needs at that time. Practitioners should know that being unwilling to challenge and address oppression in large societal systems is akin to aiding families in adjusting to their oppressors. Oppression can never be accepted as normal.

Some significant assumptions of ethnic sensitive practice include the following:

1. History affects the generation and solution of problems.
2. The present is more important than the past or the future.
3. Nonconscious phenomena affect family functioning.
4. Although ethnicity can be a source of strain, discordance, and strife, it can also be a source of cohesion, identity, and strength (Schlesinger & Devore, 1995).

A *multicultural perspective* is another component of ethnic-sensitive practice, and it necessitates practitioners learning to value and embrace the unique attributes and nuances of cultures other than their own. Philip Fellin (as cited in Lum, 2003) notes several principles that underlie a multicultural perspective:

1. It should be inclusive of all subcultural groups that are viewed as distinct yet interdependent with mainstream U.S. culture.
2. It should recognize that all people in U.S. society identify with multiple cultures with varying degrees of affiliation.
3. It should recognize that all members of U.S. society engage in various types of relationships within their various cultures and in relation to a mainstream U.S. culture.
4. It should recognize the changing nature of U.S. society as it is continually influenced by all of its subcultures (pp. 271–272).

Also key to effective practice is the practitioner's capacity to understand culture and power and the connection between the two. The practitioner needs to demonstrate knowledge of the clients' or group's culture in addition to being willing to help clients respect their own culture and the cultures of others. Hopps, Pinderhughes, and Shankar (1995) suggest the following:

> Practitioners' knowledge of their own culture should include the capacity to take responsibility for managing any biases, prejudices, learned misinformation, and distorted attitudes and stereotypes held about clients. Each client must be given the opportunity to demonstrate his or her own strengths. The flexibility in thinking and behavior that such a stance requires

means that extra steps, extra efforts, and extra time will be needed to understand differences presented by a client. This means using a way of thinking that involves application of general knowledge about various cultural groups to a specific client. A two-level process, which involves a look at the specifics within the general and vice-versa while managing the complexities involved, is a key to empowering. (Hopps & Morris, 2000, p. 89)

Efforts at problem resolution must be in tune with ethnically distinctive values and community customs. Such practice involves the concept of the *dual perspective,* or a conscious and systematic process of simultaneously perceiving, understanding, and comparing the values, attitudes, and behaviors of the larger social system with those of the family's immediate community system. This perspective recognizes that every client is part of two systems: the dominant or sustaining system, which is the source of power and economic resources, and the nurturing system, which is composed of the physical and social environment of the family and community (Norton, 1998).

As described by Anderson (2003), "The dual perspective should not be interpreted as being a concept for use only with minorities; it can be applied to all people. It should direct attention to the 'common human needs of people' and the degree to which they are not within the nurturing society and within the major society" (p. 83). The dual systems faced by all individuals are noted in Figure 3.1.

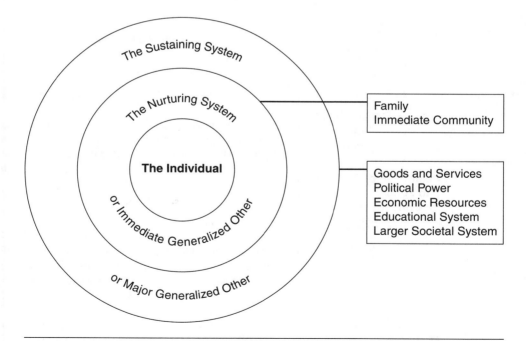

FIGURE 3.1 *The Dual Systems of All Individuals*

Source: Anderson, 2003; Norton, 1998.

In a discussion of the dual perspective, Arline Prigoff (2003) reviews the San Antonio Model (SAM), which highlights a Cultural Assessment Grid. In utilizing the grid, clients and practitioners are able to isolate elements of both clients and environmental systems that can be viewed as resources in the resolution of the clients' problems (see Types I and II in Figure 3.2) or as contributors to problems (see Types III and IV).

If the dual perspective is followed in tandem with the grid, it becomes an effective tool in discerning elements of the environment and their impact on clients. For example, the dominant sustaining system can be hostile to cultural diversity and thus correspond more closely with Type IV, whereas the sustaining system of people of color corresponds more with Type II. What this shows is how the two systems can act either as positive, nurturing forces or as negative, nonsustaining forces.

Ethnic and class history and traditions often involve institutional sources of oppression. Therefore, practice with families must pay simultaneous attention to family and community/systemic concerns. Solomon (1976) observes that we find victims of poverty and oppression caught up in a systemic process of powerlessness in which the failure of the larger society system to provide needed resources operates in a circular feedback process that entraps victims and puts in motion a malignant process. The failure of the larger system to provide necessary supports creates powerlessness in communities. And the more powerlessness in a community due to lack of resources and nutritive supplies, the more powerless are the families within, hindered from meeting the needs of their members and in organizing to improve the community so that it can provide them with more support. And the more powerless the

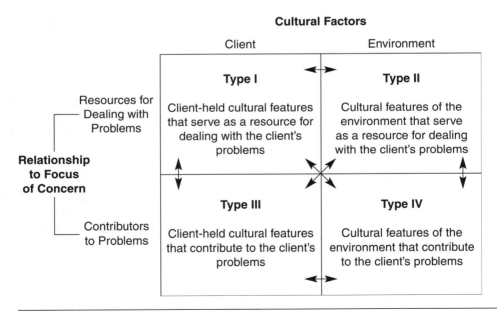

FIGURE 3.2   *Cultural Assessment Grid*

Source: Anderson & Carter, *Diversity Perspectives for Social Work Practice,* Figure 7.2, © 2003 Pearson Education, Inc. Reproduced by permission of Pearson Education Inc. All rights reserved.

families in efforts to protect their members from the stress of community failure and efforts to change its destructiveness, the more powerless are the individual members, blocked in attempts to acquire skills, develop self-esteem, and strengthen family.

Ethnic-sensitive work often requires the practitioner to think in terms of a multi-system, interactive approach as distinct from an isolated, linear approach to intervention. Many client families are challenged by complex, multiple problems (e.g., substance abuse, unemployment, underemployment, and language barriers) that demand concurrent, targeted units of intervention. What this means is that practitioners must be knowledgeable not only about clinical and group processes but also about the policies and operation of other resources, such as health care, employment and training, job placement, counseling relative to home ownership and other housing arrangements, social security, and substance abuse counseling. With this knowledge, practitioners can help connect families to needed services (Hopps & Pinderhughes, 1999; Hopps, Pinderhughes, & Shankar, 1995; Leonhardt, 2008).

Gender Justice

Family practitioners are challenged by new levels of awareness regarding gender. The subtext of gender is a priority now for the profession, due largely to advances in feminist theory and thought, broader concepts of masculinity, and the triumphant legal, economic, political, and emancipatory achievements of the civil rights movement, the women's movement, and the gay liberation movement. Gender is at the core of an ideological analysis that facilitates examination of assumptions regarding principles of hierarchy, domination, and the power of one sex over another (Hooyman, 1995).

Currently, postmodern feminism is struggling with defining its purpose and role and is being challenged to address a number of issues, including but not limited to (1) demystifying the notion of the exclusive consciousness of women as women and (2) recognizing the risks of universalizing women for the sake of solidarity. Although the latter is a needed component of change, it may also minimize individual women's uniqueness.

The feminists' theme of a universal civilizing mission both undergirded and aided their claim to legitimacy. What this meant was that feminists felt they could address the needs and interests of all women. Consequently, some women (mostly the white, Western, middle-class cohort) are being challenged by those who are not members of this cohort (poor women and women of color), who also assert that in times of multiple contested oppressions (i.e., class and race), gender might not be the deepest, most unyielding area of oppression. Unlike in the past, feminists today are increasingly able to differentiate many facets of women's identities, including not only gender but race, ethnicity, class, religion, sexual orientation, physical and mental being, and personal political orientation or political sense of self. Thus, postmodern feminism is compatible with social work in that it both respects diversity and emphasizes context, which corresponds with one of the profession's foundations: the person in environment (Forcey & Nash, 1998).

For the future, feminists must acknowledge that although there is power in viewing "women as women" and speaking as a united front in pursuit of positive social change, there is also a risk of minimizing the distinctiveness among women. What is needed is the capacity to handle this politically sensitive issue in a way that does not sacrifice women's differences or interdependence but rather enhances the goal of empowerment for all women (Forcey & Nash, 1998).

Even as women's influence reduced men's power and authority, many men continued to resist new sex-role definitions, clinging to traditional perspectives of manhood. But as time marched forward and women continued to gain economic and political power (which translated into new status arrangements), men began adapting to change and examined opportunities to address their own masculine potential. Women suggested that patriarchy diminishes feminine characteristics, such as tenderness, love, and relatedness in all people. Men, too, challenged patriarchy and stunted, insecure masculinity, which, they argued, contributes to problems related to inhibited intimacy, homophobia, the need to dominate or be dominated, and violence directed toward both men and women (Chestang, 1995; Lichtenberg, 1995).

The tasks ahead are for both men and women to move beyond old barriers and hostilities, to seek ways to explore their fullness and maturity, and to relate to their common humanity (Keen, 1991). Stories and narratives of failed experiences, tolerance and intolerance, and growth should be shared in the safe zone of mutual respect, appreciation for personal struggle, and empathy. Given new growth, both men and women should also join with other worldwide organizations in fighting servitude, sexism, and homophobia.

Another development to which therapists must be prepared to relate is the growing and increasingly open population of gays and lesbians, as well as transgenderists and bisexuals (although less is known about the latter two). This cultural subgroup has gained significant political and economic power in recent years.

The gay movement commenced with the Stonewall rebellion in 1969 and paralleled both the Black Power and women's movements. Hostility to the gay population originated with widespread and strongly held beliefs in heterocentrism, heterosexism, and homophobia, which throughout history oppressed those who could not or did not have a heterosexual identity. This belief system provided the undergirding for sociological, economic, political, and psychological factors that affected the development, sexual identity, resilience, and coping resources of the gay population. Gay people were victimized in colonial times, when sodomy was a crime punishable by death, and today still constitute the largest group of hate crime victims, suffering beatings, torture, and death in addition to discrimination in employment and access to housing, social services, and health care (Appleby, Colon, & Hamilton, 2001). Although gays and lesbians are a diverse group, they are thought to experience similar affirmative processes: namely, "identification and confrontation of sexual difference; socialization in the gay and lesbian communities; self-identification or coming out to self and others; sexual experimentation; development of a sexual identity; nurturance of sexual and intimate relationships; formulation of families . . . and life long contribution to profession and communities while under psychological duress" (Appleby et al., 2001, p. 149).

Indeed, practitioners must be able to work with the family as a member transitions through these phases. Practitioners must be prepared to help families find coping energy and perseverance when one or more of their members are confronted by and must work through internalized homophobia. This is a normative aspect of affirmative psychology that can occur at an early age with the incorporation of unavoidable noxious, negative attitudes and societal stigma into one's self-image.

It is not unusual for lesbians and gays to defend against internalized homophobia by denying who they are, distrusting and expressing anger and contempt for those who elect to be open and visible about their sexuality, becoming fearful, and withdrawing from families and associates. Many lesbians and gays experience difficulties with intimacy, affectional relationships, and sexual functioning. They may avoid managing problems such as alcoholism, drug use, safe sex, and AIDS (acquired immune deficiency disorder) and become overwhelmed with fragmentation in their lives, consequently exhibiting features of a borderline personality (Appleby et al., 2001).

Coping with stigma, discrimination, abuse, acts of violence, and internalized self-hatred, sexually divergent individuals can be prone to suicide. Family therapists must be at the forefront of efforts to minimize the influence of heterocentrism, heterosexism, homophobia, and other sexist attitudes in their practice and take the lead in helping to eradicate these discriminatory views in service delivery and society.

Power and Powerlessness

Some groups in society are oppressed because of their race and ethnicity, gender, sexual orientation, income, age, or a combination of these. Other client groups experience powerlessness because of mental, developmental, or physical disabilities.

Power is defined as the capacity to gain whatever resources are necessary to remove oneself from a condition of oppression, to guarantee one's ability to perform, and to affect not only one's own circumstances but also more general circumstances outside one's intimate surroundings (Goodrich, 1991, p. 10). Power thus involves the capacity to influence, for one's own benefit, the forces that affect one's life space. *Powerlessness* is the inability to exert such influence (Pinderhughes, 1995).

Power, as a construct, is useful in understanding the relationship between the majority group and people of color and other ethnic groups, women, gays and lesbians, as well as their interaction and role in maintaining the majority–minority status, including discrimination, racism, and sexism. A dominant group acquires and holds onto its resources and power in several ways. One is by excluding and marginalizing low-status or different groups, making it difficult for them to access and acquire what they need. Another way is by developing expectations that influence opportunities and outcomes for both lives of members of the dominant group and of those who have less power (Hopps et al., 1995; Pinderhughes, 1995).

Indeed, people who are overwhelmed and powerless may react to their role, status, and position by means that are truly unhealthy, unsafe, and unproductive. Pinderhughes (1995) offers this example:

> As individuals, minority people of color react to being tension relievers, anxiety reducers, and victims in the social system by behaviors that aim to provide them a sense of power. Many of them struggle not to accept the projections of the powerful that they are incompetent, dumb, crazy, a stud, sexual, or dependent. Considerable effort is expended to ward off a sense of powerlessness. People adopt behaviors in which they identify with the aggressor (which leads to feelings of self-hatred); are guarded (seen by the powerful as being paranoid); strike out (seen by the powerful as being violent); and are oppositional, passive-aggressive, or autonomous (seen by the powerful as being stubborn). It is important to consider that the dependency response to conditions of powerlessness does not mean ethnic minorities and people of color desire it; instead, they may adopt dependency to get a sense of power or to be close to persons who actually have power (McClelland, 1975).

They may also try to get a sense of power by assuming the negative attributions of the dominant society in an exaggerated way, for example, by being a super-stud, super dumb, or super-dependent. Although reactive, these behaviors, which Chestang (1976) identified as paradoxical mechanisms, also have meaning because they facilitate a feeling that one is the initiator. (pp. 290–291)

These reactive behaviors often inhibit individuals and families from taking proactive steps to improve their social functioning and standing and to reject designated, assigned positions. While not being able to exercise influence over one's life's chances can be painful, having such influence can be rewarding. Even so, individuals with power can exhibit fear of losing status and control and become fearful of those with little power. Powerful individuals may also experience guilt over their own privileged position; exhibit control needs; demonstrate a lack of tolerance, respect, and compassion for those who are different; and express affinity for those like themselves.

Feeling guilty because of the realities of their power, some of these individuals might be willing to give a little, but few would relinquish their power. Thus, this power conundrum is at the crux of the struggle faced by people of color, women (although they have moved well ahead of people of color), new immigrants, and gays, lesbians, and transgendered in relationship to the dominant group (Hopps et al., 1995; Pinderhughes, 1995).

Practitioners must know that power is embodied in the professional role, which is endowed with knowledge and skills and emboldened by having the license to assess, intervene in, and evaluate family functioning. Thus, there is a power differential between the practitioner and the family. The needs of some poor families of color are so great and the resources so slim that practitioners may easily become overwhelmed and anxious and fall prey to self-comforting behaviors in efforts to reduce their stress and anxiety (Hopps et al., 1995). Practitioners must assess and be realistic about their personal needs and never think of manipulating the helping/treatment encounter to meet their own status and power needs.

Practitioners can help clients and improve their functioning using relevant empowerment intervention strategies. Some of these are noted in Table 3.2.

TABLE 3.2   *Empowerment Intervention Strategies*

- Contextualize the problem. Understand how the social system has impacted one's behavior.
- Identify behavioral responses to powerless roles.
- Understand the survival nature of such behaviors; identify strengths.
- Understand the reactive nature of these responses to powerless roles. Understand costs (e.g., cannot set own goals, plan, take leadership except in reactive ways).
- Connect faulty thinking to antisocial behavior.
- Set personal and group goals.
- Take responsibility for reactive behavior that blocks teaching goals.
- Learn proactive, prosocial behavior. Change faulty thinking and antisocial behavior.
- Learn to exercise power effectively. Be a leader.
- Learn to function in collaborative roles and to negotiate.
- Learn to take action in the community as a citizen, advocate, voter, and agent of change.

Source: Adapted from Hopps & Pinderhughes, 1999, p. 89.

Poverty, Children, and Persistent Poverty

Poverty is a matter of the differentiated distribution of goods and privileges. In the preface to *The Power to Care* (Hopps et al., 1995), Wilson states,

> In an industrial society groups are stratified in terms of the material assets or resources they control, the benefits and privileges they receive from these resources, the culture experiences they have accumulated from historical and existing economic and political arrangement and the influence they yield because of those arrangements. Accordingly, group variation in resources, lifestyles and life chances is related to these variations. (p. vii)

Poverty is a major factor in the lives of many families. It is manifested not only in the lack of sufficient income but also in the lifestyle that follows. The U.S. government defines the *poverty level* using factors such as income before taxes (excluding capital gains and non-cash benefits) and family composition and size. The poverty threshold for a family of four was $11,611 in 1987, $13,359 in 1990, $17,761 in 2000, $18,811 in 2003, $20,614 in 2006, and $21,386 in 2007 (U.S. Census Bureau, 2004, 2006, 2007). The volatile economic conditions that have affected many Americans in recent years have been exacerbated for people who are poor, who depend heavily on benefits such as food stamps, rent supplements, public housing, SCHIP (State Children's Health Insurance Program), and Medicaid.

More than 10 million U.S. children under the age of six (43 percent) are from low-income families. By race and ethnicity, 63 percent of American Indian, 61 percent of Latino, 60 percent of African American, 27 percent of Asian American, and 26 percent of white children live in low-income families. Although children of color are disproportionately represented in low-income circumstances, white children represent the largest cohort of poor children (National Center for Children in Poverty, 2007). There is also a strong correlation between poverty and single-parent households, which are mostly headed by females. More than 50 percent of families in poverty are headed by females, whereas 22 percent are headed by males and 10 percent have two parents.

According to the National Center for Children in Poverty (2007), 28.6 million U.S. children are living in low-income families and 12.7 million are living in poor families. *Persistent poverty* is defined as a problem faced by families impoverished for 8 out of 10 years. In this cohort, African Americans and female-headed families are dominant (Hopps et al., 1995).

Poverty is a diversity issue that directly affects many families. Poverty and lack of housing have given rise to unprecedented rates of homelessness. Families with children are the fastest-growing element of the homeless population. Practitioners must be acutely aware that these families in poverty have needs that are at Levels I and II of family functioning. These needs must be addressed before needs at Levels III and IV can be given adequate attention.

Family Structure

As described by Hopps & Morris (2000), "the family, society's most basic institution, has changed":

The two-parent family in which the husband is the breadwinner and the wife is the home-maker is not only no longer the norm but for many, neither a hope nor an ideal. "Alternative" styles now dominate, including the two-parent home, two-earner family, the single-parent family (due to divorce or out-of-wedlock births), the blended family, the gay or lesbian fam-ily, and the common law marriage with family and extended families especially for new immigrants. Many others now simply defer marriage or remain single. (p. 7)

Changes in the role and function of the family have also occurred, with much less time and energy being allocated for nurturance and caregiving. Women are no longer as available for these roles as they were in the past, because they are in the paid labor force as dispropor-tionately low-wage workers (and are expected to constitute nearly 65 percent of the labor force between 2000 and 2010). Groups that are particularly vulnerable because of the shift-ing economy and its impact on families are the young, the elderly, and single parents (Hopps & Morris, 2000).

Families who have been marginalized because of their racial or ethnic identity have experienced a drastically sharp transition from the two-parent to the one-parent family, and a most devastating challenge for them is poverty, as noted earlier. In instances in which a single mother heads a family with children, the potential for poverty is substantial: a 50 percent likelihood, versus a 25 percent likelihood if the head of the household is male.

Practitioners must know about contraception, abstention, and sex education so they can inform families about options for delayed births. The high birthrate among unmarried African American women has historically been viewed as a main cause of poverty in this cohort; today, however, that rate is at its lowest in 40 years. The increase in the rate of chil-dren born to unmarried white women resembles that of African American women during the 1960s and 1970s. In fact, over one-third of all births are to unmarried mothers (National Center for Health Statistics, 2003).

Of particular significance is the decline of teenage pregnancy, a trend that has been noted since 1991 (Longley, 2004). The major decline has been with non-Hispanic black teenagers. The highest teenage birthrates are among Mexican American teens, and the low-est are among Asian/Pacific Islander teens (CDC, 2005).

An integral part of the evolving family structure landscape is the growing presence of same-sex couples and families. The discussion of gay unions and marriages has centered on political and economic rights, but couples often want to establish families. A growing number of children worldwide are without parents, owing to a host of circumstances, including drugs, poverty, AIDS/HIV, sex trafficking, political unrest and potential for genocide, and famine. Gay and lesbian couples are able to adopt children and thereby fulfill their parenting instincts and desires.

Same-sex parents are often victims of prejudice and stereotypes, and their parent-ing capabilities often are questioned. However, to date, research on gay/lesbian parenting has found no evidence that the psychological development of children in these unions is compromised. Additionally, the home environment of a same-sex couple is as supportive and enabling of a child's psychosocial development as that of a heterosexual couple (Patterson, 1995).

Summary

Within an ecosystems–social constructionist perspective, there are many commonalities and differences that practitioners must be aware of as they work with families who are functioning at various levels. People's common humanness is a unifying factor and a foundation on which to build a therapeutic alliance. Diversity issues must be recognized, with the goal of developing mutual respect and appreciation for differences. Thus, the focus should be on people's commonalities that unite us, not differences that divide us. The *helping relationship* or *therapeutic alliance* is a necessary condition for assuming that no harm is done and for developing a climate within which work can be done on the problems that families bring to practitioners. The core needs of clients and the core conditions of the professional relationship (including empathy, respect, genuineness, and warmth) are commonalities for all work within families. The therapeutic alliance, consisting of the practitioner and client systems, accounts for the social field in which the alliance occurs.

Diversity issues include valuing multiculturalism and engaging in ethnic-sensitive practice. A cultural assessment grid is noted for use in developing such practice. Research has addressed various dimensions of the therapeutic alliance but not focused on diversity as a significant variable in the helping relationship. Given the growing presence of people of color and the many cultural differences that exist in U.S. society, attention must be given to this topic.

In the forefront of family practice today are issues of gender justice, which go beyond just women's issues. Consciousness raising over the past few decades has served to focus attention more on the oppressiveness of patriarchy, thus precipitating changes in both genders. Oppression is felt by other groups, as well, because of race, ethnicity, sexual preference, income, age, and the like. A major factor in oppression is access to the basic economic resources necessary for the well-being of any family. Practitioners must be especially sensitive to those families who are functioning at Levels I and II.

Closely tied to oppression is poverty, which is an especially crucial issue for people of color and single-parent families. Family practitioners must be sensitive to different family structures and realize the impact of ecosystem factors on them.

Discussion Questions

1. How does the addition of the concept of *alliance* (as in the *therapeutic alliance*) alter the previous understanding of the helping relationship?

2. How can new levels of awareness regarding gender and sexual diversity influence the therapeutic alliance on the three levels of the individual, the subsystem (parents or children), and the whole family system?

3. Using a family from your practice, assess the manner in which you engaged or joined the clients. Extend this discussion of the therapeutic alliance through all the contexts of helping.

4. How can practitioners show value for and appreciation of the diverse cultures of the families with whom they work?

5. Explain and discuss issues of power, powerlessness, and empowerment in a family from your practice. Identify any power needs you might have experienced and how you managed them.

6. Discuss how you would assess a young same-sex couple that applied to your agency for adoption of children.

Internet Resources

http://ethics.acusd.edu/Applied/race
http://dir.yahoo.com/Society_and_Culture/Issues_and_Causes/Multiculturalism
http://usgovinfo.about.com/cs/censusstatistic/a/aabirthrate.htm/p=1
www.canadianheritage.gc.ca/progs/multi/what-multi_e.cfm
www.diversity-oneness.com/index00.shtml

Suggested Readings

Anderson, J., & Carter, R. W. (Eds.). (2000). *Diversity perspectives for social work practice*. Boston: Allyn & Bacon.
This book provides a broad view on diversity issues that can be helpful to all professions.
Biestek, F. P. (1957). *The casework relationship*. Chicago: Loyola University Press.
This is a classic on the therapeutic relationship and should be required reading for all helping professionals. A chapter is devoted to each of the seven principles of the helping relationship.
Boyd-Franklin, N. (1989). *Black families in therapy: A multisystems approach*. New York: Guilford Press.
The author dispels myths, focuses on strengths, and sets African American families in context. She gives major treatment interventions in a multisystemic approach and discusses diversity of family structures.
Brown, L. S., & Ballou, M. (Eds.). (1992). *Personality and psychology: Feminist reappraisals*. New York: Guilford Press.
Synthesizing over 20 years of feminist thinking, this book gives original critiques of primary psychological theories and their accompanying definitions of pathology. The authors challenge previous theories of how healthy personalities develop and point out the need to keep any theory of personality relevant to women's lives.
Encyclopedia of social work (2007, 20th ed., Vols. 1–4). Washington, DC: National Association of Social Workers and Oxford University Press.
This updated, revised, and expanded encyclopedia provides an objective overview of social work in the United States. It contains 400 articles and 300 biographies covering all aspects of social work from practice and interventions, social environments, social conditions and challenges, to social policy and history.
Hopps, J. G., Pinderhughes, E., & Shankar, R. (1995). *The power to care: Clinical practice effectiveness with overwhelmed clients*. New York: Free Press.
This book contains important discussions on diversity, power, powerlessness and oppression, poverty, and clinical practice with overwhelmed clients.
Jordan, J. V., Kaplan, A. G., Miller, J. B., Stiver, I. P., & Surrey, J. L. (1991). *Women's growth in connection*. New York: Guilford Press.
This book offers a new perspective on women's development and ways of being in the world. The authors are clinicians, supervisors, and teachers who have been searching for therapeutic models that are based on and reflect the lives of women rather than male models. It discusses women's meaning systems, values, and organization of experiences.

Pinsof, W. F., & Catherall, D. R. (1986). The integrative psychotherapy alliance: Family, couple and individual therapy scales. *Journal of Marital and Family Therapy, 12*(2), 137–151.
This article introduces the concept of the therapeutic alliance into the family and marital domain and conceptualizes individual, couple, and family therapy as occurring within the same systematic framework. The book also discussed three new scales that measure the alliance in individual, couple, and family terms.

References

Anderson, J. (2003). Strengths perspective. In J. Anderson & R. W. Carter (Eds.), *Diversity perspectives for social work practice* (pp. 11–20). Boston: Allyn & Bacon.

Appleby, G. A., Colon, E., & Hamilton, J. (2001). *Diversity, oppression, and social functioning: Person-in-environment assessment and intervention.* Boston: Allyn & Bacon.

Berlin, S. B. (2005). The value of acceptance in social work direct practice: A historical and contemporary view. *Social Service Review, 79*(3), 482–510.

Biestek, F. P. (1957). *The casework relationship.* Chicago: Loyola University Press.

Brandell, J. R., & Ringel, S. (2004). Psychodynamic perspectives on relationship: Implications of new findings from human attachment and the neurosciences for social work education. *Families in Society, 86*(1), 35–45.

Buber, M. (1958). *I and thou* (2nd ed.). New York: Scribner's.

Centers for Disease Control (CDC) and Prevention. (2005, September 8). Births: Final data for 2003. *National Vital Statistics Reports, 54*(2). Retrieved March 29, 2008, from www.cdc.gov/nchs/data/nvsr/nvsr54/nvsr54_02.pdf.

Chestang, L. (1976). *The diverse society.* Washington, DC: National Association of Social Workers.

Chestang, L. (1995). Men: Direct practice. In R. L. Edwards (Ed.), *Encyclopedia of social work* (19th ed.). Washington, DC: National Association of Social Work.

Davatz, U. (1981). Establishing a therapeutic alliance in family systems therapy. In A. S. Gurman (Ed.), *Questions and answers in the practice of family therapy.* New York: Brunner/Mazel.

Duncan, B. L., Miller, S. D., & Sparks, J. A. (2004). *The heroic client.* San Francisco: Jossey-Bass.

Florsheim, P., Shotorbani, S., Guest-Warnick, G., Barratt, T., & Hwang, W-C. (2000). Role of the working alliance in the treatment of delinquent boys in community-based programs. *Journal of Clinical Child Psychology, 29*(1), 94–107.

Forcey, L. R., & Nash, M. (1998). Women and therapy: Rethinking feminist theory and social work therapy. *Women and Therapy, 21*(4), 85–100. Retrieved August 23, 2004, from ProQuest database.

Goldstein, A. (1975). Relationship enhancement methods. In F. Kanfer & A. Goldstein (Eds.), *Helping people change: A textbook of methods.* New York: Pergamon Press.

Goodrich, T. J. (Ed.). (1991). *Women and power.* New York: Norton.

Gregory, M., & Holloway, M. (2005). Language and shaping of social work. *British Journal of Social Work, 35*(1), 37–53.

Hooyman, N. (1995). Diversity and populations at risk: Women. In F. Reamer (Ed.), *The foundation of social work knowledge.* New York: Columbia University Press.

Hopps, J. G., & Morris, R. (Eds.). (2000). *Social work at the millennium: Critical reflections on the future of social work.* New York: Free Press.

Hopps, J. G., & Pinderhughes, E. R. (1999). *How the power of groups can help people transform their lives.* New York: Free Press.

Hopps, J. G., Pinderhughes, E., & Shankar, R. (1995). *The power to care: Clinical practice effectiveness with overwhelmed clients.* New York: Free Press.

Horvath, A. O. (2000). The therapeutic relationship: From transference to alliance. *Journal of Clinical Psychology: Millennium Issue: The Therapeutic Alliance, 56*(2), 163–173.

Keen, S. (1991). *Fire in the belly: On being a man.* New York: Bantam Books.

Kilpatrick, A. (1995). Contexts of helping. In A. Kilpatrick & T. Holland, *Working with families* (p. 39). Boston: Allyn & Bacon.

Kivlighan, D. M., Jr., & Shaughnessy, P. (2000). Patterns of working alliance development. A typology of client's working alliance ratings. *Journal of Counseling Psychology, 47*(3), 362–371.

Larkin, R. (2003). African-Americans in public housing: A traditional social work approach to substance abuse treatment. *Journal of Health and Social Policy, 17*(2), 67–82.

Leonhardt, D. (2008, April 8). For many, a boom that wasn't. *New York Times,* Business Day Section, p. C-1.

Lichtenberg, P. (1995). Men: Overview. In R. L. Edwards (Ed.), *Encyclopedia of social work* (19th ed.). Washington, DC: National Association of Social Work.

Longley, R. (2004, November 18). U.S. birth rate hits all-time low. Teen birth rate also falls to record low. About.com. Retrieved March 29, 2008, from http://usgovinfo.about.com/cs/censusstatistic/a/aabirthrate.htm?p=1.

Lum, D. (2003). People of color (ethnic minority) framework. In J. Anderson & R. W. Carter (Eds.), *Diversity perspectives for social work practice* (pp. 61–76). Boston: Allyn & Bacon.

Mandin, P. (2007). The contribution of systems and object-relations theories to an understanding of the therapeutic relationship in social work practice. *Journal of Social Work Practice, 21*(2), 149–162.

McClelland, D. (1975). *Power: The inner experience.* New York: Wiley.

Miehls, D., & Moffatt, K. (2000). Constructing social work identity based on the reflexive self. *British Journal of Social Work, 30*(3), 339–348.

Minuchin, S. (1974). *Families and family therapy.* Cambridge, MA: Harvard University Press.

National Center for Children in Poverty. (2007). *Basic facts about low-income children.* Retrieved April 6, 2008, from http://nccp.org/publications/pub_762.html.

National Center of Health Statistics. (2003). *Births: Final data for 2002* (DHHS Publication No. PHS 2004–1120). Hyattsville, MD: Government Printing Office. Retrieved November 10, 2004, from www.cdc.gov.nchs/data/nvsr/nvsr52/nvsr52_10.pdf.

Norton, D. (1998). *The dual perspective.* New York: Council on Social Work Education.

Palmer, N., & Kaufman, M. (2003). The ethics of informed consent: Implications for multicultural practice. *Journal of Ethnic and Cultural Diversity in Social Work, 12*(1), 1–26.

Patterson, C. J. (1995). Summary of research findings. In American Psychological Association, *Lesbian and gay parenting: A resource for psychologists.* Washington, DC: Author. Retrieved October 17, 2004, from www.apa.org/pi/parent.html.

Pinderhughes, E. (1995). Diversity and populations at risk: Ethnic minorities and people of color. In F. Reamer (Ed.), *The foundation of social work knowledge.* New York: Columbia University Press.

Pinsof, W. F. (1994). An integrative systems perspective on the therapeutic alliance: Theoretical, clinical and research implication. In A. Horvath & L. Greenberg (Eds.), *The working alliance: Theory, research and practice.* New York: Wiley.

Pinsof, W. F. (1995). *Integrative problem-centered therapy: A synthesis of family, individual, and biological therapies.* New York: Basic Books.

Pinsof, W. F., & Catherall, D. R. (1986). The integrative psychotherapy alliance: Family, couple and individual therapy scales. *Journal of Marital and Family Therapy, 12*(2), 137–151.

Prigoff, A. W. (2003). Dual perspective framework. In J. Anderson & R. W. Carter (Eds.), *Diversity perspectives for social work practice* (pp. 77–92). Boston: Allyn & Bacon.

Rogers, C., Gendlin, E. T., Kiesler, D. L., & Truax, C. B. (1969). *The therapeutic relationship and its impact.* Madison: University of Wisconsin Press.

Ruch, G. (2005). Relationship-based practice and reflective practice: Holistic approaches to contemporary child care social work. *Child and Family Social Work, 10*(2), 111–123.

Schlesinger, E. G., & Devore, W. (1995). Ethnic-sensitive practice. In R. L. Edwards (Ed.), *Encyclopedia of social work* (19th ed., pp. 902–908). Washington, DC: National Association of Social Workers.

Solomon, B. (1976). Social work in a multi-ethnic society. In M. Solemyer (Ed.), *Cross-cultural perspectives in social work practice and evaluation* (pp. 167–176). New York: Council on Social Work Education.

Truax, C. B., & Carkuff, R. R. (1967). *Toward effective counseling and psychotherapy: Training and practice.* Chicago: Aldine de Gruyter.

U.S. Census Bureau. (2004). *Poverty thresholds—2003.* Washington, DC: U.S. Department of Commerce. Retrieved November 10, 2004, from www.census.gov/hhes/poverty/threshold/03prelim.html.

U.S. Census Bureau. (2006). *Poverty thresholds—2006.* Washington, DC: U.S. Department of Commerce. Retrieved August 12, 2008, from www.census.gov/hhes/poverty/threshold/06prelim.html.

U.S. Census Bureau. (2007). Poverty thresholds—2007. Retrieved March 29, 2008, from www.census.gov/hhes/poverty/threshold/07prelim.html.

4

Ethically Informed and Spiritually Sensitive Practice

Allie C. Kilpatrick, Ph.D., Thomas P. Holland, Ph.D., and Dorothy S. Becvar, Ph.D.

The entire therapeutic venture is fundamentally an exercise in ethics, involving the inventing, shaping, and reformulating of codes for living together (Efran, Lukens, & Lukens, 1988). Thus, in addition to recognizing the need for adherence to professional codes of ethics, practitioners must also recognize that family interventions constitute a dialogue whose goal is to create a context that facilitates accommodating the needs and desires of all the participants. Fundamental to this context is the dimension of spirituality. Indeed, although seldom recognized, some form of spirituality is common across humanity (Becvar, 2001). At varying times in a person's life, this aspect of being may seek expression, and, even when implicit, it inevitably influences beliefs and behaviors. This chapter provides suggestions for creating a practice that is well informed relative to ethical issues and sensitive to the role of spirituality in the lives of both professionals and clients.

Ethically Informed Practice

Most professional groups that work with families have their own codes of ethics by which members are expected to abide. It is essential that students and practitioners know and practice according to these codes. Among the ethical issues discussed in the following section are some of the more complex challenges confronted in family practice, as well as several models for dealing with them.

Ethical Practice

Working with families requires awareness of several important areas of ethical considerations and challenges. These involve tensions related to separating interventions from the larger ecosystems, focusing on individual or family welfare, using informed consent, respecting confidentiality, avoiding deception and inappropriate manipulation, and deciding who should participate in therapy.

1. *Separating interventions from the larger ecosystems.* For many years, family therapists have spoken of problems as being symptoms of family system dysfunction rather than manifestations of individual illness. Interventions have focused on first-order change (i.e., change within a system that remains unchanged) and second-order change (i.e., changes of the system and the rules governing it) (Watzlawick, Weakland, & Fisch, 1974). However, as noted by Doherty and Boss (1991), practitioners do not always consider the wider implications of the community, social, cultural, and political systems in the creation of problems or the ripples their interventions may produce in this larger pond on either level of change.

An illustration of how both society and the practitioner's interventions may play roles in exacerbating problems for clients can be seen in work with abusive families. For many years, society tolerated abusive behavior toward women and children. Now, society has changed, and practitioners label such behavior "bad" or "mad." If abusive behavior is part of a family's heritage, however, then their forebears, too, now may be seen as being bad. Further, if practitioners tell clients that the negative consequences of the abuse will likely remain with them all their lives, then they probably will, inasmuch as people participate in the creation of their own reality based, at least in part, on perceptions such as these shared by professionals (Becvar, 2001; Becvar & Becvar, 2009).

Appropriate rules of conduct evolve in a society, and practitioners contribute to defining acceptable and unacceptable behaviors and problems. Practitioners also play a role in defining what constitutes an ethical issue. Perhaps the ethical imperatives here are for practitioners to avoid narrowing the range of focus to the point there is little they see that is *not* illness, thus limiting preventive activities (Becvar & Becvar, 2003; Becvar, Becvar, & Bender, 1982), and to ensure that they do no harm. Indeed, practitioners must be careful not to create more problems than their interventions solve. Further, they should remain aware of ethical dilemmas that arise in practice concerning such issues of social justice as institutional racism, societal gender bias, and accessibility to resources.

2. *Focusing on individual or family welfare.* In a survey of members of the American Association for Marriage and Family Therapy (AAMFT; Green & Hansen, 1989), the ethical dilemma rated as the second most frequently encountered and the second most important was the tension between family versus individual needs (second only to reporting child abuse). Practitioners are concerned with protecting the rights and promoting the welfare of all clients. When there are multiple clients, an intervention that serves one person's best interests may be counterproductive for another person. The ethical imperative here is to attempt to balance therapeutic responsibility toward individuals and the family as a unit (Doherty & Boss, 1991).

The basic philosophy of Western medicine and the medical code of ethics implies that a clinician's primary loyalty is to the patient as an individual; broader issues of public welfare are relegated to public health. By contrast, in the Eastern European tradition, the clinician's first obligation is to the community, and the individual is of secondary concern. Another aspect of this dilemma emerges from the fact that society also defines the roles of men and women. Practitioners have been guilty of subordinating the rights of women and children to the family good, even when it is to these individuals' detriment. It is not surprising that the issue of individual versus family rights was first raised by feminists, who have argued convincingly that balancing individual and family welfare requires practitioners to see beyond the therapy room to the family context (Doherty & Boss, 1991).

3. *Using informed consent.* The idea of informed consent involves "a knowledgeable decision based on adequate information about the therapy, the available alternatives, and the collateral risks" (Bray, Shepherd, & Hays, 1985, p. 53). State laws and professional association codes of ethics have made informed-consent procedures standard practice. Disclosure documents are often read by family members before they see the practitioner (Huber & Baruth, 1987). In order to make informed choices, clients should have information about the therapy setting, their rights and responsibilities, the therapist's credentials and competence, complaint procedures, the content and process of the professional relationship, the potential risks and benefits of change, limits of confidentiality, and record-keeping procedures and fees (Burkemper, 2004).

4. *Respecting confidentiality.* With passage of the Health Insurance Portability and Accountability Act (HIPAA) in 1996, guidelines regarding the preservation of client confidentiality (unless the client grants permission to reveal personal information) became even stricter. At the same time, practitioners continue to have the right to disclose information when necessary to prevent a serious threat to the health of a client and/or to the safety of another person or the general public. Examples of the latter include incest, child abuse, and dangers such as those addressed by the *Tarasoff* decision (Health Insurance Privacy and Accountability Act, 2002), which ensures protection for intended victims.

In addition, when working with families, the practitioner may not reveal information unless all parties to the therapy have given their consent. In other words, even if one member of the family gives written permission to share information with a third party, the practitioner may not do so unless everyone who participated also gives written permission. The exception, of course, is when a parent or legal guardians signs for a minor child.

Another ethical challenge also may emerge relative to family members' relationships and the handling of secrets. Whether the practitioner is willing to keep private revelations fully confidential, to allow no confidentiality among family members, or some combination of the two, his or her position must be clearly communicated to the family as early as possible in the therapeutic encounter. This position must reflect the *Code of Ethics* of the American Association for Family and Marriage Therapy (AAMFT, 2001), which requires written permission to reveal one individual's confidence to other members of the client system in the context of therapy. The ethical imperative is to disclose the practitioner's policy on confidentiality as part of initial informed consent for treatment (Doherty & Boss, 1991).

5. *Avoiding deception and inappropriate manipulation.* According to Doherty and Boss (1991), deception is, along with gender bias, a central ethical issue in contemporary family practice. According to some theories, manipulation should be avoided at all costs. Others state that manipulation is unavoidable (Watzlawick et al., 1974). For example, all practitioners influence clients by sharing or withholding thoughts and feelings about them.

Given the universal influence practitioners have on clients and the continual decisions practitioners make about what to disclose, the issue is not the nature of the intervention but whether any concealment is ethical and whether the therapist remains trustworthy (Doherty & Boss, 1991). The practitioner must not deceive the family about his or her beliefs or intentions or conceal family realities that members deserve to know.

6. *Deciding who should participate in therapy.* Ethical issues arise around the coercion of reluctant adults or children in the family, especially when it violates the autonomy of a skeptical family member. Refusing to see the family unless all members are present could also be coercive to willing members, who may feel obligated to make successful efforts to engage the other members. Doherty and Boss (1991) assert that refusing treatment if family members do not participate would be unethical in public mental health centers, which are often the last resort for troubled families.

Handling these ethical issues builds on the principles of relationships, ecosystems, and social constructionism discussed in earlier chapters. These principles consistently focus on the integrity of practitioners in respectful, genuine, and caring relationships with family members and with themselves. Underlying these principles are the basic ethical values of respecting autonomy, acting fairly and justly, promoting benefits, and limiting harm.

Guiding their application may be ethical theories such as *utilitarianism,* which emphasizes seeking outcomes that maximize positive changes and minimize negative ones. Another is *duty theory,* which emphasizes the ethical principles and obligations one has, such as telling the truth, deciding fairly, and keeping promises. Another is *virtue theory,* which looks at the motives and intentions of the actor. Professional codes of ethics tend to be constructed on the basis of duty theory, setting forth a variety of principles that practitioners are obligated to follow. Because practitioners may encounter the challenge of competing principles, many ethicists advocate consideration of motivations and results as well as obligations.

Guides for Decision Making

The variety of ethical issues faced by family practitioners may be examined in terms of several underlying dimensions. Woody (1990, p. 135) proposes a pragmatic approach to dealing with ethical concerns in family practice, drawing on theories of ethics, codes of professional conduct, practice theories, sociological context, and the professional identity. These components serve as five decision-making bases for practitioners to use in a comprehensive analysis aimed at preventing ethical problems and reaching defensible ethical decisions. The assumption is that practitioners draw from several bases in the process of weighing competing values and coming to a decision and use both intuitive and critical thinking.

Another perspective on the ways family practitioners deal with ethical issues was drawn from qualitative research by Holland and Kilpatrick (1991). They developed a three-dimensional framework based on their findings from a *grounded theory* study of practitioners and how they defined and made ethical decisions. Holland and Kilpatrick's model of clinical judgment has been refined since publication and now consists of three bipolar dimensions: (1) the focus of a decision, ranging from means to ends; (2) the interpersonal orientation, ranging from autonomy to mutuality; and (3) the locus of authority, ranging from internalized to externalized.

The first dimension focuses directly on the practitioner's decisions and identifies a tension between pursuing solutions that maximize benefits regardless of risk versus complying with principles and procedures that are seen to reflect the values of the profession. The issues of deception and inappropriate manipulation may be involved here.

The second dimension examines the interpersonal orientation in the decision-making process. It reflects the practitioner's struggle between the protection of individual freedom and self-determination and the responsibility of mutual caring, which urges active intervention in the service of protection and improvement for the good of all. Here, the issues of separating interventions from the larger ecosystem and focusing on individual family welfare come into play.

The third dimension involves the source of authority in the decision-making process. It focuses on the grounds for making decisions and represents the conflict of allegiance to values that lie within the individual or the client/worker relationship and the obligation to comply with external sources, such as agency policy or existing norms. Issues of informed consent and confidentiality are applicable here (see Figure 4.1).

Crossing these three dimensions permits examination of each area in relation to the other two, which yields a comprehensive look at one's ethical orientation. Such a perspective

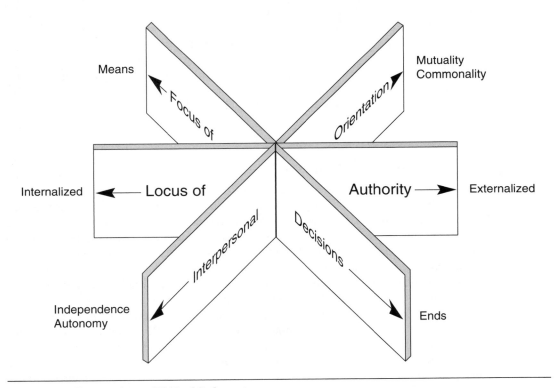

FIGURE 4.1 *Dimensions of Ethical Judgment*

suggests looking for interactions across these three dimensions in specific practice situations. A professional or a family may have a pattern of dealing with ethical problems that emphasizes following standard policies and procedures, exercising centralized control, and protecting the security of his or her position or the internal stability of the family. Another approach to ethical dilemmas may emphasize a pattern that seeks to distribute power more broadly, to emphasize the attainment of ends at the expense of following standard procedural rules, and to advance individual autonomy.

Posing these dimensions in terms of polar extremes does not entail their opposition or mutual exclusion. One may attempt to balance them by seeking both group stability and individual flexibility, by encouraging both productivity and cohesiveness, and by being both nurturing and powerful. The importance of balance along each dimension may be highlighted by the extreme form that any of these values can take if unchecked.

In addressing ethical problems, dimensions such as these should be thoughtfully considered. Before trying to apply them to a decision or dilemma in practice, the practitioner should be aware of his or her own values, prior socialization, and influences from others involved in the situation. Stereotypes and biases can influence judgment, especially if they are not explicitly recognized. In addition, the professional must take into consideration the cultural perspectives of the clients, which may vary from his or her own. If circumstances allow, the practitioner should not take up complex problems when fatigued, ill, or unduly influenced by pressures from others. If he or she has a personal stake in the outcome of the decision, a trusted but disinterested outside party should be invited into the deliberations to guard against self-interest bias.

Understanding the facts of the situation is essential, even though one cannot know everything about it. The practitioner should know and consider reasonably complete information bearing on the case. Likewise, he or she is responsible for identifying the relevant technical and professional issues present and the possible choices available, including what options are feasible and what the relevant research indicates about them. Codes of professional ethics provide important guidance regarding what choices to make and principles to follow.

The ethical dimensions of the situation must be identified explicitly and weighed reflectively. The decision maker specifies, evaluates, and measures the possible courses of action and the potential consequences of each. Who is involved, and what is at stake for each of them? The practitioner should identify the duties, obligations, and interests of each party in the situation. What are the alternative courses of action (including doing nothing)? Then he or she should weigh the principles involved in each alternative and their probable results. This includes consideration of the costs and benefits of alternatives, their long- and short-term effects, required resources and limitations on them, prior commitments and other constraints, justice and fairness for all parties involved, and the possible need for reparations for those who may suffer losses.

Based on such considerations, it is often possible for the practitioner to identify one or two main courses of action. These should be examined for universality and consistency: Would it be appropriate for anyone in a similar situation to apply these principles and come to the same conclusion? If no alternative passes this examination, then the practitioner may select the option that results in the least undesirable net consequences. If others have not already been engaged in the deliberations, it is often helpful to test conclusions and check for biases (remembering to safeguard the confidentiality of clients). These steps of ethical decision making are illustrated in Figures 4.2 and 4.3.

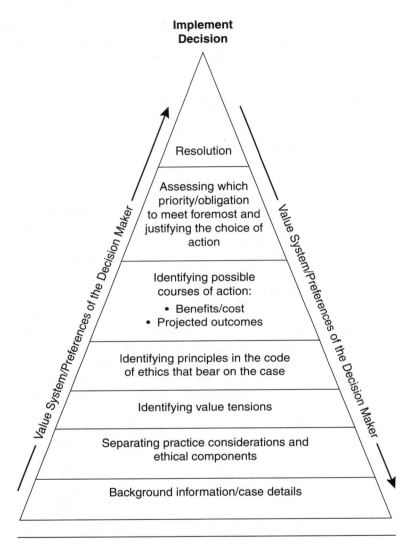

Implement Decision

Resolution

Assessing which priority/obligation to meet foremost and justifying the choice of action

Identifying possible courses of action:
• Benefits/cost
• Projected outcomes

Identifying principles in the code of ethics that bear on the case

Identifying value tensions

Separating practice considerations and ethical components

Background information/case details

Value System/Preferences of the Decision Maker

Value System/Preferences of the Decision Maker

FIGURE 4.2 *Framework to Analyze Ethical Dilemmas*

Source: Mattison, 2000, Ethical decision making: The person in the process. *Social Work* *45*(3), 206. Copyright 2000, National Association of Social Workers, Inc., Social Work.

Codes of Ethics

Every profession has the responsibility to articulate its basic values and ethics through principles and standards that are relevant to all professional functions, settings, and populations served. These *codes of ethics* serve to guide decision making and conduct relative to practice in general and, more specifically, when ethical issues arise. As discussed previously, ethical decision making is a process. Keeping in mind the guides for decision making and

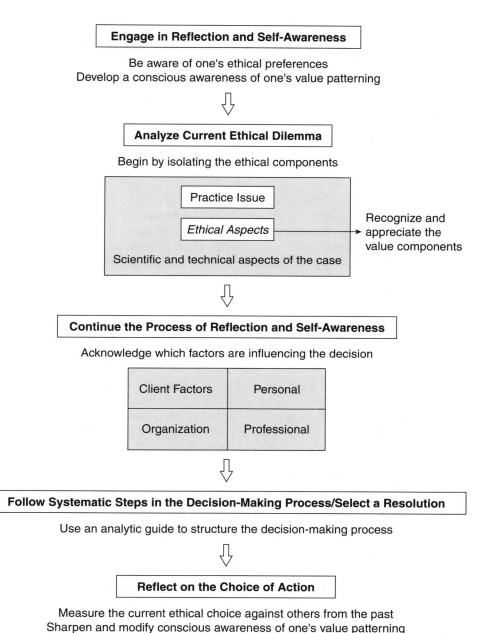

FIGURE 4.3 *Cycle of Reflection*

Source: Mattison, 2000, Ethical decision making: The person in the process. *Social Work 45*(3), 210. Copyright 2000, National Association of Social Workers, Inc., Social Work.

the dimensions for clinical judgment, we note that all professions that include working with families have their own codes of ethics. For illustrative purposes, the following sections will discuss the codes of ethics of the National Association of Social Workers (NASW) and the American Association for Marriage and Family Therapy (AAMFT). (See the Internet Resources at the end of this chapter for various codes of ethics.)

NASW Code of Ethics (1999).   The broad ethical principles in the code of ethics of the NASW are based on social work's core values of service, social justice, dignity and worth of the person, importance of human relationships, integrity, and competence. The code was updated in 1999 and serves the following six purposes:

1. to identify the core values of social work
2. to summarize broad ethical principles reflecting these values and set standards
3. to identify relevant considerations and conflicts
4. to provide ethical standards for which the profession is accountable
5. to socialize new practitioners to social work's mission, values, ethical principles, and ethical standards
6. to articulate the standards used to assess unethical conduct

The NASW code sets forth standards that are relevant to the professional activities of all social workers and to which all social workers should adhere. The standards include the categories of social workers' ethical responsibilities to clients, to colleagues, in practice settings, as professionals, to the social work profession, and to the broader society.

The longest and most in-depth standard is the first one, the responsibility to clients. It covers the following: the commitment to clients, which is the primary obligation; self-determination of clients; the provision of valid informed consent to clients; the necessity of competence in providing services; the understanding of cultural competence, oppression, and social diversity; sensitivity to conflicts of interest, including dual relationships; the limits of privacy and confidentiality; guidelines for client access to records; sexual relationships with clients, which are strictly forbidden; rules for physical contact; prohibition of sexual harassment; ban on derogatory language; appropriate payment for services; dealing with clients who lack decision-making capacity; interruption of services; and termination of services. Special attention must be paid to each of these as practitioners discharge their professional responsibilities to clients in a respectful, caring manner.

AAMFT Code of Ethics (2001).   The code of ethics of the AAMFT, which was revised in 2001, is binding on members in all categories, including students, clinical members, and approved supervisors; also included are applicants for both membership and for the approved supervisor designation. It is similar in many respects to the NASW code. Eight categories are addressed: responsibility to clients; confidentiality; professional competence and integrity; responsibility to students and supervisees; responsibility to research participants; responsibility to the profession; financial arrangements; and advertising.

The code requires that marriage and family therapists report any alleged unethical behavior of colleagues so that the profession can be self-regulating and maintain the highest standards of ethical practice. Reports are to be made to the AAMFT Ethics Committee and/or to state or provincial regulatory bodies, as appropriate.

Other professionals who work with families, such as psychologists, counselors, chaplains, and nurses, have their own codes of ethics. State and provincial licensing boards also have their own codes. In some cases, these boards may have an umbrella code that covers several helping professions. All family practitioners are required to know the relevant codes that govern their practice.

Although a code of ethics cannot guarantee ethical behavior, it provides an important set of guidelines. Ultimately, however, the ethical behavior of practitioners must come from their personal commitment to engage in informed ethical practice. Similarly, to practice in a manner that is spiritually sensitive requires knowledge of this dimension and a commitment to be aware of it and act in a responsible manner.

Spiritually Sensitive Practice

A greater emphasis is currently being placed on the role of spirituality in working with families, not only within social work but in all the health and mental health professions. Indeed, practitioners now recognize that avoiding this realm in work with clients may do them a grave injustice. Much of this change in perspective has taken place since the first edition of this book was published in 1995.

For example, prayer, contemplative practices, and the role of spirituality have gained attention within organized medicine. Whereas in 1993, only 3 of 125 U.S. medical schools offered courses on spirituality and health, in 2006, over 100 did (Dossey, 2006). Similarly, many medical schools today include spiritual histories in patients' charts. This occurred after the Joint Commission on Accreditation of Health Care Organizations strongly recommended in 1997 that every health care institution have a vehicle in place to include this perspective (Joint Commission on Accreditation, 1997).

Also, in 1993, Rachel Naomi Remen, M.D., developed an elective medical school course called The Healer's Art, which gives medical students an opportunity to explore the human dimension of medicine and the deeper meaning of their work. This course is now being replicated at 53 medical schools nationwide (see ISHI Programs and Workshops, 2008). Similarly, Harold Koenig, M.D., is overseeing the study of spirituality and health at Duke University (IONS, 2007). In a survey conducted by the Institute of Noetic Sciences (IONS, 2007) of self-selected respondents, 88 percent said they "believe in a universal energy of oneness that pervades all life," and 76 percent reported having had "a moment of clarity or profound insight that changed my life."

Some people experience spirituality in what are seen as more nontraditional ways. A Baylor University Religion Survey (2005) found that a significant percentage of Americans polled believed in one or more of the following: extrasensory perception (ESP), ghosts, telepathy, astrology, communication with the dead, witchcraft, reincarnation, clairvoyance, and channeling. Koerner and Rich (1997) reported in *U.S. News & World Report* that approximately 15 million Americans have had a near-death experience (about 5 percent), with 10 to 20 percent of those believing they were at death's door. Among children close to death, more that 70 percent have had a near-death experience. About 17 percent of near-death experiences are distressing to the experiencer and described as hell-like, guilt laden, or inverted (Atwater, 2007). In a related study in 2001, the international medical journal *The Lancet* published a 13-year study of 10 different Dutch hospitals in which 18 percent of "clinically dead" patients reported having a near-death experience (van Lommel, van Wees, Meyers, & Elfferich, 2001).

Surprisingly for some, Hamer (2004) suggests there is a genetic tendency toward spirituality, and he identifies a so-called God gene. The IONS survey (2007) draws this conclusion:

> Because we are wired for mystical and spiritual experiences, we can be inspired to act from a higher sense of morality and a renewed passion for what is possible. Our brains are wired to facilitate cooperation, compassion, love, and altruism. Historically we have reserved these positive emotions and behaviors for those with whom we feel a personal affiliation. But the evolutionary trend is increasing—rather than decreasing—the scope of that affiliation. (p. 73)

Since 1994, the Council on Social Work Education has required that all master's degree programs in social work provide practice content that includes approaches and skills for clients from varying religious and spiritual backgrounds (CSWE, 1994). And the social work profession has been described as "undergoing a resurgence of interest regarding the issue of spirituality in social work" (Rice, 2002, p. 303).

Past Barriers and Future Directions

In the past, there have been several barriers to addressing the spiritual dimension with families. One is that, in order to become more scientific, practitioners assumed they had to separate themselves from nonscientific spiritual constructs. The spiritual dimension was seen as esoteric and unobservable (Cornett, 1992), allowing the entrance of bias and subjectivity. Although subjective constructs such as spiritual power, psychic energy, and divine intervention are hard to observe and measure, from a social constructionist perspective (Prest & Keller, 1993), we recognize that subjectivity is inevitable. Further, as Cornett notes, the failure to integrate spirituality into clinical thinking represents an impoverishment in practice.

A second barrier has been fears about imposing a particular frame of reference on clients. Effective practice is predicated on the practitioner having a nonimposing, nonjudgmental stance. Practitioners' spiritual commitments are better expressed through caring behavior. However, rather than attempt to monitor appropriate spiritual expression in clinical work while monitoring other areas, many practitioners have simply discounted the need to explore the spiritual aspect of clients' lives, often with the assumption that these aspects are conflict free, functional, or comfortable (Cornett, 1992). Rigid conceptions of spirituality and biases against formal institutions have also been barriers (Prest & Keller, 1993).

The last two decades saw a gradual breakdown of these barriers and an increase in attention to the spiritual dimension in people's lives, as well as permission to include religious and spiritual issues in therapeutic conversations (Becvar, 1997a, 1997b; Frame, 2000). However, several areas relevant to ethical issues have accompanied this shift. These include the fact that a focus on spirituality in therapy is rarely included in professional training programs (Bowman, 1989); that there are many potential pitfalls requiring attention when including such a focus (Benningfield, 1997); that professionals must respect the autonomy of clients, safeguard their welfare, protect them from harm, and treat them in a just and honest manner when dealing with spiritual issues (Haug, 1998); and that therapists must recognize the limits of the knowledge it is possible to have relative to spirituality (Becvar, 2001). Thus, the mandate for the future relative to the ability to practice in a spiritually sensitive manner is paying attention to each of these dimensions.

Definition of Spirituality

A definition of *spirituality* needs to encompass the person's understanding of and response to meaning in life (Cornett, 1992). It must include faith and values as spiritual dimensions (Kilpatrick & Holland, 1990), as well as the process of conceptualizing the individual's connection with others, the world, and the creator (Campbell & Moyers, 1988). *Spiritual expression* can also be defined as the individual's response to the events in life over which he or she has no control.

Atwater (2007) distinguishes between spirituality and religion. She states that *spirituality* is most commonly defined as a personal relationship with God that can involve direct revelation, while recognizing and honoring the sacredness of all created things. *Religion* is seen as a systemized approach to spiritual development based on set standards or dogmas that provide community support while establishing moral upliftment and behavior (p. 96).

Canda and Furman (1999) note that definitions of spirituality in the social work literature include the following six attributes:

1. An essential or holistic quality of a person that is considered inherently valuable or sacred and irreducible.
2. An aspect of a person or group dealing with a search for meaning, moral frameworks, and relationships with others, including ultimate reality or life after life.
3. Particular experiences of a transpersonal nature.
4. A developmental process of moving toward a sense of wholeness in oneself and with others.
5. Participation in spiritual support groups that may or may not be formally religious.
6. Engagement in particular beliefs and behaviors, such as prayer or meditation, in a spiritual or religious context. (pp. 44–45)

Implementation

As practitioners think about acknowledging spirituality in practice, it is important to be aware that conflicts in values and the search for direction, meaning, integration, and faith underlie many of the problems presented by clients. Moreover, despite the difficulty of dealing with such elusive and complex issues, few areas are more important than them. Even in poor communities, according to Aponte (1994), the challenge to the family is not only about bread or basic resources but also about the spirit. Practitioners must encourage a sense of dignity, purpose, and future in families that have given up hope, meaning, and self-worth and succumbed to a sense of despair. Here, optimism and hope are the core elements in building the resilience so necessary when working with Level I family needs.

Practitioners might begin to address this realm by including in the initial assessment questions about the clients' belief system, asking, for example, "Where are you on religion or spirituality?" or "How important is or what role does religion or spirituality play in your life?" Practitioners might also ask about the spiritual resources clients have available to them, both personal, such as prayer or meditation, and professional, such as a member of the clergy or spiritual guide.

At the same time, it is important for practitioners to understand and be aware of their own spirituality in order to be helpful to family members in their pilgrimage of life. Indeed, like other personal issues, the practitioner's spirituality can be an obstacle or an asset. Thus, practitioners must be sensitive to their own biases to avoid value imposition or an inappropriate intrusion on the therapy process.

Effective practice also includes recognizing clients' desires and readiness to deal with spiritual concerns, accepting them, and being as comfortable with discussing this dimension as with discussing the physical, emotional, and intellectual dimensions of practice (May, 1982). Further, whatever the client's belief system may be, a spiritual orientation on the part of the practitioner should focus on helping the client define meaning in life and achieve ultimate satisfaction; as such, the practitioner may also participate in facilitating deeper levels of healing (Becvar, 1997a). Indeed, as Bardill (1997) states, a failure to account for the spiritual reality in practice means that a powerful reality of life has been ignored.

Hodge (2001) presents a two-dimensional framework for spiritual assessment. The two components are a narrative spiritual history outline and an interpretive anthropological framework, as shown in Table 4.1. Using this assessment tool could help "elicit what may

---

TABLE 4.1   *Framework for Spiritual Assessment*

Initial Narrative Framework

1. Describe the religious/spiritual tradition you grew up in. How did your family express its spiritual beliefs? How important was spirituality to your family? Extended family?
2. What sort of personal experiences (practices) stand out to you during your years at home? What made these experiences special? How have they informed your later life?
3. How have you changed or matured from those experiences? How would you describe your current spiritual or religious orientation? Is your spirituality a personal strength? If so, how?

Interpretive Anthropological Framework

1. *Affect.* What aspects of your spiritual life give you pleasure? What role does your spirituality play in handling life's sorrows? Enhancing life's joys? Coping with life's pain? How does your spirituality give you hope for the future? What do you wish to accomplish in the future?
2. *Behavior.* Are there particular spiritual rituals or practices that help you deal with life's obstacles? What is your level of involvement in faith-based communities? How are they supportive? Are there spiritually encouraging individuals that you maintain contact with?
3. *Cognition.* What are your current religious/spiritual beliefs? What are they based on? What beliefs do you find particularly meaningful? What does your faith say about personal trials? How does this belief help you overcome obstacles? How do your beliefs affect your health practices?
4. *Communion.* Describe your relationship to the Ultimate. What has been your experience of the Ultimate? How does the Ultimate communicate with you? How have these experiences encouraged you? Have there been times of deep spiritual intimacy? How does your relationship help you face life challenges? How would the Ultimate describe you?
5. *Conscience.* How do you determine right and wrong? What are your key values? How does your spirituality help you deal with guilt (sin)? What role does forgiveness play in your life?
6. *Intuition.* To what extent do you experience intuitive hunches (flashes of creative insight, premonitions, spiritual insights)? Have these insights been a strength in your life? If so, how?

Source: D. R. Hodge, 2001. Spiritual assessment: A review of major qualitative methods and a new framework for assessing spirituality. *Social Work, 46*(3), 208. Copyright © 2001, National Association of Social Workers, Inc., Social Work.

be the most untapped strength among consumers, their spirituality" (p. 211). At the same time, Hodge (2003) notes that no single assessment instrument is right for all clients and that practitioners should be familiar with several to be able to respond appropriately in each individual situation. In 2005, Hodge gave additional qualitative assessment tools from which to select. These include the following: (1) *spiritual lifemaps* illustrate the clients' relationship with God over time; (2) *spiritual genograms* illustrate the flow of spiritual patterns across at least three generations; (3) *spiritual ecomaps* focus on clients' current, existential, spiritual relationships; and (4) *spiritual ecograms* combine the assessment strengths of the spiritual ecomaps and genograms in a single assessment approach and tap information that exists in space and across time.

Having determined the importance of spirituality to the client, the practitioner may then include this aspect of life as a regular part of the therapeutic conversation. The practitioner may also wish to consult with or refer clients to others who have greater expertise in this area. In addition, the practitioner may engage in self-disclosure as appropriate, sharing the ways in which spirituality has helped him or her in the journey toward health and healing.

At the same time, the practitioner also must be able to accept the fact that for many clients, such explicit discussions may be neither desirable nor useful. Even though spirituality is an important part of many clients' lives, they may not see it as relevant to the problems at hand. Some may feel it is just too personal or simply feel uncomfortable discussing this topic with a therapist. Other clients may express lack of belief in any kind of spirituality. Some also may have experienced trauma in the context of their faith tradition (Hickson & Phelps, 1997).

Nevertheless, a spiritual orientation on the part of the practitioner, which includes a nonjudgmental attitude as well as a focus on such issues as clients' values and search for meaning and purpose in life, may result in the creation of both a more effective therapeutic encounter and a more meaningful reality for the clients (Becvar, 1997a).

Canda and Furman (1999) present the following as specific examples of spiritually oriented helping activities:

Active imagination
Art, music, dance, and poetry therapies
Assessing spiritual emergencies
Assessing spiritual propensity
Biofeedback
Caring for the body
Cooperation with clergy, religious communities, and spiritual support groups
Cooperation with traditional healers
Creating a spiritual development timeline and narrative
Developing and using multicultural teams
Developing mutually beneficial human–nature relationships
Developing and participating in rituals and ceremonies
Dialoguing across spiritual perspectives
Differentiating between spiritual emergencies and psychopathology
Dissolving inner chatter and distractions
Distinguishing between religious visions and hallucinations or delusions
Dream interpretation

Exploring family patterns of meaning and ritual
Exploring sacred stories, symbols, and teachings
Family brainstorming
Focused relaxing
Forgiveness
Guided visualization
Intentional breathing
Journaling and diary keeping
Meditation and prayer
Mindful paying attention
Nature retreats
Physical disciplines for spiritual cultivation, such as hatha yoga or t'ai chi
Reading scripture and inspirational materials
Reflecting on beliefs regarding death and afterlife
Reflecting on the helpful or harmful impact of religious participation
Win-win solution making (p. 291)

Regardless of the activities chosen, however, the practitioner's intentional use of spirituality in practice is unique, not because of his or her words or actions but because of his or her assumptions about how these words or actions interface with the transcendent dimension. According to Anderson and Worthen (1997), three assumptions are basic to a spiritual perspective: (1) an awareness that God or a divine being exists; (2) a recognition that humans have an innate yearning for a connection with this being; and (3) a belief that this being is actively interested in humans and acts on relationships to promote beneficial change. Working from these assumptions, practitioners share their own spiritual selves, and then the range of available resources and possibilities for change expands for everyone.

Accordingly, the practitioner is kind and operates from a place of integrity. Compassion for clients is expressed through a nonjudgmental stance, focused attention, and the creation of meaningful relationships. Humility and respect for everyone involved in the process also characterize spiritually sensitive practice. For example, despite the fact that certain client behaviors are socially unacceptable, the practitioner attempts to focus on understanding the context of clients and their behavior, rather than assume a blaming or demeaning attitude. Questions such as "How did you learn that it was okay to hit/abuse your spouse?" provide important information about areas in which further learning may be useful and help to move in the direction of potential solutions. And as clients are able to experience a respectful process, they may find themselves open to growth and change.

Growth and change in other areas may be facilitated through questions such as the following that are aimed directly at understanding the degree of meaning and purpose in the lives of clients:

- Are you doing the work you want to be doing?
- Are you satisfied with the education you have obtained?
- Is there any way in which you would like to increase your education or training?
- How do you express your creativity?

- Do you have any special talents or skills that you have not fully developed or expressed?
- Assuming that money and other responsibilities were no object, what would you do with your life if you could do what you truly wanted?
- What would you like to have accomplished by the time you reach age 70 in order to feel that life has been meaningful?
- Have you developed your spiritual life to the extent that you desire?
- What are your most important values?
- What gives your life the most meaning?
- Is there anything you deeply value that you have not yet fully experienced or realized in your life?

The transpersonal or spiritual dimension involves being empowered by the energies and wisdom that flow from the greater wholeness that is attained upon recognizing that life has meaning and purpose. It is the bedrock of empowerment for the practitioner and families and for national and international practice.

Indeed, recent research (Faver, 2004) suggests that practitioners' ability to provide care is sustained by a sense of connectedness to a sacred source, to work, to supportive communities, and to clients—a phenomenon defined as *relational spirituality*. Instead of relegating issues of value to the private sphere, spiritually sensitive practice acknowledges that a transcendent dimension permeates all aspects of life, linking each individual with other individuals and with the community or public sphere. Such linkages typically prompt spiritual people into actions of concern for others (Elkins, 1990), especially the poor and the vulnerable. Although spiritual people may not always have spoken with one voice on every issue, they have affirmed in numerous ways their shared faith that the spiritual dimension of life leads to a transcendence of individualism and to a life of commitment and service to others (Leiby, 1985; Peck, 1987).

The convenient popular dichotomy between public and private morality works against the integration of communities, as well as practitioners' personal and professional lives. Shared public interests rely, in large part, on the development of private virtue. Both private and public order depend on the availability of material resources and fair systems of allocation. Therefore, being committed to the values of social justice and the difficult tasks of implementing such values in economic and political systems is essential (Siporin, 1986). Humans' spiritual heritage further emphasizes that individual self-actualization is gained through committed relationships with others, through investing one's own resources and very self in furthering the good of others (Kilpatrick & Holland, 1990).

Practitioners' recognition of the spiritual foundations of their lives and their professional practice leads to a number of implications regarding the client, the practitioner, their relationship, and the social context of the profession. Consistent with the social constructionist framework, clients are acknowledged as practitioners' peers. Practitioners recognize that clients are human beings, too, and that just as practitioners have professional expertise, clients are the experts on their personal lives and families. Exploration of spiritual issues must be undertaken with respect for the individual's, couple's, or family's spiritual framework and with the understanding that their belief systems represent their view of reality, which is just as valid for them as the practitioner's is for him or her.

The spiritual, social, emotional, and material or physical dimensions of life are all necessary for individual growth and well-being. Thus, each should be considered in the therapeutic relationship. A biopsychosocial–spiritual model of human functioning makes spiritual issues a legitimate focus for practitioners and provides for a more complete understanding of the strengths, resources, weaknesses, and problems of families. Policies and services that provide accessibility to support in all of these areas are essential for human well-being. Increased openness to addressing relevant spiritual beliefs and metaphors may often provide the practitioner with an important avenue to effective interventions that have great potential for bringing about growth and change.

Ethical Challenges

As indicated in the first half of this chapter, it is essential for practice to be ethically informed. Thus, as the practitioner attempts to function in a spiritually sensitive manner, it also is important to be cognizant of the potential dilemmas and ethical issues that may emerge in this realm for both the professional and the client. Two issues will be addressed in the following sections: conflicts arising from religious/spiritual beliefs and limits of competence/lack of training.

Conflicts Arising from Religious/Spiritual Beliefs

Given the ethical imperatives to avoid discrimination and foster client self-determination, the practitioner must be able to recognize when a conflict in religious or spiritual values and practices precludes his or her ability to practice in an unbiased manner and support the rights of clients to make decisions for themselves. Differences in beliefs around issues and behaviors such as abortion, birth control, cohabitation, divorce, homosexuality, and sex before marriage, which often emerge from an individual's religious/spiritual belief system, may challenge the ability of the practitioner to work effectively with certain clients. In such situations, the practitioner is advised to seek supervision and/or to make appropriate referrals (Becvar, 2001).

An example of such a conflict is the belief in reincarnation held by a large part of the world's population. Many families and students have come to the United States from countries that have a predominant Hindu or Buddhist orientation. Reincarnation and karma are integral parts of these individuals' belief systems, and they will likely see some personal and social issues very differently from mainstream Americans. For instance, if someone believes that in some reincarnations, one is male, and in others, one is female, making people androgynous beings, then one's sexual orientation in this life may not be an issue. If people are essentially spiritual beings and their goal is not merely survival but perfection, then the reincarnation principle makes possible a new sense of purpose. In addition, in showing how the laws of karma inexorably operate, a new sense of the ethical validity of religious percepts will become clear (Cerminara, 2007). Further, to Western beliefs about nature and nurture as determinants of personality, Eastern culture may add karma. To work with persons of this spiritual orientation, the practitioner would need to have extensive knowledge, understanding, and acceptance of their belief system. If this is not possible, appropriate referrals should be made.

Limits of Competence/Lack of Training

Given that attention to and permission to include the religious/spiritual dimension in clinical practice are relatively recent occurrences, it is not common for practitioners to have had extensive training in this area, unless they attended a seminary-based program (Becvar, 1997a). Although schools of social work are now often including at least one course on the topic in their curricula, sensitivity to the limits of one's competence is essential to prevent a code of ethics violation.

Being adequately prepared to accommodate issues and needs in this realm may require additional supervision or training through workshops or advanced study, as well as finding consultants who might provide advice should the need arise. Such training would help the practitioner learn how to prevent personal issues from intruding inappropriately along with ways to engage effectively with spiritual and religious issues as they emerge, either implicitly or explicitly, in the practice setting.

Summary

Ethics and spirituality are personal matters that provide the blueprint for inventing, shaping, and reformulating the way people are with themselves and how they relate to others. And both are an inevitable part of the therapy context.

Ethical issues influence what practitioners are able to do with families, which means practitioners must be informed in this area. Pertinent ethical issues include separating interventions from the larger ecosystems; focusing on individual or family welfare; using informed consent; respecting confidentiality; deciding who participates in the treatment sessions; and avoiding deception and inappropriate manipulation. Models of decision making address the grounds for making a decision, dimensions of clinical judgment, and codes of ethics. Such models provide guidelines for making ethically informed decisions in practice.

A final context to be considered is that of spiritually sensitive family practice. Although previously a much neglected area, spirituality is now recognized as an important aspect of people's lives as well as of the therapy process. Many of the barriers to addressing family members' spiritual concerns have been overcome, and there is much support for working in a spiritually sensitive manner. Aspects of spirituality include one's personal faith and values, how one understands and responds to meaning in life, and how one feels connected with others and the world, as well as recognition of a transcendent dimension. Increased openness in dealing with family members' relevant spiritual beliefs may enrich and enhance practice.

Spirituality is a resource to draw on not only from within the individual or family but also through places of worship within the ecosystem and the values underlying each person's or system's construction of reality. At the same time, it is important for practitioners recognize potential ethical conflicts that may arise relative to differences in value systems or limits of competence.

Discussion Questions _____

1. Describe and discuss ethical issues that may arise in an intervention with a family with a strong patriarchal tradition.

2. Regarding the ethical dilemma of meeting family versus individual needs, how would you balance the therapeutic responsibility toward both?

3. How do you effectively work with clients who present spiritual ideas that are different from or even in conflict with your own?

4. How can you assess when a client or family is ready to or needs to discuss spiritual issues?

5. What are some ethical issues of which to be aware when including spirituality in the therapeutic conversation?

Internet Resources _____

Ethics

http://ethics.sandiego.edu
www.ethics.org
www.globalethics.org
www.ethics.ubc.ca
http://pages.prodigy.net/lizmitchell/volksware/ethics.htm

Professional Codes of Ethics

www.socialworkers.org/pubs/code/code.asp
www.aamft.org/resources/LRMPlan/Ethics/ethicscode2001.asp
www.amhca.org/code
www.nbcc.org/extra/pdfs/ethics/NBCC-CodeofEthics.pdf

Spirituality

http://ssw.asu.edu/portal/research/spirituality
www.cswe.org/spirituality
www.socwel.ku.edu/canda/
http://kidshealth.org/parent/emotions/feelings/spirituality.html

Suggested Readings _____

Assagioli, T. (1990). *Psychosynthesis: A manual of principles and techniques.* Wellingborough, UK: Crucible Press.
> The author defines and maps the geography of spiritual transformation through psychosynthesis. Psychological disturbances may serve as precursors to a more ethically and spiritually refined outlook. The process of spiritual development is described in four critical phases.

Becvar, D. S. (1997). *Soul healing: A spiritual orientation in counseling and therapy.* New York: Basic Books.
> This groundbreaking book shows how a spiritual orientation (which can encompass the full range of belief systems) can be used to facilitate healing at the deepest level.

Doherty, W. J., & Boss, P. G. (1991). Values and ethics in family therapy. In A. S. Gurman & D. P. Kniskern (Eds.), *Handbook of family therapy* (Vol. 2, pp. 606–637). New York: Brunner/Mazel.
> Of special interest in this chapter is the discussion of personal and cultural values in family therapy, ideological issues, ethical issues, and gender and ethics in family therapy. Future directions are also discussed.

Dykstra, C., & Parks, L. (1986). *Faith development and Fowler.* Birmingham, AL: Religious Education Press.
> Fowler presents an overview of his faith development theory, and then other authors evaluate the theory and discuss how it can be enhanced.

Huber, C. H. (1993). *Ethical, legal and professional issues in the practice of marriage and family therapy* (2nd ed.). New York: Merrill.
> This is a very popular text used in many marriage and family therapy professional issues courses. Several chapters are devoted to ethical issues, the professional codes of ethics, and their implications for working with families.

Kilpatrick, A. C., & Holland, T. P. (1990). Spiritual dimensions of practice. *Clinical Supervisor, 8*(2), 125–140.
> This article places values and faith in a historical context within the profession of social work, presents developmental stages of faith, and gives some practical ways that students and practitioners can think about the spiritual dimensions of professional practice.

Mattison, M. (2000). Ethical decision making: The person in the process. *Social Work, 45*(3), 201–212.
> Reflective self-awareness can alert the decision maker to the ways assumptions and values influence thinking about ethical dilemmas.

May, G. (1982). *Will and spirit: A contemplative psychology.* San Francisco: Harper.
> Within Maslow's hierarchy of needs, May found that spirituality can be found at both ends of the continuum. He states, "It emerges at the bottom, when physiological needs for survival cannot be met and physical existence is threatened. It also arises when most other needs have been taken care of and one has the luxury to ask, 'What's it all for? ' or 'Is this all there is?' Thus, it is in relative affluence or in utter desolation that human spiritual longing most obviously becomes prominent." (p. 91)

References

American Association for Marriage and Family Therapy (AAMFT). (2001). *AAMFT Code of Ethics.* Washington, DC: Author.

Anderson, D. A., & Worthen, D. (1997). Exploring a fourth dimension: Spirituality as a resource for the couple therapist. *Journal of Marital and Family Therapy, 23*(1), 12.

Aponte, H. (1994). *Bread and spirit: Therapy with the new poor.* New York: Norton.

Atwater, P. M. H. (2007). *The big book of near-death experiences.* Norfolk, VA: Hampton Roads.

Bardill, D. R. (1997). *The relational model for family therapy: Living in the four realities.* New York: Haworth Press.

Baylor University Religion Survey. (2005). Retrieved from www.baylor.edu.content/services/documents .php/3304.pdf.

Becvar, D. S. (1997a). *Soul healing: A spiritual orientation in counseling and therapy.* New York: Basic Books.

Becvar, D. S. (Ed.). (1997b). *The family, spirituality and social work.* New York: Haworth Press.

Becvar, D. S. (2001). Moral values, spirituality and sexuality. In R. H. Woody & J. D. Woody (Eds.), *Ethics in marriage and family therapy.* Washington, DC: AAMFT.

Becvar, D. S., & Becvar, R. J. (2009). *Family therapy: A systemic integration* (7th ed.). Boston: Allyn & Bacon.

Becvar, R. J., Becvar, D. S., & Bender, A. E. (1982). Let us first do no harm. *Journal of Marital and Family Therapy, 8*(4), 385–391.

Benningfield, M. (1997). Addressing spiritual/religious issues in therapy: Potential problems and complication. In D. Becvar (Ed.), *The family, spirituality and social work* (pp. 25–42). New York: Haworth Press.

Bowman, E. S. (1989). Understanding and responding to religious material in the therapy of multiple personality disorder. *Dissociation, 2*(4), 231–238.

Bray, J. H., Shepherd, J. N., & Hays, J. R. (1985). Legal and ethical issues in informed consent to psychotherapy. *American Journal of Family Therapy, 23,* 50–60.

Burkemper, E. M. (2004). Informed consent in social work ethics education: Guiding student education with an informed consent template. *Journal of Teaching in Social Work, 24*(1,2), 141–160.

Campbell, I., & Moyers, B. (1988). *The power of myth.* New York: Doubleday.

Canda, E. R., & Furman, L. D. (1999). *Spiritual diversity in social work practice.* New York: Free Press.

Cerminara, G. (2007). *Many mansions: Healing the karma within you, Part II.* Virginia Beach, VA: A. R. E. Press.

Cornett, C. (1992). Toward a more comprehensive personology: Integrating a spiritual perspective into social work practice. *Social Work, 37*(2), 101–102.

Council on Social Work Education (CSWE). (1994). *Curriculum policy statement for master's degree programs in social work education.* Alexandria, VA: Author.

Doherty, W. J., & Boss, P. G. (1991). Values and ethics in family therapy. In A. S. Gurman & D. P. Kniskern (Eds.), *Handbook of family therapy* (Vol. 11, pp. 606–637). New York: Brunner/Mazel.

Dossey, L. (December 2006). *Healing between spirit and medicine.* Paper presented at the National Cathedral, Washington, DC.

Efran, J. A., Lukens, R., & Lukens, M. D. (1988). Constructivism: What's in it for you? *Family Therapy Networker, 12*(5), 27–35.

Elkins, D. (1990, June). On being spiritual without necessarily being religious. *Association for Humanistic Psychology Perspective,* 4–5.

Faver, C. A. (2004). Relational spirituality in social caregiving. *Social Work, 49*(2), 241–249.

Frame, M. W. (2000). Spiritual and religious issues in counseling: Ethical considerations. *Family Journal: Counseling and Therapy for Couples and Families, 81*(1), 72–74.

Green, S. L., & Hansen, J. C. (1989). Ethical dilemmas faced by family therapists. *Journal of Marital and Family Therapy, 15*(2), 149–158.

Hamer, D. (2004). *The God gene.* New York: Doubleday.

Haug, I. (1998). Including a spiritual dimension in family therapy: Ethical considerations. *Contemporary Family Therapy, 20*(2), 181–194.

Health Insurance Privacy and Accountability Act (HIPAA). (2002). Retrieved August 7, 2008, from www.hhs.gov/ocr/hipaa.

Hickson, J., & Phelps, A. (1997). Women's spirituality: A proposed practice model. In D. Becvar (Ed.), *The family, spirituality and social work* (pp. 43–57). New York: Haworth Press.

Hodge, D. R. (2001). Spiritual assessment: A review of major qualitative methods and a new framework for assessing spirituality. *Social Work, 46*(3), 203–214.

Hodge, D. R. (2003). Assessing client spirituality: Understanding the advantages of utilizing different assessment approaches. *Society for Spirituality and Social Work Forum, 10*(1), 8–10.

Hodge, D. R. (2005, October 1). Assessment in marital and family therapy: A methodological framework for selecting from among six qualitative assessment tools. *Journal of Marital and Family Therapy,* Retrieved August 6, 2008, from http://highbeam.com/doc1P3-914573791.html.

Holland, T. P., & Kilpatrick, A. C. (1991). Ethical issues in social work: Toward a grounded theory of professional ethics. *Social Work, 36*(2), 138–144.

Huber, C. H., & Baruth, L. G. (1993). *Ethical, legal and professional issues in the practice of marriage and family therapy* (2nd ed.). Columbus, OH: Merrill.

Institute of Noetic Sciences (IONS). (2007). *The 2007 shift report: Evidence of a world transforming.*

ISHI Programs and Workshops. (2008). *The healer's art.* Institute for the Study of Health and Illness. Retrieved August 6, 2008, from www.commonweall.org/ishi/programs/healers_art.html.

Joint Commission on Accreditation of Health Care Organizations. (1997). *Spiritual assessments.* Retrieved from www.jointcommission.org/AccreditationPrograms/HomeCare/Standards/FAQsProvision+of+ Care/Assessment/Spiritual_Assessment.htm.

Kilpatrick, A. C., & Holland, T. P. (1990). Spiritual dimensions of practice. *Clinical Supervisor, 8*(2), 125–140.

Koerner, B. I., & Rich, J. (1997, March 31). Is there life after death? *U.S. News & World Report.* Retrieved from www.usnews.com/usnews/culture/articles/970331/archive_006588.htm.

Leiby, J. (1985). The moral foundations of social welfare and social work. *Social Work, 30,* 32–33.

Mattison, M. (2000). Ethical decision making: The person in the process. *Social Work, 45*(3), 201–210.

May, G. (1982). *Will and spirit: A contemplative psychology.* San Francisco: Harper.

National Association of Social Workers (NASW). (1999). *NASW Code of Ethics.* Washington, DC: Author.

Peck, M. S. (1987). *The different drum.* New York: Simon & Schuster.

Prest, L. A., & Keller, J. F. (1993). Spirituality and family therapy: Spiritual beliefs, myths, and metaphors. *Journal of Marital and Family Therapy, 19*(2), 137–148.

Rice, S. (2002). Magic happens: Revisiting the spirituality and social work debate. *Australian Social Work, 55*(4), 303–312.

Siporin, M. (1986). Contribution of religious values to social work and the law. *Social Thought, 13,* 35–50.

van Lommel, P., van Wees, R., Meyers. V., & Elfferich, I. (2001, December). Near-death experiences in survivors of cardiac arrest: A prospective study in the Netherlands. *Lancet, 358,* 2039–2045.

Watzlawick, P., Weakland, J. H., & Fisch, R. (1974). *Change: Principles of problem formation and problem resolution.* New York: Norton.

Woody, I. D. (1990). Resolving ethical concerns in clinical practice: Toward a pragmatic model. *Journal of Marital and Family Therapy, 16*(2), 133–150.

II

First Level of Family Need: Basic Survival

Level I families are dealing with basic survival needs, such as having food, clothing, shelter, protection, medical care, and minimal nurturance. A primary issue in these families is whether there is enough parenting capacity to support and protect the family's members. Families on this level may have presenting problems of pervasive life stresses, illness of a primary caretaker, economic deprivation, alcoholism, mental illness, or homelessness.

The chapters in this part present two approaches that may be helpful to families who have Level I needs. The first approach is designed to meet basic needs in neglectful families. In Chapter 5, Gaudin presents a model for working with neglectful families. He cites empirical research but the focus is on practice guidelines. He includes strengths assessment, needs and strategies for effective engagement, and also includes methods for working with diversity and substance abuse issues, and the communication of hope.

The second approach focuses on ways to assist families and to enable them to cope with illnesses (both physical and mental), disabilities, and other primary stressors. In Chapter 6, Greene and Kropf discuss the issues of family case management. They present a coordinated, congruent, and collaborative approach that can be used with both chronic and short-term problem situations. The case presented and analyzed is applicable across diverse racial and ethnic groups.

5

Interventions with Level I Neglectful Families

James M. Gaudin, Ph.D.

Case Study

Karen Mackey is a relatively attractive 25-year-old single mother of a 9-month-old child named Kevin. Karen is not living with or married to Kevin's father, Jeff, who is a sometimes-employed construction worker. Jeff sporadically pays Karen $200 a month in child support. She also receives support from Temporary Assistance for Needy Families (TANF), food stamps, and Medicaid. Karen is a high school dropout who works part time as a server in a bar on weekend evenings. On these nights, she leaves Kevin in the care of her friend and neighbor, Lois.

Lois reported Karen to Family and Child Services after she failed to pick up Kevin one Saturday night after her evening shift at the bar. Karen says that she did not intend to leave Kevin with Lois for so long but that she just "needed to get away for a while for a break." This was the first report the agency has received about Karen and her possible maltreatment of Kevin.

For the past six months, Karen and Kevin have lived in a small, dilapidated, single-wide, two-bedroom trailer in a trailer park several miles from a small town in southern Georgia. The floor of the living room is covered with old pizza boxes and scraps of food, along with a soiled diaper, and in the kitchen, piles of dirty dishes fill the sink. There is also a problem with roaches, and a window is broken out in the baby's room.

Kevin sleeps in an old crib Karen got from a co-worker, and it has several missing and broken slats. He appears to be properly clothed, but his feeding seems irregular. There are half-filled baby bottles lying around on the floor beside his crib and also on the couch in the living room. A small pile of dirty clothes lies in the corner of the baby's room.

Karen complains of Kevin's frequent crying during the night, which causes her to lose sleep. She loses patience with him when he soils or wets his diapers and wakes up crying. She feeds him by laying him on the couch or in his crib and propping up the baby bottle on a pillow. When Karen holds Kevin, she displays no signs of cuddling or tenderness. She says she loves him dearly, but she appears to view him as a burden—an obstacle to achieving her dreams. Karen says babies are like little machines: You just have to feed them and change their diapers regularly.

Karen likes working in the bar but wants to get a more respectable, better-paying job, perhaps as an administrative assistant or receptionist. She communicates clearly and has a pleasant, outgoing personality, but she does not have the skills for an office job. She would also like to have some nice clothes to wear to work and to find better housing closer to town. Karen smokes cigarettes and drinks wine, beer, and occasionally whiskey, but she says her drinking is not a problem, since it is only now and then.

Karen is estranged from her family, who live in Florida. She left both school and home at age 16. She hints that her reason for leaving was some emotional and perhaps sexual abuse at home. She has been good friends with Lois since moving into the trailer park six months ago. Lois provides babysitting services for Karen and offers a sympathetic listening ear for her romantic and parenting problems. Lois is her only friend, except for the men she meets at the bar. Karen hopes to meet a nice guy there who will marry her and be kind to her.

Needs of Level I Neglectful Families

The Mackey family is an example of a Level I family, which is severely dysfunctional. This type of family lacks the basic energy and resources required to successfully carry out critical family functions such as parenting, having steady employment, solving problems, and providing mutual emotional support. The problems in functioning tend to be long term and chronic, rather than temporary. Many but not all families who neglect their children are typical of Level I families. They are unable to provide for the basic needs of their children.

Child neglect has been variously defined. Most basically, "child neglect occurs when the basic needs of a child are not met, regardless of the cause" (Dubowitz, Black, Starr, & Zuravin, 1993, pp. 22–23). However, most state laws define neglect in terms of the failure of the parent or another care provider to provide for the basic physical, medical, emotional, and intellectual needs of a child. This most prevalent definition clearly places the responsibility of child neglect on the child's parent or principal care provider. However, the broader definition from Dubowitz et al. highlights the fact that factors beyond the family can cause neglect. For instance, the inadequacies of critical social systems external to the family may be responsible for child neglect.

Child neglect is the most frequently reported and confirmed type of child maltreatment. Recent national studies confirm that neglect represents more than 64 percent of reported child maltreatment victims. Another 2.2 percent are medically neglected (USD-HHS, 2006). Neglect is the most prevalent type of maltreatment that professionals recognize, whether they report it or not. A study by Sedlak and Broadhurst (1996) estimates the prevalence of children harmed by neglect to be 13.1 per 1,000 children. The rate for all types of abuse was 11.1 per 1,000 children. Neglect is also 46 percent more likely to be repeated than other types of child maltreatment (USDHHS, 2004).

There are many types of neglect. Neglect can be physical, emotional, medical, intellectual, or social. It may be chronic, temporary, or episodic. Parents may successfully meet the needs of children for food, safe housing, supervision, medical care, and clothing but be incapable of providing the kind of consistent emotional support and nurturing that children need for healthy psychological development. Conversely, parents may provide adequate emotional nurturing but fail to provide safe housing, adult supervision, food, or medical care necessary for the child's health and safety.

Child neglect typically has multiple causes. Dysfunction of the family system is often the immediate factor, but there are typically contributing factors at all ecological systems levels:

● At the individual parent, or *ontogenic,* level, the causes may include the parent or caretaker's low intellectual functioning level, substance abuse, mental illness, impaired judgment or problem solving, or poor communication skills. These causes often stem from the parent or caretaker's own neglectful developmental experience.

● At the family system, or *mesosystem,* level, the cause may well be single-parent status and inadequate support from the child's father, incarceration of a parent, too many children (large family), marital conflict or domestic violence, poor communication between parents, and so on.

● Causes at the *exosystem* level can include so-called neighborhood drain (i.e., the predominance of single, poor, unemployed families in a given area) (Garbarino & Sherman, 1980); lack of access to critical supplemental child care services (e.g., child day care, supervised after-school recreation programs and facilities); an unsafe, crime-ridden neighborhood; lack of affordable transportation; lack of accessible employment; geographic and/or social isolation; and weak informal social support networks.

● At the *macrosystem* level, the contributing causes may include inadequate public funding for education, unavailability of special education services, an impoverished or underdeveloped local economy with consequent high unemployment or low local wage scales, racism and discrimination, lack of community concern for children in poor areas, and high crime and incarceration rates, especially for minorities.

Child neglect is often a result of a combination of causes at all these system levels, but dysfunction at the family system level is the most immediate proximate cause.

Poverty is highly associated with neglectful parenting. The incidence of reported child neglect is highest among low-income families. Findings from the *Third National Incidence Study* (Sedlak & Broadhurst, 1996) indicate that the likelihood of a child experiencing physical neglect is more than 1.5 times greater among families with a yearly income of $15,000 or less than in families with a yearly income of $30,000 or more. For families and children living in poverty, this fact must be considered as a major risk factor for child neglect.

Family size is another significant predictor of child neglect. Findings from the same national study reveal that children in single-parent families are at an 87 percent greater risk of physical neglect and a 74 percent greater risk of emotional neglect than those living in two-parent homes. Similarly, the number of children in the family is predictive of neglect. Children living in families with four or more children are three times more likely to be physically neglected than those coming from single-child families (Sedlak & Broadhurst, 1996).

Assessment

Clearly, a complete psychosocial assessment of a Level I neglectful family must be based on an ecological–systems conceptual model, which encompasses all the possible causes of a family's neglectful functioning. A comprehensive assessment of the family's functioning in its environment and the factors contributing to the malfunctioning is a key element in planning an effective intervention to improve the family's functioning.

Assessment must not be a one-time, single event or stage but rather an ongoing, continuous process as work continues with a Level I family. Important facts are often not evident from the initial referral information because families rarely reveal important covert issues in the initial intervention sessions. Often, details about family composition, substance abuse, mental illness, previous neglect and/or abuse, domestic violence, and other critical diagnostic information surfaces after a level of trust is developed between the family and the practitioner. Effective engagement and development of a trusting helping relationship with the family are essential for developing a comprehensive assessment of the family in its environment.

Sources of Information for Assessment

Although the parents or primary care provider will be the main source of information needed for assessment, other sources are necessary for obtaining the information needed for a comprehensive ecological assessment. Prior to the initial contact with the family, the practitioner should review information from previous records, reports, and assessments of the family's functioning. Especially important is evidence of prior neglectful parenting, substance abuse, domestic violence, mental health problems, and other indicators that reflect previous levels of family functioning and especially parenting functioning.

Following an initial exploration with the parents or primary care provider, the practitioner should obtain the perspectives of other family members. This should include extended family, who are often important influences on the parents' or principal care providers' functioning. Every effort should be made to include all adult family members, children, and adolescents in the interviews. Observation of family interactions reveals much about family communication, family conflicts, and problem-solving behaviors.

The *family system* should be broadly defined to include grandparents, other relatives, fictive kin, and friends and neighbors who often share child care tasks, give advice about child care, provide emotional support, or contribute to conflicts within the family system. Quite different perspectives on family dynamics are often gained from including these other members of the family system. Valuable insights into family dynamics may also be obtained from school-age children and adolescents. It is especially important to insist on interviewing the father, boyfriend, or other significant adult who may or may not reside in the same location as the family.

Home visits to observe the family function in its natural home environment also provide invaluable information about patterns of communication, family roles, exercise of power and control, conflict management, disciplinary practices, and the emotional content of parent–child and adult–adult interactions. Home visits also provide unique, real-world understanding of the organization, cleanliness, and hygiene practiced in the home and the influence of living space, sleeping arrangements, home furnishings, heating and cooling, and economic resources reflected in the home environment. These observations provide valuable diagnostic and baseline information, which is necessary to set reasonable, specific, clear, achievable goals for improved parenting practices.

Assessment Information

Assessment of factors contributing to the family's neglectful parenting should be based on the ecological model (Belsky, 1993; Belsky & Vondra, 1989). The practitioner should assess both risk factors that serve as obstacles to adequate family functioning and protective factors that can at least potentially support and enhance family functioning (DePanfilis, 2006; Thomlinson, 1997). The relevant contributing factors at all four ecological systems levels must be included in the assessment.

Factors at the Ontological Level

Children.　The number of children in the home (and out of the home in the care of others), the ages of the children, and the developmental progress of the children are all critical items of information. In cases of neglect, the practitioner must pay special attention to the children's lack of or exaggerated attachment behaviors with the parents and any obvious physical or mental disabilities. The practitioner should observe children's age-appropriate physical, intellectual, speech/language, and social skills, as well as their interactions with their parents, siblings, and peers for unusually aggressive or passive behaviors and for the appropriate expression of emotions. Information from the children's school on attendance, academic progress, and behavior also provides essential details about age-appropriate behavior and development. Neighbors can be asked for their observations of the children's behavior and developmental progress.

Parents or Primary Care Providers.　First, it is important to identify the primary care provider or providers for the child or children in the home. Is the primary care provider the parent, grandparent, some other relative, or another person? The practitioner should also inquire about other persons living in the home. Are there family members with serious physical or mental disabilities? Finally, the practitioner should determine the identity and residence of the father or fathers of the children and/or the mother's male partner.

It is critical to make determined efforts to contact and actively involve the father or the mother's or care provider's male partner, whether he is living in the home full time, part time, or not at all. The male parent figure is often not included in the assessment and intervention, yet he is, at least potentially, a critical resource and a powerful influence on the child, the mother, and the functioning of the family system. Often, he is not mentioned as a member of the family or his participation in the family is minimized by the female care provider for various reasons. The practitioner should assertively pursue information about the father or male companion of the mother to obtain his involvement. Scheduling contacts outside normal office hours is often required to meet fathers.

In the case of Karen Mackey, what roles does Jeff, Kevin's father, play in the family? Could Karen's relationship with Jeff be strengthened so he can become a stronger support?

Was he abusive? If domestic violence is identified by the mother as a serious problem, precautions must be taken to ensure her safety before contacting the father or male parent figure.

The physical appearance of the parents or primary care providers should be noted by the practitioner as an indicator of self-esteem and self-respect. The clarity and logical sequence of the care providers' communication, the language spoken, and the appropriateness of their affect are important indicators of their level of intellectual functioning, educational attainment, and mental status. Karen Mackey's appearance reflected positive self-esteem, and her clear communication was also a strength.

Of course, strong emotions of anger and defensiveness are not unusual in initial contacts with neglectful parents, who often reject the allegations of neglect and forcefully deny that their parenting is substandard. The intensity, tone, and range of emotions expressed indicate the individual's ability to express and manage a range of emotions. Depressed affect can indicate the influence of alcohol or drugs, lack of sleep, or mental/emotional problems. The family members' communication with the child welfare professional is an indicator of their communication and social skills.

The practitioner should look for signs of depression, a mental health problem that is found frequently with neglectful parents (Polansky, Ammons, & Gaudin, 1985). Clinical depression is indicated by a persistent pattern of depressed affect, hopelessness, lack of appetite, sleep problems, lack of energy to get out of bed or to perform normal tasks of daily living, or pattern of constant sleeping, nervousness, anxiety, and agitated feelings.

The family or child welfare professional must assess the parent or primary care provider's level of knowledge about parenting and child care, including his or her awareness of children's age-appropriate physical and emotional needs. What is the care provider's level of knowledge and skills about the nutritional and health care needs of infants and children? Can he or she perceive the signs of a child's need for medical attention or physical or emotional comforting? Can the care provider recognize the signs of need from the child's behavior (e.g., crying or reaching out) and then appropriately interpret and respond to them? The practitioner's choice of interventions may be different depending on which of these levels of perception and action the parents need help (Crittenden, 1993). (Practitioners should use Lutzker and Bigelow's [2002] infant and child health care training program for assessing and teaching these critical parenting skills.)

The parents' or care provider's general knowledge about community services and resources, as well as their physical and social environment, should be assessed to determine their general fund of knowledge and awareness about the world they live in. The practitioner should assess whether their level of knowledge indicates some social isolation or mental handicap.

Since substance abuse is a major factor in an increasingly larger number of neglectful families, the practitioner must look closely for indicators of alcohol and/or other drug use. Available written records from previous abuse or neglect interventions should be checked for indications of previous substance abuse. Obvious symptoms include slurred or illogical speech, sluggishness, signs of sleep deprivation, extreme passivity or hyperalertness, expression of inappropriate emotions, lack of physical balance or steadiness, repeated and compulsive cigarette smoking, red or watering eyes, needle marks on arms. The practitioner should also look for evidence of beer or hard liquor containers, numerous prescribed drug containers, and needles and other drug paraphernalia.

The practitioner should ask the primary care provider directly about her use of alcohol and other drugs and that of other members of the family, including children and adolescents. The practitioner should expect denial on the part of the substance abuser. Assertive questioning should continue if the abuse of alcohol or drugs is revealed by physical evidence, behavior, or information from others. The practitioner should challenge the abuser's denial with this evidence. If substance abuse is indicated, this must become the primary focus of intervention. The effect of the substance abuse on the parent or primary care provider's ability to adequately care for the children must be carefully assessed to determine the need for supplemental child care or substitute parenting by relatives or foster care.

A psychosocial history should be taken. The practitioner should ask the parents or primary care providers about their own experiences growing up. Questions should address the kind of relationship they had with their parents, the stability of the family over time, the economic resources of the family, and the employment history of the primary income provider. The practitioner should also ask about the kinds of discipline the parents or care provider experienced and the expressions of love and the consistency of the emotional nurturing they received from their parents or primary care providers. He or she should ask about their memories of any child abuse or neglect they received, as well as their school experiences, employment history, marital history, and history of romantic relationships as indicators of stability in adult relationships.

Finally, the child welfare or family intervention professional must critically assess the parents' or primary child care provider's level of awareness of the need to improve their parenting and their level of motivation to provide more adequate care for their children. Very often, neglectful parents are in denial of or honestly do not view their care for their children to be substandard. Cultural differences may account for some variation in standards for child care, discipline, and supervision. The child welfare professional must be sensitive to cultural differences but be prepared to confront the denial or lack of knowledge with the facts of normal child development and the age-appropriate needs of children, their observations, and the report of neglect.

Factors at the Mesosystem Level

The practitioner should begin by determining the family composition. The term *family* should be broadly defined to include the children living in the home or out of the home, the children's primary care provider, the children's father(s), the mother's current male or female partner (whether in the home full or part time), and other adult or adolescent relatives or friends living in the home. The practitioner should determine the current marital status of the primary care provider and his or her marital history as an indicator of the stability of the family system. In addition, the practitioner should assess the quality of the relationship between the primary care provider and his or her spouse or intimate partner.

What is the level and consistency of mutual emotional support and the clarity of verbal communication among family members? The practitioner should ask about and observe the communication and verbal and nonverbal expressions of emotions in the family. He or she should ask and observe how conflicts are handled and how decisions are made (e.g., how money is spent or what TV programs will be watched). These are indicators of the distribution and exercise of power among family members. Another important topic is how tasks are allocated among family members. Who cooks, cleans, and handles the money? Who cares for and disciplines the children? How much are parenting and housekeeping tasks shared, and who shares them?

The practitioner should observe the verbal and nonverbal interactions between the children and their parents or care providers. How much positive affection is expressed verbally and behaviorally by the parents toward the children and the children toward the parents? Do the parents show affection by physically embracing and holding their young children? Do the children show positive affection toward their parents or care providers, or do they appear withdrawn or fearful? How much negative expression of feeling, such as scolding, is expressed between them? (Practitioners should use Lutzker and Bigelow's [2002] parent activities training procedures for assessing parent–child bonding and for improving parent–child interactions.) Discipline should be considered as well. How is discipline exercised? Is it age appropriate? How are sibling and peer conflicts handled by the care provider? How consistent is the discipline? Which adult or adults supervise the children? Are these care providers physically and emotionally capable? Is the supervision consistent and adequate?

What is the quality of the children's sibling relationships? Do their interactions indicate positive emotional connections along with the usual sibling conflicts? What are the levels of positive interaction versus conflict among siblings when at play? Are their expressions of frustration and anger appropriate or extreme?

The practitioner should assess the quality of relationships among other adults in the family. What is the dominant emotional tone in the family? Is there a positive, hopeful tone or a negative, hopeless, depressed, or angry tone? Is there appropriate expression of a range of emotions?

How is the home environment structured? The practitioner should ask about the sequence of normal daily routines and observe the cleanliness and orderliness of the home. (To systematically assess the cleanliness of the home, practitioners should utilize Lutzker and Bigelow's Checklist for Living Environment to Assess Neglect [2002, pp 96–129].) What are the mealtime routines? Is there a definite time for the major evening or noontime meal? Is there a clear rule about when children are to be in bed, do their homework, watch television, or perform household chores? Are these rules consistently enforced by the parents or primary child care providers? Who gets up and makes sure the children are fed and leave for school on time? What are the sleeping arrangements for the children and adults in the home? How safe is the home environment for children? (To assess hazards, the practitioner should use Lutzker and Bigelow's Home Accident Prevention Inventory [2002, pp. 96–128].)

Economics is another key area for assessment. How adequate are the family's economic resources? Is one or more of the adults in the family employed consistently? What is the recent employment history of the primary income provider? What level of education and job skills or training do the primary income provider and other adults in the family have? Does the primary care provider receive child support payments from the father(s) of the children? Does anyone in the family receive TANF, Social Security, disability, retirement, survivor, SSI, veterans, or pension benefits? Does the family own their home or rent? Does the family own a drivable car? Do they have a telephone to use at least for emergencies?

Factors at the Exosystem Level

Research on neglectful families has fairly consistently identified weak relationships and limited supports in the linkages between the neglecting family and relatives, neighbors, and friends (DePanfilis, 1996, 1999, 2006; Gaudin & Polansky, 1986; Polansky et al., 1985; Thompson, 1994, 1995). Neglectful families often also lack strong linkages with formally organized community services that could support and supplement parenting. However, empirical research indicates that parental functioning can be improved significantly by interventions to strengthen informal linkages, along with teaching social skills, and other interventions to effectively connect neglectful families (DePanfilis, 1996, 1999; Gaudin, Wodarski, Arkinson, & Avery, 1991).

It is therefore important to assess the relationships between neglectful families and their relatives, neighbors, and friends. Doing so offers the potential for supporting and supplementing the family's resources for improved parenting. The practitioner should ask about the family's relationships with close relatives, neighbors, and friends and how frequently they speak to these potentially supportive people. What is the emotional content of these contacts? Are the relationships positive, negative, or conflicted? How enduring are these relationships? Is there anyone the parent or care provider feels that he or she can call on for help with parenting or household tasks? How much can the parent or care provider count on the neighbor or relative to help with child care, provide transportation to the doctor, give the parent emotional support and advice about parenting, or loan him or her money to help to buy food or diapers? If the connections are conflicted, weak, or nonexistent, the practitioner should ask about the duration and the issues that precipitated the conflict or the reasons for the weak relationships. How do the parent's or care provider's feelings about the person or past experiences or his or her biases play into the weak relationship with a potentially supportive relative, neighbor, or friend?

It is also important to assess the parents' or primary care provider's relationships with formally organized helping resources. Where does the family go for medical care? Is there a consistent relationship with a physician, pediatrician, or clinic for the children? What kind of relationship does the family have with the children's school? Has the family received services from other community agencies—from churches, from family support programs, from child care centers, or from a public health or assistance agency? To what extent is the family involved with a church, mosque, or synagogue? To what extent are the children involved with organized neighborhood, community, church, or social programs? The practitioner should ask about neighborhood organizations that might offer potential social support to the parents and children. What has been the family's relationship and involvement with neighborhood groups? It's also important to ask also about the parents' perception of the safety of the neighborhood, including the frequency of crime in the area.

Asking these kinds of questions will allow the worker or therapist to assess the parents' or care provider's perception of the social supports currently available to the family and to offer some direction for interventions to strengthen these vital social network linkages and improve parenting. The child welfare professional must investigate the potential availability to the family of affordable child care, after-school care, health care, and recreation programs in the neighborhood.

A visit to the children's school is also essential for the practitioner to assess the school's experience and attitude toward the family and the kinds of services the school can offer to the children in terms of special education and needed support services. Often, school personnel have had negative experiences with neglectful families and hold negative attitudes toward them, which constitute significant barriers to the family's receiving needed supportive services. Conflict resolution may be needed to resolve these issues.

Factors at the Macrosystem Level

A comprehensive ecological assessment must also include factors in the larger social–economic environment that are determinants of family functioning and may be significant contributing causes of neglectful parenting, requiring community, rather than family-focused, interventions. The health of the larger economic environment of the country, the state, and the local area determines the availability of jobs, the amount of tax monies available to support high-quality schools with special educational and support services, the level of crime and delinquency, and the funds needed to support affordable child care, medical care, and social and recreational services.

Racism causes discrimination in jobs, recreational opportunities, and social relationships and can be a significant barrier for minority families who want to access public and privately operated family support services. In addition, the lack of priority that the federal, state, and local governments place on the needs of poor families and their children is reflected in how tax monies are allocated to support public health, education, and social services. The unavailability of affordable, subsidized housing for low-income families is a major factor in the quality and safety of homes that families can provide. The availability and accessibility of public transportation can be a major determinant of access to jobs and medical, social, and recreational services. The ready availability of alcohol and other drugs in the community and neighborhood enhances the abuse of these addictive substances by parents who thus are inattentive to or unable to attend to the needs of their children.

Strategies for Effective Engagement

Level I neglectful families are frequently difficult to engage in a collaborative helping relationship. The identification of deficits in parenting is the presenting problem, but other issues pose formidable obstacles to establishing a trustful relationship with the child welfare worker or family therapist. Those issues include the parent or care provider's implied failure as a caregiver, previous negative experiences with child welfare investigators or other professional helpers, distrust of bureaucratic organizations, and mental health or substance abuse. To establish the level of trusting relationship that is essential to effective helping, the practitioner must be completely conscious of these issues and initiate interventions to overcome them.

At the initial contact, it is essential for the practitioner (most often a female protective services worker) to clearly identify herself and the agency or organization he or she represents and the purpose of the visit, which is most often in the family home. Not understanding these facts increases the anxiety of the family members and creates an obstacle to trust and openness. Trust is enhanced when the child welfare worker or therapist is honest and clear about the reason for the visit. The reason for intervention must be concern about the child's welfare, but the practitioner must also communicate understanding and empathy to the parents or other care providers.

It is reasonable to expect that parents, when confronted by an inquiring child welfare worker, will be defensive about their care for their children and angry about the intrusion into their lives. The anger must be accepted and empathy must be communicated to normalize it. The practitioner should imagine being in the parents' position to gain empathy for their resentment and anger. Communicating empathy often reduces the anger and begins to build a more positive relationship.

The practitioner should also expect and anticipate the parents' denial of neglectful parenting. Many neglectful parents do not view their parenting as neglectful. Their parenting frequently reflects that which they received as children or that is normative among their friends and relatives. To challenge the denial, the practitioner should confront the parents or care provider with the facts of the physical or emotional neglect and the lack of supervision or necessary medical care. The need for knowledge about child development and the age-appropriate needs of children must be clearly stated, and the facts of the referral, as cited by an anonymous source, should also be used to counter the denial of neglect.

Differences in age-appropriate norms for child care are often related to ethnic or social class differences. For instance, in the author's experience, low-income, poorly educated African Americans and Mexican immigrants often leave toddlers in the care of very young children or rely on folk remedies to treat illnesses that require professional medical care. The practitioner must be sensitive to these cultural mores and communicate understanding. However, he or she must also clearly state child care norms that reflect what is considered adequate care in the larger American culture. Legal authority should be used as a last resort to motivate cooperation.

It is important for the practitioner to listen empathically to the parent's or care provider's perspective, story, and concerns. The practitioner should communicate interest, empathy, and respect for the individual's view of the situation, his or her history, his or her story about the children, and his or her efforts to meet the needs of the children. The practitioner must temper judgments of the family's functioning by gaining an understanding of what experience from their past might be contributing to their current problems. Their stories provide highly valuable information about past levels of functioning and factors that contribute to the current level of functioning. Understanding the family's stories is also critical for building honest communication and an open, trusting relationship, which is necessary to achieve an accurate, comprehensive assessment and effective intervention.

While listening to the family's story, the practitioner should identify and affirm their strengths (DePanfilis, 1999, 2006). Sometimes, strengths are difficult to identify in chronically neglectful parents, but the practitioner must make an effort to identify them. In the case study about Karen Mackey, her desire to get a better job and her friendship with Lois are both strengths to be affirmed. The ability of parents and children to survive against formidable obstacles with little help is often an amazing strength that can be affirmed. Most neglectful parents want to be good parents. The practitioner should affirm the sincerity of their desire and their efforts to be good parents.

Although the primary focus on improved parenting must be maintained, the needs, desires, and wants of the parents must be solicited, identified, validated, and, if possible, pursued. Karen Mackey's desire to get a better job and home should be affirmed and included in the intervention plan. Level I neglectful parents, who are often the products of neglectful parents, are often self-centered and have difficulty acknowledging, empathizing with, or responding effectively to the needs of their children. Their own pervasive unmet social, emotional, and physical needs take precedence.

By focusing exclusively on the needs of the children, while dismissing the parents' own pressing needs, the practitioner communicates disrespect, and the result is often failure to effectively engage the parents. While the primary focus must be on the critical needs of the child, it is also important to address the expressed needs, wants, priorities of the parents. Doing so communicates that their needs are important and will be given serious attention. However, the parents' needs are often many and can be overwhelming. The practitioner should identify one priority need or desire of the parent (e.g., a job, improved housing, or clothing) and make that a goal to be pursued as a part of the intervention plan.

Epstein's (1988; Epstein & Brown, 2002) task model is useful for intervention with Level I families. It begins with the clear requirement that there be at least one want or client-specified need that can be mutually agreed on and pursued as a prerequisite for an effective working relationship between the family and the social worker or therapist. This clearly expressed parent want or need must be included in the goals to be pursued by the family member and the practitioner. The goal may be, as in the case of Karen Maxey, a better job or some new clothes. Or it may just be the parent's desire that the professional terminate contact with the family. In this latter case, the practitioner accepts this as a goal and involves the parent in identifying the obstacles to that happening—namely, the improvements in parenting that must first be made to assure the basic needs of the children are met.

The communication of hope is a critical tool for engaging neglectful families. Polansky, Chalmers, Buttenweiser, and Williams (1981) characterize one type of neglectful family as the *apathetic, futile family*. This type of family has a long history of failure and lack of success in many areas of their lives. They have encountered so many obstacles and failures in life that they have lost all hope of ever functioning successfully as parents or spouses or of achieving anything.

To overcome the pervasive hopelessness and apathy of many chronically neglectful families, the child welfare worker or therapist should strive to communicate hope of success in at least one small area of functioning as a parent. For this reason, it is critical that at least one limited, clearly stated, achievable goal be mutually agreed on and pursued. Accomplishing such a goal will encourage and motivate chronically neglectful parents and thus generate hope.

Goals and Basic Tenets

Goals for intervention with Level I families must be clearly related to the critical contributing factors at all ecological system levels and the practitioner's resulting understanding of the family dynamics. Given the severely impaired functioning and personal and social resource deficits of these families, it is critical that goals be clear, mutual, realistic, achievable, and measurable. Setting and then pursuing goals that do not meet these criteria will overwhelm and discourage the family, create another failure for them, and doom the intervention to failure.

The overarching goal of intervention with a Level 1 neglectful family must be to enable them to achieve adequate parenting and family functioning, not to make them into superior parents. The overall goal is for the family to provide their child or children with food, clothing, housing, emotional nurturance, medical care, and education that is adequate to meet their individual needs. The practitioner may wish for a higher level of functioning, but again, goals must be realistic and achievable.

For example, for the Mackey family, the goals may be (1) to eliminate the dangerous element of Kevin's sleeping situation by repairing the broken slats in his bed and (2) to increase the number of positive verbal and nonverbal interactions during the day between mother and child (e.g., nurturing, physical hugging). Another goal may be to increase the number of days per week the parent prepares one balanced hot meal a day for the child or keeps dangerous cleaning materials in a secure area. A goal for Karen Mackey may be to enroll in classes teaching office skills. Although the critical care needs of the children cannot be ignored or postponed, the effort is to identify clear, mutually desired, limited goals that are within the family's ability to achieve and that will provide them some experience with achievement.

The safety of the child or children who are being neglected must be given priority. It is usually necessary for the practitioner to challenge the parent or care provider's denial of the problem to raise the priority of the child's critical needs. Karen Mackey is not aware of her infant's need for being tenderly held and emotionally nurtured or the danger posed by the broken crib slats.

Similarly, a denial of substance abuse by the parents or primary care providers must be challenged by the practitioner with facts gathered through observation or other information substantiating abuse. Reducing or stopping the substance abuse must be a high-priority goal to ensure the child's adequate care and supervision. Provisions may need to be made for other competent adult family members, relatives, or friends to provide the necessary care and supervision of the children.

Goals may also be set to remedy problems at other system levels. For Karen Mackey, a goal may be to make amends with her friend Lois and renew their mutually supportive relationship. For another parent, a goal may be to end a destructive relationship. Whatever the goal, it must be clearly stated and mutually agreed on with the parent and realistic and achievable by him or her with the social worker or therapist's help. Successful goal achievement builds hope, self-confidence, and motivation to achieve more.

Interventions with Level I Families

Interventions with Level I neglectful families must be based on the comprehensive ecological assessment of the contributing causes at all system levels. Since there are usually multiple contributing causes at various system levels, a variety of interventions are needed. No single intervention will work with these multiproblem families.

What is usually required is a combination of concrete, material resources to meet the family's critical basic needs for food, clothing, shelter, medical care, and substitute or supplemental parenting services along with psychosocial support services (DePanfilis, 1999,

2006; Gaudin et al., 1991; Gaudin, 1993; NRC, 1993). The provision of concrete assistance to meet basic needs may be needed to remove the immediate danger to the child and/or address a critical need of the parent (e.g., food, housing, substitute or supplemental child care, emergency medical care). Providing this assistance also builds the positive relationship with the practitioner by demonstrating his or her willingness and ability to provide help to the family.

Since Level I families often have a number of critical needs, the practitioner, with the family members, must review the range of needs and set clear priorities for which needs to pursue first. The parents' or care provider's critical needs must be addressed along with those of the children, but the health and welfare of the children must be given priority. In the Mackey case, the practitioner must pay attention to Karen's desire for some nicer clothes and a better job, but he or she must prioritize helping Karen understand the importance of meeting Kevin's nutritional needs and need for emotional nurturing.

The process with the parents or care provider begins by listing their expressed needs and wants, such as a new job, new clothes, better housing, and so on. It is important that the wants be solicited and listed, not dismissed as nonpriorities. The list should be complete but not so long as to be overwhelming to the parents or the practitioner.

A written contract should be developed between the practitioner and the family. The contract must include (1) clearly stated, mutual, realistic, achievable, measurable goals to be achieved; (2) specific action steps or tasks to be done by the parents, older children, and practitioner to achieve the goals; (3) the tangible or emotional payoffs for each task accomplished; and (4) specific timeframes for accomplishing the tasks and goals. The contract must be jointly developed by the parents (and older children, if appropriate) and the professional worker or therapist and signed by all family members who have tasks to be accomplished. Again, special efforts must be made to involve absent fathers and other significant male figures in the family. The contract clarifies the joint effort to be made to achieve clearly stated goals and the specific actions to be taken by each person involved (see Figure 5.1).

Obstacles to accomplishing the identified tasks must be anticipated by the practitioner and the family members, and strategies should be developed for overcoming those obstacles. For instance, the task for Karen Mackey might be to spend at least 10 minutes twice each day holding, playing with, and talking to her 9-month-old child. The obstacles would likely include Karen's lack of knowledge, comfort, and skills for doing this. The practitioner's task would be to discuss with Karen her feelings about her child and to provide some verbal instruction and printed information about the needs of infants of this age, including their need for physical and verbal stimulation and positive, nurturing, physical contact with a caregiver. The practitioner should also model this kind of interaction with the infant for Karen and then coach her in imitating the behaviors, giving her positive feedback for what she does well along with suggestions for improving her techniques. The payoffs for Karen will be her more positive feelings about herself as a parent, less crying from Kevin, and positive reinforcement from the practitioner. (Lutzker and Bigelow's [2002] Planned Activities Training Model offers highly organized step-by-step procedures for teaching parents positive, playful, nurturing ways to interact with their children.) This kind of cognitive-behavioral intervention, which is based on behavioral and social learning theory (see Chapter 8), has proven most effective with neglectful families (DePanfilis, 1999, 2006; Howing, Wodarski, Kurtz, & Gaudin, 1989; Lutzker, 1990; Lutzker & Bigelow, 2002; Lutzker, Frame, & Rice, 1982).

FIGURE 5.1 *Task-Centered Contract*

Family Name _____

Priority Family Needs/Wants	**Goals**
1._____	A._____
2._____	B._____
3._____	C._____

	Family Member Tasks	**Person Responsible**	**Completion Date**	**Professional Tasks**
Goal A.	1._____	_____	_____	1._____
	2._____	_____	_____	2._____
	3._____	_____	_____	
Goal B.	1._____	_____	_____	1._____
	2._____	_____	_____	2._____
	3._____	_____	_____	
Goal C.	1._____	_____	_____	1._____
	2._____	_____	_____	2._____
	3._____	_____	_____	

Contract Begin Date _____   **End Date** _____

Family Members' Signatures   **Professional's Signature**

_____   _____

_____

_____

_____

Other knowledge and skills deficits that can prove formidable obstacles to task accomplishment may include lack of social skills for a job interview, poor anger management or problem-solving skills, poor assertiveness skills, and lack of knowledge of the public transportation system. All of these obstacles to successful task accomplishment require effective teaching by the professional worker or therapist using social learning principles. Anticipated racial or ethnic bias on the part of service providers may also be a significant obstacle requiring the anticipatory teaching to parents of assertive communication and anger management skills. It may also call for use of active listening, empathy, and assertiveness skills by the practitioner with the service provider to mediate conflicts and to reduce barriers to facilitate the referral. Some structural family therapy approaches (see Chapter 7) can also be effective in helping the family to develop some basic rules for daily activities, role clarification for parents and children, appropriate reallocation of power, task sharing, and more effective communication.

Social network interventions may also be required to help the family develop more supportive linkages with neighbors, relatives, and friends (DePanfilis, 1996, 1999; Gaudin et al., 1991; Gaudin et al., 1993, Gaudin, 2001; Thompson, 1994). Based on the child welfare worker's or therapist's assessment of the family's social support system, the practitioner may need to teach the parents basic social and communications skills; convene networks to redefine the content of linkages; employ conflict resolution skills to solve conflicts that have weakened linkages with relatives, neighbors, or friends; help the parents to identify potentially supportive neighbors, friends, and relatives; or recruit natural neighborhood helpers to strengthen social network supports (Gaudin et al., 1991).

Poor family linkages with formally organized family support services requires brokering by the practitioner, providing information, and making effective referrals to services that can support or supplement parenting. Effective referral of neglectful parents to services requires that the practitioner (1) have specific knowledge about the service resource's hours of operation, eligibility criteria, fee schedule, location, phone number, and access to public transportation and clearly communicate this information, if necessary in writing, to the parents; (2) if possible, identify a specific person for the parents to contact at the service resource; (3) rehearse with the parents their initial contact with the resource by phone or in person and coach them, as needed; and (4) ask the parents about any obstacles or problems that concern them about following through on the referral and problem solve these issues with them. The practitioner should make appropriate use of cognitive restructuring to overcome the parents' fears or concerns (i.e., challenging irrational thoughts and suggesting substitute positive thinking).

Successful intervention with Level 1 neglectful families is usually not accomplished in a short time period. Because of these families' multiple problems, relatively few strengths, and limited emotional and economic resources, as well as their tendency to repeat neglect after intensive intervention ceases, intervention over an extended period of time or at least periodic follow-up interventions are required to maintain adequate family functioning (Gaudin, 1993; Gaudin et al., 1991; DePanfilis, 1999).

Over the course of interventions, the practitioner and the family together must continuously evaluate the effectiveness of the interventions for achieving the mutual goals stated in the contract and to alter the contract, as needed. Over time, changes are often needed in the tasks assigned family members. For the practitioner, strategies may need to be altered for overcoming obstacles to task completion, and goals may need to be revisited because they are too ambitious or no longer relevant. Because Level I neglectful families lack resources and are prone to frequent crises, the practitioner often must decide whether to agree to change, add, or subtract goals, tasks, and strategies in view of failures or changing family needs. For example, newly discovered information revealing a parent's substance abuse problem or a pending eviction obviously calls for revising priority goals and tasks. The challenge is to maintain the priority on the basic needs of the child while responding to changing family circumstances and needs.

Termination of contact with the family should be made when the goals stated in the contract have been accomplished and the basic minimum needs of the child are being met. The practitioner reviews the contract with family members to assess the progress made on the goals and positively reinforces them for the tasks accomplished and goals achieved. It is important that the family members own both their accomplishments and their disappointments for the goals and tasks they did and did not achieve. Because Level I neglectful families have likely experienced few successes in life, receiving recognition, praise, and self-congratulation for goals and tasks accomplished is empowering and builds much needed self-esteem.

Anticipating future obstacles and problem solving to overcome the anticipated obstacles is also an important part of the termination process. Using the skills learned through the task model interventions, parents and care providers can learn to problem solve and plan strategies to overcome anticipated obstacles to maintaining the positive parenting practices they have learned.

Family members should be given information about supportive services and resources to call on in the future and encouraged to access them when needed. Family members should be encouraged to make use of informal social support from family, friends, and neighbors. Because neglectful families have higher rates of recidivism than families who commit other types of maltreatment, the practitioner can anticipate the need for periodic interventions over time to reinforce, supplement, or repeat interventions after services have been terminated. Such follow-up is necessary in guiding these fragile families as they face new life circumstances and challenges that create new issues and needs.

Application to Families on Levels II, III, and IV

Families at Levels II, III, and IV generally have the basic social and economic resources needed to function well and do not require the same kind of help with concrete needs that Level I families require. However, as noted in Chapters 7 and 8, Level II families require help with structuring family relationships and learning skills in communication, conflict resolution, and problem solving, which calls for the social learning approach also needed with Level I families. And because of their social skills deficits, Level II families may also require interventions to strengthen their formal and informal social support networks.

The needs of Level III and Level IV families are quite different. They already have many of the necessary social and communication skills, and they have established patterns of roles, relationships, and communication, although these may be dysfunctional and in need of modification. Level III families share with Level I families the need for role clarification between parents and children, but Level III families generally have the basic knowledge and skills needed to do so. The needs of Level IV family members for self-actualization and greater intimacy, insight, personal autonomy, and spiritual fulfillment call for highly different intervention strategies.

Evaluation of Effectiveness

The practitioner must continuously evaluate the effectiveness of the interventions against the goals and tasks listed in the contract between him or her and the family. When there is insufficient task and goal accomplishment, the mix of interventions must be evaluated, obstacles identified, and new strategies developed with the family.

Structured measures for evaluating the adequacy of parenting may be used for more quantitative assessment. Polansky et al.'s (1981) Childhood Level of Living Scale and Trocme's (1996) Child Neglect Index are structured observational measures of neglect that are simple for practitioners to use. Caldwell and Bradley's (1984) HOME is also a helpful structured observational rating scale that has been widely used to assess the adequacy of the home environment and parent–child interactions. Magura and Moses's (1986) Child Well-Being Scales are anchored observational rating scales that are often used to evaluate parent and child functioning. Finally, Lutzker and Bigelow's (2002) procedures for assessing and teaching parent–child interaction activities, home cleanliness, home hazard assessment and accident prevention, and infant and child health care skills contain structured observation and parent self-report protocols for periodic assessment of progress in these areas.

The absence of another report of neglect is also an obvious indicator of the effectiveness of interventions. However, reoccurrence can be expected in Level 1 neglectful families whose personal, social, and economic resources are limited and whose life situations involve highly stressful living conditions with many recurring life crises.

Ethical Challenges

The primary ethical challenges involved in working with Level 1 neglecting families include the following:

1. determining neglectful versus minimally adequate parenting in a multicultural society
2. preserving family autonomy in decision making while ensuring the safety of children
3. selecting priority needs and goals from the many wants and needs of parents and the pressing needs of children
4. intervening authoritatively when neglect has been reported yet developing a trusting, helping relationship with the identified family
5. making the decision to remove a child from the family to assure his or her safety

Summary

Level I neglectful families present a formidable challenge to child welfare workers and other practitioners who seek to help them improve their functioning. The combination of poverty, limited personal and social resources, and an often nonsupportive or toxic living environment calls for multisystemic interventions, based on an ecological systems model. A combination of helping with concrete needs and psychosocial interventions is required. Specific, planned interventions are required from the practitioner to overcome the expected denial of neglect and anger about the obvious implication of failure as a parent.

Suggested interventions are based on social learning, cognitive-behavioral, family systems, and social network theories and the task-oriented model of working with resource-poor families (Epstein, 1988; Epstein & Brown, 2002). Teaching parenting and social skills and brokering community services are required of the practitioner. Social network interventions are also suggested to strengthen the family's informal social supports.

A rich resource for interventions with Level 1 families is Lutzker and Bigelow's (2002) series of empirically validated programs for assessing and teaching parent–child bonding and interaction skills, infant and child health care skills, and home cleanliness and hazard reduction assessment. These programs are contained in one affordable paperback manual. The interventions are based on social learning and behavioral theories, which have proven to be effective with Level I neglectful families (Lutzker, 1990; Lutzker & Bigelow, 2002; Lutzker et al., 1982; Wolfe, 1994).

Discussion Questions

1. Is 9-month-old Kevin Mackey being neglected? Which of his basic needs are not being adequately met?

2. How might you seek to engage Karen Mackey to overcome her denial of neglect and to gain her trust and active involvement in working with you to improve her parenting?

3. What strengths do you see in Karen Mackey that could be highlighted and built on?

4. What other facts would you want to obtain about the Mackey family to complete your comprehensive assessment? What issues require further exploration?

5. What appropriate priority goals might you be able to set with Karen Mackey?

6. What efforts might you make to involve Jeff, the father of Karen Mackey's child?

7. How might use Lutzker and Bigelow's (2002) Safe Families program with the Mackey family for assessment and intervention?

Internet Resources

http://ncadi.samhsa.gov
www.childwelfare.gov/pubs

Suggested Readings

Breshears, E. M., Yeh, S., & Young, N. (2006). *Understanding substance abuse and facilitating recovery: A guide for child welfare workers* (DHHS Publication no. PHD1092). Washington, DC: U.S. Department of Health and Human Services.
A useful guide for working with families for whom substance abuse is a problem. Available free of charge from The National Clearinghouse for Alcohol and Drug Information, P.O. Box 2345,

Rockville, MD, 20847-2345. Or call (800) 729-6686 or e-mail info@health.org (see also website in Internet Resources).

Child Welfare Information Gateway. (2004). *Child neglect demonstration projects: Synthesis of lessons learned.* Washington, DC: U.S. Department of Health and Human Services.

This publication provides the findings and conclusions from nine federally funded projects targeting families or families at high risk of neglect along with suggestions for addressing family needs and engaging families. (Available online at www.childwelfare.gov/pubs/candemoe/candemoe.cfm.)

DiPanfilis, D. (2006). *Child neglect: A guide for prevention, assessment, and intervention.* Washington, DC: U.S. Department of Health and Human Services.

This is a very practical, useful handbook, which offers directions for professionals for effective assessment and intervention with neglectful families. (Available online at www.childwelfare.gov/pubs/usermanual.cfm. Also available free of charge by calling (800) 394-3366 or e-mailing info@childwelfare.gov.)

Dubowitz, H. (1999). *Neglected children: Research, practice, and policy.* Thousand Oaks, CA: Sage.

This book contains a collection of chapters by well-known experts in child neglect that focus on the implications of neglect on the children. The book includes chapters on assessment, intervention, maternal prenatal alcohol and drug use, prevention of neglect, and recommended research and policy.

Epstein, L. (1988). *Helping people: The task-centered approach.* Columbus, OH: Merrill.

Epstein, L., & Brown, L. B. (2002). *Brief treatment and a new look at the task-centered approach.* Boston: Allyn & Bacon.

These two volumes describe a time-limited, task-centered approach that was developed specifically for helping impoverished Level I families. The model begins with family-expressed wants or needs that can be translated into mutually agreeable, realistic goals. It employs a task-centered, problem-solving approach to consider alternative strategies and tasks to meet goals, use of positive reinforcement for task achievement, and development of alternative task strategies to overcome anticipated and encountered obstacles to task and goal achievement.

Gaudin, J. M., Wodarski, J. S., Arkinson, M. K., & Avery, L. S. (1991). Remedying child neglect: Effectiveness of social network interventions. *Journal of Applied Social Sciences, 15*(1), 97–123.

This article provides an empirically validated model for a mix of interventions to strengthen families' informal social support linkages, teach them social skills, and improve parental functioning.

Lutzker, J. R., & Broadhurst, K. M. (2002). *Reducing child maltreatment: A guidebook for parent services.* New York: Guilford Press.

This paperback publication provides an empirically validated, hands-on ecobehavioral treatment model for intervening with neglecting or abusing parents or parents at high risk for committing maltreatment. The 15-session model includes parent activities training to improve parent–child bonding and interaction, infant care and health care skills training, and home cleanliness and safety assessment and training. The manual includes the Home Accident Prevention Inventory, the CLEAN Checklist (for assessing and teaching household management skills), and complete instructions for assessing parent–child bonding and teaching the Planned Activities Training and Infant and Child Health Skills Training programs.

References

Belsky, J. (1993). The etiology of child maltreatment: A developmental-ecological analysis. *Psychological Bulletin, 114*(3), 413–434.

Belsky, J., & Vondra, J. (1989). Lessons from child abuse: The determinants of parenting. In D. Cicchetti & V. Carlson (Eds.), *Child maltreatment: Theory and research on the causes and consequences of child abuse and neglect* (pp. 53–202). New York: Cambridge University Press.

Caldwell, B. M., & Bradley, R. H. (1984). *Administration manual: HOME observation for the measurement of the environment* (Rev. ed.). Little Rock: University of Arkansas at Little Rock.

Crittenden, P. M. (1993). Characteristics of neglectful parents: An information processing approach. *Criminal Justice and Behavior, 20,* 27–48.

DePanfilis, D. (1996). Social isolation of neglectful families: A review of social support assessment and intervention models. *Child Maltreatment, 1,* 37–52.

DePanfilis, D. (1999). Intervening with families when children are neglected. In H. Dubowitz (Ed.). *Neglected children: Research, practice, and policy* (pp. 211–236). Thousand Oaks, CA: Sage.

DePanfilis, D. (2006). *Child neglect: A guide for prevention, assessment, and intervention.* Washington, DC: U.S. Department of Health and Human Services.

Dubowitz, H. (Ed.). (1999). *Neglected children: Research, policy, and practice.* Thousand Oaks, CA: Sage.

Dubowitz, H., Black, M., Starr, R., & Zuravin, S. (1993). A conceptual definition of child neglect. *Criminal Justice and Psychology, 20*(1), 8–26.

Epstein, L. (1988). *Helping people: The task-centered approach.* Columbus, OH: Merrill.

Epstein, L., & Brown, L. B. (2002). *Brief treatment and a new look at the task-centered approach.* Boston: Allyn & Bacon.

Garbarino, J., & Sherman, D. (1980). High-risk neighborhoods and high-risk families: The human ecology of child maltreatment. *Child Development, 51,* 188–198.

Gaudin, J. M. (1993). Effective interventions with neglectful families. *Criminal Justice and Behavior, 20,* 66–89.

Gaudin, J. M. (2001). The role of social supports in child neglect, In T. D. Morton & B. Salowitz (Eds.), *The CPS response to child neglect: An administrator's guide to theory, policy, program design, and case practice* (pp. 105–114). Duluth, GA: Child Welfare Institute.

Gaudin, J. M., & Polansky, N. A. (1986). Social distancing and the neglectful family: Sex, race and social class influences. *Children and Youth Services Review, 8,* 1–12.

Gaudin, J. M., Wodarski, J. S., Arkinson, M. K., & Avery, L. S. (1991). Remedying child neglect: Effectiveness of social network interventions. *Journal of Applied Social Sciences, 15*(1), 97–123.

Howing, P. T., Wodarski, J. S., Kurtz, P. D., & Gaudin, J. M. (1989). Effective interventions to ameliorate the incidence of child maltreatment: The empirical base. *Social Work, 34*(4), 330–338.

Lutzker, J. R. (1990). Behavioral treatment of child neglect. *Behavior Modification, 14*(3), 301–315.

Lutzker, J. R., & Bigelow, K. M. (2002). *Reducing child maltreatment.* New York: Guilford Press.

Lutzker, J. R., Frame, R. E., & Rice, J. M. (1982). Project 12-Ways: An ecobehavioral approach to the treatment and prevention of child abuse and neglect. *Education and Treatment of Children, 5,* 141–155.

Magura, S., & Moses, B. S. (1986). *Outcome measures for child welfare services.* Washington, DC: Child Welfare League of America.

National Research Council (NRC). (1993). *Understanding child abuse and neglect.* Washington, DC: National Academy Press.

Polansky, N. A., Ammons, P., & Gaudin, J. M. (1985). Loneliness and isolation in child neglect. *Social Casework, 66,* 38–47.

Polansky, N. A., Chalmers, M. A., Buttenweiser, E., & Williams, D. P. (1981). *Damaged parents.* Chicago: University of Chicago Press.

Sedlak, A. J., & Broadhurst, D. D. (1996). *The third national incidence study of child abuse and neglect.* Washington, DC: U.S. Department of Health and Human Services.

Thomlinson, B. (1997). Risk and protective factors in child maltreatment. In M.W. Fraser (Ed.), *Risk and resilience in childhood: An ecological perspective.* Washington, DC: NASW Press.

Thompson, R. A. (1994). Social support and the prevention of child maltreatment. In G. B. Melton & F. D. Barry (Eds.), *Protecting children from abuse and neglect: Foundations for a new national strategy* (pp. 40–130). New York: Guilford Press.

Thompson, R. A. (1995). *Preventing child maltreatment through social support: A critical analysis.* Thousand Oaks, CA: Sage.

Trocme, N. (1996). Development and preliminary evaluation of the Ontario Child Neglect Index. *Child Maltreatment, 1*(2), 145–155.

U.S. Department of Health and Human Services (USDHHS), Administration for Children and Families. (2004). *Child maltreatment: 2002.* Washington, DC: U.S. Government Printing Office.

U.S. Department of Health and Human Services (USDHHS), Administration for Children and Families. (2006). *Child maltreatment: 2006.* Washington, DC: U.S. Government Printing Office.

Wolfe, D. (1994). The role of intervention and treatment services in the prevention of child abuse and neglect. In G. B. Melton & D. Barry (Eds.), *Protecting children from abuse and neglect: Foundations for a new national strategy* (pp. 224–303). New York: Guilford Press.

6

A Family Case Management Approach for Level I Needs

Roberta R. Greene, Ph.D., and Nancy P. Kropf, Ph.D.

Case management is a process for assisting families who have multiple service needs. In reality, it may be appropriate for families who have Level I through IV needs whenever they experience multiple complex difficulties that require a range of services from numerous providers. The goals of family case management are to mobilize a family's strengths, to marshal resources, and to maximize family functional capacity. This chapter discusses family-centered case management and focuses on the Level I family.

Family Needs

Throughout the life of the family, members must negotiate changes, shifts, and alterations in their relationships with one another. This movement through the life cycle, known as *family development,* requires family members to establish, maintain, and adapt to new roles. In making these life transitions, the family builds on strengths and faces stressful challenges.

Case management can help families cope with and adjust to the stress related to unexpected, or nonnormative, situations. An example of a Level I situation that requires reorganization in the family system is a severe illness. For example, case managers who work with clients who have HIV (human immunodeficiency virus) or AIDS (acquired immune deficiency syndrome) provide support and skill development to help these individuals disclose their status to friends and family (Kalichman et al., 2007). In addition, people isolated and debilitated by crack cocaine or HIV require assertive outreach services (Greene, 2000). Other Level I needs experienced by families include homelessness (Nelson, Aubry, & Lafrance, 2007), chronic mental illness (Buck & Alexander, 2006), and having a frail older adult (Gellis, 2006; Hseih, 2006).

Case management services can also help families adapt to normative transition phases across the life span. Structural changes that occur at family transition points, such as births, reaching adulthood, and retirement, also can disturb the family's balance. For example, a case manager can play an important role in helping a young single mother with childrearing and household responsibilities (East, 1999; Sun, 2000). Similarly, a case manager can be instrumental in identifying and linking a new mother with emotional, financial, and medical support services for her new role as a caregiver to a young infant.

Case managers need to understand that the family is a social unit that faces a series of developmental tasks. These tasks vary along the parameters of cultural differences but, at the same time, have universal roots (Minuchin, 1974). According to Tseng and Hsu (1991), the stages of the life cycle have been defined for "intact nuclear families in contemporary Western societies" (p. 8) as the unattached young adult, the formation of the dyadic relationship, the family with young children, the family with adolescents, the family launching children, the family with older members, and the family in later years (Becvar & Becvar, 2009; Goldenberg & Goldenberg, 1980; Rhodes, 1980).

However, the structure and development of the family may vary because of diverse needs and interests (Greene & Riley, 2005). Coontz (2005) chronicles the history of marriage across the centuries, from ancient to current times. Her research integrates the sociopolitical impact on the changing structure and function of the family as a social system. As Walsh (2003), states, "The very concept of the family has been undergoing redefinition as tumultuous social and economic changes in recent decades have altered the landscape of family life. Amid the turmoil, couples [partners] have been forging new and varied arrangements as they strive to build caring committed relationships" (p. 4).

Family developmental patterns may be affected by the geographical origin and birthplace of the members and where they are in the cycle of acculturation to mainstream U.S. society. Ho (1987) proposes that practitioners should be aware that behaviors differ depending on whether a family and its members are foreign or native born and on the degree to which they are bicultural. Falicov and Karrer (1980) recommend that studies of the family life cycle should consider the effects of cultural variables such as social class, ethnicity, and religion. For instance, it is often assumed that divorced fathers—in particular, African American fathers—are distant and uninvolved in the lives of their children. However, Leite and McKenry (2006) found that African American fathers strive to remain connected to their children through various social interactive patterns.

Therefore, when making applications to family assessment, it would be more appropriate for the case manager to think of several typical family life cycles. In addition, the case manager must be open to disputing the predominant social narratives that diminish the strengths and realities within families, especially multicultural and multiethnic family systems.

Family Case Assessment

An important principle in family case management is that a biopsychosocial change in any one member affects the balance of the whole family group. Greene (2008) points out that most elderly clients come to the attention of an agency at a time of crisis. At that time, the practitioner must ask, Who is the client? The answer is that the elderly individual's entire family is the client, because they are all involved in the crisis. Consequently, the case manager's assessment and treatment interventions must consider both the elderly person's biopsychosocial needs and the family's role allocations and adapting and coping capacities.

The following case example involves a family with a member who has a chronic mental illness (Kelly & Kropf, 1995). The son, who is now in middle adulthood, is being cared for by his aging parents. This case clearly illustrates the usefulness of addressing the issues and needs from a whole-family perspective.

> Philip Jordan is a 40-year-old single male diagnosed with schizophrenia. He lives at home with his 75-year-old parents in a small Southern town, where his father is a retired pastor from the local Baptist church. Philip, who has a 22-year history of mental illness, has experienced many psychiatric hospitalizations but has remained out of the hospital for the past two years. Currently, he has a flat affect, depressed mood, and mild paranoid ideation concerning his parents. He reports bizarre hallucinations involving religious themes and sexual thoughts.
>
> At the time of his first psychotic break, Philip's parents were in their late fifties. They blamed themselves for Philip's illness and prayed for him to be "cured and return to being normal." Instead of regaining his emotional health, Philip's condition worsened over time. His father retired prematurely, believing that if he devoted all his time to caring for his son, Philip would improve. However, the retirement caused the parents to be estranged from their supports and placed a financial burden on the family.
>
> The family went to the local mental health center to discuss their situation. Their family physician had suggested that they contact the mental health program, because Philip's mother's health had been deteriorating. The parents had begun to realize that their advancing age was creating difficulties in providing care for their son. They were also concerned about Philip's lack of social contacts and the family's worsening financial circumstances due to additional medical expenses.
>
> The mental health center intake worker gathered extensive information about the family's functioning. Philip's physical, emotional, and social functioning and medication management were discussed. Beyond Philip's functioning, information was acquired about the other family members, including the parents' own health status, their knowledge of mental illness, their social support system, and their feelings of competence in managing Philip's caregiving needs in this life stage. Spiritual issues were also explored with the family and were especially significant because religious participation was such an important aspect of family life in early phases. Based on a model developed for older adults (Hayes, Meador, Branch, & George, 2001), information about the family's spiritual history was gathered, including their practices, social participation, and social support.
>
> As a part of this family-focused assessment, the parents discussed the stress of this caregiving role and its effects on their physical and emotional health. Of particular concern was the evaluation of functional areas in which Philip's competence may be furthered or fostered (Bandura, 1997). Mr. Jordan spoke about his disappointment over his early retirement, subsequent financial

worries, and loss of status in the community. He also reported that he struggled with the idea that having a son like Philip was God's way of testing his faith. In particular, Mr. Jordan seemed to miss the fellowship that came from being with other members of the congregation. Mrs. Jordan discussed her worries about Philip's future care and her worsening hypertension and digestive problems. Through her discussion with Philip, the case manager also became aware of his own anxiety over the health of his parents and his fears about his own future.

The interviews with the total family unit allowed the case manager to form a holistic impression about the family's past functioning, their present situation, and their future needs.

Treatment Goals

Building on the assessment data about the Jordan family, the case manager and family discussed service goals that were formalized into a service contract. The plan included goals that addressed the individual members, the parents as a couple, and the family as a household unit. Additionally, the plan overtly specified the relationship between the mental health service personnel and the family.

The contract addressed the issues of independence, family functioning, and spirituality that had been discussed by the family during the assessment. For Philip, goals were constructed to assist with vocational training and placement. This plan was intended to decrease Philip's isolation, provide him with structured time during the day, and allow him to contribute to the household finances. To provide the parents with a temporary break from caregiving, the family decided to have Philip begin taking respite care weekends at a group home. This plan also allowed Philip to experience a residential situation before a family crisis might force him to do so.

Other goals were constructed that related to the parents' issues. Mr. and Mrs. Jordan were interested in becoming involved in a psychoeducational group sponsored by the mental health center to learn more about schizophrenia and behavior management. They were also interested in attending an upcoming session on estate planning led by a local attorney. In addition, the case manager discussed spiritual needs within the family, such as reconnecting to their family of faith.

The role of the case manager with the parents was to provide information about the resources they might use to assist in their relationship to Philip. They were also assured that their service plan would be periodically reviewed and that the family would have a voice in formulating future goals.

The case manager and family discussed future plans for Philip. The short-term goals were to have the family begin the process of exploring and considering options for Philip's future care. As an initial step in this process, they prepared a plan that helped the family specify and clarify values and preferences as a part of the process of determining what type of future care arrangements were best suited for a person with a disability (Mount & Zwernik, 1988). Intermediate goals for the family were to visit the group homes in their county, to discuss Philip's care with other relevant family members (i.e., one other son who lived out of state), to begin to use respite care to familiarize Philip with residential living experiences, and to work with an attorney who could explicate financial issues relevant to the eventuality of parental death. These steps were all part of the long-range goal of helping the family make arrangements for the time when the parents could no longer continue as Philip's care providers.

Treatment Approach: A Generalist Model of Case Management

A variety of case management models exist, and the choice of using a particular approach depends on numerous factors, including the target client group, staff capabilities, financial resources of the agency, and organizational structure. Rothman (1992) describes four models, each having a different structure or focus:

1. In the *generalist model,* one case manager performs a variety of roles to facilitate a client's movement through the service delivery system (Robinson, 2000). The generalist case management model most closely resembles traditional social casework (Levine & Fleming, 1984).

2. With a *case management team,* a multidisciplinary group functions as the case management system for a client. Each team member is responsible for performing a specialized function (e.g., social work, physical therapy, speech therapy, psychology).

3. A *therapist case manager* is used extensively in the mental health system. This model infuses a therapeutic relationship into the case manager role.

4. The *supportive care model* is based on the natural environment of the client (e.g., neighborhood, cultural group). In this model, case management is provided to the client through the natural helping network.

To be effective practitioners, generalist case managers must have a broad perspective on human services, one that moves beyond the boundaries of the social welfare agencies in which they work. The use of a social system model can assist the case manager in practice with actual clients.

Kuhn (1974) has identified three elements of a social system, and Dattalo (1992) has taken each and operationalized it in the case management process (see Figure 6.1). The first is the *detector function,* which is an information-gathering phase. The case manager gathers information about both the client problem and available resources and service options. The second element is the *selector function,* in which information is screened for use in the treatment process. The case manager uses theoretical frameworks and practice principles to organize information in understanding client preferences, values, and behaviors. The final function, the *effector function,* is the "doing" function. After gathering information about the problem and possible solutions, the case manager constructs a plan of action about treatment goals.

Key Features of Case Management

Another way of examining the case management process is to outline its key features. While case management serves as a process to link clients with services it is also "a principle that guides the provision of a full range of services" (Frankl & Gellman, 2004, p. 5).

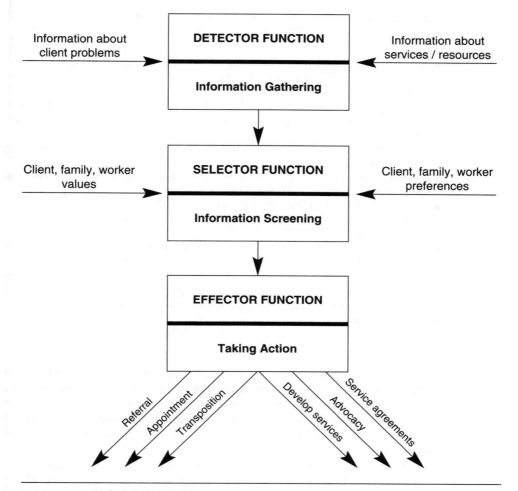

FIGURE 6.1 *Kuhn's Social System Model*
Source: Schneider & Kropf, 1992, p. 141.

This practice approach is aimed at ensuring that clients with complex, multiple problems and service needs receive all services in a timely and appropriate way. This process has traditionally required the case manager to conduct a skillful assessment of the client's functional capacity and support network and plan and then advocate for and obtain a range of suitable community-based services encompassing economic, health and medical, social, and personal care needs (see Table 6.1). Such screening takes on more importance when case managers work with clients who are at high risk, such as those with catastrophic conditions and costly injury or illness.

Community-based case-managed services have been used in all fields of practice, including child welfare, aging, and mental health. Although the presenting problem of the

TABLE 6.1   *Key Features of Social Work Case Management Practice*

Social work case management practice

- is a process based on a trusting and enabling client–social worker relationship.
- utilizes the social work dual focus of understanding the person in the environment working with populations at risk.
- aims to ensure a continuum of care to clients who have complex, multiple problems and disabilities.
- attempts to intervene clinically to ameliorate the emotional problems accompanying illness or loss of function.
- utilizes the social work skills of brokering and advocacy as a boundary-spanning approach to service delivery.
- targets clients who require a range of community-based or long-term care services, encompassing economic, health/medical, social, and personal care needs.
- aims to provide services in the least restrictive environment.
- requires the assessment of the client's functional capacity and support network in determining the level of care.
- affirms the traditional social work values of self-determination and the worth and dignity of the individual and the concept of mutual responsibility in decision making.

Source: B. S. Vourlekis & R. R. Greene (Eds.), *Social work case management* (New York: Aldine de Gruyter, 1992). Copyright © 1992 by Aldine Publishers. Reprinted by permission of AldineTransaction, a division of Transaction Publishers.

person at risk may vary, the purpose of a case management system is to provide the client with service options along a continuum of care. The concept of a continuum of care suggests that clients may need any one of a comprehensive range of services, depending on each person's ability to function relatively independently. Clients who have greater impairments and lower levels of functioning will require more structured environments and higher levels of care.

Case managers increasingly use a *strengths perspective practice model* (Fast & Chapin, 2000; Myers, Kropf, & Robinson, 2002; Saleebey, 1992; Sun, 2000; Whitley, White, Kelley, & Yorker, 1999). The strengths perspective documents a client family's present daily-living situation and determines what they want to change, achieve, or maintain. The strengths perspective also is based on an empowerment theme that seeks ways for clients to set their own agendas and further engage with others in their environment (Rose, 1992). For example, Kisthardt (1992) has suggested that people who have persistent mental illness not be labeled as being "resistant to treatment" or "lacking in social skills." Rather, such clients should be understood as unique, complex individuals, coping with social pressures as well as their "talents, desires, and hopes" (p. 61).

Case management reflects the historic struggle to effect change in the person, the environment, or both (Greene, Cohen, Galambos, & Kropf, 2007). In this approach, the case manager assesses the client within the context of his or her environment and provides both direct and indirect service. *Direct service* is based on a mutually trusting, therapeutic client–social worker relationship, in which the case manager evaluates the client's circumstances and intervenes to ameliorate emotional problems accompanying illness or loss of functioning. The emotional problems and stress associated with loss of functional capacity require the case manager to combine intrapsychic and interpersonal strategies with environmental interventions. Such *indirect service* involves community-based strategies for resource allocation and advocacy on behalf of the client at risk.

Far too often, clients with many service needs become disconnected from narrowly defined programs, such as those that provide only housing, cash, or nutritional supports (Nelson et al., 2007). Key features of the case manager's role are responsibility for the development of a mutually agreeable care plan that offers continuity in services and assisting the client in mediating systems problems that create disruption in service delivery (Roberts-DeGennaro, 1987). Because the case manager needs to understand how systems work and how to access them and often must coordinate the work of multiple service providers by intervening across service systems' boundaries, case management has been called a "boundary-spanning" approach (Hearn, 1969; Rubin, 1987). Key aspects of a boundary-spanning approach are developing resource systems, linking clients to resource systems, and making systems more accessible and responsible. Central to carrying out this social work approach are *advocacy,* or negotiating for the equitable distribution of resources, and *brokerage,* or locating and obtaining needed resources.

Interventions: Family Case Management

Family services and case management have long been important components of social work practice. Family-focused social work, with its mission to resolve families' social and emotional difficulties, can be traced to the Charity Organization Societies (COSs) of the 1880s. During those early years, pioneer social workers were noted for meeting with families in their homes to discuss their difficulties and to assess the need for financial relief and other tangible assistance (Hartman & Laird, 1987; Richmond, 1917).

Because COS social workers also were concerned with the lack of coordination among services and fund-raising activities, case management shares similar roots with these organizations as one of the profession's earliest means of linking clients to service delivery systems (Naleppa & Reid, 2003; Rubin, 1987; Weil, Karls, & Associates, 1985). These common beginnings reflect a strong interest in the family as the focus of intervention, an emphasis on a systematic approach to information collection and assessment, a belief in the value of equity in resource allocation, and an emphasis on case coordination. Although case management and family-centered practice have a surprising amount of common ground, little has been written about the relationship of these core practice functions.

Although most people in need of case management assistance are receiving the bulk of their care from families and other primary groups, the role of the family in the case management process is ill defined. Informal helpers are an important source of support for many individuals who are in need of case management and need to be integrated into a comprehensive care plan. Examples of social networks that can be enlisted to offer assistance and aid include informal helpers who live in rural areas (Bisman, 2003), at-risk youth (Franklin, Garner, & Berg, 2007; Hilarski, 2005), and older adults (Stevens, Martina, & Westerhof, 2006).

Nonetheless, when discussing case management services, some theorists have considered the individual client's resources and natural supports. For example, the National Association of Social Workers' (NASW, 2005) *NASW Standards for Social Work Practice in*

Health Care Settings has defined the family as critical to the assessment process. Similarly, Bertsche and Horejsi (1980) recommend that the family be involved in the initial interview, the formulation of the psychosocial assessment, the decision-making process related to the care plan, follow up of service delivery problems, and counseling and emotional support. These authors go on to describe the case manager's role vis-à-vis the family as a "liaison . . . to help the client make his or her preferences known and secure the services needed" (p. 97).

In addition, Moore (1990) suggests that a key role of the case manager is to integrate formal and informal services provided by the family and other primary groups. He notes that health and social services, families, and formal organizations have complementary goals and that the coordination of shared resources is necessary. According to Nelson (1982), the goal of coordination is to achieve a fit between formal services and primary-group caregiving, not to substitute for family care. Moore (1990) maintains that it is often the practitioner who acts as a facilitator among the client, the family, and formal caregivers. In addition, Cantor, Rehr, and Trotz (1981) suggest that, wherever possible, members of the family should be the case managers and that professionals should offer training to support this family responsibility. In this way, the service package is designed to support the family and to maximize its caregiving potential.

Principles for Family-Focused Case Management

Although the literature on family case management is limited, the literature on family-centered practice is rich and often consistent with a systems perspective. This perspective generally views the family as promoting positive interdependence and problem resolution and uses intervention strategies aimed at developing the family as a system of mutual aid. By focusing on the family, the family social work literature recognizes it as the "primary social service institution" and network for planning and problem solving (Hartman, 1981, p. 7). From a family systems perspective, interventions and case management care plans are designed to preserve and enhance functioning and to modify dysfunctional family patterns (Greene, 1999) (see Table 6.2).

Since no two families are alike, once the case manager has reached out to the family as a unit, it is necessary to assess the family as a group that makes up a causal network. Systems theory suggests that to understand a family, it is necessary to examine the relationships among family members. Any one individual's behavior is considered as the consequences of the total situation (Shafer, 1969). Family members cannot be examined in isolation.

To achieve the most effective and culturally sound plan of care, the case manager who works with families must recognize differences in family forms. For example, persons with AIDS who also are gay or lesbian may want to receive care in conjunction either with their family of origin or their family of choice. Therefore, it is critical for the case manager to establish a helping relationship unique to that particular family.

Application to Families on This Level of Need

Families in need of case management services have a range of needs for flexibility, adaptability, and goal achievement. Although some families may be relatively high functioning, other families may experience high levels of tension, use outside resources poorly, and tend to be insufficiently organized to meet their goals. These are examples of Level I and II

TABLE 6.2   Key Features of Family-Focused Social Work Case Management

Family-focused social work requires that the case manager

- identify the family as the unit of attention.
- assess the frail or impaired person's biopsychosocial functioning and needs within a cultural sound family context.
- write a mutually agreed upon family care plan.
- refer client systems to services and entitlements not available within the natural support system.
- implement and coordinate the work that is done with the family.
- determine what services need to be coordinated on behalf of the family.
- intervene clinically to relieve family emotional problems and stress accompanying illness or loss of functioning.
- determine how the impaired person and family will interact with formal care providers.
- integrate formal and informal services provided by the family and other primary groups.
- offer or advocate for particular services that the informal support network is not able to offer.
- contact client networks and service providers to determine the quality of service provision.
- mediate conflicts between the family and service providers to empower the family when they are not successful.
- collect information and data to augment the advocacy and evaluation efforts to ensure quality of care.

Source: Greene, 1999.

needs where attention to basic resources is indicated (e.g., financial, medical) and structural and organizational changes are required within the family. These families may appear disordered and often require many services and clinical interventions.

Because most programs have limited resources, *case finding* is critical in providing case management services. This process involves delineating a target population and determining who is especially suited to receive a service because their informal support network is unable to provide a particular resource. Some families may require case management briefly during a transition in development, such as discharge from the hospital after an acute illness. Other families may need ongoing services, with the goal of maintaining functioning or preventing regression to the greatest possible extent.

Interventions

The purpose of case management is to provide the client system—in this case, the family—with service options that promote group and individual functioning. To accomplish this task, Dattalo (1992) has identified three sets of roles that a case manager performs:

1. *counselor roles,* which are client focused, such as being an educator and enabler
2. *coordinator roles,* which involve matching clients with services, such as being a service broker and developing information about the resource network
3. *advocacy roles,* which focus on the service system, such as being a mediator and community organizer

Using these role clusters, the case manager can establish interventions with the family to help them engage in the service system, provide support once services have been initiated, and address shortcomings in the way services are organized. Specific interventions used by case managers in working with families include building positive relationships with the family system, completing a comprehensive assessment, structuring a case plan, linking the family to needed services, monitoring service delivery, and serving as an advocate.

Building Relationships.   In all practice situations, building positive relationships with clients is an important initial component. In family case management, the practitioner has the task of promoting alliances to engage all members of the family system in the service contract. Relationship building with a family may include a number of tasks for the case manager, including education about the expectations and responsibilities of the client role and the practitioner roles, assurance about the nature and use of information shared between the family and practitioner, and listening and discussing the perceptions of the family toward using services.

Establishing rapport and trust, an important phase of any helping relationship, is especially crucial with these families (Cummings & Kropf, 2000). For example, a case manager who works with the parents of a child with a disability can employ several methods in the process of building relationships with the family. Part of the beginning phase is to determine the family culture and meaning around the child's disability and methods to cope with any stress that is experienced. In addition, information can be shared with the family to provide education about raising a child with a disability.

Completing a Comprehensive Assessment.   Case managers use a format for examining the person who is frail or impaired within a family context. The NASW standards (1999) suggest that assessment and practice must be done with cultural competence and respect for the social diversity of their clientele. Because the family is a unit or interdependent group, it is necessary to assess how a change in one member's functioning affects role expectations throughout the family system (Greene, 1999).

To gather this tremendous amount of information, data should be collected from a variety of sources. These include records from other formal service providers in addition to information from the family members themselves. Within a family case management situation, the perspectives and experiences of all members of the system must be incorporated. In addition, case managers can incorporate standardized instruments that promote comparisons to others who are in similar situations. Case managers can select instruments from a number of resources for part of the assessment phase (e.g., Cohen, Underwood, & Gottlieb, 2000; Kane & Kane, 2000; Roberts & Yeager, 2004).

Structuring a Case Plan.   A thorough assessment of a family provides the foundation for a case plan. A service plan is based on a psychosocial study of the client and his or her family. It is a mutually agreed upon blueprint for deciding what services need to be mobilized on behalf of the impaired person and family (Naleppa & Reid, 1998). It also involves the way in which the family will interact with formal care providers and the cost of that care.

For example, an ecomap can be constructed with a family to determine resources and needs. A family that is raising a child with disability may have many ties to formal resources, such as the child's school, health care providers, specialized support services, and so on. However, the ecomap may determine that the parents have relatively few

informal supports, such as a friendship group and leisure pursuits. If most of their tim
spent on caregiving tasks for their child, the parents may feel a sense of isolation or
called caregiver burnout. A case plan may include respite care services to promote add
tional social connections for the parents.

Linking Clients to Services.   Linking involves referring or transferring client systems to
services and entitlements that are indicated in the family care plan as being necessary and
available. This process includes identifying available services and gathering information
about service access issues. The case manager can also be involved in helping families
learn about other resources and transitioning into another type of service program. Case
managers can enable clients to use available resources by demonstrating how to take appropriate and effective action—for example, how to seek out and join a caregiver support
group.

Monitoring Service Delivery.   The relative success of case management practice is
based on seeing whether work among the various services involved in a case is performed
in a harmonious fashion (Greene, 1992). The case manager is the coordinator of this effort,
making certain that information is exchanged among the numerous service providers who
may be involved with a family. Monitoring service delivery to determine if client systems
are receiving allocated resources requires that the case manager keep in ongoing contact
with the client and his or her network and service providers. Where the family is not successful, it may mean that there are mediating conflicts between the family and service
providers. Troubleshooting to resolve these conflicts can fill much of the case manager's
day (Steinberg & Carter, 1983).

In working with families, monitoring service delivery is intertwined with a dynamic
assessment process. Changes that affect the family system precipitate changes in service
needs for the family. In the Jordan family, for example, Mrs. Jordan suffered a stroke a few
months after the family visited the mental health center. Her illness had a dramatic impact
on the family's ability to carry out their service goals. The case manager maintained a key
role in making certain that services were not disrupted during this family emergency. The
case manager was also pivotal in helping the family receive resources that lapsed as a result
of the mother's illness, such as homemaker services and transportation.

Being an Advocate.   Frankl and Gelman (2004) define *advocacy* as when "a case manager acts on behalf of clients who are unable or unwilling to act on their own behalf . . . or
when clients are able to act on their own, but when it is judged that a case manager could
intervene more effectively" (p. 38). In addition, other advocacy issues for case managers
involve negotiating and eradicating barriers to services for clients, integrating disparate
service networks for clients who do not clearly meet eligibility for one service sector, and
serving as change agents to promote a comprehensive service system that is structured to
sensitively meet the needs of clients (Greene et al., 2007). Clearly, the advocacy role
involves a number of skill areas and competencies for case managers.

The Jordan family exemplifies a situation that is becoming an increasing concern in
mental health: older parents who provide care to a chronically disabled son or daughter. At
this life stage, the older family is concerned with the ability to continue to provide extended

care for a person who has a chronic mental illness. Case managers who work with older families may need to advocate for services that are specific to issues faced by older families (Cummings & Kropf, 2000). Examples of advocacy efforts include establishing legal/ residential workshops specifically oriented to late-life caregivers, structuring an emergency respite care program to be used in instances of health crises experienced by care providers, and exploring the concept of retirement for older people who have chronic psychiatric disabilities.

Evaluation

Evaluation of services and service delivery systems is necessary for accountability to the client system, to the funding source, and to policymakers (Greene, 1992). Measures of quality delivered to the client system help ensure that service conforms to acceptable methods of practice. Case managers engage in effort on two levels: (1) evaluating the progress of the family in the established treatment goals and (2) evaluating the comprehensive quality of available services.

The evaluation of the family's advancement involves measuring progress toward treatment goals. Case plans that are constructed using behavioral objectives and time-frames lend themselves to the evaluation phase. Consider the following goal for Mr. and Mrs. Jordan:

> *Goal:* Become involved in a support group for caregivers of people with chronic mental illness.
>
> *Objective 1:* Contact the support group leader to discuss the content and structure of group. (Completed in one week)
>
> *Objective 2:* Contact neighbors, friends, relatives to identify a companion for Philip so parents can attend meeting. (Completed in two weeks)
>
> *Objective 3:* Parents attend first support group meeting. (Completed in one month)

Using these types of behavioral objectives within specified timeframes, the case manager can help the family partialize and evaluate progress. Points of inertia, or inactivity in the family, can suggest to the case manager areas where additional support is needed. For example, the inability of the Jordans to accomplish Objective 2 suggested that they lack social support or have difficulty asking for support from others. This discovery led to enhancing the treatment plan to address this issue with the family.

Evaluating progress with a family is an empowering experience in itself. Families that cannot partialize problems may feel immobilized and overwhelmed. The case manager can motivate families by presenting them with their own progress.

As evidence-based practice becomes more integrated into social work, additional methods to evaluate the outcomes of case management (and other service delivery roles) are being stressed. Numerous examples of case management evaluation are currently available within the literature (see Counsell et al., 2007; Kropf & Cummings, 2008). Using these resources, case managers can structure evaluation protocols that include standardized instruments and appropriate scientific methods that allow comparison with the outcomes of other studies.

Application to Families at Other Levels of Need

Case management may be used with families operating at Levels III and IV. These families appear to have a high level of organization and are well prepared or differentiated in meeting their tasks (Goldenberg & Goldenberg, 2003). Very often, however, the resources secured by the case manager make the critical difference, restoring the functional capacity of the family group in crisis.

In working with clients, regardless of their level of need, the case manager must be acutely aware of the psychosocial effects of the problem situation. For example, families who are dealing with economic survival issues may require help understanding their feelings of fear and anger. Living from day to day can be stressful, and children, in particular, may experience great anxiety. Such families may benefit from structural family interventions that work to realign hierarchical power positions: Do the parents continue to be seen as providers? Who are the breadwinners (Levels I and II of family functioning)?

The Jordan case, which discusses a family with a member who is chronically mentally ill, provides an example of how the case manager will have to fill a number of different roles. He or she needs to build a relationship with and seek resources for the identified client: the member with the mental illness. The practitioner also may examine how other family members are adjusting to the member who is mentally ill, as well as explore what intimacy, conflict, and self-realization issues may warrant attention (Level IV of family need). In addition, families who are highly functioning may have their equilibrium severely disrupted when important resources are not available.

The key to making appropriate choices of intervention rests with assessment of family need. The selection of an intervention model from among an eclectic array is made carefully and is often a blend of approaches, depending on the particular constellation of family issues.

Ethical Challenges

By definition, case management involves access to and rationing and distributing health and social service resources. With the graying of the American population, the number of individuals needing case management services continues to increase dramatically. At the same time, case managers must make do with the amount of money budgeted for their total caseload. Such budget constraints create an informal rationing process at the local delivery level. In addition, financial constraints may hamper a social worker's outreach efforts to those invisible potential clients most in need. These ethical challenges necessitate explicit discussions among policymakers.

In addition to resource issues, ethical challenges also involve making decisions about services. For example, decisions about involvement with services involve a number of value-based determinations, such as self-determination and autonomy (Greene et al., 2007). Along with the aging of the population, these issues are especially relevant for populations of people with physical and psychiatric disabilities. As part of a treatment team, case managers will have to evaluate these multiple and competing ethical concerns in service delivery.

Summary

Although family-focused interventions and case coordination have existed simultaneously since the beginning of social work practice, a family-centered approach to case management has not been widely addressed. This chapter has promoted an inclusive model of working with a family whose needs are primarily on Level I. The model of practice is built on the active premise that one person in the family does not "own a problem." His or her issues affect all members. The case of the Jordan family provided an example of how a case manager could take a whole-family approach within a mental health context. The service goals did not reduce the family to the identified client and parents but defined the client system as the family unit.

→The role of the case manager in family-focused practice is to meet family needs and promote family harmony. The case manager has the responsibility to empower family members to activate and augment their support network. Formal services are introduced where the support system cannot accomplish tasks and meet the family's needs. The case manager helps the family identify and clarify their service needs and construct a plan of action. The case manager is also responsible for determining that the plan is being implemented and for evaluating its success.

Discussion Questions _____

1. What features are common to both individual- and family-focused case management? How would the Jordan case study differ if the approach used was individual focused?

2. What are the advantages and disadvantages of having a single case manager, as opposed to team case management?

3. Describe the roles of a case manager using a family approach.

4. How do you maintain a trusting relationship in a case management role in a difficult setting (such as public housing) when you feel you have done all you can to obtain trust?

5. How would a case manager address the spirituality needs of the family as part of treatment goals?

6. Beth is a 28-year-old female with a history of substance abuse and incest as a child. She recently attempted suicide. Would the family case management approach be useful in working with her situation? What would be the short-term goals? The long-term goals?

7. Identify a family from your practice whose primary needs are at Level I and with whom you think the case management approach would be particularly relevant. Briefly identify the family's current supports and needs, and list at least five specific ways in which you could potentially assist this family using relevant family case management methods.

8. Is case management a type of family therapy? Why or why not?

9. Why would the case management approach be used with Level I and II families more often than with Level III and IV families?

Internet Resources

www.cmsa.org
www.cfcm.com
www.casemanagement.com
www.sinai.org/who/sci_programs/chicago_fam_case_mgmt.asp
www.help.org
http://support.codegear.com/case

Suggested Readings

Bowers, B. J., & Jacobson, N. (2002). Best practice in long-term care case management: How excellent case managers do their jobs. *Journal of Social Work in Long-Term Care, 1,* 55–72.
This article reports on a study of case managers who have been identified as excellent in carrying out their role. Based on findings, the authors provide recommendations about how case managers can enhance their performance.

Frankl, A. J., & Gelman, S. R. (2004). *Case management.* Chicago: Lyceum
This book addresses case management practice. The authors describe various roles that case managers assume and provide content to enhance case management skills.

Hegar, R. L. (1992). Monitoring child welfare services. In B. S. Vourlekis & R. R. Greene (Eds.), *Social work case management.* New York: Aldine de Gruyter.
This chapter of an edited text on case management focuses on case management in the child welfare area. It addresses such concepts as permanency planning, protective services, and family preservation.

Genrich, S. J., & Neatherlin, J. S. (2001). Case manager role: A content analysis of published literature. *Care Management Journal, 3,* 14–19.
This research selected articles within the professional literature that focused on case management practice. Based on findings, the authors provide a summary of practice roles that are common across different practice contexts where case managers work.

Greene, R. R., Cohen, H. L., Galambos, C. M., & Kropf, N. P. (2007). *Foundations of social work practice in the field of aging* (chapter on Geriatric Case Management). Washington DC: NASW Press.
This chapter uses a competency-based approach to teaching students case management skills. In addition, various case examples are included.

Naleppa, M., & Reid, W. J. (1998). Task centered case management for the elderly: Developing a practice model. *Research on Social Work Practice, 8*(1), 63–85.
These authors use a task-centered approach to case management. They describe how to establish tasks with older clients and motivate clients to achieve goals.

Vourlekis, B. S., & Greene, R. R. (Eds.). (1992). *Social work case management.* New York: Aldine de Gruyter.
This book discusses the eight basic functions of case management through an examination of different fields of practice.

Walsh, F. (2003). *Normal family processes: Growing diversity and complexity.* New York: Guilford Press.
The third edition of this book provides a broad overview of family systems. Chapters address diverse family systems, multicultural issues, and family life course and development. In addition, challenges that face contemporary families, such as divorce, same-sex family units, and single-parent families are also addressed.

References

Bandura, A. (1997). *Self efficacy: The exercise of control.* New York: W. H. Freeman.

Becvar, D. S., & Becvar, R. J. (2009). *Family therapy: A systematic integration* (7th ed.). Boston: Allyn & Bacon.

Bertsche, V. A., & Horejsi, C. R. (1980). Coordination of client services. *Social Work, 25*(2), 94–98.

Bisman, C. D. (2003). Rural aging: Social work practice models and intervention dynamics. *Journal of Gerontological Social Work, 41*(1/2), 37–58.

Buck, P. W., & Alexander, L. B. (2006). Neglected voices: Consumers with serious mental illness speak about intensive case management. *Administration and Policy in Mental Health, 33*(4), 470–481.

Cantor, M., Rehr, H., & Trotz, V. (1981). Workshop II case management and family involvement. *Mount Sinai Journal of Medicine, 48*(6), 566–568.

Cohen, S., Underwood, L. G., & Gottlieb, B. H. (Eds.). (2000). *Social support measurement and intervention: A guide for health and social scientists.* New York: Oxford Press.

Coontz, S. (2005). *Marriage: A history.* New York: Penguin.

Counsell, S. R., Callahan, C. M., Clark, D. O., Tu, W., Buttar, A. B., Stump, T. E., & Ricketts, G. D. (2007). Geriatric care management for low-income seniors: A randomized controlled trial. *Journal of the American Medical Association, 298*(22), 2623–2633.

Cummings, S., & Kropf, N. P. (2000). An infusion model for including content on elders with chronic mental illness in the curriculum. *Advances in Social Work, 1*(1), 93–103.

Dattalo, P. (1992). Case management for gerontological social workers. In R. L. Schneider & N. P. Kropf (Eds.), *Gerontological social work: Knowledge, service settings, and special populations* (pp. 138–170). Chicago: Nelson-Hall.

East, J. F. (1999). Hidden barriers to success for women in welfare reform. *Families in Society, 80,* 295–304.

Falicov, C. J., & Karrer, B. M. (1980). Cultural variations in the family life cycle: The Mexican American family. In E. A. Carter & M. McGoldrick (Eds.), *The family cycle* (pp. 383–426). New York: Gardner Press.

Fast, B., & Chapin, R. (2000). *Strengths-based care management for older adults.* Baltimore: Health Professions Press.

Frankl, A. J., & Gelman, S. R. (2004). *Case management.* Chicago: Lyceum.

Franklin, C., Garner, J., & Berg, I. K. (2007). At-risk youth: Preventing and retrieving high school dropouts. In R. R. Greene (Ed.), *Social work practice: Risk and resiliency in childhood and adolescents* (2nd ed.). Washington, DC: NASW Press.

Gellis, Z. (2006). Older adults with mental and emotional problems. In B. Berkman (Ed.), *Handbook of social work in health and aging* (pp. 129–139). New York: Oxford University Press.

Goldenberg, I., & Goldenberg, H. (2003). *Family therapy: An overview* (5th ed.). Monterey, CA: Brooks/Cole.

Greene, R. R. (1992). Case management: An arena for social work practice. In B. S. Vourlekis & R. R. Greene (Eds.), *Social work case management* (pp. 11–25). New York: Aldine de Gruyter.

Greene, R. R. (1999). *Human behavior theory and social work practice* (2nd ed.). New York: Aldine de Gruyter.

Greene, R. R. (2000). *Case management with older adults: Developing a new paradigm.* Paper presented at the Indiana Social Services Administration, Division of Addiction and Mental Health Services, Building Case Management in the New Millennium.

Greene, R. R. (2008). *Social work with the aged and their families* (3rd ed.). New York: Aldine de Gruyter.

Greene, R. R., Cohen, H. L., Galambos, C. M., & Kropf, N. P. (2007). *Foundations of social work practice in the field of aging: A competency-based approach.* Washington, DC: NASW Press.

Greene, R. R., & Riley, J. (2005). Family and group approaches to interventions with older adults and their caregivers. In B. Berkman & S. Ambruosco (Eds.), *The Oxford handbook of social work in aging.* New York: Oxford University Press.

Hartman, A. (1981). The family: A central focus for practice. *Social Work, 26,* 7–13.

Hartman, A., & Laird, J. (1987). Family practice. In A. Minahan et al. (Eds.), *Encyclopedia of social work* (18th ed., pp. 575–589). Washington, DC: National Association of Social Workers.

Hayes, J. C., Meador, R. G., Branch, P. S., & George, L. K. (2001). The Spiritual History Scale in four dimensions (SHS-4): Validity and reliability. *Gerontologist, 41,* 239–249.

Hearn, G. (1969). Progress toward an holistic conception of social work. In G. Hearn (Ed.), *The general systems approach: Contributions toward an holistic conception of social work* (pp. 63–70). New York: Council on Social Work Education.

Hilarski, C. (2005). Exploring predictive factors for substance use in African American and Hispanic youth using an ecological approach. *Journal of Social Service Research, 32*(1), 65–86.

Ho, K. H. (1987). *Family therapy with ethnic minorities.* Newbury Park, CA: Sage.

Hsieh, C. (2006). Using client satisfaction to improve case management services for the elderly. *Research on Social Work Practice, 16*(6), 605–612.

Kalichman, S. C., Klein, S. J., Kalichman, M. O., O' Connell, D. A., Freedman, J. A., Eaton, L., & Cain, D. (2007). *Health and Social Work, 32*(4), 259–267.

Kane, R. L., & Kane, R. A. (Eds.). (2000). *Assessing older persons: Measures, meaning, and practical implications.* New York: Oxford Press.

Kelly, T., & Kropf, N. P. (1995). Stigmatized and perpetual parents: Older parents caring for adult children with life-long disabilities. *Journal of Gerontological Social Work, 24*(1,2), 3–16.

Kisthardt, W. E. (1992). A strengths model of case management: The principles and functions of a helping partnership with persons with persistent mental illness. In D. Saleebey (Ed.), *The strengths perspective in social work* (pp. 59–83). New York: Longman.

Kropf, N. P., & Cummings, S. M. (2008). Evidence based treatment with older adults: Concluding thoughts. In S. M. Cummings & N. P. Kropf (Eds.), *Handbook of psychosocial interventions with older adults: Evidence-based treatment.* New York: Haworth Press.

Kuhn, A. (1974). *The logic of social systems: A unified deductive, system-based approach to social science.* San Francisco: Jossey-Bass.

Leite, R., & McKenry, P. (2006). A role theory perspective on patterns of separated and divorced African-American nonresidential father involvement with children. *Fathering, 4*(1), 1–21.

Levine, I. S., & Fleming, M. (1984). *Human resource development: Issues in case management.* Baltimore: University of Maryland, Center for Rehabilitation and Manpower Services.

Minuchin, S. (1974). *Families and family therapy.* Cambridge, MA: Harvard University Press.

Moore, S. T. (1990). A social work practice model of case management: The case management grid. *Social Work, 35*(5), 444–448.

Mount, B., & Zwernik, K. (1988). *It's never too early, it's never too late: A booklet about personal futures planning* (Publication no. 421-88-109). St. Paul, MN: Metropolitan Council.

Myers, L., Kropf, N. P., & Robinson, M. (2002). Grandparents raising grandchildren: Case management in a rural setting. *Journal of Human Behavior in the Social Environment, 5*(1), 53–71.

Naleppa, M., & Reid, W. (1998). Task centered case management for the elderly: Developing a practice model. *Research on Social Work Practice, 8*(1), 63–85.

Naleppa, M., & Reid, W. J. (2003). *Gerontological social work; A task-centered approach.* New York: Columbia University Press.

National Association of Social Workers (NASW). (2005). *NASW Standards for Social Work Practice in Health Care Settings.* Retrieved on August 7, 2008, from www.socialworkers.org/practice/standards/NASWHealthCareStandards.pdf.

Nelson, G. (1982). Support for the aged: Public and private responsibility. *Social Work, 27*(7), 137–143.

Rhodes, S. L. (1980). A developmental approach to the life cycle of the family. In M. Bloom (Ed.), *Life span development* (pp. 30–40). New York: Macmillan.

Richmond, M. (1917). *Social diagnoses.* New York: Russell Sage Foundation.

Roberts, A. R., & Yeager, K. R. (Eds.). (2004). *Evidence-based practice manual.* New York: Oxford Press.

Roberts-DeGenarro, M. (1987). Developing case management as a practice model. *Social Casework, 68*(8), 466–470.

Robinson, M. (2000). Case management for social workers: A gerontological approach. In R. L. Schneider, N. P. Kropf, & A. J. Kisor (Eds.), *Gerontological social work: Knowledge, service settings, and special populations* (2nd ed., pp. 136–166). Belmont, CA: Wadsworth.

Rose, S. (1992). Case management: An advocacy/empowerment design. In S. M. Rose (Ed.), *Case management and social work practice* (pp. 271–298). New York: Longman.

Rothman, J. (1992). *Guidelines for case management: Putting to professional use.* Itasca, IL: Peacock.

Rubin, A. (1987). Case management. In A. Minahan et al. (Eds.), *Encyclopedia of social work* (18th ed., pp. 212–222). Washington, DC: National Association of Social Workers.

Saleebey, D. (1992). *The strengths perspective in social work.* New York: Longman.

Schneider, R. L., & Kropf, N. P. (Eds.). (1992). *Gerontological social work: Knowledge, service settings, and special populations.* Chicago: Nelson-Hall.

Shafer, C. M. (1969). Teaching social work practice in an integrated course: A general systems approach. In G. Hearn (Ed.), *The general systems approach: Contributions toward a holistic conception of social work* (pp. 26–36). New York: Council on Social Work Education.

Steinberg, R. M., & Carter, G. W. (1983). *Case management and the elderly.* Lexington, MA: D. C. Heath.

Stevens, N. L., Martina, C. M. S., & Westerhof, G. J. (2006). Meeting the need to belong: Predicting effects of a friendship enrichment program for older women. *Gerontologist, 46*(4), 495–502.

Sun, A. P. (2000). Helping substance-abusing mothers in the child welfare system: Turning crisis into opportunity. *Families in Society, 81*(2), 142–151.

Tseng, W. S., & Hsu, J. (1991). *Culture and family problems and therapy.* New York: Haworth Press.

Weil, M., Karls, J. M., & Associates. (1985). *Case management in human service practice.* San Francisco: Jossey-Bass.

Whitley, D. M., White, K. R., Kelley, S. J., & Yorker, B. (1999). Strengths based case management: The application to grandparents raising grandchildren. *Families in Society: The Journal of Contemporary Human Services, 80,* 110–119.

Part III

Second Level of Family Need: Structure, Limits, and Safety

Level II families have their basic survival needs met and are dealing primarily with issues of family structure, limits, and safety.

The first approach to working with families at this level is structural family interventions, discussed by Aponte in Chapter 7. This approach is based on family systems theory and has been used with a wide range of families in diverse racial, ethnic, and socioeconomic groups, as well as with single-parent and foster care families. It is one of the approaches that is used more internationally.

In Chapter 8, Horne and Sayger present the social learning family interventions approach to families who have needs on Level II. This approach deals with both internal and external or environmental factors that affect family needs and focuses on learning more effective social skills.

Second Level of Family Needs: Structure, Limits, and Safety

7

Structural Family Interventions

Harry J. Aponte, M.S.W.

Structural family therapy (SFT) is a systems-based model that places a special focus on the internal organization of relationships within families vis-à-vis their functioning. This model aims to solve problems of dysfunction by making changes in the underlying structure of personal relationships through intervening actively in client experiences.

Levels of Family Need

SFT was developed to meet the needs of troubled inner-city youth and their families. The model was first presented in a book whose title spoke to the original target population, *Families of the Slums* (Minuchin, Montalvo, Guerney, Rosman, & Schumer, 1967). What most directly influenced the emerging character of this new model was the *underorganization* (Aponte, 1994b, pp. 13–31) of these families with Level II needs. The structures of the target families were often underorganized, lacking "the *constancy, differentiation,* and *flexibility* they need[ed] to meet the demands of life" (Aponte, 1994b, p. 17). The model focused on bringing effective organization to the families so their members could find better solutions to their problems.

Given that the original families were "products of slums" (Minuchin et al., 1967, p. 6), it is no wonder that the model also lent itself from the very beginning to work with families with Level I needs. Families needed to be able to organize themselves with effective authority and hierarchy, clear personal boundaries, and stable relationship alliances and to possess communication skills to negotiate these structural components in order to meet their most basic needs in the midst of socioeconomic deprivation. Because of the social conditions within which these disadvantaged families faced their problems, the model looked not only at the internal relationship context of the family but also at the structure of the social environment within which these families struggled with life (Aponte, 1994b, pp. 13–31).

It was not long, however, before the original proponents of the model began to discover how the family's relationship structure was relevant to other problems, such as anorexia nervosa (Minuchin, Rosman, & Baker, 1978). Predictably, families in which youngsters were starving themselves to manage their emotional distress and family conflict did not tend to come from the lowest socioeconomic strata. For the most part, they were middle-class families with Level III needs. The factor these families had in common with lower-income families was the direct impact that a dysfunctional family structure had on the functioning of its members.

Moreover, today's devolution of U.S. society's traditional consensus of values made it apparent to some that it is not enough to speak only of structure and function in relation to people's life struggles. In the current cultural milieu, neither families nor their therapists share a common base of values on which they can base their efforts to solve problems. This awareness brought about an incorporation into the structural model of notions of values and spirituality (Aponte, 1994b, 1996, 2002a, 2002b). The Level IV spiritual needs of life relating to moral standards, philosophical perspective, and the social base of spirituality are all relevant to families in the current age, regardless of socioeconomic status (Aponte, 1999).

Assessment

The core focus of an assessment in SFT is how families are organized in relation to the problems they experience in the present. SFT views the past as "manifest in the present and . . . available to change by interventions that change the present" (Minuchin, 1974, p. 14). The assessment demands a clear identification of the focal issue, preferably in the operational terms in which it is currently manifested (Aponte & VanDeusen, 1981, p. 316). In SFT, *enactment* is the basic context in which family assessments take place (Aponte, 1994b, p. 21; Minuchin, 1974, p. 141). Structural therapists have families relive in the therapy the struggles they have at home. Witnessing and engaging with an actual interaction and its underlying relationship structure is a more reliable source of information than what people report about their lives.

Three underlying structural dimensions draw a structural therapist's attention (Aponte & VanDeusen, 1981):

1. *Boundaries:* what defines who is in or out of a family relationship vis-à-vis the focal issue, as well as what their roles are in this interaction
2. *Alignment:* who is with or against the other in the family transactions
3. *Power:* the relative influence of each person in the family interactions (pp. 312–313)

Therapists formulate *structural hypotheses* at the level of the current boundary, alignment, and power organization of the family in relation to its issues (Aponte & VanDeusen, 1981, pp. 314–315; Minuchin, 1974, p. 130). They also formulate a second level of hypotheses, called *functional hypotheses,* that "speak to the *meaning* and *significance* of the current structure" (Aponte, 1994b, p. 36). The present structure of family relationships has a history and a purpose. Functional hypotheses describe the historical background of the family that brought it to the present difficulty and the current motivations that drive family members to relate to each other as they do now around the current issue.

Because structural therapists work through the interactions they witness in the present, their every action with families is intentionally based on hypotheses about what they are observing. In fact, SFT considers change-inducing interventions to be not just techniques but technical interventions ensconced in relationships "occurring through the process of the therapist's affiliation with the family" (Minuchin, 1974, p. 91). In other words, structural therapists promote change through specifically aimed techniques within strategically shaped relationships. Consequently, therapists' every action should flow from their diagnostic hypotheses, and these hypotheses should be confirmed or altered according to the feedback garnered from the impact of therapists' actions (Aponte, 1994b, p. 38).

Consider the following case about the Gonzagas, a Mexican American family. During an interview, a consultant was presented with a set of parents and five children, ages 4 to 16 (Aponte, 1994b, pp. 32–57):

> The identified patient was an 11-year-old boy, Pancho, who was having school problems. In the initial presentation of the case, the mother was outspoken and articulate about the problem. The father, a packer, had been described by the family's co-therapists as relatively uninvolved in raising the children and not active in the therapy, although he had attended every session.
>
> The consultant began the session hypothesizing that the father's regular attendance indicated that, although silent, he cared about what was happening with the children. Yet the consultant hypothesized that in terms of *boundaries,* the father was peripheral to the mother's handling of Pancho's school problems. The mother exercised the *power* of the executive parent in relation to this boy's school problems by being the one who communicated with the school and oversaw his school performance. However, in terms of *alignment,* Pancho resisted her guidance. The consultant hypothesized that the boy was likely triangulated between parents who had a conflictual marriage.
>
> The consulting therapist had little family history to formulate his functional hypotheses but did speculate that this Latin-cultured father, who had relatively limited education, was not comfortable in the American world of professional agencies that are mostly populated by highly educated women, as were this family's co-therapists. He remained relatively reserved and silent in their presence, much like he was at home with his articulate wife.
>
> Seeing how little control the mother had over Pancho, the consultant further hypothesized that at the heart of her powerlessness was the absence of the father's backing in dealing with the boys. To probe the father's willingness and ability to help his son, the consultant invited him to engage Pancho in a discussion about his troubles, hoping for an *enactment* of the current father–son relationship. What emerged from the interaction was that the boy was frightened of his father, who was slow to talk but quick to hit. When the consultant gave the other two boys in the family the opportunity to join the discussion, the father was confronted by the 16-year-old's painful plea to have his father quit calling him a "liar" and to stop hitting him because he felt humiliated and intimidated. The father came to the realization that he was important to his sons and that

they needed him to treat them with both affection and respect. The father, with emotion, concluded that *he* was the problem in this situation and quietly said he understood the boys' reactions because he "too had a father."

The consultant worked to bring the father into the parenting in a way that would convince him how needed he was by his wife and children. The original therapists were to follow up with the couple about their marital difficulties to help them work more cooperatively as parents.

Goals

SFT aims to engage clients in an active experience of change, beginning with the enactment by family members around current, concrete issues. The approach looks to achieve palpable results by building on family members' strengths as they renegotiate their relationships around their issues with the active, personal engagement of the therapist. This new experience is meant to form the basis for better future patterns of relating and solving problems.

Intervention Approach

There are basically seven principles of intervention that form the foundation of SFT.

A Focus on Concrete Issues

SFT focuses on the urgent issue that holds the family's attention and intensity of concern (Aponte, 1998b). With the Gonzaga family, it was Pancho's school problems that brought the family to therapy. What hurts becomes an impulse for change.

However, the concrete issue that impels a need to change also carries with it motivation based on the clients' values. Those values can be drawn from clients' family traditions, culture, or spirituality. In the Gonzaga family, it can be assumed that education was important to them. In addition, affection and respect were valued in the family. The therapist looks to connect not only to the pain and particular circumstances motivating the drive to change but also to the ideals and values that inspire that drive.

Location in the Present

For SFT, the current issue contains within it (1) the focal point of today's concern, (2) the dynamics immediately generating the distress, and (3) traces of the family's past experience that help explain the "why" of today's problem. In other words, today's issue carries with it the immediate pain urging relief, as well as the deeper structural and dynamic forces that are driving the problem. The present issue is alive with the emotions, history, and spirituality that give that experience its meaning and importance. The therapeutic process itself is fashioned by the practitioner into a safe context for the family to speak to and reenact its issue in the immediacy of the present, accessible to the therapist's observations and interventions.

Mediation of the Client's Experience in Session

The most powerful field of intervention for SFT is the family's enactment of their issue in the session (Aponte & VanDeusen, 1981, p. 329; Minuchin & Fishman, 1981, pp. 78–97). The structural therapist looks to seize the moment when family members spontaneously enact some aspect of their struggle in the session. Failing a spontaneous enactment, the therapist attempts to create a situation that draws family members into their characteristic interaction around the issue. Talking about an issue draws from the intellect and memory. The drama, or enactment, of the struggle during a therapy session embodies all the affect and energy that infuses the family's interactions. By becoming alive on the therapeutic stage, the issue becomes more readily understandable and accessible to the therapist.

With the Gonzaga family, the consultant directly asked the father to talk with Pancho about how they relate around the boy's school problems. When Pancho told of his fear of his father and the oldest brother spontaneously spoke of how hurt he was by the father's disrespect of him, the consultant held still and let the father respond with his own intensity to his sons. The situation became an opportunity to see how they interacted but also to suggest a new way for the father to engage with his boys. That enactment is both material for assessment and a chance to intervene.

Achieving Change through Restructured Relationships

The structural family therapist pays special attention to the organization of family relationships with respect to the focal issue. This transactional structure is the skeleton undergirding the dynamics that generate the family's problem.

There are essentially two species of structural dysfunction: conflict driven and underorganized. The *conflictual structure* reflects competing interests among family members. The *underorganized structure* represents a lack of the stability, flexibility, or richness of development needed in family relationships to meet the demands of the family's functions. Structural therapists intervene to resolve conflict, repair what is broken, and build new strength in the family's underlying structure.

As noted earlier, at least one perspective on the structural model has evolved to incorporate the spiritual dimension of life into a three-part vision of human social functioning that includes structure, function, and values. People organize themselves psychologically and in relationships to carry out life's functions but always in relation to their morals, ideals, and philosophy of life. This spiritual dimension can take a secular form without reference to a transcendent spiritual world, or it can be embodied in a formal religious belief system and faith community. In either case, people's spiritual framework is vital to the process in which they choose how to think about and contend with life's challenges. In practice, the structural therapist who has a spiritually sensitive perspective brings to the therapeutic effort a recognition of moral choice, personal philosophy, and faith community in the dynamics that influence how people approach solving their problems (Aponte, 1996, 1998b, 2002a, 2002b).

Building on Client Strengths

SFT centers the therapeutic process on the resources and power of clients to grow and change, whether within themselves or in their family relationships (Aponte, 1999). The model works through a "search for strength" (Minuchin & Colapinto, 1980). Structural therapists actively engage with families to block old pathological transactional patterns (Aponte & VanDeusen, 1981, pp. 335–336) while also working to build on families' strengths to achieve new effective solutions to life's problems. People's resources reside within their characters, family relationships, and communities, including faith communities (Aponte, 1994b, pp. 58–82; Aponte, 1996).

The spiritual dimension of therapy pivots on the ultimate resource of positive, personal power for clients: free will, the seat of people's moral choices. Individuals who are poor and disenfranchised can discover within themselves, their families, and their communities, however distressed, the personal power in freedom of the will that Frankl (1963) experienced in the Nazi concentration camps. "For the powerless and invisible, acting on the freedom to choose is to claim their potential and importance in the face of daunting circumstances" (Aponte, 1999, p. 82).

Speaking to clients' strength begins with relating to their personal value and dignity and ultimately hinges on acknowledging their personal power and responsibility to freely choose the actions that will determine their destiny. Clients' belief systems contain the strength, standards, and ideals behind their will to choose, and their families and faith communities are their most intimate personal supports.

Aiming at Palpable Outcomes

While SFT looks into the underlying structure of people's actions and relationships, the model is practiced in real-life experience and aims for outcomes that make a perceptible difference in how people live. The initial formulation of the problem takes the form of action and interaction that makes clear the concern of the family (Aponte & VanDeusen, 1981, p. 316). The structural therapist then enters the family's struggle through the *enactment,* an actual reliving of the family drama in session, and follows up with interventions aimed at creating new transformative experiences during session. When the consultant had Mr. Gonzaga talking with his boys in session in ways that elicited mutuality instead of stifling through intimidation, both father and sons discovered in that moment's encounter a warm reciprocal affection.

As a follow-up to the in-session experience, structural therapists also assign tasks as homework (Minuchin, 1974, p. 151), moving the therapeutic experience back into the home, where the family drama normally takes place. Finally, when structural therapists formulate goals, they think in terms of day-to-day experiences that embody the structural and dynamic changes that family members tested in the therapist's office (Aponte, 1992b).

Understanding a problem and communicating effectively with regard to it are means to an end. Living life more successfully is the goal.

Intervention through the Practitioner's Active Involvement with the Family

Structural therapists actively engage with families to create experiences both among family members and between practitioner and family as a means of generating change. Initially, therapists look to join (Minuchin, 1974, pp. 133–137) families "in a carefully planned way" (p. 91). This is not only an effort to gain the trust of family members but also a strategic therapeutic opportunity to relate in new ways that draw out new interactions within families.

In more stubborn and chronic situations, practitioners may themselves engage with families with greater intensity (Minuchin, & Fishman, 1981, pp. 116–141) or heighten a conflictual interaction among family members (Aponte & VanDeusen, 1981, p. 335) to induce reactions that bring clients out from behind their defensive walls. Therapists may attempt to block (Aponte & VanDeusen, 1981, p. 335) or unbalance (Minuchin & Fishman, 1981, pp. 161–190) inflexible patterns of interaction to challenge family members to adopt more functional modes of operating. However, when clients are more readily disposed to change, practitioners may promote healthier attitudes, behaviors, and patterns of interaction (Aponte & VanDeusen, 1981, p. 336) through what they simply encourage, point out, or suggest.

Therapists may intentionally employ themselves in purposeful personal interactions with clients within their professional roles to coax different therapeutic experiences for clients (Aponte, 1992a). This use of self calls for the practitioner to be emotionally free to use his or her own person deliberately and more fully for therapeutic purposes. The practitioner must be able to utilize his or her personal assets, as well as flaws and life struggles, to both identify with and differentiate from clients. In SFT, this active use of self is employed with specific strategic goals within the person-to-person interactions between client and practitioner.

Evaluation

As noted earlier, the structural model grew out of research on the treatment of poor, underorganized families. The results of the research, as published in *Families of the Slums* (Minuchin et al., 1967), demonstrated the effectiveness of interventions on the family structure in resolving specific issues. These interventions challenged old structures and created new ones through constructing fresh client experiences in session. The initial research on underorganized families was immediately followed by research on families with children suffering from psychosomatic conditions, most of whom were not economically or socially disadvantaged (Minuchin et al., 1978).

The impact of family structure on psychosomatic illness has been studied further (Kog, Vertommen, & Vandereycken, 1987; Northey, Griffin, & Krainz, 1998; Onnis, Tortolani, & Cancrini, 1986; Wood et al., 1989), and SFT has been examined in application to such disparate topics as drug addiction (Allen-Eckert, Fon, Nichols, Watson, & Liddle, 2001; Stanton, Todd, & Associates, 1982), family therapy with children (Abelsohn & Saayman, 1991; Kerig, 1995), family and culture (Fisek, 1991; Jung, 1984; Santisteban et al., 1997), and business and industry (Deacon, 1996). There has also been exploration, within the framework of SFT, of the role of the wider system on the treatment of families (Peck, Sheinberg, & Akamatsu, 1995).

The concept of structure in systems has broad application. However, research on structural interventions in family and social institutions should also take into account the personal, cultural, and social values of the observers, the practitioners, and the clients.

Family and social structure cannot be studied or evaluated outside the values that determine what is healthy or unhealthy and morally right or wrong.

Application to Families at Other Levels of Need

The structural model has clearly demonstrated its relevance to Levels I, II, and III needs. The theory and intervention techniques are well adapted to address concerns about concrete issues, hierarchical family structure, and personal boundary issues. While SFT is not specifically tailored to therapeutic foci about intimacy in relationships and personal self-actualization, it clearly addresses these issues as part of the work on relationships within families and couples. Individual self-actualization is integral to an understanding of the evolution of the individual's psychological structure in the contexts of family and society. Values and spirituality, which relate most strongly to Level IV concerns, historically have been a later addition to SFT for the understating of human relationships.

Ethical Challenges

Because of the active posture of the therapist, SFT faces two ethical challenges: (1) the imposition of the therapist's values on clients and (2) the blurring of boundaries between therapist and client. In SFT, therapists actively engage in helping clients identify their issues, set goals, and determine the therapeutic approach needed to reach those goals. All this work is built on a value platform, or the morals and ideals that set the foundation of values for the therapy. Ideally, these values are explicitly or implicitly agreed on by therapist and client without coercion or manipulation on the part of the therapist. However, because of the active posture of the therapist, vigilance and sensitivity are required to make this a truly mutual process.

In addition, the active role of structural therapists can make them vulnerable to blurring boundaries in the therapeutic process between therapist and client. These therapists may be prone to an investment in outcomes that overreach clients' readiness or commitment to change. In the interest of joining, therapists may also be vulnerable to identifying with clients beyond what is called for in understanding them and gaining their trust.

Structural therapists, like other active therapists, should engage in training on the use of their person in therapy. They should make an ongoing commitment throughout their professional careers to do the following:

1. Deepen their understanding of their own personal issues in the context of their family history, signature themes (personal struggles), and cultural, political, and moral values.
2. Work on their own personal growth and development through efforts to resolve their own personal emotional struggles and relationship issues within their families of origin and procreation.
3. Gain ever-greater mastery of their personal selves in the therapeutic process with clients, enabling them to better observe and pilot themselves in the therapeutic context.

Doing this work on themselves will help practitioners avoid the temptation of trying to work out their personal issues through their clients' lives. In addition, doing this personal work can help practitioners learn to appropriately, purposefully, and effectively both identify with clients and differentiate from them in the clients' best interests.

Summary

Structural family therapy is not a single, tightly organized model of intervention with a unitary, orthodox theory. However, virtually all approaches to the model have in common the emphasis on family structure, the clients' experience in the session, the here-and-now issues and their underlying dynamics, the building on client strengths, the focus on real-life outcomes, and the active style of client engagement and intervention by practitioners. Some perspectives on the model emphasize technique over therapeutic relationship, whereas others stress the therapist's personal involvement.

Structural therapists also differ in their views on normal family structure and in their opinions about the importance of spirituality to the work of therapy. These differences are incidental to the essence of the model, however, which focuses on actively addressing today's issues in session through the enactment of the structures of the underlying relationships. The model continues to be a dominant approach in the field of family therapy.

Moreover, amid today's eclecticism in therapy, it is rare to find practitioners who practice a single, orthodox approach. For example, structural therapists commonly utilize Murray Bowen's thinking about the family of origin. From the earliest days, structuralists have employed strategic techniques. What structural therapists today ignore the psychoanalytic concept of the unconscious?

On the other hand, SFT has influenced practitioners from other orientations. The insights of SFT about structure in family systems are no longer the exclusive concerns of the structural model. SFT has made its contributions to the field of family therapy and has learned from the contributions of other family therapy models, as well as models of therapy for individuals—as it should be.

Discussion Questions

1. What are the essential components of the structural model?

2. How can elements of other models be utilized in SFT, and how can components of SFT be incorporated into other models of family therapy?

3. How is SFT applicable to Level III and IV needs?

4. Why is the work on the person of the therapist of particular importance for the structural family therapist?

5. How does one incorporate the diversity of values and spirituality among practitioners and clients into the structural model?

Suggested Videotapes

Clinical application of forgiveness. (1996). National Conference on Forgiveness, University of Maryland (Frederick A. DiBlasio, Ph.D., School of Social Work. University of Maryland at Baltimore, Phone: 410-706-7799).

This videotape shows the actual session that is discussed in Aponte's (1998b) article "Love, the spiritual wellspring of forgiveness: An example of spirituality in therapy."

A daughter who needs a mother. (1991). AAMFT Master Series (Website: www.aamft.org).

Aponte works with an African American family in which the focus is on the relationship between a mother and her emotionally alienated adolescent daughter. The mother struggles with the effects of her own emotionally deprived childhood on her relationship with her daughter.

Family therapy with the experts: Structural therapy with Harry Aponte. (1998). Allyn & Bacon (Allyn & Bacon, video no. 3208L8. Phone: 800-278-3525).

This videotape is from the series *Family Therapy with the Experts.* It contains not only a full clinical session by Aponte demonstrating structural family therapy but also an interview in which he discusses the structural model.

A house divided: Structural family therapy with a black family. (1990). Golden Triad Films (Phone: 800-869-9454).

Aponte works with an African American family in this complex family situation of a married couple who have children from previous marriages. The father was released from jail for this interview.

Tres madres: Structural family therapy with an Anglo/Hispanic family. (1990). Golden Triad Films (Phone: 800-869-9454).

Aponte works with a three-generation family that has both Anglo and Latino family members. The presenting issue is a young, unhappy, sleepwalking girl. The focus of the therapy is a young mother valiantly struggling to survive a dysfunctional family background, poverty, and cultural difficulties.

Williams family: Strength and vulnerability. (1995). Research and Education Foundation, AAMFT (Child Development Media, #20929P-Vb-X, Phone: 800-405-8942).

This film features Aponte's interview with the family from Chapter 11 of his book *Bread and Spirit* (Aponte, 1994b). It portrays a family that has courageously overcome the overwhelming trials and tragedies of racism, sickle cell anemia, drug addiction, and untimely, violent deaths. Their spirituality has been a key source of their strength.

Suggested Readings

Aponte, H. J. (1992). Training the person of the therapist in structural family therapy. *Journal of Marital and Family Therapy, 18*(3), 269–281.

This article attempts to apply the notion of the person-of-the-therapist to structural family therapy and is the first effort to address more fully the use of self in this model.

Aponte, H. J. (1994). *Bread and spirit: Therapy with the new poor.* New York: Norton.

This book contains updates to Aponte's basic structural writings, along with some new material. The particular emphasis of the book is on therapy with disadvantaged families and the place of values and spirituality in this work.

Aponte, H. J. (1998). Love, the spiritual wellspring of forgiveness: An example of spirituality in therapy. *Journal of Family Therapy, 20*(1), 37–58.

Using the example of setting the value platform for a therapeutic contract, this article demonstrates a method for incorporating spirituality into therapy.

Aponte, H. J. (1999). The stresses of poverty and the comfort of spirituality. In F. Walsh (Ed.), *Spiritual resources in family therapy* (pp. 76–89). New York: Guilford Press.

This chapter in Froma Walsh's book is a more recent elaboration of the application of a spiritual perspective to therapy with a particular population.

Aponte, H. J. (2002). Spiritually sensitive psychotherapy. In R. F. Massey & S. D. Massey (Eds.), *Comprehensive handbook of psychotherapy: Vol. 3. Interpersonal/humanistic/existential approaches to psychotherapy* (pp. 279–302). New York: Wiley.

Minuchin, S. (1974). *Families and family therapy.* Cambridge, MA: Harvard University Press.
This book is the most complete representation of Minuchin's concept of structural family therapy.
Minuchin, S., & Fishman, H. C. (1981). *Family therapy techniques.* Cambridge, MA: Harvard University Press.
This book contains Minuchin and Fishman's most comprehensive compendium of structural family therapy's technical interventions.

References

Abelsohn, D., & Saayman, G. (1991). Adolescent adjustment to parental divorce: An investigation from the perspective of basic dimensions of structural family therapy theory. *Family Process, 30*(2), 177–191.

Allen-Eckert, H., Fon, E., Nichols, M. P., Watson, N., & Liddle, H. A. (2001). Development of the family therapy enactment rating scale. *Family Process, 40*(4), 469–478.

Aponte, H. J. (1992a). Training the person of the therapist in structural family therapy. *Journal of Marital and Family Therapy, 18*(3), 269–281.

Aponte, H. J. (1992b). The black sheep of the family: A structural approach to brief therapy. In S. H. Budman, M. F. Hoyt, & S. Friedman (Eds.), *The first session in brief therapy* (pp. 324–342). New York: Guilford Press.

Aponte, H. J. (1994a). How personal can training get? *Journal of Marital and Family Therapy, 20*(1), 3–15.

Aponte, H. J. (1994b). *Bread and spirit: Therapy with the new poor.* New York: Norton.

Aponte, H. J. (1996, Fall). Political bias, moral values, and spirituality in the training of psychotherapists. *Bulletin of the Menninger Clinic, 60*(4), 488–502.

Aponte, H. J. (1998a). Intimacy in the therapist-client relationship. In W. J. Matthews & J. H. Edgette (Eds.), *Current thinking and research in brief therapy: Solutions, strategies, narratives* (Vol. 2, pp. 3–27). Philadelphia: Taylor & Francis.

Aponte, H. J. (1998b). Love, the spiritual wellspring of forgiveness: An example of spirituality in therapy. *Journal of Family Therapy, 20*(1), 37–58.

Aponte, H. J. (1999). The stresses of poverty and the comfort of spirituality. In F. Walsh (Ed.), *Spiritual resources in family therapy* (pp. 76–89). New York: Guilford Press.

Aponte, H. J. (2002a). Spirituality: The heart of therapy. *Journal of Family Psychotherapy 13*(1,2), 13–27.

Aponte, H. J. (2002b). Spiritually sensitive therapy. In R. F. Massey & S. D. Massey (Eds.), *Comprehensive handbook of psychotherapy: Vol. 3. Interpersonal/humanistic/existential approaches to psychotherapy* (pp. 279–302). New York: Wiley.

Aponte, H. J., & VanDeusen, J. M. (1981). Structural family therapy. In A. S. Gurman & D. P. Kniskern (Eds.), *Handbook of family therapy* (pp. 310–360). New York: Brunner/Mazel.

Aponte, H. J., & Winter, J. E. (2000). The person and practice of the therapist. In M. Baldwin (Ed.), *The use of self in therapy* (2nd ed.). New York: Haworth Press.

Deacon, S. (1996). Utilizing structural family therapy and systems theory in the business world. *Contemporary Family Therapy, 18*(4), 549–565.

Fisek, G. O. (1991). A cross-cultural examination of proximity and hierarchy: A dimension of family structure. *Family Process, 30,* 121–133.

Frankl, V. E. (1963). *Man's search for meaning.* New York: Washington Square Press.

Jung, M. (1984). Structural family therapy: Its application to Chinese families. *Family Process, 23*(3), 365–374.

Kerig, P. K. (1995). Triangles in the family circle: Effects of family structure on marriage, parenting, and child adjustment. *Journal of Family Psychology, 9*(1), 28–43.

Kog, E., Vertommen, H., & Vandereycken, W. (1987, June). Minuchin's psychosomatic family model revisited: A concept-validation study using a multitrait-multimethod approach. *Family Process, 26*(2), 235–253.

Minuchin, S. (1974). *Families and family therapy.* Cambridge, MA: Harvard University Press.

Minuchin, S., & Colapinto, J. (Eds.). (1980). *Taming monsters* [Videotape]. Philadelphia Child Guidance Clinic.

Minuchin, S., & Fishman, H. C. (1981). *Family therapy techniques.* Cambridge, MA: Harvard University Press.

Minuchin, S., Montalvo, B., Guerney, B., Jr., Rosman, B., & Schumer, F. (1967). *Families of the slums.* New York: Basic Books.

Minuchin, S., Rosman, B., & Baker, L. (1978). *Psychosomatic families.* Cambridge, MA: Harvard University Press.

Northey, S., Griffin, W. A., & Krainz, S. (1998). A partial test of the psychosomatic family model: Marital interaction patterns in asthma and non-asthma families. *Journal of Family Psychology, 12*(2), 220–233.

Onnis, L., Tortolani, D., & Cancrini, L. (1986, March). Systemic research on chronicity factors in infantile asthma. *Family Process, 14*(2), 107–121.

Peck, J. S., Sheinberg, M., & Akamatsu, N. N. (1995). Forming a consortium: A design for interagency collaboration in the delivery of service following the disclosure of incest. *Family Process, 34*(2), 107–121.

Santisteban, D., Coatswroth, J. D., Perez-Vidal, A., Mitrani, V., Jean-Gilles, M., & Szapocznik, J. (1997). Brief, structural/strategic family therapy with African American and Hispanic high-risk youth. *Journal of Community Psychology, 25,* 453–471.

Stanton, M. D., Todd, T. C., & Associates. (1982). *The family therapy of drug abuse and addiction.* New York: Guilford Press.

Wood, B., Watkins, J. B., Boyle, J. T., Noguiera, J., Zimand, E., & Carroll, L. (1989, December). The psychosomatic family model: An empirical and theoretical analysis. *Family Process, 28*(4), 399–417.

8

Social Learning Family Interventions

Arthur M. Horne, Ph.D., and Thomas V. Sayger, Ph.D.

Family life has become increasingly stressful during the past century. There has been more isolation of family members due to the urbanization of American society and a move toward small nuclear families instead of extended families. The urbanization process has led to a focus on work outside the home for most adults. Increased costs of living have resulted in more parents working longer hours out of the home, with fewer support systems available to provide parenting and child care.

There is a significant level of violence in American society. This, coupled with drug and alcohol abuse, a concomitant increase in sexual experimentation among young people, and more teenage parenting and single-parent households, has resulted in a dramatic growth in the numbers of children and family members living below the poverty level and a corresponding increase in suicidal and homicidal behavior among young people. In many communities, gang membership has supplanted family membership as the primary source of identity.

Family Needs

Within American society, there is a substantial number of families that are functioning above the crisis level, the level at which families need support from the community for their very survival needs. Although the survival needs of these families have been met, they still have very real and serious problems. Examples of families with problems that fall within the second level of need include families with disruptive, acting-out children; families that are experiencing considerable disarray in the form of poor family organization and structure; families with difficulties in communicating and effective problem solving; families that have children in difficulty with school or community agencies; and families experiencing a high level of disruptive affect, as in violent anger or disabling depression.

Many of the families that have Level II needs are there because of internal and external (environmental) factors that have affected them. These include the following child, family, and school risk factors:

Child
Perceives that parents support fighting as a way of solving conflict
Expects success and no negative consequences for aggression
Lacks problem-solving skills
Attributes aggression where there is none
Holds beliefs that support violence
Is depressed
Uses drugs and alcohol
Has low academic achievement
Carries a weapon
Has negative parental relationships

Family
Lack of supervision
Lack of attachment, connection, and effective communication
Lack of discipline or consequences
Negative relationships
Psychopathology of one or both parents
Antisocial behavior of family members
Susceptibility to stressors
Unemployment
Marital conflict
Divorce
Few opportunities for pleasurable or play activities

School
Lack of supervision
Lack of attachment and communication
Lack of discipline or consequences
Negative relationships

Families that have sought help have included ones like those in the following case studies:

The Hartmans
The Hartmans called the counseling center requesting to be seen because of a referral from the school psychologist. Their son Kevin had experienced high rates of behavioral conduct problems in school for a number of years. Now that he had reached sixth grade, he had become a serious enough problem to be perceived as a danger to other children.

Mr. Hartman was a carpenter who worked long hours when employed and who had little time for the family. Mrs. Hartman, a waitress, worked afternoons and was seldom home when the children came home after school. Kevin, the oldest child, had been a behavioral problem throughout his school career and had been referred for testing several times.

Each time he was evaluated, Kevin was identified as marginal in terms of special needs; consequently, he had not received any special placement. The two younger Hartman children, also boys, had behavioral problems but had not demonstrated the extent of physical aggression that Kevin had shown.

The initial interview with the family indicated that the father was quite removed and distant from parenting, seeing the role of parenting as the mother's responsibility. He was angry that he had been called into the situation. The mother, who scored in the clinical range on a depression inventory, indicated that she loved the children but that they had been a disappointment, causing her more pain than pleasure. Kevin was antagonistic to being involved in treatment, whereas the two younger boys were curious and rambunctious.

The Gonzaleses

The Gonzales family was referred because Selena Gonzales, a 15-year-old, had been caught shoplifting. She had a history of aggressive behavior, including attempting to extort money from children at school, threatening to hurt other children if they didn't pay her for protection, and stealing items from school. Selena had been arrested at a convenience store and held overnight at a juvenile detention center. She had attended juvenile court, and the judge had ordered Selena, her single-parent mother, and the siblings living at home to participate in family counseling.

Mrs. Gonzales was angry at the inconvenience, and Selena was quite rebellious. None of the family members indicated that they saw counseling as a positive experience. They indicated that they would participate in counseling only by showing up for the minimum number of times the judge had ordered.

The Yunuses

The Yunuses contacted the center and requested marriage counseling. They indicated that Mr. Yunus came from a Mediterranean background and that Mrs. Yunus was of Irish heritage. They had been married for six years.

Although the marriage had started out amicably, the last two years had been marked by conflict, arguments, and recently physical aggression. They had attempted religious counseling with their priest, and he had encouraged them to follow the traditional roles of husband and wife, with the wife deferring to the husband as the head of the household. Mrs. Yunus indicated that she had been willing to accept that role when they were first married but that it was no longer tolerable for her. Both partners reported significant conflict in the area of sexuality within the marriage. There were no children.

Marty Acree

Marty Acree, a recent university graduate, came for his first session at the counseling center and reported that his male lover had just left him for another man. Marty was distraught and reported the possibility of inflicting personal harm on himself. He stated that he had experienced a number of lovers during his university education but that his recent partner had been with him for more than a year. The two had been very close and trusting with each other.

Marty was devastated that his lover left him after having such a close and involved relationship. He indicated that his family had not been told about the partnership because he did not want his fundamentally religious family to know he was gay.

Assessment and Treatment Goals

Each family described presented very real pain and need for assistance in addressing the pressing problems that they were experiencing in their lives. The following general goals are established for all families receiving treatment:

1. Develop a sense of optimism and hope about their particular situation.
2. Appreciate the universality or general nature of their situation.
3. Become aware of the alternative ways of addressing the problems they are experiencing, so that they see more options available to them.
4. Learn more effective basic living skills: communication, problem solving, decision making, and environmental interaction.
5. Develop independence in living skills.

The goals of treatment become focused as each family member presents his or her unique and individual issues.

The Hartmans

The Hartmans require a careful negotiation to determine the level of change and restructuring that will be acceptable and agreeable. Mr. Hartman has reported little interest in participating in treatment, seeing the problem as one primarily for the mother. Here, the therapist must make a decision about family responsibility and power: Should the therapist support the traditional roles that have been assigned and accepted by family members, or should he or she focus on realigning the roles and responsibilities of the parents? The goals for the Hartman family might include these:

- empowering the mother to take greater control over how family members spend their time (father absent, chaotic family schedule)
- teaching both parents more effective parenting skills
- helping the boys learn anger-control skills

- identifying problem-solving skills and, especially important, couples communication skills

The Gonzaleses

The Gonzales family does not want to participate in treatment. A goal for this family will be to identify ways in which they are functioning well and to help them see that they are not bad or sick but doing the best they can, given their economic and social circumstances. However, the family needs assistance in learning more effective ways of dealing with their environmental circumstances. Specific goals for the Gonzales family might include the following:

- empowering the mother to be able to take greater responsibility for the behavior of the children
- teaching the family effective disciplinary techniques
- assisting the children in learning self-control strategies that will help them stay out of trouble
- establishing better communication skills within the family
- addressing environmental issues (e.g., employment, leisure time)
- working with school issues such that greater success is experienced in the school environment

The Yunuses

The Yunuses have demonstrated difficulties in maintaining and enhancing intimacy. They need to learn more effective communication and problem-solving skills. Their relationship is evolving and developing, but they have become stuck at a level that is not acceptable and is, in fact, detrimental to their growing closer. Goals might include these:

- developing more effective problem-solving skills
- learning better communication skills
- addressing the beliefs or narratives they have about their relationship
- discussing the power and role relationships that have become troublesome

Marty Acree

Marty Acree is having difficulty managing his needs for intimacy and relationships in light of his sexual orientation and negative social pressures. He needs assistance in learning to manage issues of intimacy (being discarded) and sexuality, developing personal strength to manage his loneliness, and learning communication skills, both to facilitate meeting other persons and to learn ways of talking with his family members. Goals might be as follows:

- learning to develop the strength to manage developmental passages, such as the loss of a loved one
- developing effective coping skills to manage his loss and fear

- practicing communication skills that will enhance his socialization with others and sharing with his current family and friends
- developing self-control skills to manage his life more effectively

Consistent with other families at Level II, the four families in the case examples are experiencing difficulties with inefficient and ineffective family structures. In turn, these faulty structures inhibit the effective solving of current problems; cause confusion with family rules, roles, and responsibilities; and exacerbate the low level of functioning. As a result, these kinds of confusion limit the families' capacity to overcome their life challenges and their feelings of insecurity, dissatisfaction, and discomfort with the level of intimacy within the family.

Social Learning Family Interventions

Several principles aid in practitioners' understanding of family needs and the contingencies on which current family interactions are based. The *social learning* family treatment approach (Fleischman, Horne, & Arthur, 1983; Horne & Sayger, 1990, 2000; Tolan & Guerra, 1994) has been successfully employed with a variety of families and with many levels of family needs. This model enables the practitioner to utilize a well-structured series of intervention strategies yet allows for the necessary flexibility when working with diverse, chaotic, and unique family systems. Because social learning family interventions allow for unique family structures and flexibility in implementing change according to the expressed needs of each family, this approach can be effective across racial and ethnic categories and with varying gender roles and responsibilities.

The effectiveness of social learning family interventions has been researched in a variety of clinical settings. It has been shown to be useful in the remediation of difficult child behavior problems, marital conflict, ineffective power structures and coalitions, and poor community–school–home relations (Horne, Glaser, & Calhoun, 1998; Sayger, Horne, & Glaser, 1993; Sayger, Horne, Walker, & Passmore, 1988; Szykula, Sayger, Morris, & Sudweeks, 1987).

Theoretical Base and Basic Tenets

Many theoretical approaches to family intervention have been used with Level II families, with varying degrees of success. All of these models have attempted to approach clinical work with families from a positive viewpoint and to focus on the families' strengths and current abilities to cope with chaotic and challenging living environments. Clearly, no one theoretical approach provides the answer for all families experiencing difficulties; thus, family practitioners must be clear about the needs of each family they plan to assist and how they will develop their intervention to meet those needs. An underlying knowledge of how one believes individuals and families develop and learn their behavioral patterns is the cornerstone for effectively implementing a family intervention.

For those practitioners who practice social learning family interventions, the following beliefs and assumptions about human/family development are the bases for intervention:

1. People learn within a social context (e.g., culture, community, family, school, work) through watching how other people in their environment behave, reacting to these behaviors, and interacting with those individuals in their social system (e.g., spouse, partner, child, parent, extended family members, teachers, co-workers).
2. The problem behaviors demonstrated by the individual or family are logical from a learning perspective, given the contingencies within that family's or person's environment and his or her personal beliefs.
3. People behave the way they do either because they have learned that behavior or because they have not learned alternative, and often more positive, ways to behave.
4. People's beliefs and cognitive processes influence their affective and behavioral responses.
5. People attempt to maximize the rewards of their behavior while minimizing the costs. People are more likely to perform in ways that result in what they perceive to be the best outcome for them.
6. To change how someone else behaves, a person has to change the way he or she typically responds to that behavior.
7. The more consistent the consequence and the more immediately it occurs after the behavior, the faster the person will learn. Inconsistent consequences make learning harder, because people do not know what to expect.
8. Because people rarely learn from only one act of behaving and receiving a consequence, repeated trying or testing is a necessary part of learning.
9. The family is the expert on what is happening in their life, and each family is unique.

This framework is appropriate for families at the second level of functioning. The intervention focuses on the development of effective communication skills, establishes appropriate limits and levels of authority, encourages strong parental alliances, and aids families in the development and use of self-control and problem-solving skills. It also addresses the cognitive thought processes needed to replace dysfunctional thoughts with more facilitative thinking. In essence, social learning family interventions help family members learn not only how to survive family life but also how to make their family life healthier from a psychological perspective and more enjoyable in general.

Applications and Intervention Strategies

Social cognitive learning intervention strategies focus on families at Level II and fall into three general categories:

1. *Cognitive restructuring* addresses any disruptive or maladaptive thoughts that might result in painful or disturbing feelings and, consequently, maladaptive behaviors.
2. *Coping skills training,* such as relaxation training, self-control strategies, behavior rehearsal, and modeling, addresses inappropriate learning experiences.

3. *Problem-solving skills training,* such as behavioral contracts, negotiation, and brainstorming, assists families in developing alternative strategies for resolving current and future conflicts or concerns.

Perhaps the most important objective of intervention with Level II families is to focus on creating a structured learning environment in which family members can learn and practice new behaviors that will alter their currently ineffective family structure.

Therapeutic Relationship.   The development of a positive therapeutic relationship is central to effective family intervention. The relationship between the practitioner and client develops in much the same way as all social systems are formed—that is, through modeling appropriate social behavior, coaching the family members in effective social communication, and setting up positive consequences for establishing the therapeutic alliance.

To accomplish these goals, the family practitioner must first help the family establish positive expectations for change. Level II families are characterized by a negative view of their chances for remediation. They feel that they have tried everything they know how to do and that nothing has worked. Thus, it is important for the practitioner to communicate to each family that he or she believes that the family can successfully deal with its current problems. The process of preparing the family for success can be initiated by taking these steps:

1. *Defining all members in the family as being hurt by their circumstance.* Most families attempt to find someone or something to blame for their problems. Objects of blame may be the child, parent, judge, social service system, neighborhood, teacher, school, social caseworker, extended family members, or therapist. In defining all members in the family as being in pain, everyone acknowledges that each family member is affected by hurtful ways and that blaming will not solve the problem.

2. *Normalizing the family problems.* Families may communicate hopelessness or feelings of "Why me?" when they are first referred for treatment. It is important to inform the family in treatment that all families have problems and that, although the family's current problems may seem to be overwhelming and uncontrollable, families in similar situations have been successful in overcoming their conflicts.

3. *Emphasizing the family's strengths and positive motivation.* Although many families may initially proclaim their reluctance to participate in treatment, the fact that they have attended a session shows that they have some concern for their family and hold some hope for change.

4. *Communicating empathy.* The family must believe that the practitioner understands what it is like for them to be experiencing these problems. Assuming the position that family members are the experts on their own family can assist the practitioner in communicating positively to the family that he or she is there to listen, understand, and help them successfully overcome their concerns.

5. *Communicating hope.* Although the problems facing the family may be enormous and difficult, having a positive attitude and an ability to see the hope and irony in the situation is necessary. Most families at Level II have forgotten how to laugh and enjoy themselves; thus, the practitioner must attempt to make the treatment intervention enjoyable and even fun, without diminishing the seriousness of the problems being addressed.

The practitioner can also use these relationship-building skills:

- breaking complex problems into manageable units
- dealing with one issue or task at a time
- giving everyone a chance to participate
- teaching new skills in specific, nontechnical language
- modeling new skills
- personalizing in-session rehearsals
- predicting feelings and behavior changes
- soliciting and anticipating concerns
- encouraging client initiative and giving credit for positive changes
- determining reasons for client resistance
- checking for comprehension and understanding when teaching new skills
- sharing the treatment or session agenda
- gathering information about what family members do
- gathering information about cognitive and emotional reactions
- gathering information about behavioral sequences and patterns

Structuring for Success.   Structuring for success begins with the initial contact between the family and the practitioner. Not only does the professional want to be successful in assisting the family to function in a more effective manner, but the family must also establish a belief in their own ability to succeed.

To establish this positive expectation for change and success, the intervention begins with clearly and objectively defining the problem, establishing specific behavioral goals, emphasizing consistency and persistence in developing family routines, interacting with respect and dignity, emphasizing family strengths, and enhancing the couple's and/or the parent–child relationship. The family is encouraged to begin tracking the instances of problem behaviors to determine patterns, sequences, frequency, intensity, and duration.

Usually, the family discovers that the incidence of problem behavior is less frequent than they had perceived, yet the discomfort, anger, pain, and disruption created by the behavior are no less real. However, in discovering that the behavior occurs less frequently, the family becomes more hopeful that positive change can be achieved, and thus their motivation and commitment to treatment will increase.

Self-Management Skills Training.   Individuals who cannot gain and maintain control of their emotions and behaviors find it very difficult, if not impossible, to interact with family members in a positive and respectful manner. A study conducted by Morris et al. (1988) found that fathers of aggressive boys reported five times more negative thoughts about their families and eight times more negative thoughts about their child than did fathers of well-behaved boys. This finding further supports the belief that the maladaptive thought processes that family members have about one another must be altered if they hope to develop a more functional family environment.

These self-control strategies might be utilized to assist family members in gaining and maintaining self-control:

1. *Relaxation training.* Learning self-control by learning to control bodily reactions through training in deep-breathing exercises, progressive muscle relaxation, or other relaxation strategies is very effective.

2. *Positive reframing.* Individuals will typically react to a behavior based on some perception they have regarding the intent of that behavior. For instance, a parent who is constantly being interrupted by a child may assume the child is being an ill-mannered pest. This belief might lead the parent to respond in a negative manner. However, if the child's reaction were reframed as an attempt to gain the parent's highly valued attention, the parent might respond more positively. Functioning under a more positive frame of reference, the parent can then teach the child more appropriate ways of gaining parental attention. This reframing can also be identified as an attempt to replace upsetting and possibly irrational thoughts with calming thoughts that allow the family members to interact in healthier ways.

3. *Child self-control strategies.* The most effective way to implement and train children to use self-control strategies is by aiding the parent in instructing the child. The so-called turtle technique (Schneider & Robin, 1976) assists younger children in gaining control over impulsive, aggressive, and disruptive behaviors and teaches them to slow down, "pull into their shell," calm down, and think of their behavioral goal. This strategy encourages the child to think before he or she acts.

4. *Disciplinary strategies.* For families in which parental authority has been undermined, it becomes important to assist parents in gaining control through consistent and effective disciplinary methods. Many Level II parents have relied on spanking, lecturing, or grounding to punish children for their misbehavior. These punishments are typically ineffective, particularly if the parents' authority is not secure or respected. By emphasizing modeling, direct instruction, and rehearsal to develop effective discipline, parents can be instructed in the development of strategies that allow the child to fully experience the consequences of his or her misbehavior. The following disciplinary strategies are often recommended:

Time-out. Time-out is useful for general child noncompliance or defiance or when immediate cessation of the behavior is important. Short-term time-out is most effective with children younger than age 10 and requires the parent to send the child to a nonreinforcing environment for a specified length of time to cool off and gain self-control.

Premack principle. Often referred to as "Grandma's law," the Premack principle requires the child to complete a desired or expected activity before doing something he or she prefers to do. A form of contract, this strategy is often misused and reversed and therefore rendered ineffective. For example, the child must eat his or her vegetables before he or she has dessert; this is an appropriate contract. However, because the child is whining or yelling, many parents will allow the child to eat the dessert to make him or her quiet. Typically, the child will continue to refuse to eat his or her vegetables. In essence, the child has won the battle.

Natural and logical consequences. Particularly useful with irresponsible children, natural and logical consequences allow children to experience the consequences of their behavior; thus, children learn which behaviors have negative costs and which provide positive rewards.

Assigning extra chores. Effectively used with older children and adolescents, extra chores are assigned for children who lie, damage property, or steal. The child should be assigned to do one hour of work for each transgression. It is important that the chore be something that would not disrupt other family functions if not completed (e.g., cooking dinner). Additionally, the child is restricted from the telephone, friends, food, and fun until the work is completed. In instances of property damage or stealing, the child should also be expected to pay restitution.

Loss of privileges. To be effective, the loss of a privilege must involve something the child values. For instance, telling the child that he or she cannot use the car on the weekend when he or she does not have a driver's license will not be effective. Also, parents must not go overboard. If the child loses a privilege for too long, he or she will soon find a replacement of equal or greater value, and the suspended privilege will lose its effectiveness. Loss of privileges is often effective when other disciplinary strategies have been unsuccessful.

Communication Skills Training. Healthy and functional family communication begins with ensuring that the message that is intended to be sent is the message that is being heard. Uruk, Sayger, and Cogdal (2007) found a strong relationship between family cohesion and flexibility, trauma symptomology, and psychological well-being. This finding suggests that family members must be specific and brief and utilize "I" messages instead of "you" messages if they hope to increase the effectiveness of their communication and become happier and psychologically healthier.

Effective communication involves the following:

1. *Speaking your piece.* Individuals in the family must express their desires and opinions instead of relying on others to read their minds.
2. *Finding out what others are thinking.* Many individuals make the mistake of believing they know what other family members are thinking. To be sure, family members must ask others what they are thinking.
3. *Showing others that they are being heard.* Maintaining good eye contact and otherwise indicating interest and trying to understand what others are saying will communicate concern and commitment to clear communication.
4. *Asking questions when confused.* If family members do not understand what other members are trying to communicate, they should ask for clarification.
5. *Stopping and letting others know when communication is breaking down.* During arguments, many things that are said in haste and anger may cause others to feel hurt or angry in return. It is best to stop the interaction before it progresses to this stage and to wait until a more calm and rational discussion can occur.

Other behaviors can derail communication and should be avoided. Such behaviors as criticizing, blaming, denying, being defensive, mind reading, sidetracking, and giving up only lead to the demise of effective communication.

Problem-Solving Skills Training.   Most families at Level II are relatively unskilled problem solvers in many aspects of their lives. To overcome these deficiencies, intervention will lead family members through problem-solving exercises designed specifically to address their unique problems. Basic to problem-solving skills training is the act of brainstorming alternative solutions for specific problems. An approach that seems particularly useful with Level II families is to ask these questions:

1. What is your goal? What would you like to see happen?
2. What are you doing to achieve this goal?
3. Is what you are doing helping you to achieve this goal?
4. If not, what are you going to do differently?

At first, most families will require a great deal of assistance to generate positive alternatives to their current behavior. However, through modeling this four-step process, the family will soon be able to generate many alternative solutions. The task for the practitioner then becomes helping the family evaluate the potential consequences of each solution and selecting and implementing the alternative deemed most satisfactory in resolving the problem.

Evaluation of Effectiveness

A number of researchers (Sayger et al., 1988, 1993; Smith, Sayger, & Szykula, 1999; Szykula et al., 1987) have measured the effectiveness of social learning family interventions in a variety of settings with children with behavior disorders and their families. The results have been impressive, with significant decreases in negative child behaviors and corresponding increases in positive child behaviors both at home and in school. Sayger et al. (1988) also report that these behavioral changes were maintained after a 9- to 12-month follow-up. In a comparison of strategic and behavioral family therapies in an outpatient child psychiatric facility, Szykula et al. (1987) report that 100 percent of the families participating in social learning family intervention demonstrated gains toward their treatment attainment goals, whereas 67 percent of those in the strategic family therapy group made gains toward treatment goals.

In a study of the impact of social learning family treatment for child conduct problems on the level of marital satisfaction of parents, Sayger et al. (1993) note that those parents reporting low marital satisfaction prior to treatment reported scores in the maritally satisfied range after treatment. Sayger, Szykula, and Sudweeks (1992) found that parents participating in social learning family interventions reported significantly more positive than negative side effects of their participation in treatment. These studies suggest that consumer satisfaction ratings show that family treatments are both efficacious and effective in the positive treatment of many aspects of poorly functioning families with problems ranging from marital conflict to child behavior problems.

Application to Families on Levels I, III, and IV

Social learning family treatment offers a structured approach to dealing with a variety of family concerns. As such, it can be effectively employed with families at all levels of functioning.

Families functioning at Level I can benefit from the positive focus on structure, organization, and problem solving. Even with families at levels higher than Level I, instances may occur in which their safety and security are challenged through unemployment, death, divorce, or other life events. The need to define and develop a new family structure and organization can become a focus in treatment.

Families at Level III can benefit from the focus on establishing clear boundaries and communication skills building. Level IV families can benefit as they develop self-knowledge and awareness regarding their behavior patterns, goals for the future, and general understanding of family systems and structures.

Ethical Challenges

Social learning family therapy has a strong research- and evidence-based background that demonstrates considerable effectiveness, particularly when working with families that have skills deficits (i.e., those who do not have adequate skills for the family work that needs to occur). A challenge for the practitioner, however, is to determine whether the skills are lacking because of lack of knowledge, lack of valuing of the skills, or other reasons, such as being incompatible with the cultural norms of the family being seen.

Social learning family therapy has an implied value of how families should function and approaches family deficits as just that: *deficits.* In some cultural groups, the specific approaches used in social learning therapy are not valued or endorsed; rather, they are seen as being white or middle class or incompatible in other ways.

Social learning family therapy is often seen as easy because it has, to some extent, been "manualized" (i.e., described in manuals). Social learning is, at times, seen as something anyone can do because the manual gives directions. And so, the ones who carry out the therapy are often poorly trained, particularly in the important clinical skills necessary to be effective with families in need of support and therapy.

Social learning family therapy is often seen as a first step (as in "Let's try to teach them some basic family skills and see if that works") rather than an attempt to understand the dynamics of the family and how systemic issues may continue the dysfunctional interactions among family members. Social learning family therapy may be effective with first-order changes (behavioral) in the family using this approach, but to accomplish second-order changes (rules/systemic), the family dynamics must be incorporated into the process.

Summary

Social learning family interventions with Level II families focus on learning more effective social skills. People learn in social settings, with the family being the primary such setting. Through live and vicarious modeling, family members learn to interact in more positive and constructive ways. The goal is to replace the "Nastiness begets nastiness" approach with that of "You attract more bees with honey than with vinegar." People seek the maximum pleasure and least pain that they can experience in life, and as a result, they often use aversive methods of interacting to obtain the greatest payoffs. Frequently, this tendency results in an environment focusing on aversive interactions, the abuse of family members, and a lack of family (community) happiness because individual desires at times take precedence over the best interests of the group.

Social learning family interventions present a relearning opportunity, helping family members learn to interact with one another in more pleasant, affirming, and respectful ways. Two primary contributions are (1) teaching family members how to interact in positive rather than aversive ways by showing respect and dignity for all members of the family and (2) providing structure and organization that brings order to chaos, predictability to uncertainty, and trust rather than fear.

Although this approach is not proposed as the only intervention for all families, it has been demonstrated to be highly effective for assisting families experiencing considerable chaos, with clinicians using aversion to control family members. When families are functioning with inadequate or inappropriate social skills, social learning family interventions facilitate the learning of more adaptive and fulfilling ways of living together.

Discussion Questions

1. Identify the particular population that the social learning family intervention model has been used with the most. Why has this population been targeted? What about the social learning family intervention model is particularly well suited to working with this population?

2. The authors provide evidence substantiating the efficacy of social learning family intervention. Describe why behavioral research methods have been especially applicable to this model of intervention, and discuss whether the information is useful for the clinical practitioner.

3. It often appears that clinicians' adherence to particular models is guided more by intuition and feel than by research. Family treatment adheres to a research model for evaluating the development and application of principles. Discuss why social learning family treatment makes use of this research model, whereas many other models do not.

4. The authors note that the social learning family treatment model is not necessarily the only or the best intervention to use. Describe guidelines that could assist you in deciding whether the social learning family treatment model is applicable to a given case.

5. The authors address the softer clinical skills necessary to be effective with families. Discuss the importance of relationship skills to a program that is predominantly technique and intervention oriented.

6. Explain from an ethical/professional position how you can justify using or not using a model that is less appealing but more efficacious.

7. Identify the aspects of treatment that seem to be key for families at Level II.

Internet Resources

http://umdrive.memphis.edu/tvsayger/public/LIFECardiff.ppt

Suggested Readings

Goldstein, A., & Huff, C. (1993). *The gang intervention handbook.* Champaign, IL: Research Press.
This handbook describes interventions useful for addressing gang problems, including two chapters describing family interventions.

Horne, A., & Sayger, T. V. (2000). Social learning family therapy. In A. Horne (Ed.), *Family counseling and therapy* (3rd ed.). Itasca, IL: Peacock.
This text presents an overview of models and theories of family therapy intervention. The chapter on social learning family therapy includes a historical foundation for the model and reviews the research supporting the model. The chapter also describes applications to marriage work.

McDonald, L., & Sayger, T. V. (1998). Impact of a family and school-based prevention program on protective factors for high-risk youth. In J. Valentine, J. A. DeJong, and N. J. Kennedy (Eds.), *Substance abuse prevention in multicultural communities* (pp. 61–85). New York: Haworth Press.
Presents research results from a drug abuse prevention program.

Sayger, T. V., & Heid, K. O. (1991). Counseling the impoverished rural client: Issues for family therapists. *The Psychotherapy Patient, 7,* 161–168.
Discusses the problems facing family therapists when working with the rural poor and possible strategies for family intervention.

Sayger, T. V., Szykula, S. A., & Laylander, J. A. (1991). Adolescent-focused family counseling: A comparison of behavioral and strategic approaches. *Journal of Family Psychotherapy, 2,* 57–79.
This article presents a hypothetical case and discusses the application of social learning and strategic family therapy in addressing the family issues.

References

Fleischman, M., Horne, A., & Arthur, J. (1983). *Troubled families: A treatment program.* Champaign, IL: Research Press.

Horne, A., Glaser, B., & Calhoun, G. (1998). Conduct disorders. In R. Ammerman, C. G. Last, & M. Hersen (Eds.), *Handbook of prescriptive treatments for children and adolescents* (2nd ed.). New York: Pergamon Press.

Horne, A. M., & Sayger, T. V. (1990). *Treating conduct and oppositional defiant disorders in children.* Elmsford, NY: Pergamon Press.

Horne, A., & Sayger, T. V. (2000). Social learning family therapy. In A. Horne (Ed.), *Family counseling and therapy* (3rd ed.). Itasca, IL: Peacock.

Morris, P. W., Horne, A. M., Jessell, J. C., Passmore, J. L., Walker, J. M., & Sayger, T. V. (1988). Behavioral and cognitive characteristics of fathers of aggressive and well-behaved boys. *Journal of Cognitive Psychotherapy: An International Quarterly, 2,* 251–265.

Sayger, T. V., Horne, A. M., & Glaser, B. A. (1993). Marital satisfaction and social learning family therapy for child conduct problems: Generalization of treatment effects. *Journal of Marital and Family Therapy, 19,* 393–402.

Sayger, T. V., Horne, A. M., Walker, J. M., & Passmore, J. L. (1988). Social learning family therapy with aggressive children: Treatment outcome and maintenance. *Journal of Family Psychology, 1,* 261–285.

Sayger, T. V., Szykula, S. A., & Sudweeks, C. (1992). Treatment side effects: Positive and negative attributes of child-focused family therapy. *Child and Family Behavior Therapy, 14,* 1–9.

Schneider, M., & Robin, A. (1976). The turtle technique: A method for the self control of impulsive behavior. In J. Krumboltz & C. Thoreson (Eds.), *Counseling methods.* New York: Holt, Rinehart & Winston.

Smith, W. J., Sayger, T. V., & Szykula, S. A. (1999). Child-focused family therapy: Behavioural family therapy versus brief family therapy. *Australian and New Zealand Journal of Family Therapy, 20,* 83–88.

Szykula, S. A., Sayger, T. V., Morris, S. B., & Sudweeks, C. (1987). Child-focused behavior and strategic therapies: Outcome comparisons. *Psychotherapy: Theory, Research, Practice and Training, 24*(3S), 546–551.

Tolan, P. H., & Guerra, N. G. (1994). *What works in reducing adolescent violence: An empirical review of the field.* Boulder: Center for the Study and Prevention of Violence, University of Colorado.

Uruk, A. Ç., Sayger, T. V., & Cogdal, P. A. (2007). Examining the influence of family cohesion and adaptability on trauma symptoms and psychological well-being. *Journal of College Student Psychotherapy, 22,* 51–64.

IV

Third Level of Family Need: Boundaries and Control

Families with needs on Level III have their basic survival needs met and have achieved some success in dealing with the issues of family structure, limits, and safety. They have a structure and style that usually works for them. As a result, they are able to focus on more specific needs, such as setting clear and appropriate boundaries and control. In the "house" analogy for Level III, the primary focus is on the inner architecture, because the presence of the outer structure and basement are assumed.

In Chapter 9, Koob discusses solution-focused interventions, one of the brief intervention approaches appropriate for families at this level of need. The emphasis on health and strengths in this approach make it an especially useful model for families functioning at Level III.

The second intervention approach for such families is presented by Walsh in Chapter 10. Family systems interventions draw heavily on Murray Bowen's family theory, which is an intergenerational approach. This theory shows how emotional ties within families of origin influence the lives of individuals in many crucial ways. This approach has been widely used internationally.

9

Solution-Focused Family Interventions

Jeffrey J. Koob, Ph.D.

Solution-focused brief therapy (SFBT) is, as the name implies, a postmodern intervention that focuses on solutions rather than problems. For example, if a child frowns, one could focus on the child's not frowning (problem focused), or one could focus on the child's smiling (solution focused). If the child smiles more, then by definition he or she frowns less. To obtain this dynamic interplay, however, certain assumptions must be made (de Shazer, 1985, 1988, 1994, 1997; de Shazer et al., 1986; O'Hanlon & Weiner-Davis, 1989).

Assumptions

Solution-focused brief therapy is based on the following assumptions:

1. *The family is the expert.* Unlike problem-focused therapies, in which the therapist is viewed as the expert, SFBT therapists believe that families have the knowledge, resources, and strengths to find their own solutions. The therapist is there to help guide them toward those solutions. In other words, the therapist is the expert in knowing the therapeutic techniques, but the family is the expert in defining their solution. In addition, because the therapist is not constructing the solution from his or her own cultural perspective, SFBT is sensitive to families' cultural identification, thus allowing cultural differences to help shape the solution.

2. *Problems and solutions are not connected.* If one can accept this assumption, then issues of diagnosis and assessment become moot (although not to managed care). SFBT maintains that, at one time, a problem emerged due to an antecedent. It is unnecessary, however, to discover that antecedent or to help the client gain insight surrounding the antecedent. Rather, the therapist can determine what the clients would prefer to be doing instead of continuing the problem, and that exception becomes the solution. It is, in fact,

unnecessary for the therapist to know the presenting problem; it is necessary, however, for him or her to ask what the clients would prefer to be experiencing instead of the problem.

3. *Make unsolvable problems solvable.* The clients present the therapist with what are, in their view, unsolvable problems. The therapist's task, therefore, is to redefine or reframe the problems into solvable terms. Take, for example, a client who says, "I cannot be happy, because I am a depressed person." Now suppose that the therapist asks, "Are there times when you are less depressed?" This represents a slight change in the definition, and this definition, unlike the client's, is amenable to change.

4. *Change is constant and inevitable.* This assumption questions the idea of a system struggling to maintain homeostasis. From this view, problems can be seen not only as necessary for change but as part of the change process. The notion is not to eliminate a problem so the system can go back to a steady state; rather, it is to define the problem as part of the change process. Doing so allows the system to become unstuck within the change process (problem) and prompts the system to complete the present change (solution). In other words, "Your child frowns because he or she is sad" (problem) becomes "Your child frowns as a means of communicating with you" (new definition). "How would you like your child to communicate with you?" (client as expert). "I would like my child to smile more" (solution).

5. *Only a small change is needed.* De Shazer (personal communication, September 15, 1985) uses the analogy of a person walking in the desert. He says that if the person makes a one-degree angle to the right, it will not seem like much at first, but as time passes, the walker will end up miles away from the original destination. This implies that the therapist needs only to affect a small change in the system, not solve each problem individually or even attack the most serious problem, and that small change over time will snowball into dramatic changes.

6. *Keep it brief.* Due to the focus on solutions rather than problems, the time spent in assessment, clinical diagnosis, and facilitating insight are frequently bypassed. Rather, with an emphasis on how a client would like life to be, the interaction becomes positive, motivating, and future oriented. This shift, however, from problem talk to solution talk must follow the client's lead, an issue that will be dealt with later in this chapter.

7. *Stay in the future.* The more the therapist keeps the focus on the future, the more effectively therapy will proceed. Insights, feelings, and past history are not areas SFBT therapists encourage clients to explore. In general, these are viewed as areas that make clients feel worse and deflated. Instead, the focus is toward the future: "How would you like your life to be different? When this change happens, what will your family be saying about you?" The challenge is that most therapists were taught how to assess the past, so assessing the future can be difficult. Asking questions that begin with w*ho, what, when, where,* and *how* is a good start.

8. *Focus on perceptions.* Perceptions are the culmination of feelings, thoughts, and behaviors. Asking about the miracle, coping, exceptions, and other SFBT questions helps clients keep their focus on their perceptions. Asking about feelings, however, tells clients that the therapist believes that their feelings are the important issue here, irrespective of thoughts and behaviors. Focusing on problems tells clients that they should come to therapy and have problems to discuss, because that is what the therapist has suggested to them is important.

Typical Needs of Level III Families

Level III families tend to have "a structure and a style that is often perceived as working" (Weltner, 1985, p. 46). The analogy for this level is the inner architecture of the "house." When one is working with the inner structure, the presence of the outer structure is assumed. In Level III families, it is assumed that "there is sufficient strength and health to allow for resolution" (p. 47). This assumption is congruent with the use of a solution-focused approach to family treatment (Cleveland & Lindsey, 1999).

Assessment

Consider the following case study (based on Berg, 1995):

A mother, daughter, and father present at an SFBT clinic. The clinician asks what prompted them to make an appointment. The mother explains rather emphatically that her daughter (who appears to the therapist as being in junior high) "needs to be in school." The mother further asserts that if it were not for her daughter's boyfriend, her daughter would be in school. She concludes that her daughter "needs to be bad, because her boyfriend is bad." Rhetorically, the mother asks, "Where has my little girl gone, and who is this stranger now living in the house?" The father and daughter sit quietly. The therapist agrees that it is difficult for mothers to lose their "little girls."

The daughter explains, "I know I should be in school." The therapist shows surprise and gives some praise to the daughter for knowing the importance of education: "Wow, how do you know this? Most children your age don't know this. Mom, did you know your daughter knew this?" The daughter further explains that perhaps if her mother were not so confrontational, she would feel less stressed and then be more comfortable about attending school.

The father diplomatically summarizes the interaction: "If our daughter attended school, perhaps my wife would be less confrontational. If my wife were less confrontational, perhaps our daughter would attend school." The mother and daughter sit quietly.

The therapist asks about exceptions to the rule—times when the daughter does manage to get to school, times when the mother and daughter have a non-confrontational conversation. Both mother and daughter agree that their relationship was nonconfrontational prior to the boyfriend. The daughter contends that she is able to get to school when there is a test. The therapist shows surprise, gives praise that she is able to do this, and asks the daughter to elaborate further.

Finally, the therapist asks each of them what is known as the miracle question—namely, "When you go to sleep tonight, imagine that a miracle happens, but because you are sleeping, you are not aware of it. The miracle is that when you wake up, you will no longer have the problem that brought you to therapy. Upon awaking, what will be the first sign to you that a miracle has happened?" For the mother, it is her daughter going to school and having meaningful conversations with her; for the daughter, it is hearing laughter in the house and everyone talking to one another in a tension-free environment; and for the father, it is getting a job. (He is currently unemployed and, to the therapist, looks depressed.) The therapist then asks each person to rate on a scale from 1 to 10 how close he or she is to achieving that miracle, with 10 representing the miracle.

The therapist takes a consulting break and returns to the family with a list of compliments, normalizations, reframes, and a task. The task is that each of them is to choose a special day to pretend that he or she has achieved his or her miracle. It will be the task of the other two to guess which day was the special day for each person.

Theory Base and Basic Tenets

Beyond Milton Erickson

SFBT, similar to strategic (Haley, 1976), structural (Minuchin, 1974), and communication therapies (Satir, 1964), derives its roots from the teachings of Milton Erickson (Short, 2001). All of these therapies have in common the use of joining, normalization, reframing, paradox, systems focus, nonpathologizing, a focus on small change, and a small number of sessions. SFBT, however, differs from these other therapies in two major aspects.

The first difference relates to the roles of the client and therapist. In these other therapies, the therapist is the expert who directs the clients toward resolution of a problem. In SFBT, however, the clients are viewed as the experts, and the therapist assists them in constructing the solution (de Shazer 1985, 1988; O'Hanlon & Weiner-Davis, 1989; Walter & Pellar, 1992). In other words, the clients possess all of the building materials (strengths), and the therapist first helps them decide what they want to build (solution) and then helps them to build it. De Shazer (personal communication, September 15, 1985) explains that practitioners can follow in the footsteps of Milton Erickson or stand on his shoulders and see what lies beyond. In other words, practitioners can improve on what Erickson started.

This notion of improvement lends a dynamic structure to SFBT. A group of students once asked de Shazer what they should read to prepare to learn SFBT. De Shazer said, "Read what I have yet to write" (personal communication, September 15, 1985). The best the student or practitioner can do, however, is to read what De Shazer has written recently. As an illustration, if one were to read de Shazer's earlier works (1985), in which he discusses skeleton keys, where one key (solution) can fit many different locks (problems), he or she would find that they are not entirely consistent with his later works. De Shazer's (1997) more current idea—that problems and solutions are not related—may make the use of the key obsolete. In other words, SFBT is a continuously evolving treatment method in which some earlier tenets can later become obsolete.

Miracle Question Is the Heart

A tenet not likely to become obsolete is the use of the *miracle question*. It could be said that the miracle question is the heart of SFBT. Remember the question: "When you go to sleep tonight, imagine that a miracle happens, but because you are sleeping, you are not aware of it. The miracle is that when you wake up, you will no longer have the problem that brought you to therapy. Upon awaking, what will be the first sign to you that a miracle has happened?"

The miracle question has strong theoretical underpinnings in the works of Polak (1973), Toffler (1974), and Frankl (1963). These researchers conclude that when people have a positive vision of their future, they will succeed, and when they do not have a vision, they will fail.

Polak (1973) set out to discover why some nations survive and others perish. He found that this had no relationship to the country's size, wealth, strategic location, or natural resources. Nations that had a powerful vision of their future (for example, as stated in a document such as the United States' Constitution and Declaration of Independence and Great Britain's Magna Carta) survived; those that did not perished.

Toffler's (1974) writings inspired teachers to discover which students excelled in life and which students failed. Teachers found that having a high grade-point average (GPA) and high scores on standardized tests and being brought up in an advantaged family (e.g., with wealth, education, resources) were not keys to students' success. Rather, success was linked to students' having a positive vision of the future (strong goals for what they wanted to accomplish in their lives).

Finally, Frankl (1963) found that the prisoners who survived the World War II concentration camp experience were not the youngest and the healthiest. Rather, the survivors were those individuals who had something important yet to accomplish in their lives. They had a positive vision of the future.

The purpose of the miracle question in SFBT is for the clients, with the help of the therapist, to build a positive vision of their future. That future is one in which the presenting problems do not exist and in which the clients would derive additional positive experiences not present in their current lives. This positive vision of the future, therefore, becomes the motivating factor for clients to improve their lives.

"The Cup Is Half Full"

When clients come to the therapist with problems, those problems have become the major foci of their lives. The clients have, for all intents and purposes, stopped focusing on any positive experiences in their lives.

SFBT therapists believe that a cup that is half empty is a cup that is half full. The clients have been focusing on the empty part; it is the work of the therapist to refocus their attention on the full part. Take for example the coping question "Given all of these difficulties in your life, how are you able to cope?" This changes the focus from problem talk to solution talk (i.e., the positives in their lives). The formula first-session task from the case assessment is also an example of refocusing the client toward the positives (de Shazer & Molnar, 1984).

Language Constructs Reality

SFBT places a great deal of significance on the use of language. Sentences are constructed in such a way as to create an alternative future—for example, "When the problem is solved, what will you be doing differently?" *When* is used instead of *If* to suggest a positive future to the client.

This use of language is consistent with Milton Erickson's (Short, 2001) use of hypnotherapy. However, de Shazer contends that this same suggestive state can be reached through the proper choice of words, rather than through formal induction. In fact, de Shazer (1994) wrote a book entitled *Words Were Originally Magic,* in which he described how the German philosopher Ludwig Wittgenstein (1974) unraveled Bertrand Russell's (1959) problems of philosophy (i.e., we can know nothing for sure) by focusing on words when used in context (which creates meaning) and words when used out of context (which creates problems), with context being the key. In other words, Russell's asking how we can know anything for sure takes the word *know* out of the context in which it is normally used. Wittgenstein argues that Russell makes the question unanswerable. Wittgenstein's asking if we know our name uses the word *know* in context and makes the question answerable. Consider this example:

> *Therapist:*   How do things need to change to make you happy?
>
> *Client:*   I can never be happy, because I am a *depressed person.*
>
> *Therapist:*   Then what needs to happen to make you *less depressed?*

Treatment Goals

In an ideal SFBT setting, the therapist meets with the family in front of a two-way mirror. The family signs consent forms, agreeing to be videotaped and observed by a two-member consulting team on the other side of the mirror. In the room is a telephone that can be used by the team to call the therapist with questions to ask the family. In addition, the family is informed that after approximately 45 minutes, the therapist will leave the room, consult with the team, and return with some recommendations.

To illustrate a classical SFBT treatment process, a prototype can be illustrated in three sessions.

Session 1

In Session 1, the therapist must find the clients' way of cooperating with him or her. Because motivation and other client characteristics constitute 40 percent of why they get better (Garfield, 1994), it is worth the small effort. In other words, the clients either made an appointment to see the therapist, which tends to suggest cooperation, or someone sent them to see the therapist, which tends to suggest cooperation.

In the latter case, it may seem otherwise, but if the clients are sitting in front of the therapist, they are cooperating with someone. If someone else sent them (e.g., court, teacher, parent), it just means the therapist must ask relationship questions until he or she discovers the clients' way of cooperating—for example, "What has to happen to convince the court that you no longer need to see me?" Eventually, the therapist should be able to ask the clients, "What has to happen here today to convince you that it was a good idea to see me?" When the client made an appointment to see the therapist, in fact, this was the first question asked. It is designed to elicit preliminary goals.

Depending on the goal, the interview can take different directions initially. For example, in a crisis, coping questions should be used: "How do you cope? How did you get out of bed this morning?" What the therapist should experience is the clients talking about their strengths. If marital or relationship issues have brought the clients to therapy, relationship questions should be asked: "What would your spouse say? When you are happy, how is your spouse different?" What the therapist will notice is that the clients keep their focus on the relationship, rather than their individual differences. When the first session is going well, much of the focus will be on the miracle. The therapist encourages the family to expound on the miracle—for example, "After the miracle happens, what will you notice first? What will you notice next? What will your spouse notice?"

Once the miracle question has been elaborated, the therapist asks if even a small piece of this miracle has already happened. The scaling question can then be used to gauge how close the clients are to achieving their miracle. If the clients say they are at a 5, the therapist expresses praise in that they are halfway there. Next, the therapist asks what has to happen for them to move from a 5 to a 6. If the clients say that is too far a move, the therapist asks about moving from a 5 to a 5.1.

Finally, the therapist takes a consulting break, whether he or she has a team behind the two-way mirror or not, and then comes back with a prescription (recommendation). The therapist starts with compliments, normalizations, and reframes. The formula first-session task can then be prescribed: "When people enter therapy, they begin to change. There are things in your life, however, that you do not want to change because they are positive. So, between now and the next time we meet, pay attention to those positive things in your life, and we will discuss them next week." (For more customized prescriptions, see DeJong and Berg [2008].)

Session 2

The therapist begins by asking "What's better?" (elicit). When the clients mention positive changes, the therapist amplifies (encourages the clients to elaborate) these changes. For example, if the clients say they went to a movie, the therapist asks, "Is this a new behavior? How do you explain it? How were you able to do it? How can you continue to keep it happening?" If the clients say nothing is positive and puzzled prompting does not help ("Nothing!?" "Are you sure!?"), the therapist meticulously unravels every detail of the family's activities that occurred since leaving the therapist's office the week before. Positive changes will surface. These changes are reinforced by the therapist through compliments (reinforce), and then the process starts over again with "What else is better?" until all changes have been exhausted. This technique is referred to as EARS (**e**licit, **a**mplify, **r**einforce, **s**tart over).

Assuming that this session focuses primarily on positive changes, the therapist again asks the scaling question, comparing it to last week's. The rating usually goes up; at the worst, it stays the same. If it happens to go down, the therapist should ask "What did you do to keep it from going further down?"

Finally, the therapist takes a consulting break. When he or she returns, the clients are again given compliments, normalizations, and reframes. The formula second-session task can then be prescribed: "Progress is often two steps forward and one step back. If you find yourself taking a step back this week, pay attention to what you do to keep moving forward again."

Session 3

The therapist begins by using the EARS protocol. Namely, he or she asks "What's better?" (eliciting), followed by as many questions as possible about the change (amplifying), complimenting their progress (reinforcing), and asking "What else is better?"(start over). Using the formula second-session task, if the clients took steps back, the therapist asks "What did you do to move forward again? How were you able to do this? It must have been difficult, but somehow you were able to do it. How will you continue to do this in the future?" In this fashion, the therapist continues to address all of the steps back, one step at a time.

For issues where steps back were not taken or if no steps back were taken, the therapist asks the clients how they were able not to take a step back. It may be possible to close the case at this time or at least extend the time of the next visit.

Epilogue

As a final note, this is a prototypical treatment process. If clients do not feel bad about what is happening in their lives, it is doubtful that they will be in therapy. If the therapist is not sensitive and empathetic to the clients' feelings, the clients will not return. Although SFBT therapists do not encourage problem talk ("Tell me more about how the problem is interfering with your life") and elaboration of feelings ("Tell me more about how that made you feel"), it is a serious mistake to move from problem talk to solution talk until the clients are ready. If these are feelings clients have never expressed or stories they have never told, SFBT does not move to solution talk until they are ready. These issues are probably the most common reasons for a necessary and appropriate increase in the number of sessions.

Application

Using this prototypical treatment process, the process can be customized for the previous family case study.

Session 1

In recalling the family case assessment, the therapist asks "How old is the daughter? What grade is she in at school? How many days a week does she miss school? How long have the parents been married? How long has the father been unemployed?" Some might argue that for a family case assessment, the SFBT therapist missed a lot of critical information. However, if the family is the expert, how does it help them if the therapist asks questions to which they already know the answers? In addition, because problems and solutions are not connected, why ask for information that is not relevant to the solution? These last two questions are consistent with an assessment by an SFBT therapist.

After the mother has explained the situation, the daughter agrees that she should be in school. Because this solution was introduced by the mother, the therapist encourages the daughter to discuss this further. In addition, the therapist wants the mother to hear why the daughter thinks she should be in school and the fact that the mother and daughter agree. Already, the family has introduced some material that will become compliments during the recommendation or prescription segment. First, both the mother and the daughter agree on something. Second, the daughter is smart enough to realize that school is important. Third, the parents have raised an intelligent daughter.

When the father is asked for his perspective, he is able to briefly summarize the situation between the mother and the daughter. His awareness and diplomacy will also be material for compliments during the prescription segment.

Next, the therapist asks about exceptions to the rule—times in the past or in the present when these problems did not exist or were easily solved. This discussion provides a source of solutions. It may be discovered that the family had solutions in the past but has forgotten them. Because the family is the expert, the therapist is using the resources of the family. In addition, exceptions to the rule tell the family how the circumstances need to be different for the solution to emerge (e.g., the daughter goes to school when she has a test). The daughter's ability to understand the importance of taking tests can also lead to a compliment during the prescription segment.

Because the family members are able to talk about the positives in their lives and to voice positive things about one another, the therapist can introduce the miracle question. If the members reject the question ("Miracles don't happen" or "I cannot think of anything"), then it may be that the question was asked too soon. The therapist needs to continue with problem talk. Another explanation is that the clients do not entertain the possibility of miracles. In that case, the therapist can ask, "If you were very lucky . . ." or "If you won the lottery . . ." for example. Generally, the clients' mood state is perhaps the best indicator of when it is time to ask the miracle question.

In this case study, the family members are able to elaborate their miracle. If there are similarities in their miracles (the daughter's hearing laughter), this becomes a possible compliment for the prescription section.

To determine how close family members are to achieving their miracle, a scaling question is asked. If a family member says the family is at a 5, then the therapist expresses praise in that they are halfway there. (Every number can be defined in a positive way.) Even at a 1, the clients can be told that they are on track toward their miracle or that they are in the game. (There are techniques for never getting a 1 as a response.) Next, the therapist asks what has to happen for the family to move from a 5 to a 6. If they say that is too far a move, the therapist asks about moving from a 5 to a 5.1.

In the case assessment, the mother says she is at a 5, so the therapist expresses encouragement that the mother is halfway to her miracle. The daughter is at a 6, so the therapist expresses encouragement that she is over halfway there. The father is at a 5, so he is also encouraged. All of these rankings, of course, provide further material for the prescription section.

Finally, the therapist takes a consulting break, meets with the team to write a prescription, and then returns to the family to administer the prescription. This break is consistent with the suggestive state achieved in Ericksonian hypnotherapy. When the therapist leaves the room, the family is wondering what the therapist and consulting team will have to say on their return. De Shazer (1985) believes that this puts the family in a susceptible state, thus making them more receptive to the prescription. Keeping in mind the case study, the prescription may sound like what follows (except that the clients' names would be used).

End-of-Session Feedback

Here is feedback that the therapist could give each family member, the parents together, and the family as a whole:

"Mother, the team agrees with you that it is difficult for a parent to see a daughter grow up and wonder where her little girl has gone. A child who was once easy to talk with becomes a daughter who now seems like a stranger. This must be very hard for you. The team is impressed with your hard effort and dedication to deal with this situation."

"Daughter, the team sees your difficulty in juggling school, family responsibilities, and a social life. It seems early for someone your age to try to do this on your own, but given how bright you are and your potential, we can see why you are trying. It seems that you must have inherited your hard effort and dedication from your mother."

"Father, your diplomatic way of looking at the situation between your wife and daughter is impressive. You manage to stay neutral, and by doing so, you may become the diplomat between your wife and daughter."

"Parents, the team congratulates you on raising such an intelligent daughter. She is aware of the importance of school. Few children her age are intelligent enough to understand how important school is to their future."

"All of you have formed miracles that consider not only your own happiness but also the happiness of the other family members. Mother, your daughter's going to school; daughter, hearing laughter in the house; father, obtaining a job. All of these situations bring happiness to your family. In addition, all of you are already halfway or more to achieving your miracle. Although achieving miracles is not easy, this family possesses the capacity for hard work and the dedication that are needed to achieve miracles."

"Finally, we want to give each of you a homework assignment. Each of you will choose a special day on which you will pretend that you have moved up your scale 1 point. For Mother and Father, this means you have moved from a 5 to a 6; for Daughter, this means you have moved from a 6 to a 7. You cannot tell the other two what day you have chosen as your special day. It will be the additional task of the other two to guess which day you have chosen as your special day."

Session 2

The therapist enters the room, sits down, and notices that the family members are smiling. The mother is dressed in more relaxed clothing than in the last session (jeans rather than a suit), and the daughter and husband are dressed more neatly (new jeans rather than ripped jeans).

The therapist starts by asking "What's better?" The mother begins by explaining how she got up in the morning, went to the kitchen to make breakfast, and had an enjoyable conversation with her husband and daughter, who in reality were still in bed. When the daughter came home late, the mother made believe that her daughter and daughter's boyfriend were out buying her a gift, and it caused them to be late. When she watched a movie, the mother told her daughter and husband all about it, as if they were interested. The mother said that it was fun. The therapist praised the mother for her creativity. The daughter and father told similar stories, with the father "cracking jokes" and making the mother and daughter laugh (for real, not pretend). Not surprisingly, they were able to identify each family member's special day.

The mother and father went on a date that included dinner and a movie. The daughter smiled, turning to look at both of them, as they told their story. The therapist showed encouragement and asked, "Is that different for the two of you to go on a date? What did you both do to make it happen? How will you continue to keep it happening in the future?" After exhausting all the material regarding the date, the therapist asked, "Are there other positive changes that occurred in the past week?"

The daughter smiles and explains that she has gone to school every day. The therapist gives encouragement and asks, "Wow, how were you able to do that?" The daughter explains that she knows the importance of school.

The father explains that he is willing to take a temporary or part-time job until something better comes along. The therapist gives encouragement and asks, "Is that new for you—your willingness to look for a part-time job until a full-time job comes along?" He states that, yes, it is new for him.

Finally, the therapist asks the family members to remember when they rated how close they were to achieving a miracle on a scale from 1 to 10. The therapist then says to the mother, "Last week you were at a 5—more than halfway to achieving your miracle. Where are you now?" The mother says that she is at a 6. The therapist gives encouragement, asks the father and daughter the same question, and finds that each has moved up his or her scale by 1 point.

Epilogue

The family was complimented and given the formula second-session task, regarding progress being two steps forward and one step back. At session 3, they continued to show improvement (e.g., school attendance, conversations, dates), so a fourth session was scheduled for two weeks later, at which time the therapy ended.

Application to Spirituality

The words *spirituality, morality, ethics,* and *religion* commonly have different definitions, depending on who is using them. In SFBT, these concepts become important to therapy only if they are important to the clients. Because the therapist is attempting to learn the clients' culture, language, and vision of a positive future, he or she learns the clients' view of these concepts only if the clients believe that they are necessary for a positive solution.

As an example, a client with HIV (human immunodeficiency virus, the virus that can lead to AIDS) said, "I am so angry that I am going to f**k everyone at the bar." The client has introduced an ethical, moral, religious, or spiritual issue, depending on his definition. It relates to the "cup half empty" approach. The cup half empty for this client is to use his disease to harm others; the cup half full is to use his disease to help others. The SFBT therapist's response was "And how will this help you?" The client looked puzzled and said, "Well, it won't help me." This nonconfrontational stance tends to puzzle the client, who may have expected the therapist to be confrontational. With nothing to fuel the client's anger, the anger dissipates. Seeing the cup half full and being nonconfrontational, therefore, are ways to deal with spiritual issues.

In a similar case, another client with HIV who was asked by the therapist "And how will this help you?" replied, "I'll feel better." The therapist then asked, "When will you stop feeling better?" (future orientation). The client looked puzzled and said, "When I feel guilty for what I did." The therapist replied, "So what could you do instead—that, instead of making you feel guilty, it *might* make you feel proud? And it would keep you feeling better?" The client said, "Help them not to make the same mistake that I did." *Might* is used as a hedging word to suggest the word *proud* to the client, because the client had not used the word. This approach makes the client more amenable to the suggestion. This future orientation is leading toward the miracle question, in which spiritual issues may play a part in the miracle construction.

Later, both clients spoke of getting involved in social change as a way of helping others affected by HIV and AIDS ("How will this help you?" became "How will this help others?"). The therapist complimented the clients on their evolving sense of social consciousness. One client responded that he had never considered himself *religious* (which he defined as following the teachings of an organized religion) but did consider himself *spiritual* (which he defined as believing there is something greater than humanity). The therapist used this to compliment the client in the delivery of the prescription, stating, "As you find your body becoming less healthy, you will find your mind, on the other hand, becoming more healthy. Or, as you would say, more *spiritual*." (Both the therapist and the client were aware of the effects of the virus on the brain; therefore, the concept of a healthy mind was not misconstrued to mean that the virus would leave the brain.)

This movement from expressing the desire to harm others toward a spiritual desire to help others assisted these clients in finding meaning in their lives. This meaning helped them deal with end-of-life issues.

Interventions

Joining

Joining is basically the therapist's means of establishing rapport with the family. Sometimes, the therapist engages in small talk with the clients before the session begins as a way of breaking down formality and giving an indirect compliment—for example, "People sometimes have difficulty finding us. Did you find our location OK?" or "It is often difficult to park around here. Were you able to find a spot OK?" Using the clients' language (i.e., actual phrases they use) is critical to joining with the family. When the family hears their words, they know you are listening.

An SFBT therapist takes the stance of being nonconfrontational. Therapists may say that they are confused or puzzled by some clients' information that seems inconsistent, but an SFBT therapist never confronts. Finally, discarding the notion that clients resist (de Shazer, 1984) helps the therapist join with the clients. Berg (1995) states that even clients labeled as "involuntary" do not resist therapy. She contends that if they were resisting, they would not be sitting in the therapist's office.

Normalizing

For clients, problems are issues that are not normal. It stands to reason, therefore, that if the therapist can suggest to them that the issue is normal, by definition, then it will cease to be a problem—for example, "How do you know this is rebellious behavior and not just being a teenager?" Rebellious behavior is a problem; acting like a teenager is normal behavior.

Circular Question

People may act based on what they believe others think, rather than on what others are actually thinking. To unravel this mystery, an SFBT therapist might ask a *circular question,* such as "What do you think your mother thinks about your missing school?" Hearing the answer to this question will help the mother see how the daughter believes she views the situation.

In the family case study reviewed earlier, if the daughter were to say that she believes her mother sees her as stupid, this would likely lead to a compliment from the mother regarding the daughter's intelligence. It would also help to clear up misunderstandings. A further level of difficulty would be to ask, "What do you think your mother thinks *you* think about your missing school?" In essence, these types of questions help members understand how and why other family members act in certain ways.

Relationship Question

Perhaps more common and less convoluted than the circular question is the *relationship question,* which is any question that keeps the focus on the relationship. Examples include "When you are happy, how is your mother different?" and "Who in your family will be the first to notice your change?" This type of question includes the clients and someone in or potentially in their environment. It is important to use with dyads and families.

Coping Question

A *coping question* helps the family move from problem talk to solution talk. At a point in the session when it seems that the clients have described all of their problems, this question can be used—basically, "Given all of these problems [list all of them], how are you able to cope?" If the clients are able to mention positive aspects and can sustain this positive direction, then they are becoming ready for the miracle question. If, on the other hand, the clients have little to say or say some positives but keep going back to the problems, then the therapist needs to continue to listen to the problems until the clients are ready. It may be that positives cannot be discussed until the second session. When the therapist gives the task, it should be dirsected toward looking for positives (formula first-session task). This sets the stage for asking the miracle question in session 2. It is often the question of choice when dealing with crises.

Miracle Question

The *miracle question,* as stated earlier, provides the clients with a positive vision of the future. This vision becomes a motivating factor and a description of when therapy has been successful (i.e., when the miracle has been reached or the family agrees they are close enough).

One serious caution regarding the miracle question is that it must deal with the possible, never the improbable. For example, the therapist would not say to an AIDS patient that the miracle is that he or she will no longer have AIDS. Similarly, the therapist would not say to a person in a wheelchair that the miracle is that he or she will be able to walk. Instead, the therapist would say to each of these individuals that the miracle is that he or she will be able to *cope* with AIDS or *cope* with being in a wheelchair. Doing so helps clients establish goals.

Scaling Question

A *scaling question* is used to gauge a baseline and measure progress in a behavior, goal, or construct—essentially, "On a scale from 1 to 10, with 1 being that you are so depressed you can't even leave your house, given that you are at least at a 2 and that 10 would be that you are so happy that you don't need to see me anymore, how would you rate your level of happiness?" This example includes a means of not having the clients say they are at a 1, and it changes the scale to one of happiness, which may not work for all clients (i.e., those who believe they cannot be happy).

If the clients say they are at a 1, you can mention how they are on the track to success or in the game for achieving happiness, for example. At 2, they are almost halfway to being halfway there; at 3, they are halfway to being halfway there; at 4, they are almost halfway there; at 5, they are halfway there; at 6, they are over halfway there; and so forth. Obviously, the therapist can make other comments to represent the numbers. When the clients give a number on the scale, the therapist then asks what has to happen to move up one number. If a whole number is too large a move for the clients, a decimal increase can be used (from a 5 to a 5.1). It will get an answer.

Exceptions to the Rule

This is a team search between the therapist and the clients to discover solutions to a problem that either the clients forgot or never considered using for a different problem—for example, "Was there a time in your life when this problem did not occur? When was the last time the problem did not happen? In the time that the problem has surfaced, has there been a time when you have been able to stop the problem from occurring? Have you had problems in the past that were similar to this problem? How were you able to stop those problems from happening?" This is the one time that an SFBT therapist goes to the clients' past. As such, it is an exception.

Who, What, When, Where, and How Questions

In SFBT, the therapist must learn to ask questions in a different manner. Many questions in SFBT begin with the words *who, what, when, where,* and *how.* If the therapist keeps these questions positive and oriented toward the future, then he or she is likely asking an SFBT question: "Who will be the first to notice your change? What will your friends be saying about you? When you smile, how is your spouse different? Where would you like to be on the scale that would tell you that you no longer need to see me for therapy? How will you know when things are better?"

Hypnotic Situations

Hypnotic situations are those that make the family more susceptible to what the therapist suggests. It was discussed previously how the consultation break serves to make the family more susceptible to the prescription—namely, they are wondering what the team has to say. During the compliment segment of the prescription, the therapist attempts to produce a "yes set." If the family nods and agrees to several compliments in a row, they are more likely to agree to the statement that follows. This may be a statement that the family has struggled to agree on during the session—for example, "Your daughter wants to go to school."

Finally, the therapist may word a sentence in such a way that it comes out as a command rather than a suggestion—for example, "You may find that as you look for exceptions, that you, *Matt, stop overeating,* you will make the right choices for yourself." The italicized words are said as a statement while looking directly at the client. The sentence is clumsy and another sentence follows, so the statement (hypnotic suggestion) is more hidden to the client.

Hedging Words

Berg and DeJong (1996) suggest using hedging words. They contend that using words such as *seems, might,* and *perhaps* plants suggestions in the clients' minds that later grow to fruitful solutions—for example, "It seems that perhaps you might change too fast." Using hedging words also allows the SFBT therapist to drop the suggestion if the clients reject it. This allows the clients to maintain their position as experts and keeps the therapist from creating a milieu of resistance.

Compliments

The therapist should give clients as many compliments as possible. Basically, there are three kinds of compliments:

1. *Direct compliments* are what people commonly use, such as "You are really smart," "You did a great job," and "That is fantastic!"
2. *Indirect compliments* are given in the form of question, such as "How is it that you are so smart?" or involve another person in the clients' life, such as "Your parents must be very proud of you."
3. *Self-compliments* are when clients compliment themselves—for example, "I am really smart."

In general, the strength of the compliment increases as one moves from direct to self.

Tasks

Tasks are the assignments that are suggested at the end of an SFBT session as the final part of the prescription. The first two described here are very generic, and could be used in most situations. They are considered *formula tasks.* The first-session formula task is as follows: "When people enter therapy, they begin to change. There are things in your life, however, that you do not want to change because they are positive. So, between now and the next time we meet, pay attention to those positive things in your life, and we will discuss them next week." Other first-session tasks might include "Do not change anything" and "Do something different."

All of these tasks accept the assumption that the client is the expert and therefore can find a solution to the problem. The traditional task encourages the family to make changes. "Do not change anything" is more vague and suggests that the clients can keep the situation from getting worse and therefore can, at some point, make it better. "Do something different" encourages the family to find a solution. Whatever it is that they do differently may, in fact, resolve the problem.

The second-session formula task is "Progress is often two steps forward and one step back. If you find yourself taking a step back this week, pay attention to what you do to keep moving forward again." Another possibility is "Pay attention to what you do when you overcome the urge to [engage in that behavior]."

Both of these tasks encourage clients to pay close attention to the solution. The first option provides the additional value of normalizing or reframing relapse. If there is a step back, some families disregard any progress made at that point, thinking "It's right back to the way it used to be." By acknowledging that people do take steps back, this is reframed as part of progress and as an acceptable route toward it. Moreover, families sometimes progress quickly, and members worry or express a fear of relapsing. This task helps them.

As a variation on this task, the therapist may suggest that the family take a step back in the next week. This becomes a no-lose situation. If they take a step back, they are following the normal route toward progress; if they do not take a step back, that is certainly positive. Sometimes when a family is asked to take a step back, they will argue with the therapist, adamantly stating that they will not do it. That is certainly a positive sign. Besides the formula tasks, there are two tasks that are more tailored to clients: perception tasks and behavioral tasks. *Perception tasks* are tasks of observation, not action. They typically begin with "Notice" or "Pay attention"—"Notice what you are doing to make things better" or "Pay attention to what else you are doing but have not noticed yet that is making things better." *Behavioral tasks* require the clients not only to notice change but also to do something about it: "Pick a day and pretend that your miracle has happened" or "When she comes to visit, do something different." (When to use these tasks is explained later in the section End-of-Session Feedback.)

The Team

When the therapist has the luxury of working with a team, he or she realizes that they are an invaluable source of intervention material. They may keep track of the clients' pet phrases, possible compliments, and suggestions for tasks. In addition, they can call the therapist when he or she is meeting with a family and offer suggestions for change. Finally, a team can allow the therapist to join with the family against the team—for example, "I agree with you. You should not take a step back. But the team thinks you should." In this way, the team can also parallel the struggles that the family is experiencing regarding the possibility of relapse.

End-of-Session Feedback

Providing feedback at the end of the session is critical to the intervention. When clients first see a SFBT therapist, they are told that after 45 minutes the therapist will leave the room and take about 5 minutes to review what was said (alone or with a team). Different combinations of events result in different feedback. The therapist must first define the type of client. There are three types of clients:

1. A *visitor* is a client who was sent to the therapist by someone else (i.e., court, teacher, parent). If this client remains reluctant by the end of the 45-minute period, the therapist should only compliment him or her (i.e., at least three to five compliments suggested).

2. A *complainant* is a client who is complaining about the behavior of someone else in his or her life and who wants that person to change. This client does not see a role for himself or herself in the change process, however. If he or she continues to complain by the end of the session, the therapist should offer compliments, use a statement to bridge the compliments with the task ("Seeing that your son sometimes behaves the way you want him to . . ."), and give the client a perception task ("When your son behaves the way you want him to, notice what you are doing differently").

3. A *customer* is someone who is motivated to see the therapist. If after 45 minutes, the visitor or complainant becomes motivated, he or she should then be considered a customer. At the end of the session, the therapist should give the customer compliments, a bridging statement, and a task. The tasks will depend on whether the client has clear exceptions to the problem or a clear goal. If he or she does not, then perception tasks are suggested. If the client does have clear examples, then behavioral tasks are suggested.

The pretend task in the preceding End-of-Session Feedback application is a common example of a perception task. It is important to note that tasks should be as general as possible. Clients should be able to individualize a task to their liking. The therapist would not want to say, for example, "The two of you should go out to dinner one night this week." Instead, the therapist could say, "When the two of you do things together, notice how your children are different." Even this task would only be suggested, however, if the clients had mentioned doing things together as a goal or this idea had been uncovered from an exception question.

Evaluation

Gingerich and Eisengart (2000) reviewed all of the controlled outcome studies on SFBT ($N = 15$) through the year 1999. Although all 15 of these studies met the criteria for controlled outcomes, 5 of them were determined to be superior to the other 10 in terms of degree of experimental control. Those 5 studies will be reported here.

Sundstrom (1993) randomly assigned 40 female college students who were suffering from depression to one of two groups: SFBT group ($N = 20$) or interpersonal psychotherapy for depression group ($N = 20$). Sundstrom found a statistically significant treatment effect for both groups from pre to post. Sundstrom did not, however, find any differences between groups. It was concluded, therefore, that SFBT is as effective as a well-established treatment for depression (ITP) but not superior to that treatment.

Zimmerman, Jacobsen, MacIntyre, and Watson (1996) compared 30 parents in an SFBT parenting group to 12 parents on a waiting list. Their results indicated more statistically significant differences in the SFBT group than in the waiting-list group; namely, the SFBT group improved on parenting skills.

Cockburn, Thomas, and Cockburn (1997) randomly assigned 48 orthopedic patients to one of four groups: Groups 1 and 3 were SFBT plus standard rehabilitation, and groups 2 and 4 were standard rehabilitation only. The results showed statistically significant differences between the two SFBT groups and the two comparison groups. The SFBT groups improved on their ability to cope with their disability. In addition, and more importantly, the SFBT groups were able to return to work in a shorter period of time.

Lindforss and Magnusson (1997) randomly assigned 60 serious criminals with high recidivism rates to one of two groups: an SFBT group ($N = 30$) or a control group ($N = 30$). Comparing the two groups on recidivism rates, the results indicated that the SFBT group had a statistically significant lower recidivism rate compared to the control group, in addition to less serious offenses and shorter sentences for the SFBT reoffending prisoners compared to the control reoffending prisoners.

Seagram (1997) matched 40 adolescent offenders on severity of antisocial behaviors to form two groups: an SFBT group ($N = 21$) and a standard institutional care group ($N = 19$). Seagram reported several statistically significant findings for the SFBT group compared to the comparison group; namely, the SFBT group improved in prosocial behaviors. The improvements were only modest, however.

Later Gingerich and Eisengart (2000) studies on the effectiveness of SFBT have included children (Corcoran & Stephenson, 2000; Franklin, Biever, Moore, Clemons, & Scamardo, 2001), the elderly (Dahl, Bathel, & Carreon, 2000), married couples (Nelson & Kelley, 2001; Pomeroy, Green, & Van Laningham, 2002), and substance abusers (Mott & Gysin, 2003).

Corcoran and Stephenson (2000) used SFBT with 136 children, aged 5 to 17, who were referred for classroom behavioral problems. Results indicated positive changes on the Conners' Parent Rating Scale and mixed results on the Feelings, Attitudes, and Behaviors Scale for children. Franklin et al. (2001) obtained similar results with seven children, aged 10 to 13, who were diagnosed with learning disabilities and classroom behavioral problems. Employing single-system design techniques, the study found positive changes on a range of behavioral problems measured by Conners' Teacher Rating Scales.

Dahl et al. (2000) used SFBT with 74 patients, aged 65 to 89, who were suffering from depression, anxiety, and marital problems. Results showed positive outcomes on self-rating scores, motivational scores, the Global Assessment of Functioning (GAF) scale, and patient satisfaction.

Pomeroy et al. (2002) used SFBT with 12 HIV/AIDS, serodiscordant, heterosexual couples. Results indicated positive outcomes for increased marital satisfaction and decreased depression and anxiety. Nelson and Kelley (2001) obtained similar results with five couples (10 participants) who were attending group therapy. Employing single-system design techniques, the study found positive outcomes for increased marital satisfaction and goal attainment for 8 of the 10 participants.

Mott and Gysin (2003) transformed a residential substance abuse treatment center from a problem-focused approach to a solution-focused approach. Results indicated improved quality and effectiveness of substance abuse treatment and improved staff morale.

More recent studies on the effectiveness of SFBT have included assessment of individual and family counseling (Fischer, 2004), at-risk high school students (Newsome, 2005), a meta-analysis of SFBT outcome studies (Kim, 2006), and classroom-related behavioral problems (Franklin, Moore, & Hopson, 2008).

Fischer (2004) collected data on 40 professional counselors using SFBT with 3,920 cases over a period of two years. Outcome data consisted of the responses to two scaling questions asked at every session about daily functioning and coping. Fischer's analysis demonstrated statistically significant improvements on both scales regardless of number of sessions or system size (i.e., individual, dyad, family).

Newsome (2005) evaluated the effectiveness of eight-week SFBT groups for 26 junior high school students. Students completed behavioral and social scales at pretreatment, posttreatment, and a six-week follow-up. Students scored higher on all scales at posttreatment and follow-up. In addition, triangulation of results were achieved by obtaining similar outcomes from parents and teachers.

In 2006, Kim conducted a meta-analysis of SFBT outcome studies. Kim included the studies evaluated by Gingerich and Eisengart (2000), as well as outcome studies from 2000 through 2006. Although Kim's tables included 109 studies, only 22 met criteria for his analysis. He found that SFBT resulted in small but positive treatment effects.

Franklin et al. (2008) evaluated the effects of SFBT on the behavior problems of 67 children in a classroom setting. The children were administered the internalizing and externalizing subscales of the Child Behavior Checklist before and after treatment. In addition, a comparison group was used. The researchers found that the children in the treatment group improved on both scales, while those in the comparison group remained the same from pre- to posttreatment.

Applications to Families on Levels I, II, and IV

Weltner's (1985) "house" analogy for the issues of those families who might be considered at Level I is the basement. These families are facing life-and-death issues, such as obtaining housing and health care and providing sufficient parenting to nurture and protect the family. The goal for intervention is to add resources. The Level II analogy is the framing and roof and refers to authority and limits within the family unit. At Level IV, the goal is "the development of an inner 'richness'—insight, more sensitive awareness of the relational world, an understanding of legacies and heritage" (p. 47).

The utility of this approach in dealing with these issues has not been established. It is probable that this approach is more effectively used with issues at Level III than with those at Levels II and IV (Cleveland & Lindsey, 1999).

Ethical Challenges

Social work ethics speak to the elimination of oppression, sensitivity to human diversity, empowerment, confidentiality, and a strengths perspective, to name a few. When the therapist is the expert, he or she uses his or her own cultural lens to assess, diagnose, and treat the problem. When the client is the expert, these issues are not relevant to helping him or her.

When the practitioner takes the stance of not being the expert or not knowing, he or she puts the client in the position of being the expert. This does not mean an expert with regard to therapy but rather an expert with regard to the contextual framework shaped by his or her human characteristics. The therapist's taking this approach closely resembles that of an anthropologist immersing himself or herself in a culture. That is, the therapist, from a position of not knowing, must learn the solution from the client. This is accomplished through asking the right questions (i.e., through exception finding, miracle, scaling); that is, the practitioner is expert in asking the right questions, following the right leads (toward strengths), and ignoring the wrong leads (toward problems).

Social workers from a traditional perspective argue that ethically, "one size does not fit all." Through their lens, they are correct. If the therapist is the expert, he or she must learn as many therapies and aspects of human diversity as possible to be effective. This could be quite a challenge. Social workers from an SFBT perspective, on the other hand, argue that the therapist must learn the contextual framework of each client system he or she is seeing in therapy to be effective. After all, even two clients from the same culture will not likely share the same contextual situation.

Finally, this traditional perspective of "one size does not fit all" argues that the practitioner can alter treatment to be culturally sensitive, much as a tailor would alter a suit. SFBT, on the other hand, argues that the therapist must be the tailor that asks the client, "What would you like to have made? What material shall we use? I will need to take your measurements." It is the shift from therapist as expert to the client as expert that makes this situation possible. That shift, however, is a shift in paradigm.

Summary

Solution-focused brief therapy (SFBT) stands in contrast to mainstream approaches with its rejection of insight, problem focus, detailed assessments, and expert stance. Rather, SFBT learns the language, culture, and expertise of the clients to assist them in constructing a positive vision of their future. Once this vision has been formed, it becomes the task of the therapist to help lead the clients toward it from a stance that is one step behind.

SFBT is more than the sum of its techniques. Once the therapist looks through the SFBT lenses and sees that resistance does not exist, that the cup is always half full, and that change is constant, he or she will never see the world as it used to be. The significance of this change is that the therapist does not use SFBT; he or she becomes SFBT. The caution, however, is for the therapist not to accept SFBT until being convinced that it is right for him or her.

Discussion Questions

1. How can treatment be successful if the therapist does not know what problem has brought the family to therapy?

2. Because there is no clinical diagnosis for normal, how does the therapist know when a family no longer needs therapy?

3. How does language change perception?

4. How does believing that resistance does not exist help the family?

5. How does SFBT respect cultural differences?

Internet Resources

www.brief-therapy.org
www.brieftherapysydney.com.au
http://billohanlon.com
www.brieftherapynetwork.com
www.weiner-davis.com
www.gingerich.net

Suggested Readings

DeJong, P., & Berg, I. K. (2008). *Interviewing for solutions* (3rd ed.). Belmont, CA: Brooks/Cole.
This is an excellent resource for teaching solution-focused brief therapy to practitioners. It is particularly valuable because the authors use the model with clients who are generally considered to be multiproblem, difficult, and unmotivated. In addition, the book has a companion student workbook, an instructor's manual, and a CD (sold separately).

de Shazer, S. (1997). *Putting difference to work.* New York: Norton.
As with any of de Shazer's books, this one is more for the theoretician than for the clinician. It has been selected here only because it is more recent than the others. Anyone who is interested in the theory of solution-focused brief therapy will find any of de Shazer's books a logical choice.

Miller, G. (1997). *Becoming miracle workers: Language and meaning in brief therapy.* New York: Norton.
This book was written by an ethnomethodologist who for 12 years sat behind a team that sat behind the mirror watching the therapist. A clinician will see therapy through different eyes, but readers should be warned that it is possible they will never look at therapy the same way again.

Walter, J. L., & Pellar, J. E. (1992). *Becoming solution-focused in brief therapy.* New York: Brunner/Mazel.
For anyone who is looking for an SFBT primer, this is it. The authors use common cases, explain the model clearly, and offer step-by-step instructions on how to do it.

References

Berg, I. K. (1995). *I'd hear laughter* [Film]. (Available from Brief Family Therapy Center, P.O. Box 13736, Milwaukee, WI 53213-0736.)

Berg, I. K., & DeJong, P. (1996). Solution-building conversations: Co-constructing a sense of competence with clients. *Families in Society, 77,* 376–391.

Cleveland, P. H., & Lindsey, E. W. (1999). Solution-focused family interventions. In A. C. Kilpatrick & T. P. Holland (Eds.), *Working with families: An integrative model by level of need* (2nd ed., pp. 139–154). Boston: Allyn & Bacon.

Cockburn, J. T., Thomas, F. N., & Cockburn, O. J. (1997). Solution-focused therapy and psychosocial adjustment to orthopedic rehabilitation in a work hardening program. *Journal of Occupational Rehabilitation, 7*(2), 97–106.

Corcoran, J., & Stephenson, M. (2000). The effectiveness of solution-focused therapy with child behavioral problems: A preliminary report. *Families in Society, 81*(5), 468–474.

Dahl, R., Bathel, D., & Carreon, C. (2000). The use of solution-focused therapy with an elderly population. *Journal of Systemic Therapies, 19*(4), 45–55.

DeJong, P., & Berg, I. K. (2008). *Interviewing for Solutions* (3rd ed.). Belmont, CA: Brooks/Cole.

de Shazer, S. (1984). The death of resistance. *Family Process, 23,* 11–17.

de Shazer, S. (1985). *Keys to solution in brief therapy.* New York: Norton.

de Shazer, S. (1988). *Clues: Investigating solutions in brief therapy.* New York: Norton.

de Shazer, S. (1994). *Words were originally magic.* New York: Norton.

de Shazer, S. (1997). *Putting difference to work.* New York: Norton.

de Shazer, S., Berg, I. K., Lipchik, E., Nunnally, E., Molnar, A., Gingerich, E., & Weiner-Davis, M. (1986). Brief treatment: Focused solution development. *Family Process, 25,* 207–222.

de Shazer, S., & Molnar, A. (1984). Four useful interventions in brief family treatment. *Journal of Marital and Family Treatment, 10*(3), 297–304.

Fischer, R. L. (2004). Assessing child change in individual and family counseling. *Research on Social Work Practice, 14*(2), 102–111.

Frankl, V. E. (1963). *Man's search for meaning.* Boston: Beacon Press.

Franklin, C., Biever, J., Moore, K., Clemons, D., & Scamardo, M. (2001). The effectiveness of solution-focused therapy with children in a school setting. *Research on Social Work Practice, 11*(4), 411–434.

Franklin, C., Moore, K., & Hopson, L. (2008). Effectiveness of solution-focused brief therapy in a school setting. *Children and Schools, 30*(1), 15–26.

Garfield, S. L. (1994). Research on client variables in psychotherapy. In A. E. Bergin & S. L. Garfield (Eds.), *Handbook of psychotherapy and behavior change* (4th ed., pp. 190–228). New York: Wiley.

Gingerich, W. J., & Eisengart, S. (2000). Solution-focused brief therapy: A review of the outcome research. *Family Process, 39*(4), 477–498.

Haley, J. (1976). *Problem solving therapies.* New York: Grune & Stratton.

Kim, J. S. (2006). *Examining the effectiveness of solution-focused brief therapy: A meta-analysis using random effects modeling.* Unpublished doctoral dissertation. University of Texas, Austin.

Lindforss, L., & Magnusson, D. (1997). Solution-focused therapy in prison. *Contemporary Family Therapy, 19,* 89–103.

Minuchin, S. (1974). *Families and family therapy.* Cambridge, MA: Harvard University Press.

Mott, S., & Gysin, T. (2003). Postmodern ideas in substance abuse treatment. *Journal of Social Work Practice in the Addictions, 3*(3), 3–19.

Nelson, T. S., & Kelley, L. (2001). Solution-focused couples group. *Journal of Systemic Therapies, 20*(4), 47–66.

Newsome, W. S. (2005). The impact of solution-focused brief therapy with at-risk junior high school students. *Children and Schools, 27*(2), 83–90.

O'Hanlon, W. H., & Weiner-Davis, M. (1989). *In search of solutions.* New York: Norton.

Polak, F. (1973). *The image of the future.* San Francisco: Jossey-Bass.

Pomeroy, E. C., Green, D. L., & Van Laningham, L. (2002). Couples who care: The effectiveness of a psychoeducational group intervention for HIV serodiscordant couples. *Research on Social Work Practice, 12*(2), 238–252.

Russell, B. (1959). *The problems of philosophy.* Oxford, UK: Oxford University Press.

Satir, V. (1964). *Conjoint family therapy.* Palo Alto, CA: Science and Behavior.

Seagram, B. C. (1997). *The efficacy of solution-focused therapy with young offenders.* Unpublished doctoral dissertation. York University, North York, Ontario, Canada.

Short, D. (2001). *Milton H. Erickson, M.D.: Complete Works 1.0, 2600 pages* [CD_ROM] ISBN: 978-0-9716190-3-6.

Sundstrom, S. M. (1993). *Single-session psychotherapy for depression: Is it better to focus on problems or solutions?* Unpublished doctoral dissertation. Iowa State University, Ames.

Toffler, A. (1974). *Learning for tomorrow: The role of the future in education.* New York: Random House.

Walter, J. L., & Pellar, J. E. (1992). *Becoming solution-focused in brief therapy.* New York: Brunner/Mazel.

Weltner, J. (1985). Matchmaking: Choosing the appropriate treatment for families at various levels of pathology. In M. Marikin & S. Koman (Eds.), *Handbook of adolescents and family treatment.* New York: Gardner Press.

Wittgenstein, L. (1974). *Philosophical investigations.* Oxford, UK: Basil Blackwell.

Zimmerman, T. S., Jacobsen, R. B., MacIntyre, M., & Watson, C. (1996). Solution-focused parenting groups: An empirical study. *Journal of Systemic Therapies, 15*(4), 12–25.

10

Family Systems Theory

Joseph Walsh, Ph.D.

Since its introduction in the 1960s and 1970s, *family systems theory* has thrived as an influential and widely used theory of family assessment and intervention. The theory provides a comprehensive conceptual framework for understanding how emotional ties within families of origin (including extended family members) influence the lives of individuals in ways they often fail to appreciate and may tend to minimize. The theory is sometimes called *family emotional systems theory* to underscore this point and to distinguish it from the generic *family systems* term. Family systems theory is unique in its attention to multi-generational family processes and in its prescriptions for working with individuals in a family context (Bowen, 1978; Kerr & Bowen, 1988).

Murray Bowen, creator of the theory, was trained as a psychoanalyst. This helps to explain why family systems theory has implications for the treatment of individuals as well as families. The nature of healthy human functioning in the theory includes the acquisition of a balance of emotion and reason. The concept of *differentiation* is used to characterize one's ability to achieve this balance. The concept also describes one's ability to function effectively both apart from and within the family of origin. Differentiation is made possible by a facilitative family environment in which the person can establish an identity related to but also separate from that of the nuclear family.

Within most cultures of American society, people typically accelerate the processes of physically and emotionally separating from their family of origin during late adolescence. This is a major life transition for those who leave and for those who stay behind. According to family systems theory, people who have achieved differentiation will be successful in this transition, and those who have not (or are *enmeshed*) will have difficulty. One's capacity to develop positive new relationships in adulthood is affected by learned patterns of managing family-of-origin relationships. In every case, positive or negative, the influence of the family is pervasive throughout life.

Needs Presented by Level III Families

As discussed in Chapter 1, families come to the attention of clinical practitioners for a variety of reasons. Their concerns may be related to a lack of material resources, a family crisis or disorganization, relationship difficulties, or a desire for greater self-actualization. The concepts from family systems theory may be useful to the practitioner with families at *all* levels of need as a means of assessing the nature of family interactions.

Understanding the quality of family relationships, a hallmark of this theory, may be significant in treatment planning regardless of the family's specific needs. For example, a family's struggles with poverty might be characterized in part by emotional conflicts among certain members. The intervention strategies suggested by family systems theory, however, are not appropriate for all problem situations.

Family systems interventions are generally appropriate when the focus will be on the quality of nuclear or extended family interpersonal processes and on the desire for one or more family members to become more differentiated. Level III families often appear to be functioning well to the outside observer. It is their interpersonal lives—including issues of boundaries, enmeshment, and emotional distance—that is the source of their problems. The practitioner will require some structural stability in the family to help members become aware of patterns of behavior that may be contributing to problem situations.

Titelman (1998) edited a book that includes examples of a range of problems for which family systems interventions may be appropriate. These include family problems related to marital fusion, emotional dysfunction in children, a child with a medical problem, college students with adjustment problems, concerns about elderly members, depression, phobias and obsessive compulsive disorder, alcoholism, incest, divorce, and remarriage. More recently, the theory and its interventions have been found useful for issues encountered in adolescent substance abuse and other risky behaviors (Knauth, Skowron, & Escobar, 2006), child abuse (Skowron, 2005), homelessness (Hertlein & Killmer, 2004), and couples violence (Stith, McCollum, Rosen, & Locke, 2003; Walker, 2007).

Assessment

The following sections address the major concepts of family systems theory that are central to the process of assessment. These concepts are drawn primarily from Bowen (1978) and others, as noted.

The Multigenerational Perspective

One of Bowen's greatest contributions to the field of family theory was his principle that individual personalities and patterns of interaction among family members have their origins in previous generations. Additionally, he demonstrated that extended family relationships might be as important to personal development as nuclear family relationships. In these ways, Bowen foreshadowed recent developments in the field of family therapy—of moving beyond the nuclear family unit and considering other influences on family life. His broad definition of *family* also accommodates diverse family forms.

Bowen recommended a three-generation assessment of families, partly because of realistic limits on the availability of information and partly because of his early career work with families that included a member with schizophrenia (Bowen, 1959; Dysinger & Bowen, 1959; Howells & Guirguis, 1985). In that work, he observed that the type of family anxiety that results in one member's developing schizophrenia required three generations to unfold.

It is now understood that schizophrenia is largely biological in origin. Still, Bowen's work of that time helped family therapists to understand the manner in which anxiety can be passed down through generations. For example, McKnight (2003) found in a study of 60 mothers that a cutoff of parents from the previous generation has an impact on the mothers' parental functioning and on the well-being of their adolescent children. The more cut off a mother is from her own mother, the less well she functions, and cutoff between a mother and father is likely to result in a child who is cut off from his or her own father.

The practitioner does not need information about three generations to effectively provide family interventions. Family structures in American life are more diverse and fragmented today than they have ever been. Clinical practitioners experience reconstituted families, dissolving families, single-parent families, and gay and lesbian families. Geographic mobility is such that many people have limited awareness of their blood or territorial origins. It is always important to acquire as much information as possible about nuclear, extended, and cross-generation family relationships, but the practitioner can proceed with whatever data are available. In fact, the trend in family systems theory in the past 20 years has been developing strategies to work with families with a focus on only one or two generations (Titelman, 2003).

Differentiation of Self

Healthy or adaptive individual functioning is characterized by *differentiation of self.* This is a key concept in family systems theory that has two meanings.

First, the concept of differentiation represents a person's capacity to distinguish between and balance his or her thinking and feeling selves. Both aspects of experience are important. The thinking process represents one's ability to detach from, or look objectively at, personal reactions or biases. Emotional processes provide important information about the significance of the situation. The total human experience involves both emotion and reason. While Bowen advocated for a balance of reason and emotion, he did not think this was really an attainable condition because emotional feeling, unlike intellect, is a pervasive life force. For this reason, it must also be emphasized that differentiation is an ideal that can never be fully attained.

The term *differentiation* also refers to the individual's ability to physically differentiate from his or her family of origin in a manner that preserves aspects of those emotional ties while not being constrained by them. Differentiation is thus a characteristic not of a person but of a relationship. The person develops the capacity to maintain a balance in being able to separate self and maintaining old and new emotional ties. It will be shown later that this idea has been amended by some feminist thinkers who perceive the self as being more connected than separate in nature (e.g., Knudson-Martin, 2002).

In one major review of the literature, Bowen's concept of differentiation was supported as a consistent relationship was found between differentiation and chronic anxiety, marital satisfaction, and psychological distress (Miller, Anderson, & Keala, 2004). Further, it was found that more differentiated persons experience more intimate relationships with their parents. In a study of 23 men and women over the age of 30, the more differentiated group's greater intimacy resulted in a deeper sense of loss during the initial grief response to a parent's death but also a corresponding absence of regret and guilt in the months that followed (Edmondson, 2002). Higher levels of differentiation even affect one's response to physical illness, as the severity of the symptoms of fibromyalgia have been correlated with lower levels of differentiation and perceived stress (Murray, Daniels, & Murray, 2006).

In some ways, it is ironic that family systems theory provides such a rich understanding of the emotional lives of people within their families because it emphasizes the importance of reason in the formulation of health. Highly charged emotional interactions can cloud a person's ability to appropriately separate his or her feelings from those of others and to have an independent existence. Bowen felt that it was important for one's reasoning ability to develop so that it could keep emotional experience from becoming the only basis for decision making.

Triangles

In family systems theory, the interpersonal *triangle* is the primary unit of analysis. All intimate relationships are inherently unstable; they require the availability of a third party to maintain their stability.

On first glance, this might seem paradoxical, but it makes common sense. The price of intimacy in any relationship is the experience of occasional conflict. People cannot exist in harmony all the time. When in conflict, people usually rely on a third person (or different third persons, depending on the circumstances) for mediation, ventilation, or problem-solving assistance. Entin (2001) has written about the pet-focused family, in which the pet can become a part of the triangle in these same ways. This is a natural, healthy process.

Serious problems related to one's differentiation may develop, however, when he or she is drawn into certain types of triangles within the family. When a weaker (undifferentiated) person is drawn into a triangle in a way that does not facilitate the original two people's resolution of their conflict, that person may be deprived of the opportunity to become a unique individual. He or she may assume the ongoing role of helping the other two people avoid their problems with each other. For example, a study of 150 families in Japan and the United States found that triangled daughters in both cultures had lower scores on a measure of ego development (Bell, Bell, & Nakata, 2001). Problematic triangulation in families occurs when conflicted adults draw in weaker family members, often the children, to maintain the stability of their relationship.

Anxiety and the Nuclear Family Emotional System

Anxiety is an unpleasant but normal and functional affect that provides people with warning signs for perceived threats (Marks, 1987). Its symptoms include tension and nervous system hyperactivity. An anxiety-producing situation may be perceived as an opportunity for growth or as a threat to well-being. Anxiety becomes problematic when it interferes with one's capacity for problem solving. The concept of anxiety is central to psychodynamic theory, and Bowen adapted it to family systems theory. Family systems feature levels of anxiety, just as individuals do.

The nuclear family's emotional system includes four relationship patterns that may foster problem development (Georgetown Family Center, 2008). With marital conflict, each spouse projects his or her anxiety onto the other and attempts to control him or her. With the problematic emotional functioning of one spouse, the other spouse makes accommodations to preserve relationship harmony but may develop heightened anxiety as a result. If one or more children exhibit a physical or emotional functional impairment, the parents will focus their anxieties on that child, who in turn may become emotionally reactive to them. With *emotional fusion,* family members distance themselves from one another to reduce the intensity of their relationships, and they may become isolated in the process.

A family system that is characterized by psychological tension for any of these reasons may produce an atmosphere of anxiety that is shared by all members. As described earlier, this system anxiety can be passed on and increased through generations. An individual who is not differentiated experiences relatively high levels of tension in family relationships and will tend to be drawn to friends, spouses, and partners with similar levels of anxiety. In fact, one recent study concluded that anxiety is the best predictor of differentiation of self, emotional reactivity, and emotional fusion (Cocoli, 2006).

Parental Projection

Psychological defenses are processes by which people protect themselves from intolerable anxiety by keeping unacceptable impulses out of their awareness (Goldstein, 1995). Defenses are positive coping mechanisms when they help the person function effectively and do not significantly distort reality.

Projection is a common defense mechanism in which one person attributes to someone else his or her unacceptable thoughts and feelings. The projector is not aware of having the feelings or thoughts but believes instead that the person on whom they are projected is experiencing them. For example, a wife may feel anger toward her husband for spending too little time in the household. If she is threatened by the idea of being angry with her spouse, she may project that feeling onto a child. She may decide that the child is angry with the father and report that to her husband.

Projection may involve significant distortions of others' feelings, attitudes, and behaviors. Parents often use the projection defense with their children as targets, because children are vulnerable family members. Children tend to accept and internalize the pronouncements, insights, and beliefs of their parents. Within family systems, children may suffer if the parents project negative feelings and ideas onto them. The children may believe that they possess the negative thoughts and feelings attributed to them and behave as such. In family systems theory, parental projection is a major source of transmitted family anxiety.

Fusion and Emotional Cutoff

Emotional cutoff is an instinctual process between generations. It involves the ways people separate themselves from the past to start their lives in the present generation (Titelman, 2003). Cutoff may be manifested in physical distance, internal distance, or a combination of both.

While emotional cutoff may be natural and healthy, emotional *fusion* is the opposite of differentiation. It is a shared state involving two or more people, the result of a triangulation in which one member sacrifices his or her striving toward differentiation in the service of balancing the relationship of two other people. When one person is emotionally fused with another, his or her emotional reactivity to the other person becomes strong. The person does not think but feels and does so in response to the emotional state of the other person. The feelings of the mother, for example, become those of the son. When she is happy, he is happy, and when she is sad, he is sad. The son does not have an emotional life apart from that of his mother.

Neither person in a fused relationship is consciously aware of this state because the individuals lack the capacity to reason about or reflect on the situation. This happens because for a significant length of time during childhood and adolescence, prior to having an opportunity to differentiate, the fused person began to serve an ongoing function within a triangle that served the needs of two other family members.

People tend not to recognize the fact that they are fused, but they experience high levels of emotional reactivity to the other person and may attempt to extricate themselves from the relationship. A common strategy is the emotional cutoff, a person's attempts to emotionally distance himself or herself from certain members of the family or from the entire family. Emotional cutoff is the result of a person's inability to directly resolve issues of fusion, which in turn prevents him or her from forming a unique identity or satisfying relationships with others.

In situations in which the family is living together, emotional cutoff may be characterized by physical avoidance of another person or, more commonly, not discussing emotionally charged topics. For example, a son in conflict with his mother may be pleased to talk about what happened at school, but the two may avoid discussing how they feel about each other or the family. This pattern can continue after the family member leaves home. The son and mother may enjoy each other's company to an extent but have superficial interactions. The son may look for substitute families at work, at college, or at church.

Emotional cutoff is often seen in physical distance. Adolescents may be eager to leave home as a solution to their family problems. Again, this may represent a normal family transition. However, when distance alone is seen as a solution to ongoing family tension, the person may be disappointed. A first-year college student may feel that he or she can at last be an individual, when in fact, being fused with another family member prevents him or her from fully experiencing other people. An important aspect of emotional cutoff is that the person experiencing it is usually not aware of the strength of the pull of the primary relationship. The process is denied or minimized.

Other Concepts

Bowen believed that *sibling position* within a nuclear family is a partial predictor of a child's personality development. For example, oldest children tend to be more responsible and conservative, whereas younger children are more sociable and rebellious. These differences are due in part to the constellations of triangles that exist in families of different sizes.

Research during the past 10 years, however, has tended to dispel the notion that personality types can be validly predicted on the basis of family position alone (Steelman,

Powell, Werum, & Carter, 2002). Many other variables must be considered, including gender, number of years between siblings, innate temperaments, and the nature of external environments. Still, being alert to the different triangulation possibilities for each sibling is useful in assessing family systems.

Societal emotional processes are the manner in which social systems can be conceptualized as analogous to those of the family regarding the rules that govern interpersonal behavior within and among them. Family systems concepts may be helpful for understanding these other systems. For example, the social service delivery system has been described as one-third of a triangle, along with participating individual members and the family, with implications for the differentiation and fusion of participants (Moore, 1990). The church congregation has also been conceptualized as a family (Howe, 1998). Each member's relationship patterns acquired in the family of origin may be replicated with the congregation, and it is this body from which the individual must strive for appropriate differentiation. Although interesting, the concept of societal emotional processes is not yet as well developed as those concepts specific to the family unit.

The Genogram

A major tool for assessment is the multigenerational *genogram,* a visual representation on one sheet of paper of a family's composition, structure, member characteristics, and relationships (McGoldrick, Gerson, & Petry, 2008). It typically covers a span of three generations.

The information provided on a genogram includes basic facts about family members (e.g., dates of birth and death, marriages, moves, and illnesses); the primary characteristics and level of functioning of each member (education, occupation, health status, talents, successes, and failures); and relationship patterns among members (closeness, conflicts, and cutoffs). Overall family characteristics that may be assessed include structure (roles, rules, and boundaries) and the impact of life events, life transitions, and relationship patterns across generations. The advantage of using a genogram as an assessment tool is its presentation of complex family data on one page. It is also an excellent means of eliciting family medical information (Sawin & Harrigan, 1995).

Some practitioners are reluctant to construct genograms at the level of detail suggested by family systems theory because doing so is time consuming and may be annoying to clients who are eager to move into problem resolution activities (McGoldrick, 1996). Despite these concerns, it is important to understand that, in the first session, constructing a genogram engages all family members in the discussion and usually represents an interesting new way for them to think about the family system.

Assessment Questions

The questions asked by the clinician during assessment include the following:

- What are the family's current stresses? How are they expressed?
- What physical and emotional symptoms are evident in this family?
- How do the evident symptoms affect family relationships?
- What is the nature of this family's relationship system?

- How does the nuclear family interact with the extended family?
- How stable is the family now? How successfully does it handle anxiety?
- How well differentiated are the family members?
- What triangles exist in the family? Which are primary? Are they functional?
- Are any emotional cutoffs operating?
- How has the family handled stress historically?

Goals of the Intervention

The nature of change in family systems theory involves opening up the system (Kerr & Bowen, 1988). Presenting problems involve triangles, fusion, and emotional cutoff. Change requires detriangulation and new alliance building among members of the nuclear and extended family. The practitioner attends to the following goals:

- lowering family system anxiety
- increasing the reflective capacity (insight) of all members
- promoting differentiation of self by emotionally realigning the family system (which includes the opening of closed relationships)
- making members sensitive to the influences of multigenerational family patterns
- enhancing habits of problem sharing
- redressing inequalities within the family by inhibiting dominant members

Intervention Approaches

Family systems therapists do not work with a set of explicit, concrete intervention techniques. Rather, the theory offers intervention strategies with which the practitioner can design techniques according to a family's particular concerns (Bowen, 1978; Kerr & Bowen, 1988). These are summarized in the following section.

The Clinical Relationship

As a prerequisite to change, family members must experience the clinical setting as safe, comfortable, and relatively free of the anxiety that tends to characterize their natural environment. The practitioner acts as a coach. He or she remains on the sidelines of family interaction, asking questions and making suggestions that the family members discuss and enact with each other. The practitioner strives to be the focus of the family's attention and to set the tone of their exchanges. He or she must be calm, promote an unheated atmosphere, and maintain professional detachment. The purposes of this posture are to avoid emotional reactivity and negative triangulation with family members. The practitioner also serves as a model for rational interaction.

In the early stages of intervention, the practitioner may ask family members to talk directly to him or her about sensitive issues, rather than to one another, to minimize interpersonal tensions. If tensions are so high that productive interaction is impossible, the therapist can use *displacement stories* as a means of taking the family's focus off itself and giving it some distance from its own concerns. This is a technique in which the practitioner provides an example of a hypothetical family with processes and problems similar to those of the actual family. The therapist asks the actual family to share observations and suggest interventions.

The Genogram

By participating in the construction of the genogram, family members gain insight into their family processes. They learn about interpersonal patterns and how triangles operate within the family. With these insights, family members learn to appreciate that their behavior is related to larger systemic processes and the ways in which those processes support or inhibit member functioning. The process normalizes some family problems, particularly those related to transitions. Family members may become able to identify their own strategies to enhance family functioning. The genogram often stimulates a process of life review among older adults.

Another way in which the genogram serves as an effective early intervention is that during its construction, each member is observing a diagram rather than looking at others. This brings a shared focus to the discussion and displaces any negative feelings onto an object rather than another person.

Detriangulation

Detriangulation represents any strategy by which the practitioner disrupts one triangle and opens up family members to new, more functional alliances or triangles. There are many ways in which the therapist can detriangulate the family (Guerin, Fogarty, Fay, & Kautto, 1996). He or she can shift alliances with tasks to be performed within the session or when members are at home. Within the session, the practitioner might encourage role reversals or situations in which members interact with each other in different ways.

For instance, a child who is accustomed to complaining to his mother about the annoying behavior of a sibling might be asked to confront the sibling. When a couple is triangled with a child as a means of avoiding issues in their relationship, they might be instructed to spend a certain amount of time together talking about whatever is on their minds that day. If they need the assistance of a third party to bring an issue to resolution, they might be encouraged to talk with a different adult family member. In these ways, members are guided into new functional attachments with nuclear or extended family members.

Any strategy that contributes to members' opening up the family to new attachments can be pursued. The therapist should always encourage the development of new attachments that have the possibility of promoting a member's differentiation.

Increasing Insight

Family systems theory shares with psychodynamic theory a belief that understanding can lead to change. The clinician facilitates reflective discussions that promote insight about the effects of relationships on one's personality and behavior. Two techniques that promote insight are *person-situation reflection,* focused on the present, and *developmental reflection,* focused on the history of the person, the family, and its patterns (Woods & Hollis, 2000). Children and adolescents may appear to have less capacity for reflection, but insight can be defined for them simply as understanding that one person's behavior always affects another person's feelings and behavior.

Two related techniques that the practitioner might use are *externalizing* the thinking, or helping each member put into words what is generally kept inside, and encouraging the "I" position. In the latter practice, the clinician asks each person to speak about his or her own thoughts and feelings, label them as such, and accept responsibility for them. This works against the tendencies of many clients to blame others for what they think and feel.

Education

Families often benefit from understanding that their patterns of interaction have sources in the family's history and that improving family life may involve going backwards, in effect, to revisit relationships with various extended family members. Doing so helps family members feel less confused and guilty about their behaviors.

In teaching families about family system processes, the clinician helps each member to observe the self within triangles and to examine behavior in terms of family themes. This also serves as a normalizing strategy for families who worry that they are uniquely dysfunctional or beyond help. The practitioner must decide when to integrate teaching moments with other interventions. He or she should always provide this information in terms the family can understand.

Working with Individuals

Although this is a book about family intervention, it must be mentioned that one of the strengths of family systems theory is its utility for working with any subset of a family or even with individual clients (McGoldrick & Carter, 2001). Family systems intervention requires an awareness but not necessarily the presence of all family members.

In individual therapy, the clinician can construct a genogram with the client and examine his or her behavior in terms of emerging family themes. The practitioner helps the client observe the self in triangles and then detriangulate by developing new or different relationships with available family members. The practitioner can also help the client develop insight and use this knowledge of the effects of family relationships to disrupt the repetitions of unsatisfactory relationship patterns with others.

Applications

Normal life transitions can create problems in functioning for individuals and families. Among family systems theorists, Carter and McGoldrick (2005) have identified six general stages of a family's lifespan, including (1) young adulthood (between families), (2) the young couple, (3) families with young children, (4) families with adolescents, (5) families at midlife (including launching children), and (6) families in later life. As a family enters each new stage, its members may experience difficulty coping with the challenges inherent in that stage.

The following case provides an example of a biracial family's stresses related to two lifespan stages: adolescence and the declining health of older members. Concepts from family systems theory are useful for understanding the heightened anxiety and emotional tumult that creeps into a family with aging or dying members (Bowen, 1991; Margles, 1995). The illustration includes excerpts from the social worker's dialogues with the family. (Indicators of many of the intervention strategies are included in parentheses.)

The Charles Family

Dan Charles was a 16-year-old high school sophomore who was referred to the mental health center because of poor grades, negative attitudes about school and his peers, and reports by his parents of suicidal thinking. The Charles family (see Figure 10.1) had moved from Ohio to Virginia six months earlier when Dan's father, Jeff (age 41), accepted new employment. The Charles family was biracial, as Jeff was a Caucasian American and his wife, Jinhee, was Japanese American. This was not mentioned as an issue with regard to the presenting problem, however.

According to Dan and his parents, Dan was unhappy about living in Virginia. He was irritable, argumentative, and in persistent power struggles with them. Dan usually stayed in the house when he was not in school and had made no friends. He complained about life in Virginia and said he wanted to move back home. Dan complained about his classmates and refused to participate in school activities. Dan's two younger siblings (Adam, 10, and Kim, 8) resented Dan's anger and how he took it out on them. They enjoyed living in Virginia and had made new friends.

During the practitioner's assessment, however, other family issues emerged as significant to the present situation (see Figure 10.1). The practitioner learned that Jin (age 42), Dan's mother, was concerned about the health of her aging parents back in Ohio. Jin's mother was in the middle stage of Alzheimer's disease, and her father was physically limited by congestive heart failure. For that reason, Jin felt guilty about moving away from Ohio.

Jeff was a Caucasian, middle-class native of Ohio who grew up in a rural community, where he learned skills primarily related to hunting, farming, and construction. His interests and values reflected his outdoorsy upbringing, and his parents had not emphasized higher education. Jeff was an only child born to parents who were highly nurturing but doting, investing most of their energies into his happiness. Jeff was a popular child and adolescent, but he had never excelled at school. He stayed close to home and became a successful unskilled laborer who worked a series of factory jobs.

Jin was the middle child and only daughter of a Japanese American couple from California. Her parents were first-generation Japanese who had moved to the West Coast from Japan in the 1930s. Sadly, they had been interned with their own families in a camp for Japanese persons during World War II and spent two years in confinement. When they were released at the end of the war, their families continued to live in the Oakland area. Jin's parents

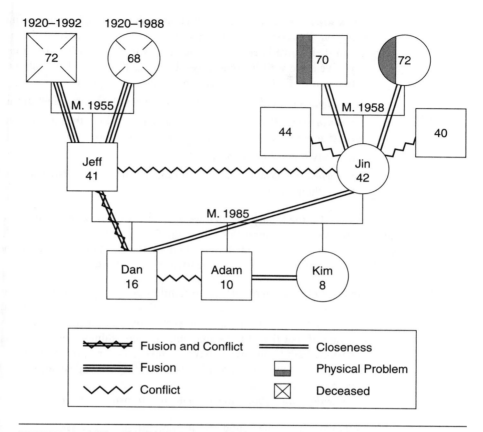

FIGURE 10.1 *The Charles Family*

met in high school and married several years later. Jin's father was an auto mechanic and eventually found work at a truck production plant in Ohio, where Jin and her brothers grew up.

Jin met Jeff in high school, and they married after Jeff finished his technical school training. He had been a devoted husband, and while Jin was embraced by the Charles extended family, her own parents had trouble accepting Jeff as a suitable husband to their daughter. He was not Japanese and was not, in their minds, sufficiently upwardly mobile. (Additional relevant family cultural dynamics will be described in the context of the intervention.)

The practitioner met with the family 10 times over a period of four months, focusing on systems issues, rather than the presenting problem of one member's maladjustment. She framed the family's functioning in a context of everyone's need to better adjust to the move, and the family was agreeable to working on this.

> *Social worker (Reframing):*   Obviously, things have been tense in the home for all of you. But consider that you've had to move several times in the last few years, and there have been real worries about money and health. Considering all that, you've done well in some ways. I can see that you all care about each other, and that you'd all like the atmosphere at home to improve.
>
> *Jeff:*   That's not quite true, though. We're not all trying. [He looks at Dan.]
>
> *Social worker:*   But you said he's been a good kid in the past. I wonder if you're all clear about what this experience has meant to him. Dan?
>
> *Dan:*   My folks should know.
>
> *Social worker:*   Maybe they do and maybe they don't. Perhaps you'll become able to tell them more about that.

One motivator for the family was that because they were now rooted in a new location, they had few choices but to support one another. The practitioner introduced the theme of life cycle stresses and complimented all of them on the good decisions they had made in their transition. Dan was pleased to have the focus taken off him.

> *Social worker (Education):*   All families go through transition periods: when there is a new child born, when a parent dies, when a child goes to school or moves away. Those things all have a big effect on everyone, even though you may not be aware of it at first. I think that, among other things, your family is in a transition period. Family members have to take some responsibility for themselves, of course, but I think you are all affected by these changes. Some of what you're concerned about is related to that. I hope you all recognize that and can maybe make some decisions about how to make this transition easier.

As they reviewed the genogram, the practitioner suggested that they could help each other with their adjustment by dealing more directly with their feelings and interacting with each other in new ways. She included attention to the grandparents in this process. Recognizing the entire family's concern for the aging couple, she integrated strategies to see that all of their needs were addressed.

> *Social worker (Education, lowering system anxiety):*   It's clear to me that you share a sense of family, especially since you're all concerned about Jin's parents. It has to be hard to be this far away from them. Again, I'm not sure if you are all aware of what each of you is experiencing, not only with this move but with other challenges over the past few years, like the family finances. With people close to us, if we don't regularly check in, we may begin to make assumptions that aren't true. Or we may decide that not talking is the easiest way to avoid stress.

The social worker then asked the family if she could share some of her observations about the genogram. She did so as a means of encouraging them to consider the entire system, but she also wanted to raise the issue of their biracial family to see if this might reveal any underlying dynamics significant to the presenting problem. The process was successful on both counts, and the following story emerged.

The couple's racial difference had several significant effects on their relationship (Romanucci-Ross, De Vos, & Tsuda, 2006). In Japanese spousal relationships, the wife takes on the mothering role toward the husband, and Jeff admitted to having been attracted by this quality in Jin, given how his own parents doted on him. And while father–child relationships in Japan are traditionally characterized as distant, parents in later life often rejoin their children's families to be cared for. This extended Jin's caregiving role beyond that of her current family and created some adjustment challenges for all three generations. This was complicated by the fact that Jin and her brothers had agreed that their parents were too ill to move, even though Jin had acted as the primary caregiver.

Japanese family values are characterized by a focus on connection and a desire to be part of the broad racial group. American family values, in contrast, focus on the immediate family, a single generation, individual achievement, and autonomy.

This values conflict created some strain in the Charles family. Jeff, in fact, viewed his in-laws' desire to be near Jin as related to their desire to interfere with his own family and marriage. Further, in Japanese culture, communication patterns are such that women are hesitant to discuss their emotions and careful not to be offensive to others. Jin had these characteristics and thus had trouble expressing any frustrations she was feeling to Jeff and the children. Jeff was outspoken in his negative reactions to what was happening in the family, but Jin was not as expressive.

Further discussion revealed that Jin's parents' confinement in an internment camp may have set up belief systems and patterns of interaction that affected Jin negatively. During World War II, 120,000 Japanese persons were interned in these camps, 60 percent of whom were U.S. citizens (Nagata, 1991). They were abruptly removed from their homes and had to give up whatever businesses and careers they had established.

The emotional effects of such experiences shaped the lives of Japanese-American children. Common outcomes were inhibited family communication, self-esteem problems, a lack of assertiveness, an emphasis on the importance of collective identity and the belief that children (especially sons) should vindicate the family's honor thought external achievement. Parents who had been interred usually maintained silence about their experiences in the camps, inhibiting cross-generational communication and creating a sense of secrecy. The messages children tended to receive from their parents were that they must finish the unfulfilled dreams of the parents to heal the pain of past loss. A strong sense of living within Japanese culture was emphasized, which caused those who married outside the race to feel guilty. Jin discussed these issues with great difficulty, and Jeff appeared anxious as she spoke.

> ***Social worker (Use of the genogram):*** As we have just seen, genograms sometimes lay out family relationships in a way that is more clear than just talking about them. For example, Jin, it looks like your brothers have put you in charge of your parents, even though they live closer. Is that accurate?
>
> ***Jin:*** Men aren't as thoughtful that way. It's my job to make sure my folks get what they need and don't become isolated. You know what it's like for older folks. If they get lonely, they give up and die. My brothers need to be concerned about their own careers. They want to do the family proud.
>
> ***Jeff:*** Men aren't thoughtful? You think I'm like your brothers?

> *Jin:*   Well, look (pointing at the genogram). It was just you and your parents. They took care of you. They died before you were able to repay that.
>
> *Social worker:*   Since we're all looking at the genogram, do any of you see anything interesting?
>
> *Jin:*   Yes. I take care of my folks, and Jeff is used to being taken care of. So now he expects me to take care of him. I want to take care of him, but I can't do everything. I have our own children, too.
>
> *Jeff (defensively):*   Jin goes overboard worrying about her parents. She gives them more attention than she gives the rest of us. Shouldn't we be number one now?
>
> *Social worker (redirecting the interaction):*   I suggest that all of you direct your comments to each other rather than to me. You're really speaking to each other. Don't worry about me, I'll follow along and participate.

Jeff and Jin argued about this issue often. Jeff was the only child in his family of origin. He was born when his parents, now deceased, were in their forties. They had been quite doting, and Jeff was accustomed to being taken care of. Jeff seemed to want Jin to attend to him in the ways she did for her parents. Jin, being a natural peacemaker, tried to see Jeff's side of the issue. Still, she resented his insensitivity to her experiencing this midlife role reversal with her parents.

> *Jin:*   He just doesn't know what it's like for me.
>
> *Social worker (use of "I" statements):*   I don't know if he does or not. It's important for you to make it clear to Jeff how you feel, Jin. In fact, all of you should try to make clear how the behavior of you parents and brothers and sister makes you feel, both good and bad. You can best get your feelings across by using what are called "I" statements. That is, always say "I feel this way" or "I feel that way" when something happens.
>
> *Adam:*   I don't get it.
>
> *Social worker:*   For example, if your sister makes a lot of noise and keeps you from getting your homework done, you might say "I get mad when you make such a racket because I can't study," instead of only saying something like "Stop making such a racket!"

The practitioner suspected that Dan tended to be triangled with his parents as a diversion from their conflicts. When they were angry with each other, they found fault with Dan and vented their feelings at him.

> *Jin:*   He used to be a good kid. But now look. The rest of us are trying our hardest to make all these adjustments, and he goes off and sulks, not helping at all.
>
> *Social worker (use of "I" statements):*   Make sure you talk to Dan instead of to me. And tell him how his behavior makes you feel.
>
> *Jin:*   Okay. Dan, I feel frustrated when you go off by yourself when I'm trying to talk to you. I feel like you're mocking me. [To the social worker] Is that okay?

The practitioner wondered if Dan willingly took on the role of troublemaker when his parents were in conflict. It was true that the recent move was hard on Dan, more so than the other children, due to his stage of life. But the combined family stress may have resulted in Dan's increased efforts to divert (1) his parents' attention from each other, (2) his mother from her guilt about not fulfilling her role in her nuclear family, and (3) his father's anger toward his in-laws and about his unmet needs to be cared for.

> **Social worker (Detriangluation discussion):**   It's normal that there would be a lot of tension in a household after a major move. Dan, I know your parents are concerned about your welfare. I'm wondering, though, how you see them reacting to, for example, a failing grade at school or your staying in your room all day.
>
> **Dan:**   Well, they yell. They yell at me. It can go on for days.
>
> **Social worker:**   Are things pretty calm between them otherwise?
>
> **Kim:**   Oh no!
>
> **Social worker:**   What's that, Kim?
>
> **Kim:**   They yell at each other a lot.
>
> **Social worker:**   You think so? Adam, what do you observe?
>
> **Adam:**   Yeah. That's just the way it is. But it's okay. It doesn't bother me much.
>
> **Social worker:**   So things can get tense in the house. That's not necessarily a problem, unless you lose sight of what you are really upset about.
>
> **Jeff:**   I don't follow you.
>
> **Social worker:**   Sometimes people use each other as outlets when they're upset but maybe not sure what exactly they're upset about. With all that's happened, is it possible that you take out some feelings on each other that might be related to your mixed feelings about moving?
>
> **[And later] Social worker (Displacement):**   Sometimes, kids might become concerned about their parents arguing and actually do things to take the parents' attention away from each other or give them something to agree on.

While the younger children did not seem to be as obviously affected by the family anxiety, the practitioner was concerned that their staying out of the situation put them at risk for emotional cutoff.

> **Kim:**   I'm doing fine. Nobody seems mad at me, except Dan sometimes. I can get away from it. It doesn't bother me, really. I can go to my room.
>
> **Social worker:**   That helps, sure. And it's okay to have your private space. But I wonder if you are able to feel comfortable being around your parents and brothers. I hope you do, most of the time.

The practitioner eventually helped the family develop plans for groups of them to travel to Ohio every three weeks to look after Jin's parents. These represented detriangulation exercises and efforts to open up the nuclear family to the extended family system. This might also help Jeff's relationship with his in-laws, as it seemed their lack of full acceptance of him into their family has produced an underlying resentment in him.

> *Social worker:*   Jin, you like to visit your parents. Have you considered taking other family members along?
>
> *Jin:*   Not much. They're all trying to get adjusted here, and it's my problem, really.
>
> *Social worker:*   But they might be interested in going along. Have you asked them?
>
> *Jin:*   No. I've been preoccupied and . . . [hesitating] I thought Jeff might get annoyed and think I was trying to keep the kids from getting settled here.
>
> *Jeff:*   Oh, come on, I'd never say that!
>
> *Jin:*   You might think I was planning to get us all back home.
>
> *Social worker (Opening up the system to extended family members):*   Jeff and Jin, if you agree that you're going to live here, as you said before, and make the best of it, perhaps you don't have to have such doubts. These short trips can be a good way for you to connect with each other and stay connected to the grandparents.

The family decided that Jin and two of the children might make one trip, enabling them to spend two full days together. Jeff and two of the children might travel to Ohio on another weekend. Jeff and Jin could not take long trips together without the entire family, so the practitioner encouraged them to spend time together close to home but away from the children. Their lives had centered on the children for years. The couple reluctantly decided to meet once a week for lunch.

> *Jeff:*   I'm not sure that lunch together can help. It seems kind of trite. We have most suppers together as it is.
>
> *Social worker:*   With the kids, though.
>
> *Jin:*   Jeff, there's less of a chance we'll get upset if the kids aren't around, sulking.

Jin felt good about this plan, and it lowered her anxiety. The practitioner helped the family appreciate Jin's need to provide support to members of two generations. In the spirit of developing new family tasks, Jeff and the children decided that they could undertake minor home renovation projects during the absences of the other members.

> *Social worker (Coaching):*   Jeff, you've mentioned that you and Dan don't spend time together anymore. What did you used to do?
>
> *Jeff:*   We camped, played sports. I don't know. He's getting older. He doesn't do as much of that stuff anymore.
>
> *Dan:*   There's the carpentry stuff, too.
>
> *Jeff:*   Yeah, we used to work on the house some—sanding the floors, building cabinets.
>
> *Social worker:*   Might you enjoy sanding floors together again?

Jeff: Actually, there's a lot to do in the new place. But he won't help.

Dan: I might.

The practitioner hoped that this would both enhance their sense of mastery and positively change the nature of their relationships. In all of these strategies, the practitioner was helping the family to form new alliances and to differentiate. The children, with the encouragement of the social worker, spent some of their time in Ohio talking with their grandparents about their mother and father's lives when they were younger. This strengthened their relationships with their grandparents. The grandparents had been rather silent about certain traumatic aspects of their history, but with Jin's encouragement, they became able to share more of those stories. All three children were fascinated and came to know their grandparents in a very different light.

Another effective intervention strategy was the practitioner's support of the family's following through with a vague desire to join a church in Virginia. The family members had not been active in their church in Ohio but were more interested in doing so now, partly because of their relative social isolation. Jin had become more conscious of her religious roots since her parents had become ill and were facing existential concerns more directly. Interestingly, she had become more interested in Christianity over the years, another issue that had disappointed her parents. She decided to embrace her religion more openly, with her parents being farther away.

Social worker: I'm getting the feeling that there's a lot of . . . intensity to what happens in the house. Is there anything that you all do that involves other people? I know you don't have family in the area.

Jin: We go to church. Sometimes. We haven't spent much time there, really.

Social worker: Did you ever? I mean, before you moved here?

Jeff: Sure. I volunteered on Sundays, too, to clean up after services.

Social worker: Churches have family activities, too. Is there anything fun the kids might do there?

The worker supported the idea, as it might provide the family with a bonding experience. This activity could also help them consider family functioning within a spiritual context. The family did participate in several church activity groups that helped them to initiate social ties. In the past, their church affiliation had not provided them with a basis for family-focused activity, but it became more a part of their lives now.

When therapy ended, the family had made a better adjustment to life in Virginia. (Note that only the clinical social worker's *active* interventions were highlighted in this vignette because of space limitations.) Relationships improved among the members, and Dan was feeling better about his parents, his siblings, and his school. Jeff had helped Jin confront her brothers about their need to be more attentive to her parents, and Jeff and Dan continued to spend recreational time together. The family had talked about possibly moving Jin's parents to Virginia if their health continued to deteriorate. They continued to make monthly trips to Ohio.

Evaluation of Effectiveness

Evaluating the effectiveness of family theories is generally difficult, and family systems theory is among the most difficult to operationalize. Bowen (1978) did not believe that empirical study was an appropriate way to determine the usefulness of his theory. He believed that such methods overlooked the theory's richness in focusing on limited variables. He believed that what people say they do is not always the same as what they actually do, so he did not put great faith in standardized clinical self-report measures (Georgetown Family Center, 2008).

Family systems theorists emphasize research on process, rather than outcome, and on single cases or small samples. Such studies are currently in progress at the Georgetown Family Center (2008) and include the topics of family violence, families and cancer, families with substance-abusing adolescents, family processes in immigrant families, relationships and physiology, relationship processes and reproductive functioning, the process of differentiation, and the workplace as an emotional system. Previous center studies have focused on AIDS (acquired immune deficiency syndrome) and the family (Maloney-Schara, 1990), aging and the family (Kerr, 1984), family violence, and managing diabetes. The theory is also used as a model for adolescent group work to promote member growth through differentiation (Nims, 1998).

The literature includes examples of tests of the utility of the theory's concepts, and several are summarized here. Roberts (2003) tested 125 college undergraduates to examine whether level of differentiation (defined as moderate levels of autonomy and intimacy with the family of origin) was associated with life stressors and social resources. She found that higher levels of differentiation correlated with lower levels of perceived life stress and more social resources; further, lower social-class status was significantly associated with more life stressors but not fewer social resources. The author concluded that social class influences the number of one's stressors but not one's social resources.

Kim-Appel (2003) examined the relationship between differentiation and psychological symptom status (somatization, interpersonal problems, depression, anxiety, hostility, and a global symptom measure) in persons aged 62 and older. Her hypotheses were confirmed, as measures of differentiation correlated negatively with emotional reactivity and emotional cutoff and correlated positively with "I" position statements. She concluded that differentiation is significant to social functioning across the life span and that psychological intervention with older adults can productively utilize family systems concepts.

Other studies have supported the validity of family systems theory's concepts. Correlations have been found between level of differentiation and risks for substance abuse and other risk behavior. Adult chemically dependent persons have lower differentiation than the control population, and people who begin using substances at age 13 or younger have significantly higher levels of emotional reactivity than those who start at age 14 or older (Pham, 2006). Among individuals in substance abuse treatment, those who report lower levels of differentiation of self are more likely to report violence in their intimate relationships, while those who report more emotional reactivity (overwhelmed by emotions of the moment) and greater emotional cutoff (threatened by intimacy) are more likely to report one instance of violence in intimate relationships during the past year (Walker, 2007). Higher levels of differentiation of self were related to lower levels of chronic anxiety and higher levels of social problem solving. Higher chronic anxiety was related to lower problem solving, indicating that differentiation influences social problem solving through chronic anxiety. Higher levels of social problem solving were related to less drug use, less high-risk sexual behaviors, and an increase in academic engagement (Knauth et al., 2006).

Several studies have focused on family-of-origin influences on career decision making. Keller (2007) studied college students and found that differentiation (and the ability to take an "I" position) was positively predictive of a student's proactive career exploration. Dodge (2001) investigated the effects of differentiation (and, from another theory, the concept of *personal authority*) on career development outcomes for 243 college students. Each concept was positively associated with a sense of vocational identity and self-efficacy in career decision making. Further, family of origin conflict was inversely associated with low self-efficacy in career decision making, low individuation, and dysfunctional career thoughts. The author concluded that addressing family conflict in therapy could have a positive impact on career development in young adults. In another study of this type, 1,006 college students were surveyed using measures of fusion, triangulation, intimidation, anxiety, and career decision making (Larson & Wilson, 1998). Results indicated that anxiety (from fusion) inhibits career development, but triangulation is not related to career decision problems.

A number of studies have considered the effects of family systems on a person's later degree of satisfaction with intimate relationships. A study of 60 married couples found that higher-differentiated couples described higher levels of marital satisfaction than lower-differentiated couples (Racite, 2001). Couples who demonstrated different levels of differentiation reported more marital problems than couples who were similar in differentiation. In one research project, men's and women's emotional cutoff scores were predictive of the nature and quality of their relationships and related depressive episodes over time (Glade, 2005). Larson, Bensen, Wilson, and Medora (1998) studied the effects of the intergenerational transmission of anxiety on 977 late adolescents' attitudes about marriage. The participants' experiences of fusion and triangulation were found to be related to negative opinions about marriage.

Timmer and Veroff (2000) studied the relationship of family-of-origin ties to marital happiness after four years of marriage for 199 black and 173 white couples. One predictor of marital happiness for wives, particularly those from disrupted families, was closeness to the husband's family of origin. When husbands' or wives' parents were divorced or separated, closeness to the husband's family reduced the risk of divorce. Avnir and Shor (1998) operationalized the concept of differentiation with a set of indicators so it could be qualitatively assessed during family intervention. Regarding parenting potential, Skowron (2005) found that greater differentiation of self (lower reactivity, emotional cutoff or fusion, and better ability to take an "I" position) predicted lower child abuse potential.

The clinician can evaluate his or her own effectiveness with family systems theory through the application of *single-systems measures* (i.e., comparing baseline and treatment measures) or *pre-experimental measures* (i.e., comparing pretreatment with posttreatment measures). All that is required to do so is a background in basic research methods. The practitioner can translate a family's goals into observable indicators that can be monitored. Coco and Courtney (1998) provide one example. They initiated and evaluated a family systems intervention for preventing adolescent runaway behavior using pre- and post-intervention measures of family satisfaction and cohesion.

Application to Families at Other Levels of Need

Family systems theory interventions require that the client, whether an individual or a family, has the capacity to interact in an atmosphere of relative calm and be able to reflect on relationships with significant others. The family structure must be stable enough that the clinician can remain detached from family processes. Because this is a historical approach to intervention, the ability to focus on several generations is desirable.

Family systems theory would not be appropriate for *most* Level I and *many* Level II families. The practitioner's focus in Level I is on meeting basic material and support needs. There is an urgency to those needs that suggests interventions that do not rely on sustained reflection. Nor is there time for multigenerational assessment in critical situations. Likewise, Level II families are often characterized by chaos that derives from structural instability. The high level of worker activity necessary to adjust the family structure is inconsistent with the family systems perspective.

Family systems theory might be appropriate for some families at other levels of need after their initial problems have been resolved. After the Level I family acquires access to basic needs, its members may struggle with issues related to enmeshment or cutoff. A structural breakdown of a Level II family may be related to a triangulation in which an adolescent accedes to an inappropriate position of power. The clinician's ability to assess those dynamics may be helpful in determining how to help the family organize problem-solving activities, strengthen certain subsystems, or plan for growth after the primary intervention ends.

Ethical Challenges

Clinicians routinely face ethical challenges in their work, regardless of their theoretical base. They are human beings first, with personal values and preferences, and they must always monitor how they adhere to the profession's ethical principles of challenging social injustice, respecting the dignity of each person (and family), supporting the importance of relationships, being trustworthy, and maintaining practice competence. Still, each theory reflects a unique orientation to practice, and social workers utilizing them may experience particular ethical challenges.

Family emotional systems interventions may give rise to these five challenges:

1. Because interventions are relatively nondirective, the practitioner must be cautious of any tendencies to step into a more directive role, especially when confronting such issues as family violence and neglect.
2. The clinician must balance the risks and benefits of getting involved in any pressing external family issues, such as advocacy for housing, employment, or health care. The theory recognizes the importance of societal processes on family functioning but does not extensively address how related goals can be incorporated into family intervention.
3. The theory warns against the practitioner becoming triangled with family members in a negative way. The practitioner must monitor his or her tendency to take sides

with or against some family member or subsystem with regard to such issues as gender discrimination and ageism.

4. The practitioner must continually assess his or her own level of differentiation, since he or she cannot help the family progress beyond that level. This does not require the practitioner to seek therapy, but he or she does need to use supervision in a way that promotes this process. This may be difficult in organizations where intensive supervision is not provided.

5. Because of the absence of clear indicators for termination, the practitioner needs to establish indicators for ending so that the intervention does not become too diffuse. Several resources have recently become available on this topic, including Walsh (2003) and Walsh and Harrigan (2003).

Summary

Family systems theory is unique in its attention to overt and subtle emotional family processes that develop over several generations. It is an appropriate guide to assessments and interventions that focus on the quality of nuclear and extended family interpersonal processes and the desire for family members to become differentiated. The theory is an effective means of working on issues related to boundaries, enmeshment, and emotional distance. It is versatile in its applicability to individuals and subsets of families. Its potential for use across cultures has also been articulated, although not yet extensively (Hines, Garcia-Preto, McGoldrick, & Weltman, 1992).

Family systems theory has been criticized, however, for two related reasons (Bartle-Haring, 1997; Knudson-Martin, 1994; Levant & Silverstein, 2001). First, it has not adequately attended to variations in how men and women experience differentiation and fusion. The theory has incorporated a male bias in its valuing of reason over emotion and prioritization of separation over connection. Beginning with Gilligan (1982), developmental theories about women have considered their relational and communication styles to be different from those of men. Women are typically brought up to empower others in the family, to respond to the thoughts and feelings of others, and to foster their growth and well-being. Men are programmed to seek extra-familial success while women are programmed to nurture and support them, often at the expense of their own development. While these are culturally supported roles, they may create a tendency to see women as enmeshed. A gender-neutral family theory would place greater emphasis on helping men increase their capacity for intimacy and balance their achievement and relationship needs (Nichols, 2009).

Second, even with its attention to societal emotional processes, family systems theory has not been sufficiently contextual in its identification of males as the dominant cultural group and their uses of power in family systems. Although these criticisms are valid, they began to be addressed by theorists in the 1990s. Family issues of gender difference and power can be productively addressed in therapy (McGoldrick, 1996).

Level III families pose a challenge to clinicians because they are well defended and cope well in many ways. These families are also a challenge because of the potential vulnerability of the practitioner to the influence of his or her own family issues on the clinical work. The struggles of the presenting family may resonate with the practitioner's family experiences, and he or she may be inclined to take sides or be blind to certain family dynamics. Titelman (1987) has written extensively about the practitioner's need to be sensitive to these forces and to utilize clinical supervision to maintain neutrality in the intervention process.

Discussion Questions _____

1. Think about your own family of origin, and identify one or two examples of relationship patterns that characterized that system. How did these patterns develop and when? It might be interesting to talk with other family members about these patterns.

2. Describe a point of fusion you have observed in your work with an individual, a family, or a family subsystem. Describe one way that you might (or did) proceed to modify that relationship.

3. Why is the triangle considered to be the smallest stable relationship system? What does attention to this concept imply about family assessment and intervention strategies?

4. Describe how a genogram can serve as both an assessment tool and an intervention strategy.

5. What is the ideal position of the practitioner in family systems work in terms of achieving both engagement and therapeutic distance?

6. One intervention strategy in family systems theory involves guiding members into new attachments with nuclear and extended family members. Why should extended family members be included in this process when possible?

7. Consider a case of family dissolution in which the primary issue in the three-member family is the adolescent child's adjustment to the divorce of her parents. Describe one possible intervention strategy if the child will be in joint custody but is disengaged from one parent.

8. Suppose you are working with a family in which the mother is dying of ovarian cancer. The two children are grown and live independently in the same city as the parents. The son, like the father, is highly involved in the mother's care. The daughter shows minimal concern with her mother's imminent death. How might you organize an intervention to help the mother communicate more openly with her daughter?

9. Consider a situation in which you are working with an individual adult client whose problem is related to an inability to risk intimacy (however you define it) in relationships with significant others. In the assessment, you learn that this person was the responsible child in a family where the father was an alcohol abuser. Describe one possible intervention strategy.

10. Consider a situation in which you are working with a single mother who is having trouble letting go of her 19-year-old daughter, who is moving toward independence in a normal way. There are two other children, ages 14 and 10. The mother fits the profile of the responsible child in her own nuclear family, in which there was an alcoholic parent. Describe one possible intervention strategy for helping the mother let go.

Internet Resources

http://plaza.ufl.edu/irma/paper2.html
www.georgetownfamilycenter.org/index.html
www.ddstats.com/fs/content/module4.htm
www.smartdraw.com/specials/genealogy.asp

Suggested Readings

Bowen, M. (1978). *Family therapy in clinical practice.* New York: Jason Aronson.
  This is the essential source of originator Murray Bowen's major writings on the topic of family systems theory.
Colucci-Coritt, M. (1999). *Feminist family therapy.* www.mindymac.com/Feminist_Family_Therapy.htm
  This essay includes a concise, useful reaction of some feminist thinkers to the prominent family systems theorists, including Murray Bowen.
Framo, J. L., Weber, T. T., & Levine, F. B. (2003). *Coming home again: A family-of-origin consultation.* New York: Brunner Routledge.
  This book is comprised of a single clinical case study of one family's struggle to come to grips with its own dynamics and losses. It embodies a contemporary Bowen theoretical perspective that takes on real life through the stories of the family as it responds to the universal dimensions of death and rebirth. The treatment sessions come to life through transcripts, reflections of the therapists, and a detailed account of the therapeutic experience.
Guerin, P. J., Fogarty, T. F., Fay, L. F., & Kautto, J. G. (1996). *Working with relationship triangles: The one-two-three of psychotherapy.* New York: Guilford Press.
  This is the most recent book by Guerin, a major proponent of family systems theory, and his associates. With its focus on the triangle, the theory's primary unit of analysis, the book has a broad clinical application.
Kerr, M. E., & Bowen, M. (1988). *Family evaluation: An approach based on Bowen theory.* New York: Norton.
  This book focuses on developments in family systems theory since the publication of Bowen's earlier volume (1978). Its coauthor, Michael Kerr, is widely acknowledged to be the theory's major proponent since Bowen's death.
McGoldrick, M., Gerson, R., & Petry, S. (2008). *Genograms: Assessment and intervention* (3rd ed.). New York: W. W. Norton.
  This well-known book is a rich and fascinating introduction to the process of genogram construction and interpretation, using the families of some well-known figures in history as examples.
Rigazio-Digilio, S., Ivey, A. I., Grady, L. T., & Kunkler-Peck, K. P. (2005). *Community genograms: Using individual, family, and cultural narratives with clients.* New York: Teachers College Press.
  While not specific to Bowenian theory, this book presents the genogram as a therapeutic tool that can be used as both an interactive assessment and intervention strategy with individuals and families. The strategies presented in this book facilitate an identification of contextual and community dynamics and resources often beyond the awareness of the clinician and client.
Titelman, P. (Ed.). (1998). *Clinical applications of Bowen family systems theory.* New York: Haworth Press.
  These books include descriptions of family systems theory interventions for a variety of presenting problems. Each chapter is authored by a different practitioner, which helps the reader get a sense of the creative approaches that can be used in family intervention.
Titelman, P. (Ed.). (2003). *Emotional cutoff: Bowen family systems perspectives.* New York: Haworth Press.
Wylie, M. S. (2004). *Family therapy's neglected prophet.* www.bowentheory.com/familytherapysneglectedprophetwylie.htm.
  An excellent biographical overview of Bowen's life and career.

References

Avnir, Y., & Shor, R. (1998). A systematic qualitative evaluation of levels of differentiation in families with children at risk. *Families in Society, 79*(5), 504–514.

Bartle-Haring, S. (1997). The relationships among parent-child-adolescent differentiation, sex role orientation and identity development in late adolescence and early adulthood. *Journal of Adolescence, 20*(5), 553–565.

Bell, L. G., Bell, D. C., & Nakata, Y. (2001). Triangulation and adolescent development in the U.S. and Japan. *Family Process, 40*(2), 173–186.

Bowen, M. (1959). The family as the unit and study of treatment: I. Family psychotherapy. *American Journal of Orthopsychiatry, 31*, 40–60.

Bowen, M. (1978). *Family therapy in clinical practice*. New York: Jason Aronson.

Bowen, M. (1991). Family reaction to death. In F. Walsh & M. McGoldrick (Eds.), *Living beyond loss: Death in the family* (pp. 79–92). New York: Norton.

Carter, B., & McGoldrick, M. (Eds.). (2005). *The expanded family life cycle: Individual, family, and social perspectives* (3rd ed.). Boston: Allyn & Bacon.

Coco, E. L., & Courtney, L. J. (1998). A family systems approach for preventing adolescent runaway behavior. *Adolescence, 33*(130), 485–497.

Cocoli, E. (2006). Attachment dimensions, differentiation of self, and social interest: A structured equations modeling investigation of an interpersonal-maturational model. *Dissertation Abstracts International, Section B: The Sciences and Engineering, 67*(6-B), 3343.

Dodge, T. D. (2001). An investigation of the relationship between the family of origin and selected career development outcomes. *Dissertation Abstracts International, 62*(2-B), 1140.

Dysinger, R. H., & Bowen, M. (1959). Problems for medical practice presented by families with a schizophrenic member. *American Journal of Psychiatry, 116*, 514–517.

Edmondson, C. R. (2002). Differentiation of self and patterns of grief following the death of a parent. *Dissertation Abstracts International, Section B: The Sciences and Engineering, 62*(12-B), 5960.

Entin, A. D. (2001). Pets in the family. *Issues in Interdisciplinary Care, 3*(3), 219–222.

Georgetown Family Center. (2008). www.georgetownfamilycenter.org/index.html.

Gilligan, C. (1982). *In a different voice*. Cambridge, MA: Harvard University Press.

Glade, A. C. (2005). Differentiation, marital satisfaction, and depressive symptoms: An application of Bowen theory. *Dissertation Abstracts International, Section B: The Sciences and Engineering, 66*(6-B), 3408.

Goldstein, E. G. (1995). *Ego psychology and social work practice* (2nd ed.). New York: Free Press.

Guerin, P. J., Fogarty, T. F., Fay, L. F., & Kautto, J. G. (1996). *Working with relationship triangles: The one-two-three of psychotherapy*. New York: Guilford Press.

Hertlein, K. M., & Killmer, J. M. (2004). Toward differential decision-making: Family systems theory with the homeless clinical population. *American Journal of Family Therapy, 32*(3), 255–270.

Hines, P. M., Garcia-Preto, N., McGoldrick, R. A., & Weltman, S. (1992). Intergenerational relationships across cultures. *Families in Society,* 323–327.

Howe, L. T. (1998). Self-differentiation in Christian perspective. *Pastoral Psychology, 46*(5), 347–362.

Howells, J. G., & Guirguis, W. R. (1985). *The family and schizophrenia*. New York: International Universities Press.

Keller, B. D. (2007). Beyond individual differences: The role of differentiation of self in predicting the career exploration of college students. *Dissertation Abstracts International, Section B: The Sciences and Engineering, 68*(1-B), 649.

Kerr, K. B. (1984). Issues in aging from a family theory perspective. In K. B. Kerr (Ed.), *The best of the family: 1978–1983* (pp. 243–247). New Rochelle, NY: Center for Family Learning.

Kerr, M. E., & Bowen, M. (1988). *Family evaluation: An approach based on Bowen theory*. New York: Norton.

Kim-Appel, D. (2003). The relationship between Bowen's concept of differentiation of self and psychological symptom status in individuals age 62 years and older. *Dissertation Abstracts International, 63*(7-A), 2467.

Knauth, D. G., Skowron, E. A., & Escobar, M. (2006). Effects of differentiation of self on adolescent risk behavior. *Nursing Research, 55*(5), 336–345.

Knudson-Martin, C. (1994). The female voice: Applications to Bowen's family system's theory. *Journal of Marital and Family Therapy, 20*(1), 35–46.

Knudson-Martin, C. (2002). Expanding Bowen's legacy to family therapy: A response to Horne and Hicks. *Journal of Marital and Family Therapy, 28*(1), 115–118.

Larson, J. H., Benson, M. J., Wilson, S. M., & Medora, N. (1998). Family of origin influences on marital attitudes and readiness for marriage in late adolescents. *Journal of Family Issues, 19*(6), 750–769.

Larson, J. H., & Wilson, S. M. (1998). Family of origin influences on young adult career decision problems: A test of Bowenian theory. *American Journal of Family Therapy, 26*(1), 39–53.

Levant, R. F., & Silverstein, L. B. (2001). Integrating gender and family systems theories: The"both/and" approach to treating a postmodern couple. In S. H. McDaniel & D. D. Lusterman (Eds.), *Casebook for integrating family therapy: An ecosystem approach* (pp. 245–252). Washington, DC: American Psychological Association.

Maloney-Schara, A. (1990). Biofeedback and family systems psychotherapy in the treatment of HIV infection. *Biofeedback and Self-Regulation, 15*(1), 70–71.

Margles, D. (1995). The application of family systems theory to geriatric hospital social work. *Journal of Gerontological Social Work, 24*, 45–54.

Marks, I. M. (1987). *Fears, phobias, and rituals: Panic, anxiety, and their disorders.* New York: Oxford University Press.

McGoldrick, M. (1996). *The legacy of unresolved loss: A family systems approach.* New York: Newbridge Communications.

McGoldrick, M., & Carter, B. (2001). Advances in coaching: Family therapy with one person. *Journal of Marital and Family Therapy, 27*(3), 281–300.

McGoldrick, M., Gerson, R., & Petry, S. (2008). *Genograms: Assessment and intervention* (3rd ed.). New York: W. W. Norton.

Miller, R. B., Anderson, S., & Keala, D. K. (2004). Is Bowen theory valid? A review of basic research. *Journal of Marital and Family Therapy, 30*(4), 453–466.

Moore, S. T. (1990). Family systems theory and family care: An examination of the implications of Bowen theory. *Community Alternatives: International Journal of Family Care, 22*(2), 75–86.

Murray, T. L., Daniels, M. H., & Murray, C. E. (2006). Differentiation of self, perceived stress, and symptoms severity among patients with fibromyalgia syndrome, *Families, Systems, and Health, 24*(2), 147–159.

Nagata, D. K. (1991). Transgenerational impact of Japanese-American internment: Clinical issues in working with children of former internees. *Psychotherapy: Theory, Research, Practice, Training 28*(1), 121–128.

Nichols, M. (2009). *The essentials of family therapy* (4th ed.) Boston: Allyn & Bacon.

Nims, D. R. (1998). Searching for self: A theoretical model for applying family systems to adolescent group work. *Journal for Specialists in Group Work, 23*(2), 133–144.

Pham, M. (2006). Differentiation and life change events I a chemical dependent population. *Dissertation Abstracts International, Section B: The Sciences and Engineering, 67*(4-B), 2237.

Racite, J. A. (2001). Marital satisfaction and level of differentiation in distressed and non-distressed couples. *Dissertation Abstracts International, Section A: Humanities and Social Sciences, 62*(2-A), 792.

Roberts, N. H. D. (2003). Bowen family systems theory and its place in counseling psychology. *Dissertation Abstracts International, 63*(12-B), 6105.

Romanucci-Ross, L., De Vos, G. A., & Tsuda, T. (2006). *Ethnic identity: Problems and prospects for the twenty-first century* (4th ed). Lanham, MD: AltaMira Press.

Sawin, K. J., & Harrigan, M. P. (1995). *Measures of family functioning for research and practice.* New York: Springer.

Skowron, E. A. (2005). Differentiation of self and child abuse potential in young adulthood. *Family Journal, 13*(3), 281–290.

Steelman, L. C., Powell, B., Werum, R., & Carter, S. (2002). Reconsidering the effects of sibling configuration: Recent advances and challenges. *Annual Review of Sociology, 28*, 243–269.

Stith, S. M., McCollum, E. E., Rosen, K. H., & Locke, L. D. (2003). Multicouple group therapy for domestic violence. In F. W. Kaslow (Ed.), *Comprehensive handbook of psychiatry: Vol. 4. Integrative/eclectic* (pp. 499–520). New York: Wiley.

Timmer, S. G., & Veroff, J. (2000). Family ties and the discontinuity of divorce in Black and White newly-wed couples. *Journal of Marriage and the Family, 62*(2), 349–361.

Titelman, P. (Ed.). (1987). The therapist's own family: Toward the differentiation of self. Northvale, NJ: Jason Aronson.

Titelman, P. (Ed.). (1998). *Clinical applications of Bowen family systems theory.* New York: Haworth Press.

Titelman, P. (2003). Efforts to bridge secondary emotional cutoff. In P. Titelman (Ed.), *Emotional cutoff: Bowen family systems perspectives* (pp. 11–137). New York: Haworth.

Walker, M. W. (2007). Differentiation of self and partner violence among individuals in substance abuse treatment. *Dissertation Abstracts International, Section B: The Sciences and Engineering, 67*(12-B), 7393.

Walsh, J. (2003). *Endings in clinical practice: Ensuring closure across service settings.* Chicago: Lyceum.

Walsh, J., & Harrigan, M. P. (2003). The termination stage in Bowen's family systems theory. *Clinical Social Work Journal, 31*(4), 383–394.

Woods, M. E., & Hollis, F. H. (2000). *Casework: A psychosocial therapy* (5th ed.). Boston: McGraw-Hill.

Part V

Fourth Level of Family Need: Family and Personal Growth

Families on Level IV of family need have their basic needs met. There is adequate parenting, and structural boundaries and limits are relatively clear. Generally, there are generational boundaries and parent–child differentiation, and personal and family growth are the primary issues. Presenting needs often focus on the wish for greater intimacy and commitment, more adult autonomy, interpersonal competence, self-actualization, more constructive resolution of conflict, or changing destructive patterns. Based on the accomplishment of lower-level needs, this higher level of need is represented by a focus on inner richness and quality of life in the house that the family is building.

The two chapters in this section offer approaches for working with families who have needs at Level IV and are experiencing growth issues at that level. The first is narrative family interventions, discussed in Chapter 11 by Williams, whose emphasis is on the meanings families make of their experiences, instead of the cause of the problem, making use of a collaborative, co-learning therapeutic relationship.

A second approach, object relations family intervention, is presented in Chapter 12 by Kilpatrick and Trawick. This approach is a bridge between working with individuals and working with families and is essentially interactional in its intervention processes.

11

Narrative Family Interventions

Nancy Rothenberg Williams, Ph.D.

Narrative therapy, referred to as the "third wave" of family therapy, is an approach to working with individuals and families within a strengths-based, social justice framework that makes it especially compatible with social work practice and values. Proponents of narrative therapy regard this approach as much more than a set of techniques. Rather, it reflects a paradigm shift that challenges the tenets adhered to in family systems theories and traditional clinical approaches to mental health treatment.

Narrative theorists focus on challenging the negative cognitions that are revealed in the ways people frame stories about their experience. These theorists hold the view that people seek out therapy when the predominant stories in their lives, otherwise called *narratives,* become oppressive and filled with pain and suffering, thus becoming oversaturated with problems (White & Epston, 1990). Therapy within this model is a process of creating a new narrative (called a *restorying process*) that challenges the status quo viewpoint, creates possibilities for alternative meanings and, correspondingly, alters negative self-defeating behaviors. As Nichols states, "Stories don't mirror life, they shape it" (Nichols & Schwartz, 2007, p. 338).

Author's Note: Michael White, considered the guiding genius behind the narrative family therapy movement, died April 5, 2008, during the revision of this chapter. The following words from Johnna Busa Paratore and Mike Nichols pay partial tribute to a man who embodied the best of the values of the social work profession—believing in people in terms of their strengths and potential: "White's leadership of the narrative movement in family therapy [was] based not only on his imaginative ideas but also on his inspirational persistence in seeing the best in people even when they've lost faith in themselves. White [was] well known for his persistence in challenging clients' negative self-beliefs and for his relentless optimism in helping people to develop healthier interpretations of their life experiences" (www.abacon.com/famtherapy/white.html).

Needs

Storytelling is the way humans capture and communicate their lived experience. It is a universal and uniquely human phenomenon that disperses seeds of cultural knowledge while shaping identity and transmitting values. Through a highly subjective and culturally influenced lens, people construct and share their stories as a way to make meaning out of their life experiences. Creating stories to convey experience has been described as a way of transmitting "cultural and family beliefs that guide personal expectations and actions" (Walsh, 1998, p. 48). Reciprocally, as people's stories have shaped culture, so, too, have people been shaped by the stories, or narratives, that the prevailing culture has adopted about them.

Narrative therapy is an approach to working with individuals, couples, and families that utilizes these stories as the point of intervention to bring about change. This theoretical model, which draws from a broad range of disciplines (e.g., philosophy, anthropology, sociology, and linguistics, as well as family therapy and psychology), has been gaining momentum in the family therapy field since the 1980s and continues to broaden its appeal and influence practice in the human service arena. In the years that this theory has been evolving, there has been a growing acceptance and respect of the significance of the narrative as a rich tool within the psychotherapeutic community (McLeod, 2006).

Goals

With its strengths perspective focusing on resiliency and social empowerment, the narrative therapy model is particularly well suited to working with traditionally underserved and/or oppressed populations. The therapist within a narrative framework is viewed as a social justice advocate, who is in the business of challenging cultural injustices that oppress or marginalize individuals. The therapist's role is to empower clients to choose preferred ways of relating that are counter to the narratives they have come to believe are their only option.

People worldwide tell stories that are grounded in their particular tradition, making narrative therapy a particularly effective approach in working with diverse cultures. Internationally, this approach has been applied to working with such diverse populations as African (Nwoye, 2006), Mexican (Sued & Amunategui, 2003), and Asian Indian (Keeling & Nielson, 2005) families, and it has been well documented in work with locally indigenous populations in the Dulwich Centre in Adelaide, Australia.

The Role of Culture

Narrative therapists take the position that the narratives people adopt act as filters that determine which features of their experience will be focused on and what meaning will be given to the experience. While narratives can offer strategies for adapting to the inevitable adversities in life, using them can also become a vehicle for cultural oppression.

A focus of concern for the narrative therapist is the notion that power is unequally distributed and held in place through cultural discourse (Marsten & Howard, 2006). Laird (2000) suggests that cultural narratives are so strong that they are, in fact, the pivotal metaphors that clinical practitioners should focus on in work with individuals, couples, and families. It is through the construction of narratives that the dominant culture is translated and becomes embedded into people's personal frames of reference as truths. These adopted truths can serve to shape self-destructive and constricting thoughts and behaviors. Thus, a narrative approach to family intervention addresses and challenges stories that disempower and pathologize individuals and families by directly addressing cultural issues of power, oppression, and social justice, which are often overlooked in more traditional, intrafamilial and intrapsychic models of practice.

The foundation of narrative therapy has been described as a "philosophy of language," in which use of language is viewed through a socially constructed lens (Leahy & Harrigan, 2006). In this approach, the impact of the cultural experience on the members of those diverse groups who remain outside the dominant cultural narrative is considered central (Goddard, Lehr, & Lapadat, 2000; Gremillion, 2004; Laird, 2000; Nylund & Nylund, 2003; O'Dell, 2000; Semmler & Williams, 2000; Waldgrave, 1998; White, 1991).

Theoretical Foundations and Basic Tenets

Michael White, a social worker from Australia, is credited with the initial conceptualization of the narrative model in the early 1980s. His ideas evolved in collaboration with David Epston, a clinician from New Zealand, who injected the notion of community empowerment, and Cheryl White, who introduced White to the feminist perspective.

The model that evolved from their collaboration is rooted in a postmodern framework while drawing from existentialist philosophy. The narrative approach recognizes social and political influences and constraints and embraces the belief that reality is socially constructed. The narrative model claims to stand theoretically distinct and independent from other traditional theories and frameworks of human behavior that view pathology as the root of people's problems. Depending on the framework, narrative theorists suggest that pathology or blame have been passed between the individual or the family system in traditional practice theories like a "hot potato." Epston (1984) argues that these approaches seek to rank individuals according to notions of pathology and correct behavior that is predetermined by external influences.

Rather than viewing one version of the truth that is possessed by the therapist, who is in effect a messenger of society, the narrative model promotes a more objective and hence nonjudgmental attitude toward human variation. This position avoids the process of imposing labels such as "dysfunctional" and "resistant" on clients. The narrative therapist places particular value on personal responsibility and empowerment and avoids pathologizing labels (Anoretic & Anoretic, 1991).

The narrative therapy approach has been described as "a perfect expression of the postmodern revolution" (Nichols & Schwartz, 2007, p. 337). This approach shares similar theoretical postmodern roots with solution-focused therapy, defined by Steve de Shazer, but the two models also have distinct differences (Chang & Phillips, 1993). Specifically, these authors note differences in therapeutic intent and stance toward problems. Despite important differences, narrative and solution-focused therapies both focus on strengths and solutions, placing these methods at the cutting edge of the social constructionist, postmodern perspective.

Some of the major theoretical and philosophical influences that profoundly impacted White and Epston include the writings of Michel Foucault, Jerome Bruner, and Gregory Bateson. Their contributions are reflected in the following three categories of assumptions that underscore the narrative model: Foucault's theory of power and oppression, Bruner's theory of change, and Bateson's theory of problems.

Theory of Power and Oppression

Michel Foucault (1965, 1979, 1980), a French philosopher, focused his work on the distribution of power within society that objectified, marginalized, and dehumanized some social groups while upholding the social status of others. He asserted that power is maintained based on standards that are set by the standard bearers of a society (i.e., doctors, teachers, politicians, therapists, celebrities), who promote oppression of deviant groups through presumed expert judgments that serve to categorize and stereotype these groups. Society adopts the position of its model experts through the internalization of a shared narrative (i.e., social construct) that perpetuates oppressive attitudes and beliefs. Thus, the culture shapes behavior and trains individuals to conform and in turn to judge those who refuse or are unable to follow the prescribed norms. Those who conform to the dominant or expert knowledge are accepted, but nonconformists come under the gaze of others and are viewed in a pejorative way.

Psychotherapists are trained to identify deviations in behavior and to assess individuals through a systematic labeling process that facilitates categorization of clinical diagnoses such as those found in the *Diagnostic and Statistic Manual of Mental Disorder* (*DSM-IV-TR*) (American Psychiatric Association, 2000). Labels such as "obsessive-compulsive," "alcoholic," "codependent," and even "borderline personality disorder" have found their way into everyday language. Family therapists also have their own language for categorizing or labeling families by using terminology such as "enmeshed," "dysfunctional," or "emotionally disengaged," which assigns pathology to the family's functioning.

Nichols and Schwartz (2007) suggest that "narrative therapists not only avoid judgments about what is normal, they reject the very idea of categorizing people" (p. 341). White (2007) argues that the search for a cause is itself a problem, leading to a vicious cycle of blame and guilt. The language of the broader society is also filled with words and phrases that convey less than acceptable or so-called abnormal behavior by categorizing out-of-the-norm roles and practices such as gay/alternative lifestyles and even single parenthood (Besa, 1994). Drewery, Winslade, and Monk (2000) emphasize the importance of recognizing the power and influence of the use of words in creating frameworks for tangible consequences that impact people's lives and become predictors of future behavior.

Drawing extensively on Foucault's ideas, White (2007) espoused forming a therapeutic coalition with individuals and families to protest oppressive social and cultural forces that become incorporated into problematic beliefs. One of the cornerstones of the narrative approach is the claim that the person/family/system is not the problem but that the problem is the problem. Creative exchanges called *externalizing conversations* (Tomm, 1993) are not merely designed to take the stigma off of the person with the problem but to create a political process of empowering individuals and families to objectify the problem and to unite with the therapist to protest its oppression.

For example, Western women have labored under the cultural construct that to be thin is to be beautiful and seek to attain physical perfection (control) through their weight. Many of these women have come to see themselves as under the influence of anorexia (rather than being anorectic) and have begun to take a stand for antianorectic ways for themselves and others. In fact, antianorexia/antibulimia leagues, the brainchild of David Epston, have sprung up in Australia, New Zealand, and Canada. The purpose of these organizations is to mobilize individuals and families who are being tyrannized by eating disorders to unite their energies (Nichols & Schwartz, 2007).

Since Epston initiated his work in the early 1990s, his ideas have spread, reframing the notion of eating disorders as a form of cultural oppression that encompasses body image as a whole (da Costa, Nelson, Rudes, & Guterman, 2007; Leahy & Harrigan, 2006; Lock, Epston, Maisel, & de Faria, 2005; Padulo & Rees, 2006; Weber, Davis, & McPhie, 2006). Padulo and Rees (2006) argue that body image difficulties that include eating disorders are a reflection of out-of control consumerism, longing for community, addiction, and the search for individuation and identity. Vodde and Gallant (2002) suggest that political activism demonstrates a unique bridge provided by the practices in narrative therapy between micro- and macropractice in the field of social work.

Theory of Change

According to Edward Bruner (1986) and Jerome Bruner (1990), stories provide the primary means for individuals to structure or organize their lived experiences. As life stories are told, with their inevitable gaps and inconsistencies, lives are changed through the process of interpreting situations and filling in gaps with both experiences and imagination. As these narratives or stories are enacted or performed, they affect lives. In fact, White (1988/1989) asserted that life is a process of reauthoring lives and relationships.

The narrative therapist who is presented with a problem-filled story subtly challenges the client's monolithic perception of the problem through a series of carefully crafted questions, which are outlined later in the chapter. In doing so, the therapist allows co-creation of a new story to occur, as new ideas, information, and perceptions around the exceptions create a context for change (Anoretic & Anoretic, 1991). Problem-saturated beliefs are challenged, and possibilities for alternative ways of behaving are enhanced. It is in this reauthoring process that the seeds of hope can be found.

Theory of Problems

Drawing on the works of Gregory Bateson (1972, 1979), narrative therapists subscribe to the notion that problems are *not* inherent in individuals or families. Problems are viewed as arising when people assign narrow and self-defeating interpretations about themselves to events that occur; these self-defeating cognitions are often culturally imposed.

Narrative therapists refer to these cognitions as the client's *dominant* or *problem-saturated story:* the primary or dominant story that the client believes. Thus, these restricted views may prevent people from noticing information about their own strengths and abilities to deal with the problems in their lives. This is the point at which families and individuals often seek therapy (White & Epston, 1990).

Much too often, well-meaning therapists reinforce a restricted view by immersing themselves in the client's problem-saturated story. This is not the only option, however. The problem and its oppression of individuals can be deliberately placed by the therapist outside the individual or family. In this method, the cause is not pursued and the focus is instead on developing a deeper understanding of how the individuals themselves understand the problem.

Since the underlying assumption is that reality is invented, narrative therapists believe that the concept of the self as a monolithic entity does not exist, since the self is essentially determined by the situation and the person with whom the self is interacting. Jerome Bruner (2002) argues, "In effect, there is no such thing as an intuitively obvious and essential self to know, one that just sits there ready to be portrayed in words" (p. 4). He suggests that the self is fluid and evolves in interaction with others and situations.

Drawing from the work of Markus and Nurius (1986) and Parry and Doan (1994), McQuaide (2000) describes this process as a "confederacy of selves." For example, the self someone is with friends is different from the self he or she is with family and is different from the self he or she is at work. Even within those groups, the individual is different with different group members and depending on his or her mood and circumstance. The individual self is constantly in flux and always in the process of being reinvented. White (1991) refers to this notion as "the constituted self" in describing how meaning is co-created between individuals and others as they communicate.

McQuaide (2000) postulates that each of these selves has its own narrative and that "the different ways a person can story [his or] her life (self-narratives) can be sources of strength and resilience or sources of weakness and vulnerability" (p. 72). Furthermore, the self can be understood as being constructed and sustained within a narrative and through the process of dialogue can be transformed (Neimeyer, 2006). Thus, it is the job of the therapist to enhance and empower the already existing, if dormant, resilient selves.

Assessment

Assessment, from the narrative perspective, is not concerned with diagnoses or classification into pathologizing categories but rather is an intervention itself, concerned with bringing forth stories from a stance of respectful curiosity. Assessment occurs through enacting a person's stories, rather than through uncovering facts. When stories and their meanings are revealed, strengths emerge at every step of the therapeutic process. Alternative stories can deconstruct and challenge old stories and are being cultivated throughout the process. Thus, assessment and treatment are not considered separate processes but intertwined and interdependent.

The concept of a symptom's function is foreign to the narrative approach (Chang & Phillips, 1993) and the labeling of such merely serves to distract from the problem and its effects on the individual or family. In the narrative model, symptom functionality is replaced by the concept that problems are inevitable and that restraints have prevented the discovery of effective solutions. As these negative explanations are explored, the pertinent question is not Why are things this way? but What has stopped things from being different? (Anoretic & Anoretic, 1991).

In the following case study, Rhonda and Jamie, a young couple dealing with the effects of an affair, went to counseling to save their marriage:

> Rhonda and Jamie, the parents of 4-year-old Dawn, have come to the family counseling center at the recommendation of their pastor. The referral came after Rhonda discovered Jamie's brief affair with her cousin, who lived with them temporarily. Devastated, Rhonda had insisted that Jamie move out, and the couple has tumultuously been dealing with the problem ever since.
>
> Because the couple live in a rural area, seeking marital counseling requires them to drive 100 miles round trip per session. Both have to take time off work to make their appointments.
>
> Rhonda and Jamie were high school sweethearts and married when Rhonda became pregnant as a junior in high school. Both grew up and continue to live in a rural area among their large extended families. Jamie works as a maintenance man at an apartment complex, a job he says he hates. He has complained to Rhonda about this issue but said little else about it.
>
> Jamie and Rhonda have been married for four years and have one child, Dawn, a daughter with whom Rhonda says she is overly attached. Dawn is cared for during the week by Jamie's mother while Rhonda and Jamie work. Rhonda says she is "paranoid" when it comes to leaving her daughter and has started worrying more about leaving her.
>
> The first few sessions of therapy were spent focusing on the presenting problem: the affair and how it has taken hold of their lives.

While the dominant culture might be inclined to view this couple as dysfunctional, *their* cultural norms include marrying young, dropping out of high school, becoming pregnant as a teen, and being involved with extended family. The difference in norms is not that they are facing marital problems but that they are seeking help in a way that is new and different for them.

Narrative therapists are not problem solvers. Rather, their purpose is to partner with people to enhance their awareness of how cultural forces have lulled them into accepting problem-saturated ways of living. Narrative therapists are less concerned with formulating therapeutic goals than they are with coauthoring with clients new preferred stories about themselves. The focus is on enabling people to separate themselves from the problem by convincing them that the *problem* is the problem and not the person. Once they are free from the old problem, people have room to rewrite new scripts for their lives.

Intervention Approaches

The Therapeutic Process

According to White (1991), a central component of the narrative approach is a *deconstruction,* which involves "procedures that subvert taken-for-granted realities and practices" (p. 121). The dominant story of a troubled family is usually characterized by a sense of helplessness and blame-filled descriptions of family members and the relationships among them. Using a narrative approach to treatment, the therapist facilitates bringing forth what is called the *problem-saturated story,* which is typically the presenting problem.

Each selected memory carries meaning or personal significance that allows people to make sense of and find continuity in their experiences. The meanings that humans attach to situations and events influence their behavior around those events. Without planning or intending to, individuals support and maintain a problem by cooperating with it until it seems to develop its own lifestyle or career (White & Epston, 1990). Through the use of empathic listening and carefully constructed questions, the narrative therapist maps the influence of the problem, thus acknowledging its influence on the family (Monk, Winslade, Crockett, & Epston, 1997).

The Role of the Narrative Therapist

The collaborative relationship between the client and narrative therapist is of pivotal importance and serves as a template for empowering the client and supporting his or her strengths. As noted earlier, narrative therapists do not view themselves as problem solvers but as facilitators who assist people in detaching from the problem-saturated version of their story that includes cultural assumptions.

Stories are carefully explored as the therapist seeks to understand the client's perception as it relates to the problem. It is through this respectful collaboration with individuals and families that clients are empowered to bring forth their alternative stories. Breaking from the more conventional view of problems being inherent either within the individual or the family, narrative therapy promotes the view that problems exist as a perception and are external to the identity of the client. Nichols and Schwartz (2006) contrast the difference between family systems approaches and the narrative approach by claiming that, instead of focusing on "self-defeating patterns of behavior, the narrative metaphor focuses on self-defeating cognitions" (p. 330).

The therapist working with Jamie and Rhonda approached the case as follows:

The therapist began by searching for meaning around the affair. She asked Jamie and Rhonda a series of questions: "What does the affair mean to you as a couple and as individuals? How has the affair affected you? What's different today when you talk about the affair than when you first found out about it? What does it mean for the affair to have involved your cousin? How has the affair affected your family relationships?"

One of the outcomes of the affair was to enable the couple to seek professional counseling and get some distance from their families. Since the couple live over an hour's drive from the counseling office, getting to and from the sessions has forced them to spend some time alone with each other. The therapist sees this as an opportunity to ask the couple further questions: "What is it about the two of you that you have been able to use this affair as an opportunity to fight for the relationship and the possibility of a different life together? What does it say about your relationship that you are willing to travel so far and make such a huge commitment to work on your relationship?"

Therapeutic Strategies

Narrative interventions include an eclectic collection of treatment methods, any or all of which may be used. One method is the use of *curious questions* to enable family members to attend to other aspects of their lived experiences. Through this process, clients are able to recall alternative stories that often draw on previous successes.

Some of the more commonly used techniques are described in the following sections. The order of techniques is intended to reflect a somewhat logical sequence, although some techniques can be repeated many times or possibly even skipped. The intervention process should be seen as progressing more in loops and curves than steps.

It becomes the therapist's job, through a process of therapeutic conversations, to assist in drawing out and identifying experiences from the past that are exceptions to the individual's problem-saturated old story. The exceptions or unique outcomes are evidence that, on occasion, the person has successfully challenged the problem and mustered the strength to overpower it. As the significance and impact of the exceptions are explored and elaborated, the individual's sense of personal efficacy intensifies. Exceptions with their new, reauthored meanings contribute to the new story's past history. The therapist, and eventually the client, can then decline to accept the validity of the old story (White & Epston, 1990).

Normalizing the Problem. The success of the narrative model depends on the collaborative bond established between the therapist and the client. One of the impacts of sharing stories is the cultivation of empathy in the listener, which has been described as a co-construction of a relational process central to developing strong helping relationships (McLeod, 1999).

Consider the case of Jamie and Rhonda:

> In addition to seeking to understand Jamie and Rhonda and their problem, the therapist began by asking many questions and phrased them in a way that helped the couple think about their situation in a slightly different way. This questioning process helped Jamie and Rhonda to feel validated and safe with the therapist and allowed the therapist, in the process, to begin to view their story more objectively. This process also enabled the therapist to shift the focus from shame and blame between the couple to uniting them against a common problem: the disrupting effects of the affair.
>
> After hearing Rhonda's detailed description of her story of betrayal and rejection, the therapist normalized the experience by making this observation: "Both of you appear to be under the influence of a great deal of sadness, anger, and loneliness because of the affair. That is completely understandable, given that your marriage has suffered such a blow."
>
> The therapist believed it was her role to hear and amplify any new version of their story that was different than the old problem-saturated version. She began by commenting on the couple's commitment in joining together to fight for their marriage. In doing so, the therapist marveled at the distance, time, and trouble the couple were investing together by coming to therapy.

Externalizing the Problem.   Frequently, individuals and families have had previous experience with therapists who have labored with them to work through or come to terms with particular labeled pathologies or dysfunctions. Given this experience, clients are often restrained by the belief that blame needs to be assigned to somebody who has intentionally maintained or caused a problem or that the problem reflects a character defect or personality weakness.

Externalizing the problem challenges these notions. Again, consider the case of Jamie and Rhonda:

> Rhonda was filled with anger toward Jamie, expressing her sense of betrayal and pain in a litany of accusations that left them both feeling helpless and hopeless. Her ruminations prevented her from being able to receive the support that she wanted from her family, her friends, and Jamie, in particular. The therapist began by asking a series of questions aimed at deconstructing the experience, such as "How has this affair affected you as individuals and as a couple?" and "What has the affair meant to you as individuals and as a couple?"

The sometimes humorous technique of naming the problem—for instance, naming alcohol "Al"—enables clients to focus their energies on combating it. This externalization process allows people to visualize the solution in terms of the collaborative process of forming a team to combat the problem. Externalization is more than a reframing and depersonalizing of the problem. It is a way for families to gain control over the problem. The therapist and family members work together to define the problem situation or pattern as something outside and distinct from the identified patient. As the problem is shaped through metaphor into an entity that can be named, the individual or family can distance themselves from it, challenge it, and defeat it (Neimeyer, 1993; Winslade & Smith, 1997).

Mapping the Problem.   During the early assessment/intervention phase, reciprocal patterns emerge and are explored in terms of how they have been supporting the problem. The problem and its impact on the individual's and family's life and relationships are scrutinized at length. The narrative therapist asks each family member to give a detailed, honest account of the distressing effects of the problem and the extent to which he or she has been supervised by it (i.e., dominated, pushed around, controlled).

Gold, Morris, and Gretchen (2003) advocate combining intergenerational aspects of the client's narrative as a way to conceptualize and intervene with the family's history. Part of the mapping process is exploring the influence (effect) of the person on the problem. White (1986) has referred to these combined questions as mapping the relative influence of the problem in the life of the person and the person in the life of the problem.

Here is how Jamie and Rhonda's therapist mapped the problem:

> The couple's therapist began by assessing the influence the problem was having on each of them as well as their marriage. Together, they discovered that the problem of the affair was bigger than they had thought. Jamie had been very unhappy in his job, and that had spilled over into his marriage. Jamie also felt quite down on himself and was extremely self-critical. Once Rhonda's anger had been explored and diminished, Jamie's story—one of desperate futility with his work situation that had little to do with Rhonda—was deconstructed. Rhonda

was able to hear how "unmanly" he felt in his limited job. Then a new narrative began to emerge as Jamie shyly shared that he had taught himself to become computer savvy, had quietly rebuilt a computer, and had dreams of studying computer science. Rhonda was able to express her pride in his knowledge.

Finding News of a Difference.   News of a difference is news that makes a difference. It provides a twist that allows the individual and family to see and experience the old story in a new way. The changed meaning provides a new storyline for daily living. The individuals are encouraged to acknowledge their progress through amplifying and recognizing the significance of small changes and shifts of behaviors away from the problem. In being helped to recognize the incremental improvements they are implementing in their life and how they are going against their dominant storyline, family members are empowered to change the story that dominates their view of themselves.

People tend to cling to the story that they are used to long after it serves them or is even an accurate depiction of their current reality. News of a difference empowers the family to recognize and acknowledge that changes are occurring and that they are responsible for the change. This is accomplished through a collaborative process of co-creating and witnessing the new or alternative stories that emphasizes optimism and empowerment. The therapist becomes a cheerleader who painstakingly amplifies successes.

Rhonda discovered news of a difference in one of her sessions with Jamie:

Since the affair had such power in Rhonda and Jamie's marriage, the therapist felt that Rhonda's rumination represented her need to be listened to. The therapist set a structured dialogue that required one partner to speak at a time and have the experience of the other partner simply repeating back what was said with guidance from the therapist to stay on track. Rhonda went first and then the therapist helped Jamie validate her feelings.

Through this exercise, Rhonda's anger significantly shifted, so that at the end, she was actually able to inject a note of empathy and hope for the future of their marriage. In this experience, Rhonda was able to viscerally experience news of a difference—the experience of being heard. Most of the rest of the session was spent exploring the couple's extraordinary triumph in being able to talk about such a loaded, painful topic.

The structured dialogue enabled Rhonda to move beyond the current story into richer, unexplored territory, and while doing so, she felt her husband genuinely struggling to understand her deeper experience. As the dialogue progressed, she moved from her rage and sense of betrayal and hopelessness to see change, allowing her to explore a sense of possibility—her needs, hopes, and expectations for the future. As the dialogue ended, Rhonda began to experience her husband as a partner who was capable of working with her to comprehend her larger vision for their future.

At the next session, there was a visceral demonstration of difference. Simply watching Rhonda and Jamie's entrance into the therapy room made it obvious to the therapist that there had been a palpable change. A sense of harmony was evidenced in the couple's eye contact, body language, level of laughter, and ease of relationship. Rhonda and Jamie reported having spent the previous weekend together on an unprecedented outing away from their town, family, and child. They were bubbling over with new energy, and there was a sense of connection and trust. In this session, Jamie began to construct a new story of possibility around his work as the therapist experienced and celebrated the couple's triumphant rewriting of their story.

Asking Therapeutic Questions.   The narrative therapist asks many gentle, curious, respectful questions in the process of interventive interviewing. These questions are intended to elicit experiences of exceptions, which is the stuff of restorying (Tomm, 1987; White & Epston, 1990).

Curious questions, by and large, are the means by which restraining patterns are revealed and challenged and new opportunities are discovered for positive, affirmative, more flexible action around the problem. As part of this search, any information that represents a positive move toward change is noticed, seized on, and highlighted. Language and metaphors are used creatively to highlight the relative influence of the problem. The following are illustrations of types of questions the therapist used with Rhonda and Jamie in laying the groundwork for the restorying of their narrative:

Opening space for possibilities
To Jamie: How have you been able to begin to see the possibility of another way of supporting your family?

To Rhonda: How have you been able to move beyond your anger?

To Both: How have you been able to see the importance of seeking counseling?

How have you been able, despite all the obstacles, to have hope for your marriage?

How have you been able to open yourself up to hear what your partner is really saying?

Effect of change questions to amplify news of a difference
So, what's it been like for you to spend a day together fighting for your family?

So, what's it been like for you to feel heard by Jamie?

How have the changes you have experienced affected your daughter and the rest of your family?

What about the two of you has made you be able to use this affair as an opportunity to fight for your relationship?

Preference questions
Do you prefer these differences or the old way?

What's it been like for you come to counseling today versus the first time?

Story development questions/News of a difference questions
If you ran a video in your head, what scenes might be there now that wouldn't have been there before?

If I was a fly on the wall, what would I hear you saying now in tone or words that might be different now than then?

They write together or the therapist writes to them to create a song, poem, or letter.

Meaning questions

What does it say about you as a couple that you were able to fight so hard for your marriage?

What does it say about you that you made the time to travel so far?

Looking to the future

As you continue on this same path, what do you imagine your relationship will look like in the future?

How do you see yourselves continuing to communicate effectively?

Scaffolding.   As clients begin the task of unraveling their stories, the storytelling process is set in motion and meaning making simultaneously occurs. It is in this process that people have the opportunity to discover past clues to support the notion of current competence. White (1991) urges therapists to treat these discoveries as "significant and intriguing mysteries that only persons can unravel as they respond to the therapist's curiosity about them" (p.30). This history of alternative stories becomes the foundation for the reauthoring of the client's narrative.

White (2005) describes these exceptions as a "point of entry into the alternate storylines of people's lives" (p. 3). He calls this process *scaffolding,* because the narrative therapist uses this history as a foundation to set the stage for the new, alternative story to evolve through exploratory questions.

In the case of Jamie and Rhonda, the couple was encouraged to remember and describe situations in which they had felt comfortable and content in their relationship. They came to see that the affair was not the norm and that they had, in fact, had many more good times than bad. Some other examples of questions from Rhonda and Jamie's sessions include the following:

- *Exceptions questions.* These questions focus on situations of successful, exceptional outcomes that do not fit with the dominant problem-filled, story. These situations are the overlooked times when the problem was not overwhelming or dominating but are not recognized yet as victories worth acknowledging by the client. Consider the use of exceptions questions with Rhonda and Jamie:

> Rhonda and Jamie's therapist also inquired about how the couple's current ability to talk to one another was different from previous occasions in their married life when they had communicated less successfully. The therapist helped bring forth the emergence of a different narrative, one in which Rhonda and Jamie were capable of discussing difficult things and becoming closer as a result. This experience helped the couple to begin to frame how they wanted their relationship to be in the future.

- *Significance questions.* These questions search for and reveal the meaning, significance, and importance of exceptions. Questions of significance help draw attention to the importance of the exception and the possibility of new meanings. For example, Rhonda and Jamie's therapist asked these questions:

What do you think these discoveries reveal to you about your motives and what is important to you and your life?

In more fully appreciating your achievement, what conclusions might you draw about what your marriage stands for?

• *Spectator questions.* This type of question is sometimes called an "experience-of-experience" question because it invites the individuals to imagine how other people they have known might experience them. For example, Rhonda and Jamie's therapist asked them these questions:

If I had been able to look in on your earlier life, what might I have seen you doing that would reveal to me how you have been able to take this step?

Of all the people who have known you, who would be the least surprised that your marriage has been able to meet this challenge, and what would they have seen that would enable them to predict it?

Collapsing Time and Raising Dilemmas.   This technique highlights the relative influence of the problem. It also allows individuals to peer into the past and the future and predict how the problem might have developed and how it is likely to evolve. They can then make a decision around the resulting dilemma. In Jamie and Rhonda's case, the dilemma was whether it was worth the effort to fight for their marriage. Some of the questions the couple's therapist asked them are as follow:

Is your marriage more of a problem for you now than, say, it was six months ago?

If you were to continue to allow this affair to get the best of you, how else would you invite your friends and future relationships to treat you as fragile and to protect you from their opinions?

Enhancing Changes.   Reinforcing changes can be accomplished through respectfully challenging a client's dominant story. Doing so serves to motivate individuals to reexamine their narratives, leading to an amplification of changes already underway. The goal here is to demolish the problem-saturated version and to begin to reauthor a more adaptive story. Children and adolescents seem particularly open to this method and respond with energy and devotion to proving the problem-saturated story wrong. Motivational questions or comments may include the following:

To a teen: But wait a minute, you told me that you were always sad, and now you're telling me that you were happy on Saturday! Are you telling me that you were able to keep sadness out of your life on Saturday?

To a parent: You said you noticed that Billy kept fear from pushing him around and that you were able to go to the mall. I don't get it! I thought you said fear controlled him all the time! Something is different here. What happened?

Predicting Setbacks.   This can be done before the dilemma has even been settled. Because the problem-saturated story still dominates, setbacks are virtually inevitable; thus, they must be anticipated and their distress expected and planned for. However, this needs to occur in a manner that highlights and encourages self-efficacy. In the following example, Jamie and Rhonda's therapist cautioned them:

> If you are really determined to make a radical change in your marriage, do you think you will be able to handle a setback? Or will you be tricked and seduced again by using something like an affair?

Letters and Audiotapes. This is a powerful tool for continuing and reinforcing the dialogue between the therapist and family members. Therapist-authored letters and tapes can be rich sources for summarizing sessions, writing up case notes and sharing them with the client, highlighting emerging new stories, and rendering lived experience into a narrative or story. The therapist can ask curious questions (such as those discussed above) that may prompt individuals to further reflect on their circumstances, and that may unearth new meanings, affirming exceptions, and unique outcomes and pose new ideas or possibilities.

The following is a copy of a letter that Rhonda and Jamie's therapist sent them following a session in which they struggled with the powerful aftermath of the affair (adapted from Winslade & Smith, 1997):

Dear Rhonda and Jamie,

I have been thinking about our meeting today and thought it would be useful for all of us if I put into writing some of the things we talked about. Please let me know the next time we meet if there are things that I missed or need to understand more fully.

When we first met, you explained that you both were fighting a particularly painful battle for your marriage. Rhonda, I am very curious how you have managed to overcome your anger and to trust the relationship again, just as I am curious, Jamie, how you have managed to find the courage to fight so hard for your family in spite of your fear. I understand that this has been far from easy. In fact, I can't help but wonder how the two of you have used the strength of your marriage to combat the effect of the affair and wondered if your marriage is not stronger as a result.

Rhonda, you also talked about how preoccupation with the affair was "leading you around by the nose," and I couldn't help wondering how you managed to stand up to that preoccupation a few weeks back in spite of the formidable power it has. I was thinking how, even in our meeting, preoccupation attempted to convince all of us that your withdrawal was the only remedy. From your experience, do you think that it's true that withdrawal is a remedy? Do you think that withdrawal and preoccupation have teamed up against you to strengthen each other's place in your life, or have they assisted you to develop your full potential?

Jamie, you have mentioned that, despite all obstacles, you have decided to continue to fight for your marriage. How have you been able to do that? Also, how have you begun to see another way to support your family, like working with computers? When did it occur to you that you had possibilities and options?

I have many more questions but am hoping I haven't already overwhelmed you. If any of these thoughts or questions are interesting to you, we can discuss them more fully when we meet, or if you feel inclined to write or draw a response, that would be great.

Using a Reflecting Team.   This method was introduced by Tom Andersen (1991) to explore available but unasked questions during family therapy conversations. A team of observers (from one to several), functioning as an audience, silently listen to the therapist and family. At a designated time, the therapist invites the team to share their observations with one another about what they have just observed.

The family and therapist silently listen to the team, who reflect on the story of the family with positive and curious comments and questions. Questions often begin with "I seemed to notice . . ." or "I couldn't help but wonder what would happen if . . ." The team attempts to be sensitive, imaginative, and respectful and to avoid any negative connotations, advice, or criticism. They introduce new ideas, bring out unnoticed exceptions, and expand the family's new story. This process usually lasts about five minutes, after which the family and therapist can reflect with each other on the reflecting team's conversation (Andersen, 1991).

Awarding Certificates and Holding Celebrations.   These acknowledgements can serve as tangible affirmations of the defeat of the problem or a new description of an individual. Certificates punctuate celebrations of victories and actual celebrations—complete with balloons, cake, and punch—signify that problems have been successfully challenged and defeated. These personal affirmations contribute to reinforcing and providing a concrete symbol of an individual's new story after the therapy is over.

Evaluation

Despite the impressive treatment effects noted in many case studies by White and others, there continues to be a dearth of empirical research examining the effectiveness of narrative methodology. This is most likely because the conclusions of traditional quantitative investigatory methods, with their emphasis on quantitative measurement and positivist thinking, are at odds with the values espoused by the narrative and postmodern school.

At the core of this dialogue is the issue of epistemology. In the narrative view, the nature of reality and accompanying normalcy become moving targets, shifting with each family's differing narrative. Thus, narrative therapists have mostly used the case study method to testify to the method's effectiveness and have been slow to experiment with ways of using quantitative methods to measure success. (See the Application section later in this chapter for illustrations of problems for which case studies have been published.) However, as qualitative methodological approaches, which are perhaps more compatible with capturing the process of change in this approach (e.g., phenomenology [Moustakas, 1994], grounded theory [Glaser & Strauss, 1967; Strauss & Corbin, 1990], and the case study method [Merriam, 1988]), continue to achieve higher credibility as vigorous methodological approaches, the literature will reflect more research.

An ethnographic study focusing on therapists' experiences in the use of narrative therapy (O'Connor, Davis, Meakes, Pickering, & Schuman, 2004) reveals that they perceive the narrative approach to be successful with clients in reducing presenting problems. These therapists also noted more enthusiastic successes as they have observed marked improvement and greater satisfaction in the development of a personal agency with their clients and viewed the narrative approach as highly respectful. Among the limitations of the narrative approach are the requirement for specialized training, the challenges to effectively address family violence, the relative density of time commitment and staff (for use of reflecting teams), and the use of consulting/reflecting teams (which, though helpful for clients, can be overwhelming and threatening for therapists).

Using an exploratory, phenomenological design with American Indian women, Keeling and Nielson (2005) employed art and writing to access their experiences and determine the suitability of narrative interventions with this population. A more recent outcome study (Weber et al., 2006) was conducted with a group dealing with eating disorder issues and employed techniques that focused on externalization of and disengagement from the problems. The participants also experienced depression and attended group weekly for 10 weeks. Pre- and posttests were administered, and the results showed a reduction in both depression scores and eating disorder risks. Additionally, all of the participants reported changes in daily practices that included less self-criticism.

Application to Families at Other Levels of Need

Examples of applications of the narrative approach used with a wide variety of individual and family problems include the following:

- Couple/relationship therapy (Blanton & Vandergriff-Avery, 2001; Brimball, Gardner, & Henline, 2003; Butler & Gardner, 2003; Freedman & Combs, 2000; Snyder, 2000)
- Working with children (Epston & Ronny, 2004; Goddard, Lehr, & Lapadat, 2000; Hurley, 2006)
- Parenting (Sax, 2007; Shalay & Brownlee, 2007; Wilkins & Donovan, 2007)
- Substance abuse (Anoretic & Anoretic, 1991; Lyness, 2002; Man-kwong, 2004; Winslade & Smith, 1997)
- AIDS (Dean, 1995; Rothschild, Brownlee, & Gallant, 2000; White & Epston, 1991)
- Domestic violence (Augusta-Scott & Dankwort, 2002; Drauker, 2003; Jenkins, 1990; Tomm, 2002; Wright, 2003)
- Gay, lesbian, bisexual, and transexual (GLBT) issues (Aman, 2007; Behan, 1999; Hurley, 2007; O'Dell, 2000; Saltzburg, 2007)
- Anorexia/bulimia (Dallos, 2004; Epston, 1993a, 1993b; Epston, Morris, & Maisel, 1995; Lock, Epston, Maisel, & de Faria, 2005; Padulo & Rees, 2006; Weber, Davis, & McPhie 2006)
- Body image (da Costa, Nelson, Rudes, & Guterman, 2007; Leahy & Harrigan, 2006)
- Grief and loss (Betz & Thorngren, 2006; McQuaide, 1995; Palmer, 2007; White, 1989a)
- Trauma (Beaudoin, 2005; Bhuvaneswar & Shafer, 2004; Charles-Edwards, 2007; Hardy, 2002; Lapsley, 2002)
- Support groups (Jones, 2004)
- Spirituality (Abels, 2000; Blanton, 2007; Faiver, Ingersoll, O'Brien, & McNally, 2001; Feinstein, 1997; Ramsey & Blieszner, 2000)

- Women's issues/sexual abuse (Gremillion, 2004; Verko, 2002)
- Men's issues/violence (Augusta-Scott, 2007a; Newman, 2007)
- Multicultural (Keeling & Nielson, 2005; Nwoye, 2006; Shalif & Makunga, 2007; Yuen & White, 2007)
- Disabilities (Begum, 2007; Eeltink & Duffy, 2004; Goddard, Lehr, & Lapadat, 2000)
- Prison population/corrections (Augusta-Scott, 2007)
- Therapeutic use of self (Cheon & Murphy, 2007b)
- Teaching/education (Eppler & Carolan, 2005; Marsten & Howard, 2006; Paquin, 2006; Speedy, 2005)

Ethical Challenges

Narrative theorists take the position that therapists are highly influenced by their own narratives as well as the dominant narratives of the culture (Semmler & Williams, 2000) and are subject to the constraints of race, gender, culture, and theoretical position (Fish, 1993; Laird, 2000; Waldgrave, 1998; White, 1989b). As such, they can never be neutral or value free, which may limit or shape what they think is relevant or important in a client's story. White and Epston (1990) and Madigan (1991) had an early caution for professionals to be aware that, because the therapeutic situation lies within the domains of power and knowledge, the therapeutic process always includes the possibility of social control and is never value free, apolitical, or context free.

Cheon and Murphy (2007) continue to emphasize the importance of the therapist's use of self within the therapeutic process. In training and supervising narrative therapists, significant emphasis is placed on the necessity of helping them to vigorously explore their own cultural narratives. This particularly relates to "depriviledging" their own stories and to the importance of focusing on use of self in the therapeutic process to be able to hear the narratives of others in a more neutral context (Cheon & Murphy, 2007).

Summary

Narrative therapy is an approach to individual and family therapy that uses storytelling as a primary therapeutic metaphor to empower people to create change in their lives. Based on social constructivist philosophy, the narrative approach was developed by Michael White, an Australian social worker, who drew from the work of theorists such as Foucault, Bruner, and Bateson. Proponents refer to the narrative therapy approach as the "third wave" of family therapy. It focuses on countering the effects that the dominant narratives of society have imposed on shaping human behavior, rather than on blaming the individual (psychodynamic approaches) or blaming the family (family systems theories).

The narrative model places great emphasis on a collaborative therapeutic alliance between the therapist and the client, in which they team together to challenge old stories and co-create new realities. Problems are investigated in terms of the meanings that a client assigns to them, rather than their causes. Assessment is intertwined with intervention as the problem-saturated story is first carefully deconstructed. Therapeutic strategies such as asking curious questions enables so-called news of a difference to emerge, and the session begins to focus on the exceptions that actively challenge the client's belief in the old story. These strategies involve carefully worded questions that are aimed at making the problem, not the person, be the problem, a process called *externalization* of the problem.

Through this process, the relative influence and power of the problem on the person is assessed and the resources of the individual in combating the problem are validated and celebrated. At this point, the influence of the person on the problem takes center stage through the uncovering of exceptions to problematic situation. Curious, gentle, respectful questions can be raised about these exceptions, involving the exception's history, significance, and spectators/audience. Setbacks are to be anticipated and plans made to deal with them. If possible, a reflecting team can provide new descriptions and previously unnoticed exceptions. Letters, certificates, and celebrations are used to amplify the content of the sessions and provide continuity to what has been accomplished between and after sessions.

Discussion Questions

1. What is meant by the notion that there is not one self but a multiplicity of selves?

2. Explain the idea that the self can only be defined in relationship with others.

3. Why does narrative therapy emphasize the meanings of problems, rather than their causes?

4. What is meant by the term *problem-saturated story?*

5. What is the role of assessment in narrative therapy?

6. What is meant by the phrase "the problem is the problem"?

7. What are some of the key ideas that narrative therapists rely on to increase the likelihood that therapy will be a collaborative process, rather than a therapist-directed process?

8. What role do oppression and power play in the context of a person's problem?

9. How can externalization of the problem be used in deescalating the oppressive story of the problem?

10. How can exceptions questions be used in helping to reauthor a person's story?

11. What value do letters, celebrations, and reflecting teams have in narrative therapy?

12. How can the narrative approach be used with families that are perceived to be functioning at each of the four levels?

13. If you used the narrative perspective, how would the way in which you see yourself working with families be different from the way it is now?

Internet Resources

www.dulwichcentre.org.au
www.narrativespace.com
www.narrativetherapycentre.com
www.centerfornarrativepractice.com
www.anxietyanddepression-help.com
www.psychnet-uk.com/psychotherapy/psychotherapy_narrative_therapy.htm

www.narrativeapproaches.com/
www.california.com/~rathbone/pmth.htm
www.psychotherapy.net

Suggested Readings

Andersen, T. (Ed.). (1991). *The reflecting team: Dialogues and dialogues about the dialogues.* New York: Norton.

The development of a new strategy in therapy is presented, in which professionals and clients trade places, exchange conversations, and open up new possibilities for change. Dialogues are exchanged in collaborative discussions among family, therapist, and reflecting team and result in the dissolving of traditional therapeutic boundaries.

Angus, L. E., & McLeod, J. (Eds.). (2004). *The handbook of narrative and psychotherapy: Practice theory and research.* Thousand Oaks, CA: Sage.

This volume presents narrative theory, applied research, and practice from a number of different disciplines. The editors have attempted to incorporate the varying voices and traditions that have contributed to the current narrative-informed therapy field.

Anoretic, M., & Epston, D. (1989). The taming of temper. *Dulwich Centre Newsletter* [Special Edition]: 3–26.

Anoretic's article discusses temper and behavior problems from a narrative viewpoint and the development of his ideas in dealing with these issues. Epson's article presents a method for dealing with out-of-control temper in children or adults. The approach is simple, economical, and amusing for all concerned, as it teaches individuals to substitute self-control for the control of others.

Anoretic, M., & Kowalski, K. (1990). Overcoming the effects of sexual abuse: Developing a self-perception of competence. In M. Anoretic & C. White (Eds.), *Ideas for therapy with sexual abuse.* Adelaide, S. Australia: Dulwich Centre.

Drawing from both the narrative approach and the model of brief solution-focused therapy, the authors approach the issue of sexual abuse as qualitatively not unlike other issues in therapy. They propose a framework for enhancing the perception of self as competent rather than as victim.

Eppler, C., & Carolan, M. (2005). Biblionarrative: A narrative technique uniting oral and written life-stories. *Journal of Family Psychotherapy, 16*(4), 31–43.

This paper explores an innovative, child-focused narrative therapy technique, biblionarrative. Relying on either talk or writing alone may produce an incomplete description of events, but biblionarrative allows researchers and clinicians access to information that may not otherwise be discovered.

Epston, D., & Ronny. (2003). Case study of client Ronny by David Epston. Available at www.narrative approaches.com/narrative%20papers%20folder/ronny.htm.

Freedman, J., & Combs, G. (1996). *Narrative therapies: The special construction of preferred realities.* New York: Norton.

Drawing from the narrative approach, the authors present practical information to the clinician. Issues of practice power, sociocultural context, and ethics are addressed in this acclaimed book.

Gilligan, S., & Price, R. (Eds.). (1993). *Therapeutic conversations.* New York: Norton.

Emerging from a conference in Tulsa (Tune, 1992), the book's contributors are well known in the narrative family therapy tradition, the solution-focused tradition, and conversational therapies. Chapter authors respond to one another's positions and perspectives. Contributors include John Weakland, David Epston, Michael White, Karl Tomm, and Michele Weiner-Davis.

Lieblich, A., McAdams, D. P., & Josselson, R. (Eds.). (2002). *Healing plots: The narrative basis of psychotherapy.* Washington, DC: American Psychological Association.

This book is the third volume in a series entitled *The Narrative Study of Lives.* This volume explores the relationship between therapy and narrative and how stories impact the therapeutic process. The selection of chapters describes therapeutic process from a variety of perspectives and settings.

Madigan, S. (2005). Narrative therapy with children (DVD). *Child Therapy with the Expert* series. Available at www.psychotherapy.net.

This video presents live case application of the narrative therapy approach with a family. Family members learn to separate themselves from their problems and retell their stories through a series of compassionate questions that uncover their repetitive patterns. Jon Carlson and Don Keat introduce Dr. Madigan and facilitate an in-depth discussion of the further impact and uses of the model.

Monk, G., Winslade, J., Crockett, K., & Epston, D. (Eds.). (1997). *Narrative therapy in practice: The archaeology of hope.* San Francisco: Jossey-Bass.

This instructive book presents the work of a collaboration of practitioners who have applied narrative therapy to diverse populations. It is filled with instructive, illustrative examples that describe the application of this approach in creative and hope-filled ways.

Ncube, N. (2006). *Tree of Life Project: An approach to working with vulnerable children* (DVD). International Journal of Narrative Therapy and Community Work, 1. Available from the Dulwich Centre, Adelaide, Australia.

This video applies narrative ideas in work with vulnerable children in South Africa. The video was filmed in Arua, Uganda, at the TPO Training Centre in November 2006 and is 70 minutes long.

Speedy, J. (2005). Using poetic documents: An exploration of poststructuralist ideas and poetic practices in narrative therapy. *British Journal of Guidance and Counselling, 33*(3), 283–298.

This article explores the use of poetic documents in narrative therapy practice while considering the ways in which feminist and poststructuralist ideas inform these practices. The text is illustrated with examples from author's own therapeutic practice.

Tomm, K. (1988). Interventive interviewing: Intending to ask lineal, circular, strategic, or reflexive questions? *Family Process, 27,* 1–15.

This article discusses questions based on circular rather than lineal assumptions. A framework is offered that distinguishes four major groups of questions and offers guidelines to their use. Lineal assumptions lead to lineal and strategic questions; circular assumptions lead to circular and reflexive questions. The categories of questions are discussed regarding their effects on families and on therapists.

White, M. (2007). *Maps of narrative practice.* New York: Norton.

This book explores in depth the underlying structure of the six primary areas of narrative therapy practice: externalizing conversations, reauthoring conversations, remembering conversations, definitional ceremonies, unique outcome conversations, and scaffolding conversations. Case examples are used to chart the flow of the therapeutic conversations with the purpose of providing a roadmap for therapists.

White, M., & Epston, D. (1990). *Narrative means to therapeutic ends.* New York: Norton.

Letters, documents, and certificates offer a respectful and often playful means to encourage the restorying of experience. The narrative approach is explained. Many examples are offered that are suitable for children, adolescents, and adults. In addition, the restraints of power and the political implications inherent in therapy are discussed.

Yuen, A., & White, C. (Eds.). (2007). *Conversations about gender, culture, violence and narrative practice: Stories of hope and complexity from women of many cultures.* Adelaide, Australia: The Dulwich Centre.

This book contains writings from women of many cultures about initiatives, projects, and ways of responding to violence. It includes practice-based chapters describing narrative ways of working with those who have experienced violence and also creative ways of engaging with men and women who have enacted violence against others.

References

Abels, S. L. (2000). *Spirituality in social work practice: Narratives for professional helping.* Denver: Love.

Aman, J. (2007). A journey towards gender belonging: Adam's story. *International Journal of Narrative Therapy and Community Work, 3,* 39–46.

American Psychiatric Association. (2000). *Diagnostic and statistical manual of mental disorders* (4th ed., text revision). Washington, DC: Author.

Andersen, T. (Ed.). (1991). *The reflecting team: Dialogues and dialogues about the dialogues.* New York: Norton.

Anoretic, M., & Anoretic, D. (1991). Michael White's cybernetic approach. In T. C. Todd & M. D. Selekman (Eds.), *Family therapy approaches with adolescent substance abusers.* Boston: Allyn & Bacon.

Augusta-Scott, T. (2007a). Conversations with men about women's violence: Ending men's violence by challenging gender essentialism. In C. Brown & T. Augusta-Scott (Eds.), *Narrative therapy: Making meaning, making lives* (pp. 197–210). Thousand Oaks, CA: Sage.

Augusta-Scott, T. (2007b). Letters from prison: Re-authoring identity with men who have perpetrated sexual abuse. In C. Brown & T. Augusta-Scott (Eds.), *Narrative therapy: Making meaning, making lives* (pp. 251–268). Thousand Oaks, CA: Sage.

Augusta-Scott, T., & Dankwort, J. (2002). Partner abuse group intervention: Lessons from education and narrative therapy approaches. *Journal of Interpersonal Violence, 17*(7), 783–805.

Bateson, G. (1972). *Steps to an ecology of the mind.* New York: Ballantine.

Bateson, G. (1979). *Mind and nature: A necessary unity.* London: Wildwood House.

Beaudoin, M. (2005). Agency and choice in the face of trauma: A narrative therapy map. *Journal of Systemic Therapies, 24*(4), 32–50.

Begum, M. (2007). Conversations with children with disabilities and their mothers. *International Journal of Narrative Therapy and Community Work, 3,* 11–16.

Behan, C. (1999). Linking lives around shared themes: Narrative group therapy with gay men. *Gecko: A Journal of Deconstruction and Narrative Ideas in Therapeutic Practice, 2.* Available online at http://www.dulwichcentre.com.au.

Besa, D. (1994). Narrative family therapy: A multiple baseline outcome study including collateral effects of verbal behavior. *Research on Social Work Practice, 4*(3), 309–325.

Betz, G., & Thorngren, J. (2006). Ambiguous loss and the family grieving process. *Family Journal, 14*(4), 359–365.

Bhuvaneswar, C., & Shafer, A. (2004). Survivor of THAT time, THAT place: Clinical uses of violence survivors' narratives. *Journal of Medical Humanities, 25*(2), 109–127.

Blanton, P. (2007). Adding silence to stories: Narrative therapy and contemplation. *Contemporary Family Therapy: An International Journal, 29*(4), 211–221.

Blanton, P., & Vandergriff-Avery, M. (2001). Marital therapy and marital power: Constructing narratives of sharing relational and positional power. *Contemporary Family Therapy, 23*(3), 295–308.

Brimball, A. S., Gardner, B. C., & Henline, B. H. (2003). Enhancing narrative couple therapy process with an enactment scaffolding. *Contemporary Family Therapy: An International Journal, 25*(4), 391–415.

Bruner, E. (1986). Experience and its expression. In V. Turner & E. Bruner (Eds.), *The anthropology of experience.* Chicago: University of Illinois Press.

Bruner, J. (1990). *Acts of meaning.* Cambridge, MA: Harvard University Press.

Bruner, J. (2002).The narrative creation of self. In L. E. Angus & J. McLeod (Eds.), *The handbook of narrative and psychotherapy* (pp. 3–14). Thousand Oaks, CA: Sage.

Butler, M. H., & Gardner, B. C. (2003). Dynamically adapting enactments to couple reactivity: Five developmental stages of enactments over the course of therapy. *Journal of Marital and Family Therapy, 29,* 311–327.

Chang, J., & Phillips, M. (1993). Michael White and Steve de Shazer: New directions in family therapy. In S. Gilligan & R. Price (Eds.), *Therapeutic conversations.* New York: Norton.

Charles-Edwards, D. (2007). Neimeyer and the construction of loss. *Therapy Today, 18*(5), 15–17.

Cheon, H., & Murphy, M. (2007). The self-of-the-therapist awakened: Postmodern approaches to the use of self in marriage and family therapy. *Journal of Feminist Family Therapy, 19*(1), 1–16.

da Costa, D., Nelson, T., Rudes, J., & Guterman, J. (2007). A narrative approach to body dysmorphic disorder. *Journal of Mental Health Counseling, 29*(1), 67–80.

Dallos, R. (2004). Narrative therapy: Integrating ideas from narrative and attachment theory in systemic therapy with eating disorders. *Journal of Family Therapy, 26*(1), 40–66.

Dean, R. G. (1995). Stories of AIDS: The use of the narrative as an approach to understanding in an AIDS support group. *Clinical Social Work Journal, 23*(3), 287–304.

Drauker, C. (2003). Unique outcomes of women and men who were abused. *Perspectives in Psychiatric Care, 3*(1), 7–17.

Drewery, W., Winslade, J., & Monk, G. (2000). Resisting the dominating story: Towards a deeper understanding of narrative therapy. In R. A. Neimeyer & J. D. Raskin (Eds.), *Constructions of disorder: Meaning-making frameworks for psychotherapy.* Washington, DC: American Psychological Association.

Eeltink, C., & Duffy, M. (2004). Restorying the illness experience in multiple sclerosis. *Family Journal, 12*(3), 282–286.

Eppler, C., & Carolan, M. (2005). Biblionarrative: A narrative technique uniting oral and written life-stories. *Journal of Family Psychotherapy, 16*(4), 31–43.

Epston, D. (1984). Guest address: Fourth Australian family therapy conference. *Australian Journal of Family Therapy, 5,* 11–16.

Epston, D. (1993a). *Workshop on anorexia.* Charter-Peachford Hospital, Atlanta, GA.

Epston, D. (1993b). *The approach of the Anti-Anorexia (Bulimia) League.* Auckland, New Zealand: Family Therapy Centre.

Epston, D., Morris, F., & Maisel, R. (1995). A narrative approach to so-called anorexia/bulimia. *Journal of Feminist Family Therapy, 7*(1/2) 69–96.

Epston, D., & Ronny. (2004, March). *Narrative therapy with children and their families: Taming the terrier.* Available online at www.narrativeapproaches.com.

Faiver, C., Ingersoll, R. E., O'Brien, E., & McNally, C. (2001). *Explorations in counseling and spirituality: Philosophical, practical and personal reflections.* Sydney, Australia: Brooks/Cole.

Feinstein, D. (1997). Personal mythology and psychotherapy: Myth-making in psychological and spiritual development. *American Journal of Orthopsychiatry, 67*(4), 508–521.

Fish, V. (1993). Poststructuralism in family therapy: Interrogating the narrative/conversational mode. *Journal of Marital and Family Therapy, 19*(3), 221–232.

Foucault, M. (1965). *Madness and civilization: A history of insanity in the Age of Reason.* New York: Random House.

Foucault, M. (1979). *Discipline and punish: The birth of the prison.* London: Peregrine.

Foucault, M. (1980). *Power/knowledge: Selected interviews and other writings.* New York: Pantheon.

Freedman, J. H., & Combs, G. (2000). Narrative therapy with couples. In F. M. Dattilio & L. J. Bevilacqua (Eds.), *Comparative treatments for relationship dysfunction* (pp. 342–361). New York: Springer.

Glaser, B., & Strauss, A. (1967). *The discovery of grounded theory.* Chicago: Aldine.

Goddard, J. A., Lehr, R., & Lapadat, J. C. (2000). Parents of children with disabilities: Telling a different story. *Canadian Journal of Counselling, 34*(4), 273–289.

Gold, J., Morris, G., & Gretchen, M. (2003). Family resistance to counseling: The initial agenda for intergenerational and narrative approaches. *Family Journal and Therapy for Couples and Families, 11*(4), 374–379.

Gremillion, H. (2004). Unpacking essentialisms in therapy: Lessons for feminist approaches from narrative work. *Journal of Constructivist Psychology, 17*(3), 173–201.

Hardy, K. (2002). Coming to terms with the events of September 11 (Interview). *International Journal of Narrative Therapy and Community Work, 1.*

Hurley, D. (2006). Internalized other interviewing of children exposed to violence. *Journal of Systemic Therapies, 25*(2), 50–63.

Hurley, E. (2007). Establishing non-criminal records. *International Journal of Narrative Therapy and Community Work, 3,* 3–10.

Jenkins, A. (1990). *Invitations to responsibility: The therapeutic engagement of men who are violent and abusive.* Adelaide, South Australia: Dulwich Centre Publications.

Jones, A. C. (2004). Transforming the story: Narrative applications to a stepmother support group. *Families in Society, 85*(1), 129–139.

Keeling, M., & Nielson, L. (2005). Indian women's experience of a narrative intervention using art and writing. *Contemporary Family Therapy: An International Journal, 27*(3), 435–452.

Laird, J. (2000). Culture and narrative as metaphors for clinical practice with families. In D. H. Demo, K. R. Allen, & M. A. Fine (Eds.), *Handbook of family diversity* (pp. 338–358). New York: Oxford University Press.

Lapsley, M. (2002). The healing of memories (Interview). *International Journal of Narrative Therapy and Community Work, 2.*

Leahy, T., & Harrigan, R. (2006). Using narrative therapy in sport psychology practice: Application to a psycho educational body image program. *Sport Psychologist, 20*(4), 480–494.

Lock, A., Epston, D., Maisel, R., & de Faria, N. (2005). Resisting anorexia/bulimia: Foucauldian perspectives in narrative therapy. *British Journal of Guidance and Counselling, 33*(3), 315–332.

Lyness, K. P. (2002). Alcohol problems in Native Alaskans: Risk, resiliency, and native treatment approaches. *Journal of Ethnicity in Substance Abuse, 1*(3), 39–56.

Madigan, S. (1991). Discursive restraints in therapist practice: Situating therapist questions in the presence of the family. *Dulwich Centre Newsletter, 3,* 13–20.

Madigan, S. (2005). *Narrative therapy for children.* DVD available at www.psychotherapy.net.

Man-kwong, H. (2004). Overcoming craving: The use of narrative practices in breaking drug habits. *International Journal of Narrative Therapy, 1.*

Markus, H., & Nurius, P. (1986). Possible selves. *American Psychologist, 41,* 954–969.

Marsten, D., & Howard, G. (2006). Shared influence: A narrative approach to teaching narrative therapy. *Journal of Systemic Therapies, 25*(4), 97–110.

McLeod, J. (1999). A narrative social constructionist approach to therapeutic empathy. *Counseling andPsychology Quarterly, 12*(4), 377–394.

McLeod, J. (2006). Narrative thinking and the emergence of post-psychological therapies. *Narrative Inquiry, 16*(1), 201–210.

McQuaide, S. (1995). Storying the suicide of one's child. *Clinical Social Work Journal, 23*(4), 417–428.

McQuaide, S. (2000) Women's resilience at midlife: What is it? How do you mobilize it? In E. Norman (Ed.), *Resiliency enhancement: Putting the strengths perspective into social work practice* (pp. 70–82). New York: Columbia University Press.

Merriam, S. (1988). *Case study research in education: A qualitative approach.* San Francisco: Jossey-Bass.

Monk, G., Winslade, J., Crockett, K., & Epston, D. (Eds.). (1997). *Narrative therapy in practice: the archaeology of hope.* San Francisco: Jossey-Bass.

Moustakas, C. (1994). *Phenomenological research methods.* Thousand Oaks, CA: Sage.

Neimeyer, R. A. (1993). An appraisal of constructivist psychotherapies. *Journal of Consulting and Clinical Psychology, 61*(2), 221–234.

Neimeyer, R. (2006). Narrating the dialogical self: Toward an expanded toolbox for the counselling psychologist. *Counselling Psychology Quarterly, 19*(1), 105–120.

Newman, D. (2007). Audience as accountability? Dilemmas in the use of outsider-witness practices in supporting men's anti-violence projects. *International Journal of Narrative Therapy and Community Work, 4,* 63–69.

Nichols, M. P., & Schwartz, R. C. (2007). *Family therapy: Concepts and methods* (7th ed.). Boston: Allyn & Bacon.

Nwoye, A. (2006). A narrative approach to child and family therapy in Africa. *Contemporary Family Therapy: An International Journal, 28*(1), 1–23.

Nylund, D., & Nylund, D. A. (2003). Narrative therapy as a counter-hegemonic practice. *Men and Masculinities, 5*(4), 386–395.

O'Connor, T., Davis, A., Meakes, E., Pickering, R., & Schuman, M. (2004). Narrative therapy using a reflecting team: An ethnographic study of therapists' experiences. *Contemporary Family Therapy, 26*(1), 23–39.

O'Dell, S. (2000). Psychotherapy with gay and lesbian families: Opportunities for cultural inclusion and clinical challenge. *Clinical Social Work Journal, 28*(2), 171–182.

Padulo, M., & Rees, A. (2006). Motivating women with disordered eating towards empowerment and change using narratives of archetypal metaphor. *Women and Therapy, 29*(1/2), 63–81.

Paquin, G. (2006). Including narrative concepts in social work practice classes: Teaching to client strengths. *Journal of Teaching in Social Work, 26*(1/2), 127–145.

Palmer, V. (2007). Narrative repair: (RE)covery, vulnerability, service, and suffering. *Illness, Crisis, and Loss, 15*(4), 371–388.

Parry, A., & Doan, R. E. (1994) *Story re-visions: Narrative therapy in the post-modern world.* New York: Guilford Press.

Ramsey, J. L., & Blieszner, R. (2000). Transcending a lifetime of losses: The importance of spirituality in old age. In J. H. Harvey & E. D. Miller (Eds.), *Loss and trauma: General and close relationship perspectives.* Philadelphia: Brunner-Routledge.

Rothschild, P., Brownlee, K., & Gallant, J. P. (2000). Narrative interventions for working with persons with AIDS: A case study. *Journal of Family Psychotherapy, 11*(3), 1–13.

Saltzburg, S. (2007). Narrative therapy pathways for re-authoring with parents of adolescents coming-out as lesbian, gay, and bisexual. *Contemporary Family Therapy: An International Journal, 29*(1/2), 57–69.

Sax, P. (2007). Finding common ground: Parents speak out about family-centered practices. *Journal of Systemic Therapies, 26*(3), 72–90.

Semmler, P., & Williams, C. B. (2000). Narrative therapy: A storied context for multicultural counseling. *Journal of Multicultural Counseling and Development, 28*(1), 51–62.

Shalay, N., & Brownlee, K. (2007). Narrative family therapy with blended families. *Journal of Family Psychotherapy, 18*(2), 17–30.

Shalif, Y., & Makunga, A. (2007). Reflections on "Stories from Rwanda." *International Journal of Narrative Therapy and Community Work, 1,* 60–61.

Snyder, M. (2000). The loss and recovery of erotic intimacy in primary relationships: Narrative therapy and relationship enhancement therapy. *Family Journal-Counseling and Therapy for Couples and Families, 8*(1), 37–46.

Speedy, J. (2005). Using poetic documents: An exploration of poststructuralist ideas and poetic practices in narrative therapy. *British Journal of Guidance and Counselling, 33*(3), 283–298.

Strauss, A., & Corbin, J. (1990). *Basics of qualitative research: Grounded theory procedures and techniques.* Newbury Park, CA: Sage.

Sued, E., & Amunategui, B. (2003). A Mexican perspective on teaching narrative ideas. *International Journal of Narrative Therapy and Community Work, 4.*

Tomm, K. (1987). Interventive interviewing: Part I. Strategizing as a fourth guideline for the therapist. *Family Process, 26,* 3–13.

Tomm, K. (1993). The courage to protest: A commentary on Michael White's work. In S. Gilligan & R. Price (Eds.), *Therapeutic conversations.* New York: Norton.

Tomm, K. (2002). Enabling forgiveness and reconciliation in family therapy. *International Journal of Narrative Therapy and Community Work, 1,* 65–69.

Verko, J. (2002). Women's outrage and the pressure to forgive: Working with survivors of childhood sexual abuse. *International Journal of Narrative Therapy and Community Work, 1,* 23–27.

Vodde, R., & Gallant, J. P. (2002). Bridging the gap between micro and macro practice: Large scale change and the work of Michael White and David Epston. *Journal of Social Work Education, 38*(3), 439–459.

Waldgrave, C. (1998). The challenge of culture to psychology and postmodern thinking In M. McGoldrick (Ed.), *Re-visioning family therapy: Race, culture and gender in clinical practice* (pp. 404–413). New York: Guilford Press.

Walsh, F. (1998). *Strengthening family resilience.* New York: Guilford Press.

Weber, M., Davis, K., & McPhie, L. (2006). Narrative therapy, eating disorders and groups: Enhancing outcomes in rural NSW. *Australian Social Work, 59*(4), 391–405.

White, M. (1986). Family escape from trouble. *Family Therapy Case Studies, 1,* 29–33.

White, M. (1988/1989, Summer). The externalizing of the problem and the re-authoring of lives and relationships. *Dulwich Centre Newsletter,* 3–21.

White, M. (1989a, Spring). Saying hullo again: The reincorporation of the lost relationship in the resolution of grief. *Dulwich Centre Newsletter,* 7–11.

White, M. (1989b, Summer). Family therapy training and supervision in a world of experience and narrative. *Dulwich Centre Newsletter,* 27–38.

White, M. (1991). Deconstruction and therapy. *Dulwich Centre Newsletter, 3,* 21–40.

White, M. (1993). Deconstruction and therapy. In S. Gilligan & R. Price (Eds.), *Therapeutic conversations* (pp. 22–61). New York: Norton.

White, M. (2005). Michael White workshop notes. Available online at www.dulwichcentre.org.au/Michael%20White%20Workshop%20Notes.pdf.

White, M., & Epston, D. (1990). *Narrative means to therapeutic ends.* New York: Norton.

White, M., & Epston, D. (1991). A conversation about AIDS and dying. *Dulwich Centre Newsletter, 2,* 5–16.

White, M. (2007). *Maps of narrative practice.* Adelaide, Australia: Dulwich Centre.

Wilkins, P., & Donovan, M. (2007). A conversation with Virus X: Outing a malevolent and subversive force in parents' lives. *Australian and New Zealand Journal of Family Therapy, 28*(3), 138–145.

Winslade, J., & Smith, L. (1997) Countering alcoholic narratives. In G. Monk, J. Winslade, K. Crocket, & D. Epston (Eds.), *Narrative therapy in practice: The archaeology of hope.* San Francisco: Jossey-Bass.

Wright, J. (2003). Considering issues of domestic violence and abuse in palliative care and bereavement situations. *International Journal of Narrative Therapy and Community Work, 3,* 72–74.

Yuen, A., & White, C. (2007). *Conversations about gender, culture, violence & narrative practice: Stories of hope and complexity from women of many cultures.* Adelaide, South Australia: Dulwich Centre Publications.

12

Object Relations Family Interventions

Allie C. Kilpatrick, Ph.D., and Elizabeth O. Trawick, M.D.

Object relations family therapy is a relatively new model of family treatment. Its origins are in two separate schools of thought whose streams have merged into a dynamic body that is having a major impact on family therapy today. Not unlike the mighty, milky-white Amazon, where it merges with the black waters of the Negro River but remains separate before finally mingling, psychoanalysis and family therapy have run together and commingled before finally merging to form object relations family therapy.

Object relations theory is considered to be the bridge between psychoanalysis—the study of individuals—and family theory—the study of social relationships. It may be defined as

> a modern adaptation of psychoanalytic theory that places less emphasis on the drives of aggression and sexuality as motivational forces and more emphasis on human relationships as the primary motivational force in life. Object relations theorists believe that we are relationship seeking rather than pleasure seeking as Freud suggested. The importance of relationships in the theory translates to relationships as the main focus of psychotherapy, especially the relationship with the therapist. (Klee, 2007)

In recognizing that the newborn baby has an *ego,* a part of the personality that copes with internal and external reality, object relations theorists have been able to understand early modes of mental functioning based on fantasies of splitting, projection, and introjection that occur in the processes of attaching to and differentiating from the family. These processes, first described by psychoanalysts, have now been recognized in families and larger social groups.

The lack of differentiation of family members has become one of the cornerstones of Murray Bowen's work (1978) in understanding families and Helm Stierlin's work (1976) in studying larger social group functioning (Slipp, 1984). When personality structure does not develop, enmeshment within the family group interferes with recognition of individual needs, which then cannot receive attention. This leads to the impoverishment of individuals and thus of the group.

To summarize this introduction, it can be stated that the term *object relations* refers to the self-structure that each individual internalizes early in childhood. This self-structure functions as a blueprint for establishing and maintaining relationships throughout life. Individual and family dysfunction is the expression of traumatic self-object internalizations from childhood that are acted out in current relationships. Object relations family interventions is the resolution of these self-destructive patterns of relating, which is necessary for people to become mature and become self-actualizing.

Family Needs

Object relations concepts developed as a way to understand psychotic, borderline, and narcissistic conditions. These concepts continue to provide the most useful tools for treatment of these conditions, in which mental functioning remains at an immature level, with massive use of defenses such as splitting and projective identification. After the recognition that groups such as families may function in ways similar to immature individuals by joining to utilize early and immature defense mechanisms, the path was paved to develop interventions that interpret these processes within the family setting.

Thus, object relations family interventions (ORFI) are indicated whenever family patterns of resolving problems and relieving emotional pain rely on defensive functioning, rather than on evaluation of reality with containment of emotional states followed by appropriate action. ORFI may be possible primarily in families functioning at Levels III or IV, where basic needs have been met and family structure is stable enough for members to meet together regularly. But ORFI may also be helpful in Level I and II families, when painful emotional states such as terror and depression are overwhelming the family's ability to maintain structural cohesiveness. Thus, ORFI is also useful for all family levels following severe trauma, when resulting emotional states overwhelm the family's usual patterns of processing emotion. At such times, the therapist's ability to know and modulate emotional states for the family may diminish actions that are damaging and may lead to deeper change in the family system.

Within the family system, the modes of mental functioning discovered by psychoanalysts may promote or disrupt attachment, bonding, love, caring, development, and intimacy, depending on whether they are used as a means of communication with self and others or as a barrier against communication. To explain, *projective identification* was first described in 1946 by Melanie Klein, an English psychoanalyst, as a way of ridding the self of unwanted painful or terrifying experiences, which were projected into the object, who then came to be experienced as identical to the unwanted part. This was thought to be essential in early infancy, allowing for nurture of the growing ego by taking in good experiences while eliminating the bad. Overreliance on projective identification in infancy or its persistence after infancy was thought to be a sign of impaired ego development.

As described by Grinberg, Sor, and Tabak de Bianchedi (1977), a student of Klein's, Wilfred Bion, recognized that for the infant, projective identification is also the means of communicating with the mother. Neuroscience researchers such as Schore (1994, 2000) have begun to describe the neural pathways through which the nonverbal infant seems to give to the mother emotional states representing needs for physical care and love. Through internal, neural processes of her own, the mother unconsciously and consciously considers the communication and responds. According to Bion, the infant introjects and internalizes the mother's response and attitude to the projection, thus learning early in life the meaning of its inner world and internalizing a listening attitude toward its self.

When this process works "good enough," a description used by Donald Winnicott (1965), another English psychoanalyst, to describe adequate mothering, the stage is set for a lifelong process of intimate communication both verbally and nonverbally with projective processes. When the process does not work between the mother and the infant, however, the stage is set for a lifelong unconscious process of using projective processes to rid oneself of unwanted inner experiences. Because the individual builds barriers against the unwanted parts that are felt to be in others, communication is interrupted. Carried to an extreme, reality may be so altered that an individual becomes psychotic. To a lesser extent, misperception of certain aspects of another person commonly occurs.

Within a family unit, systems of projective identifications develop and may persist throughout life. As with individuals, these projections may function as communications with both conscious and unconscious responsiveness to needs of individual members. Or the projections may function as a means of getting rid of the unwanted. In this case, the family develops collusive systems of projections, in which one member may carry a projection for another member in exchange for a need being met or a projection being accepted by the other. Carried to the extreme, the family using a projective system becomes poorly functioning, as reality testing is altered and action may be taken to protect against contact with the unwanted.

In a paper presented at the 2004 International Psychoanalytic Congress, Isidoro Berenstein of Buenos Aires, Argentina, described the family as a multipersonal, intersubjective organization with an unconscious structure, which he called the *unconscious family structure.* In this organization, the members are mutually linked in ways that are largely unconscious. In family therapy, the object relationships that are talked about in individual therapy are present and enacted. The presence of linked others allows the unconscious family structure to be reached in a way that is not possible in individual therapy as mental processes come to be lived out in the session. Discommunicative projective systems, which are extremely common and cause a multitude of difficulties, can then be addressed.

The three most common marital complaints—lack of communication, constant arguments, and unmet emotional needs—are understandable in this context. The remarkable and common experience of hearing several people describe one event with a totally different memory and emotional reaction can be comprehended with the recognition that each may be experiencing the other as an unwanted part of the self, thus altering reality of the interaction. Intimacy, both emotional and sexual, is blocked by these processes. To make matters worse, because the family has become a system with an unconscious structure in which members depend on each other to carry projections, the pursuit of individual goals conflicts with the pursuit of relational goals and so are undermined (Finkelstein, 1987). *Enmeshment* with unclear emotional boundaries results. To varying degrees, the family is experienced as a needed but hostile and controlling web.

As a result of these shared, unconscious, internalized object relations, children often develop symptoms and become the identified patient who is jealous, hyperactive, angry, or even ill. When a child has an illness or learning difficulty, the family may respond inappropriately and with rejection, as the child may represent an unacceptable aspect of the parents or other siblings. At other times, parents may find ambivalent pleasure in allowing gratification of unacceptable desires by their children and then will be unable to limit behavior that is also disturbing. Thus, children are confused by their parents' double messages and are truly in a bind as they sense their parents' pleased excitement with their unwanted behavior. Siblings may join parents in choosing one child as the recipient of projections. That child is then in the distressing position of accepting the role demanded by the projections in exchange for vital provisions. Not uncommonly, this child is unable to develop a sense of self and becomes depressed. ORFI is necessary in situations like this so that each family member can come to carry and be responsible for his or her own being, freeing each to develop.

Object relations family interventions deal with shared, unconscious, internalized object relations. Focusing on the interaction and interdependence of individual dynamics and family system functioning is crucial in the application of an integrated understanding to family interventions. The family is perceived not as a set of individuals but as a system comprising sets of relationships that function in ways unique to that specific family, the unconscious family structure. The immediate goal is not symptom resolution but a progression through the current developmental phase of family life with an improved ability to work as a group and to differentiate among and meet the individual members' needs. Thus, this model is especially relevant for Level IV families.

In regard to whether ORFI is indicated for a specific family, it is important to remember that psychological maturity is not necessarily related to socioeconomic status. Applegate (1990) has explored aspects of object relations theory within the sociocultural context of family constellations, childrearing practices, race, and ethnicity. The interrelationship of the internal world of object relations and the external world of multiculturalism is offered as a clinically useful way of examining issues arising from ethnic differences.

Slipp (1988) observes that ethnicity alone has not been found as an issue in ORFI's relevance. Although there are differences between ethnic and racial groups, the basic mental functioning of splitting with projection and introjection is common to all people. If the clinician is skilled and able to experience intense emotional states, these processes will be recognized and content specific to various ethnic and cultural groups will be identified and interpreted. In regard to sexual orientation, therapists generally use the same treatment methods with traditional and same-sex couples (Parker, 1996).

One must remember, however, that the lack of societal supports and resources, as well as societal sanctions imposed by the dominant culture, must be addressed within the therapeutic dialogue. Families that are functioning at Level IV may come to the clinician with problems described as internal or interpersonal conflicts, anger, blaming, lack of communication, desire for growth and greater intimacy, loss of confidence in self or spouse, depression, loneliness, or isolation. These families generally want to understand these situations and are reflective. The next section presents a case study in which ORFI is an effective explanatory and interventive method.

Family Case Assessment

Assessment of families for ORFI does not necessarily follow the common pattern of history taking, because, as with psychoanalysis, the way and order in which information is presented is essential to understanding the interactional difficulties. In other words, the mode of presentation is data that can aid in diagnosis. Furthermore, because it is essential that the therapist be available to enter into the process as a recipient of projections of emotions, he or she must remain nondirective and available from the beginning to hear the family. Although history is taken nondirectively, by the third or fourth interview, the family's ability to use ORFI can be determined based on their cooperativeness in providing linked information and their response to a holding environment and interpretive interventions.

In this context, an important source of information in assessment is the so-called countertransference reaction of the practitioner. The concept of *countertransference* has evolved in psychoanalysis. Originally, it implied an unacceptable emotional reaction on the part of the therapist that interfered with understanding. With a deeper appreciation of the power and necessity of projective processes to communicate noncognitive and unverbalized thoughts and emotional states, the emotional reaction of the therapist has come to be viewed as essential to understanding. Unless the therapist has an actual experience, the individual or family in therapy will often feel they have not been heard, even when the interpretation is intellectually correct.

Recognition of the importance of countertransference has placed a responsibility on the therapist, who must work to allow emotional reactions to be alive while maintaining the capacity to reflect and think of the reactions without responding reflexively with action. Indeed, the therapist must discern reactions that are in fact due to his or her own emotional blocks, a task that requires self-knowledge. The following case, as told by the practitioner, demonstrates this process:

> At age 68, Al, a prosperous retired executive, called to seek treatment for his 61-year-old wife, Mary, who was in the midst of her fourth severe depression. Al and his married children wished to bring her in, as she could not come herself. Indeed, when seen, Mary seemed barely functional: She spoke only in a whisper if at all, moved slowly, and had an extremely downcast, deadened expression. She said she saw no reason to live but had no suicidal plans.
>
> Al spoke for his wife, explaining that she had become depressed several weeks before during a trip to Europe with their son and daughter-in-law. Al had had a wonderful time, although it was somewhat difficult driving in strange countries, and he had depended on his competent son, of whom he was proud. Mary, however, had become more and more depressed as the trip went on, eventually withdrawing to hotel rooms and causing great discomfort in the group. They all agreed that perhaps it was the rainy weather.
>
> As Mary sat motionless, the family explained that she had always been moody, especially in the last seven to eight years, when she had begun to have severe episodes of depression. Al never felt depressed and could not understand depression. He had always worked and gotten along with people. He was a peacemaker, and it made his wife mad. He simply did not get angry. Since Al's retirement seven years before, Mary had become more depressed, wanting to be with him almost all the time. He, however, wanted time to golf with the boys and was troubled that she "punished" him by withdrawing to the back of the house after he spent a day away. On the trip, Al had wanted to be with other people; Mary had wanted to be in the room with him at night and complained that her feet hurt and she would like to put them up on his lap and relax.

As Al spoke, Mary sat motionless, and the children silently looked away, the therapist became aware of a deep feeling of hurt, angry longing that seemed to be present, drawing them together and pushing them apart at the same time. The therapist was also aware of her internal response, a wish to make peace as a mother might between two of her children, accompanied by an urge to tell them to knock it off, behave, and stop whining. On the surface, the consultation was about Mary's pain, but Al spoke for Mary, seeming to author the story of her depression as if he knew of it. The children seemed to agree that Al had the story right and wished their mother to be "corrected." The therapist made a statement recognizing the longing each experienced without assigning it to any one person and was careful to avoid labeling Mary as the "ill patient." All wished to continue, and Mary seemed to move a little more freely. Al took her arm to help her as she left the room.

In assessing this original session, the therapist thought that Mary was "holding" depression for all the family members and was overwhelmed. The therapist was also struck by the focus of the family on correcting the situation, not simply denying it. Mary seemed to accept the family's projections of emotional pain, and the therapist wondered what the family accepted for her in return, why she was willing to engage in this painful collusion.

The therapist was aware that she had a mixed reaction of wishing to be helpful but feeling annoyed and critical at the same time. She was struck by the family's level of functioning, wish to work together, and positive response to her containing the emotional pain. Thus, despite Mary's deep depression, the therapist elected to continue this approach.

In subsequent sessions, attended by Al and Mary and sometimes the grown children, Al focused on his frustration that their life was not happier since his retirement. He had thought there would be time to play golf with his friends and to travel. He wanted more time with his son and daughter and perhaps to go on a trip alone, something he had never done. Instead, he found that his children seemed more distant and that he was tied to Mary.

Mary, a homemaker who had many artistic interests and volunteer activities, quietly whispered that she thought that they would finally be together. It emerged that during their 42-year marriage, Al had worked long hours, often getting home in time to read to the children and go to bed himself, only to be up at the crack of dawn and off to work. Weekends were devoted to church and children's activities when Al was not working at home. Mary had always felt lonely but had tolerated the situation because she felt it was for the family, and the children were doing well. Moreover, she thought that some day "Al will retire and it will be my turn." Al had not noticed her loneliness or any emotional unhappiness in the family or himself. He had enjoyed the children, and Mary agreed that he was a wonderful father.

The grand picture, recreated in interactions within the first few sessions and in their perceptions of their life together, was of Mary as frighteningly sensitive, demanding, and depressive and Al as happy, content, hardworking, engaged, and devoid of unpleasant emotion other than criticism of Mary. The children had grown into competent adults but had difficulties in tolerating feelings, seeming to agree with their father that their mother felt and demanded too much. In choosing their own partners, they had responded to dynamics within the family. The daughter, always closest to her father, married a man who had not attended college but ran a blue-collar business and would always be home for dinner and weekends. The son, perceived as sensitive and artistic like his mother, was highly successful at a business that he ran from his home while his wife worked long hours away from home. They had chosen to have no children.

Dialogue of retirement and the trip was associated with a feeling of depression, which Mary silently expressed by slumping more in the chair and which Al denied by turning the focus to curing Mary's depression, perhaps with medication. Rather than label Mary as the "ill patient," interventions focused on depression as related to Al's retirement and aging. When these subjects were present, the therapist experienced feelings of sadness and fear, but family members turned to Mary and focused on her as depressed. As the therapist interpreted the feelings of loss and fear for the future that arose in relationship to Al and Mary's aging, the family was able to shift the focus from Mary and began the human process of accepting losses. The process of projective identification was operative within the family, but when painful effects were contained in the therapeutic setting and identified by interpretation, the family responded, indicating that they were good candidates for ORFI.

As the family and therapist explored the onset of Mary's depression, a similar process became apparent: Al had avoided feeling humiliated when he depended on his competent son to drive him around by focusing on his pride in his son. His son had focused on his joy at being with his kind father, rather than on worrying about his father. Mary had felt more and more incapacitated by depression, showing the way in which she carried the painful effect. In return, Al complained but remained extremely dependent on her, never leaving her side. So Mary had a constant companion, which fulfilled strong lifelong needs of dependency, thus reinforcing the pattern. Furthermore, in the third session, Mary began to evoke criticism from the family by not accepting sympathy instead of correction, indicating that she had a need to be criticized. She began to seem angry at the therapist, as if the therapist were taking something from her. In this continuing assessment, the therapist noted that the dynamics of the family were active and that she had become an observing participant. The family's ability to include the therapist indicated the ego strength to relate and to form transferences with her. Even when the therapist's comments were unpleasant, family members were able to consider them. The therapist thus knew that the ability to tolerate good and bad was present, meaning that the family could consider their emotional states.

The collusive pattern that had been present throughout the couple's long and stable marriage had limited intimacy. Only over the course of several years of therapy were the underpinnings of this pattern understood as emotional states that could be identified and located in the rightful partner. Each partner fulfilled a function of containing or fulfilling longings for the other and of representing past objects.

Both Mary and Al had grown up in large families during the Great Depression. Al was the fourth son in his family, followed by a sister, a brother, and another sister. Mary was the fifth child, preceded by four brothers and followed by one younger sister. Al presented stories of an idealized view of childhood, such as of admiring his wonderful older brothers, whom he watched run and play, and then criticized Mary's neediness. Exploration revealed that for Al, Mary represented the younger baby sister that he, as a toddler, stayed home with while he watched his big brothers run off. Most significantly, he had to watch his sister be the baby, carried and held by his mother, in a way that he had still wanted.

Originally, Al's neediness had been projected onto the baby sister, who was internalized by him as a resented representation of need. This internal representation had been reprojected (transferred) onto Mary throughout their relationship and had become more intense as Al had become more needy with aging. When his son became more competent than he, able to drive around easily in a strange country, Al's experience of his early life was strongly activated, as he again became the weak child left with baby sister and mother, who had no time for him. Mary became depressed and Al became annoyed with her, as he had felt toward his mother when she had no time to be with him.

As this picture of Al emerged, more of Mary's life experience became apparent. Her father was distant, often at work in the same blue-collar profession as their disappointing son-in-law. Her mother, remembered as a well-respected, hardworking, self-reliant homemaker, was dominant. Mary felt that her mother was not to be crossed and seemed to do little to oppose her, even though she had often longed to go off with her brothers, who always left her. Mary also experienced her mother, a fantastic housekeeper, as focused on tasks and critical of any interferences. Even though she was the first girl, she did not feel she had been enjoyed by her parents.

After high school, Mary had left home for a larger city and found employment as a secretary, where she met Al, already employed as a professional in the same company. From the beginning, Al's position paralleled that of Mary's admired older brothers, all of whom had left her. This experience primed Mary to accept the role of "wife at home waiting" but with the leftover pains of feeling that she was an unliked, bothersome baby, which were transferred into the marriage. A part of her internalized object world was a mother who did not deem feelings to be important but insisted on getting on with the tasks of maintaining a home and raising a family.

For Mary, her mother had been internalized as so critical that she would have difficulty bearing the burden of it. Inducing her family to criticize her had thus allowed her to engage in a projective identification in which others carried the criticism. Resistance in therapy occurred when the family became less criticizing and more understanding. Then Mary had to accept responsibility for her internal sense of always feeling criticized and to work through her relationship with her mother.

A significant tension arose even in the beginning sessions—that of each person waiting for another to speak or respond. Mary had said that she was always waiting for Al, and this was recreated in the therapeutic setting. As the therapist contained the painful tension and followed its lead, information arose that contributed to everyone's understanding that this was a shared internal experience of both Mary and Al, as both had felt themselves always to be waiting for Mother's attention. This common experience was dealt with in their habitual way of Al's taking actions that caused Mary to experience the feeling and then Al rejecting her if she expressed it. It was clear that each of the children had internalized parts of this pattern, which continued into the next generation. As the family and therapist worked to follow the emotional states as they became alive, the patterns were altered in all family members.

As pointed out by Thomas Ogden (1997), internal object relationships are not fixed but rather fluid sets of thoughts, feelings, and sensations that are continually in movement and always susceptible in newly experienced context. Thus, even unconscious patterns can change as the intersubjective experience of the family is altered.

Treatment Goals

The safety of each family member is always a concern. In the preceding case, the potential of suicide by Mary required evaluation. As treatment progressed, it was recognized that Al might become suicidal after being overwhelmed by intense feelings he had been avoiding throughout life. This required ongoing assessment.

Once safety has been established, the goal in ORFI is always to enable the family to engage so that the fundamental drive for relatedness will be met in the unique manner of each member. Interventions aim to support the family as a work group, so that impediments to relatedness can be identified and resolved. Impediments include family-of-origin issues, such as multigenerational transmission of conflicts and maladaptive roles, resistance to accepting and tolerating painful emotions, and attempts to control rather than empower other members.

Goals directed toward specific symptom removal or achievement of desired behaviors are incompatible with ORFI, as they usually reflect attempts to manipulate or control the group and impede the family's being with the therapist in a way that reveals interactive projection–collusion processes. As the therapist identifies the collusive processes, a potentially destructive process is broken, allowing a more constructive relativeness in which individual and group development is supported.

Intervention Approach: Theory Base and Tenets

Object relations family intervention comes from the application of object relations theory to family systems. *Object relations theory* and its therapeutic approach regard the individual's inner world and external family as components of an open system. This theory can be used to develop typologies of family interaction and treatment that take into consideration the intrapsychic influences on family patterns, which in turn affect the client's personality. Thus, psychoanalysis and family treatment complement each other to enhance the theoretical understanding in both fields and to foster an intervention approach that is dependent not on the theoretical orientation of the clinician but on the needs of the client family.

Historically, Sigmund Freud is recognized as the father of psychoanalysis and contributed theories that are the foundation of object relations. As described by Hamilton (1989), in Freud's early biological theories, infants were conceptualized as having drives directed toward an object so that the infant sought gratification from an object, usually the mother (*Instincts and Their Vicissitudes,* 1915). Psychological growth occurs when drives are frustrated and the organism seeks increasingly effective means of energy discharge. The goal is maintenance of the organism, the infant, without recognition of or focus on the object.

Freud's later theories were the beginning of object relations theory. In *Mourning and Melancholia* (1917), he described introjection following the loss of a loved person as a means of maintaining a sense of continuing to be with the person receiving fantasied gratification. In his last work, *Splitting of the Ego in the Mechanism of Defense* (1940b), Freud described *splitting* as a defense mechanism of the ego, which resulted in a lifelong coexistence of two contradictory dispositions that do not influence each other. Splitting, projection, and introjection form the core concepts of all object relations theories in psychoanalysis and ORFI.

As described by Gomez (1997), object relations theory was a British development of psychoanalysis that arose in the midtwentieth century with the recognition that relatedness is the core of all human interaction from the beginning of life. The need for others is not only biological, but it is also the need to be experienced by the other in order to develop a sense of one's own existence. The term *object* shifts from a biological concept of functions that satisfy urges to an existential experience essential for development of mind and personality, in which a person lives a dual reality, internal and external.

Working about the same time and commingling concepts, Melanie Klein (1935, 1936, 1937, 1940) and Ronald Fairbairn (1952) refined theories of splitting into good and bad objects and recognized the importance of introjection and projection for the buildup of personality structure, particularly the ego and superego. Continuing these theories, Winnicott (1965) developed the concept of the *holding environment* as an essential aspect of mother–infant relationship paralleled later in that of therapist–patient. Baliant (1952, 1968), Guntrip (1968), and Bowlby (1953, 1969, 1973, 1980) extended these ideas to concepts of attachment theory. Wilfred Bion (1962a, 1962b, 1963), working in the late midtwentieth century, extended knowledge of projective identification to recognize its importance as a normal means of communication operative in all groups. Object relations theory originally referred to internal objects but has been extended primarily by American analysts to include relations with external objects.

Although the basic tenets of ORFI are based on psychoanalysis, they continue to be modified. In the following paragraphs, specific historical tenets and concepts are presented as they are currently used in assessment and interventions.

Freud (1940a) originally mentioned *splitting* as a defense mechanism of the ego and defined it as a lifelong coexistence of two contradictory dispositions that do not influence each other, as mentioned earlier. Kernberg (1972), in tracing the process of splitting through developmental stages, states that splitting of the "all good" (organized around pleasurable mother–child interactions) and "all bad" (derived from painful and frustrating interactions) self-images, object images, and their affective links occurs from 2 to 8 months. The separation of the self from object representations occurs from 8 to 36 months. Splitting into good and bad persists, and this is seen as the fixation point for borderline patients.

Following the splitting is the integration of the good and bad emotional images so that the separate self and object representations are each both good and bad. It is at this point that the ego, superego, and id become firmly established as intrapsychic structures and that the defenses of splitting are replaced by repression. Slipp (1984) sees this stage as the fixation point for neurotic pathology. In the last stage, internalized object representations are reshaped through actual current experiences with real people. A goal of ORFI is to assist in the development of this integration and reshaping.

Introjection is a crude, global form of taking in, as if those fragments of self–other interactions are swallowed whole. It is the earliest, most primitive form of the internalization of object relations, starting on a relatively crude level and becoming more sophisticated as the child grows (Nichols, 1984). The child reproduces and fixates on its interactions with significant others by organizing memory traces that include images of the object, the self interacting with the object, and the associated affect. Good and bad internal objects are included, each with images of the object and the self.

However, the resulting internal image does not completely parallel the actual external experience, which has been altered by projection of an already existent internal state. For example, a frustrated, enraged infant is likely to perceive Mother as angry even when she is not and to store the image of her as an angry mother fused with itself as bad. To prevent this internalization, the mother must be able to provide a holding function, contain the anger, and respond in a way that alters the state of the infant and thus the perception of mother/self that is introjected.

Projective identification is a defense mechanism that operates unconsciously. Unwanted aspects of the self are attributed to another person, and that person is induced to behave in accordance with these projected attitudes and feelings (Nichols, 1984). For instance, in the case study, Al is unable to accept his sadness, anxiety, and longing to be held and supported and projects them onto Mary. Mary, unable to tolerate the internal criticism of an introjected critical mother, projects this aspect of herself onto Al and her children.

The concepts of transference (Freud, 1905), scapegoating (Vogel & Bell, 1960), symbiosis (Mahler, 1952), trading of dissociations (Wynne, 1965), merging (Boszormenyi-Nagy, 1967), irrational role assignments (Framo, 1970), and family projective process (Bowen, 1965) are all variants of Klein's (1946) concept of projective identification. The phenomenon of projective identification as a life and clinical experience is most thoroughly described by Grotstein (1981) and Ogden (1982).

Collusion is an integral part of projective identification. The recipient of the split-off part of the partner does not disown the projection but acts on the conscious or unconscious message (Stewart, Peters, Marsh, & Peters, 1975). For example, the need for a weak woman requires that both partners agree to the assigned roles. Each spouse's ego identity (which includes both good and bad objects) is preserved by having one or more bad objects split off onto the partner. Thus, each partner disowns his or her bad-object introjects and needs the other to accept the projection of these introjects in a collusive manner (Piercy, Sprenkle, Wetchler, & Associates, 1986). Dicks (1963) believes that this collusive process continues because both spouses hope for integration of lost introjects by finding them in each other. Clinicians who use object relations theory attempt in various ways to help couples own their introjects and begin seeing their spouses for the people they really are, not projected parts of themselves.

Winnicott (1958) builds on his notion of good-enough mothering with the idea of a holding environment. If the good-enough mother (or primary nurturing person) provides a holding environment that is safe, secure, responsive, nurturing, nonretaliating, and supportive of separation/individuation, the child can achieve a firm sense of identity and a lifelong capacity for developing nonsymbiotic object relations.

Scharff and Scharff (1987) develop this concept further by defining the role of the father (or secondary nurturing person) as supporting the holding of the mother physically, financially, and emotionally; the father holds the mother as she holds the baby. This contextual holding provides an environmental extension of the mother's presence that later extends outward to the grandparents and family, neighbors, and others.

Feminist-informed object relations theory additionally considers the influence of gender on the holding environment. Sex-role differentiation and shifting sex-role mores are considered to affect the holding environment that is created within the couple, marital, and family settings (Juni & Grimm, 1994). Traditional concepts of masculine and feminine roles are challenged with the emergence of new realities that defy gender specification. A holding environment that typifies excessive power imbalances between partners may be understood within the context of early object relations (Silverstein, 1994). The need for dominance and power, particularly in the area of sexual arousal and pleasure, has been suggested to evolve from excessive control or coercion by a powerful parental object during early psychosexual development.

These concepts of the holding environment also apply to working with families. The clinician needs to provide a holding environment for the family by providing safety, competence, and concern for the whole family; by engaging with the central issues of the family; and by being caring, interactive, and understanding. The concept of *containment* introduces a specifically mental ability of the therapist to allow unknown feelings, sensations, and thoughts of family members to live within the boundaries of his or her being and so be known, identified, and returned to the family in tolerable form and doses. Within this "therapeutic envelope," Al and Mary could tolerate their own experience and then accept the other as different, even if disagreeably so.

As to the current status of ORFI, there is no overall integrated theory. Various theorists have developed their own perspectives over the years, and others have made attempts at integration. One is Framo (1972), who calls his approach a "transactional" one. It leans heavily on the notion of projective identification as applied to a family system and offers a new way of presenting transference. He builds on Fairbairn's notion of the fundamental need for a satisfying object relationship. When a child interprets the parent's behavior as rejection or desertion and cannot give up him or her, the child internalizes the loved but hated parent in the inner world of self as an introject (as if swallowed whole) or a psychological representation. In the course of time, as the person begins to force close relationships into fitting this internal role model, these split-off or divided introjects become important. Framo sees the introject of the parent as a critical issue in family therapy, and one that is much neglected. Framo tries to put together a basically intrapsychic concept, *introjects,* with a systems concept. In doing so, he draws out the implications in Bowen's (1978) formulation of family theory for object relations theory.

Boszormenyi-Nagy and Spark (1973) are also concerned about introjects and object relations. They see family pathology as a specialized multiperson organization of shared fantasies and complementary need gratification patterns that are maintained for the purpose of handling past object loss experience.

Monumental groundbreaking work has been done by D. E. Scharff (1982), J. S. Scharff (1989), Scharff and Scharff (1987), and Slipp (1984, 1988). For Scharff and Scharff (1987), ORFI derives from the psychoanalytic principles of listening, responding to unconscious material, interpreting, developing insight, and working in the transference and countertransference toward understanding and growth. The immediate goal is not symptom resolution but progression through the current developmental phase of family life with improved ability to work as a group and to differentiate among and meet the individual members' needs. Slipp (1984, 1988) has studied diverse patient populations and their families to explore the interaction and interdependence of individual dynamics and family system functioning. His ultimate goal is to apply an integrated understanding to family treatment.

ORFI's basic tenet is that treatment of the individual and treatment of the family are theoretically and therapeutically consistent with each other, and both are parts of an open system. The two levels of the intrapersonal and the interpersonal are in a constantly dynamic relationship. An assumption is that resolving problems in the relationships in the client's current family necessitates intrapsychic exploration and resolution of those uncon-scious object relationships that were internalized from early parent–child relationships. Another assumption is that these early influences affect and explain the nature of present interpersonal problems (Blazina, 2001).

Application to Families on Level IV

Families who have needs on Level IV are generally introspective and reflective and yearn to be more self-actualizing. They may have problems of inner conflict or difficulties with intimacy. Although the therapist may still be treating symptomatic people, his or her goals have to do with the development of an inner richness: insight, more sensitive awareness of the relational world, and an understanding of legacies and heritage. In all cases, the purpose is to deepen awareness of the inner world and to improve understanding of history, style, and unmet yearnings.

A very important aspect is the spiritual therapies that help families discover the tran-scendent aspects of their beings. ORFI is a useful adjunct to all spiritual therapies because interventions that allow for a fuller experience of self, free of internal images or projections of others, support an engagement with transcendence and assumption of responsibility for mature spiritual experience, as described by Young-Eisendrath and Miller (2000).

Spirituality is enhanced by ORFI particularly when families share unconscious experiences of guilt. It is common for parents to feel that they have harmed their children by inadequate parenting, hostile emotions, or a failure to protect them from adverse experiences in life. Experiences of guilt lead to self-criticism and thus to a shutdown of the experience of self. The pathway to spirituality is blocked. Verbalization of thoughts and feelings that have been condemned by guilt leads to a realistic mourning and sadness and to an assumption of responsibility rather than intolerable guilt. The realization can occur that one has less than the ideal parents that were desired or is less than the ideal parent that was intended. Thus, acceptance of one's place in the world of his or her fam-ily can be enhanced. With acceptance, pain and anger diminish, leaving openness to spir-itual experience.

In ORFI, the therapeutic environment is established by the therapist's encourage-ment of open dialogue in a safe, mutually helpful atmosphere. The family practitioner generally maintains a neutral stance that respects each member's autonomy. The practi-tioner avoids assuming a directive approach but attends to other material produced in the session, as described by Slipp (1988). The past is linked to the present through interpreta-tion of the transference, particularly the ways it is acted out interpersonally in the ongoing family relationships.

To facilitate the acceptance of these interpretations, the therapist needs to join the family empathetically and to create a safe and secure holding environment where space for understanding is provided. In the research of Sampson and Weiss (1977), creating such a holding environment has been found to be the most crucial element for change and growth. The practitioner's stance with the family is one that reflects an awareness that he or she affects and is affected by the family (Slipp, 1988). ORFI fosters the kind of meaningful shared intimacy with respect for one another's individuality that the philosopher Martin Buber (1958) so aptly described as the "I-thou relationship."

Family practitioners who have not experienced Level IV work may be unprepared to deal with clients for whom meaning, awareness, and spiritual growth are issues. Some practitioners would not acknowledge the importance or even the existence of an inner world. If such practitioners encounter families who have Level IV needs, referral to a more existentially oriented practitioner would seem appropriate.

Interventions and Techniques

In ORFI, a vital part of the practitioner's role and function is assessment. Scharff and Scharff (1987, p. 155) cite six major tasks to achieve in the assessment phase to determine if ORFI would be effective:

1. The provision of therapeutic space, which includes trust and openness.
2. Assessment of developmental phase and level to determine tasks to be accomplished.
3. Demonstration of defensive functioning to determine ego strength.
4. Exploration of unconscious assumptions and underlying anxiety to determine intervention needs.
5. Testing of the response to interpretation and assessment format to see if they are ready for understanding and insight.
6. Making an assessment formulation, recommendation, and treatment plan.

These major tasks may be accomplished in a more structured assessment phase. Slipp (1984, pp. 204–205) reviews the steps in such an assessment process (see Table 12.1).

Superceding all other areas of the assessment process is the importance of each practitioner's assessment of his or her own countertransference reaction. Is one present and usable? Is the countertransference tolerable? Are there indications that the family may present situations that parallel the practitioner's own unresolved emotional distresses? Because countertransference is deeply personal, consultation may be necessary to fully assess the potential impact of a family on the practitioner's emotional life and his or her ability to tolerate and interpret the family's distresses.

In addition to the ethnic differences or conflicts mentioned earlier, attention must also be given to other sociocultural–environmental factors that influence the family. Impacts of the entire ecosystem must be considered in the assessment process.

ORFI uses some specific techniques in the beginning, middle, and last phases of treatment. Slipp (1988, pp. 199–200) has outlined them as a guide for clinicians (see Table 12.2).

Klee (2007) has developed an eight-stage model of doing object relations family interventions that is very useful:

1. Conduct a preliminary diagnosis of relational patterns.
2. Build the therapeutic alliance.
3. Identify the maladaptive relational pattern.
4. Have the patient express the maladaptive pattern.
5. Have the therapist generate an empathic confrontation.
6. Work through the confrontation.
7. Generalize the therapeutic relationship.
8. Separate and terminate.

TABLE 12.1 *Assessment Process in Object Relations Family Therapy*

- **Explore the presenting problem** of patient and its background.
  1. Does it seem related to overall family functioning and/or to stress from a family life cycle stage?
  2. What has been done so far to remedy the problem?

- **Establish an individual diagnosis** for each family member including a judgment concerning the level of differentiation and the use of primitive or mature defenses.
  1. Gather data on the client and family development.
  2. Note any ethnic differences or conflicts.

- **Evaluate family constancy** to determine if parents can maintain their own narcissistic equilibrium or if patient is needed to sustain their self-esteem and survival.
  1. Does a rigid homeostasis or defensive equilibrium exist that binds and prevents the patient from individuating and separating?
  2. Is there pressure for personality compliance within the family or social achievement outside the family?
  3. What affiliative, oppositional, and alienated attitudes exist?

- **Explore precipitating stress** and its relation to a loss or other traumatic event (negative or positive) or a transitional point in the family life cycle that has disrupted homeostasis.

- **Define individual boundaries** for members. These may be rigidly too open (a symbiotically close relationship) or too closed (an emotionally divorced and distant relationship).
  1. Are generational boundaries intact, or are there parent–child coalitions?
  2. Are the parental coalition, subsystems, and authority hierarchy intact?

- **Define the family boundary** to see if it is too open (symbiotic relations persist with family of origin) or too closed (family is isolated from community without social support system).

- **Determine the ability to negotiate differences and problem solve** through verbal dialogue involving respect for one's own and others' views, opinions, and motivations versus an egocentric controlling viewpoint resulting in coercion and manipulation.

- **Observe communication patterns** for evidence of spontaneous versus rigid stereotyping, distancing, or obfuscating; level of initiative versus passivity; rigidity of family rules; and the power-role structure.

- **Evaluate the loving and caring feelings** among members that allow for separateness (rather than acceptance only by conformity) and provide warmth, support, and comfort.

- **Define the treatment goals** in terms of difficulties that have been uncovered, and present the frame or boundaries of the treatment process.

Source: Slipp, 1984, pp. 204–205.

TABLE 12.2 *Phases of Treatment in Object Relations Family Therapy*

- **During the beginning phase of treatment,** the techniques are to
  1. Develop a safe holding environment through empathy, evenhandedness, and containment-an environment that facilitates trust, lowers defensiveness, and allows aggression to be worked with constructively.
  2. Interpret the circular positive or negative systemic interaction in a sequential nonblaming manner by
     a. defining its origin.
     b. defining what was hoped to be gained.
     c. describing its effects.

- **During the middle phase of treatment,** the techniques are to
  1. Interpret projective identification by
     a. reframing its purpose to give it a positive aim.
     b. linking it with a genetic reconstruction.
     c. clarifying why an aspect of the self needs to be disowned and projected.
     This process diminishes defensiveness, enhances the therapeutic alliance, and facilitates continued work with the reowned projective identification.
  2. Use the objective countertransference as a tool to understand the transferences and to provide material for interpreting projective identification.

- **During the last phase of treatment,** the techniques are to
  1. Work through individual conflicts and developmental arrests in the intrapsychic sphere. This process is gradual and may continue in individual therapy after the family treatment terminates.
  2. Terminate treatment.

Source: Slipp, 1988, pp. 199–200.

Evaluation of Effectiveness

Because symptom reduction is not the goal of this model, it cannot serve as the measure of effectiveness. The presence or absence of unconscious conflict, because it is not apparent to family members or outside observers, is difficult to measure. Therefore, assessment of effectiveness depends on the subjective clinical judgment of the therapist and on the family's reactions.

With the current emphasis on scientific evidence and cost effectiveness, would these measures be considered sufficient? Clinicians would answer yes, as they consider the clinician's observations to be entirely valid as a means of evaluating theory and treatment. Blanck and Blanck (1972, 1987), discussing Mahler's (1952) methods and model, state that clinicians who employ Mahler's theories technically do not question the methodology or the findings, for they can confirm them clinically. This is a form of validation that meets, as closely as possible, the experimentalist's insistence on replication as a criterion of the scientific method.

Along these same lines, Langs (1982) posits that the ultimate test of a therapist's formulation is in the use of these impressions as a basis for intervention. He states further that the patient's reactions, conscious and unconscious, constitute the ultimate litmus test of these interventions and that true validation involves both cognitive and interpersonal responses from the patient.

The views held by current eminent object relations family therapists are similar. Slipp (1988) holds that meeting the goals of treatment is the criterion that both the family and therapist use to consider ending treatment. These general goals do not lend themselves to empirical measurement but rather to subjective assessments by therapists and families. Scharff and Scharff (1987) state that at termination, the family can provide the holding environment for the members that is so necessary for attachment and growth. The family is able to return to or reach an appropriate developmental level so that they fit with the individuals' developmental needs for intimacy and autonomy. Slipp (1988) describes the end result as the restructuring of the internal world of object relations with resultant modification of the family's interpersonal relations. Each individual self is experienced as separate and less dependent on external objects to sustain self-esteem and identity. The family will be able to function as a group in a more intimate and adaptive fashion that meets each member's needs.

Although outcome studies have been primarily uncontrolled case studies, Dicks (1967) reported on a survey of the outcome of couples therapy at the Tavistock Clinic. He rated 73 percent of a random sample of cases as having been successfully treated. Others have investigated specific tenets of the ORFI theory and provided further empirical evidence of their existence (Slipp, 1984).

Application to Families Functioning at Other Levels

As discussed previously, object relations theory is very useful in understanding a vast array of needs, behaviors, problem areas, and symptomatologies. This understanding can be applied to families who have needs on any level. Although object relations theory has been utilized extensively to study and treat borderline and narcissistic personality disorders, it is now being used to understand and treat diverse populations and families.

As Slipp (1988) has stated, although ORFI is appropriate for families who desire and can tolerate intensity and closeness, it is certainly not restricted to those families. As families develop trust and become closer in the intervention process, the treatment itself can serve as a model for more open and intimate relationships. Thus, the growth produced could enable the family to move to a higher level of relating.

A significant, though not the only, variable in selecting the most suitable type of family therapy for a specific family's level of need is the family's socioeconomic level. Clients who have Level I needs with overriding poverty and social problems want help that is more immediate and less abstract. Slipp's (1988) study showed that the ORFI approach is particularly fitting for and effective with middle-class and blue-collar families. These families would typically have Level II, III, and IV needs. On the basis of Slipp's findings, ORFI with lower-socioeconomic-level families is least effective and not recommended.

Scharff and Scharff (1987), however, caution clinicians that they should not assume that the poor or the culturally or intellectually disadvantaged cannot benefit from ORFI.

Some families will fit cultural stereotypes of concrete thinking and dependency on directives and gratification, but others will take a more reflective approach. Although this type of intervention is not for all families, it is for those that demonstrate an interest in understanding, not just in symptom relief.

More recently, ORFI has proved useful in treating families of all levels who have experienced traumatic events. During and after a traumatic experience, intense, distressful emotions are stimulated. These emotions resonate with past experiences, remembered in the unconscious of the family, so that established patterns of splitting and projection are activated or intensified. Many families do not have well-established, useful psychological processes for dealing with these experiences. Therefore, after a trauma, family members may become more distant and alienated.

Interventions that are effective in preventing the fracturing of the family following a trauma provide a holding of the emotions followed by accurate verbalizations that allow each member to become more aware of his or her individual experience. This allows for the development of a space within the mind where the experience is felt and represented or, in analytic terms, held. This process, described by Fonagy and Target in several publications (1996a, 1996b; also Fonagy, Gergely, Jurist, & Target, 2002), promotes emotional experiences that would otherwise be projected or put into action, rather than become processed thought.

Ethical Challenges

Some ethical challenges need to be considered when using object relations family interventions. A primary concern is that of maintaining a central position with the family. This means that the therapist should be allied equally with all members of the family and not become invested in or identified with the perspective of one member. Doing so is especially challenging when the practitioner allows his or her own feelings to be active in the process. Monitoring countertransferences is essential to prevent favoritism.

Along the same lines, confidentiality may become an issue. A family member may call the practitioner outside the boundaries of the family session time to request information or help. Maintaining the boundaries of the family is essential. Having confidential information from one or more members compromises the practitioner's central position within the family. All information belongs to the family.

Summary

Object relations family treatment can be effective with families who have their basic physical and nurturing needs met, are capable of abstract thinking and insight, and are interested in understanding and changing destructive patterns of behavior, achieving greater intimacy and commitment, reworking meanings, and rewriting their life stories. These patterns may involve poor communication, conflict, lack of differentiation, weak personal and intergenerational boundaries, inconsistent family structure, and rules.

Therefore, ORFI is ideally suited for many Level IV families and can be very effective with Level II and III families. It is generally not recommended for Level I families.

Discussion Questions

1. What are ORFI's basic tenets, and how do they apply to the case study given?

2. What are the similarities and differences among introjection, projective identification, and collusion?

3. Do ethnicity and gender issues impact the use of ORFI? Explain your response.

4. How are family object relations interventions different from those of individual object relations interventions?

5. From your own practice, identify an individual or family that demonstrates *splitting*. Briefly explain why the defense mechanism is evidenced in the person's behavior. Can you find projective identification and collusion, as well?

6. What is the *holding environment,* and how can it be developed and utilized in applying the techniques of ORFI?

7. How is the pain of Level IV families different from that of Level I, II, and III families in view of object relations theory?

Internet Resources

http://object-relations.com/metprog.html
www.objectrelations.com
www.sonoma.edu/users/d/daniels/objectrelations.html

Suggested Readings

Applegate, J. S. (1990). Theory, culture and behavior: Object relations in context. *Child and Adolescent Social Work Journal, 7*(2), 85–100.
   Aspects of object relations theory are explored within the sociocultural context of family constellations, childrearing practices, race, and ethnicity.
Fairbairn, W. R. D. (1954). *An object-relations theory of the personality.* New York: Basic Books.
   This is a seminal work in object relations theory that has had a significant influence on the later work of Dicks, Bowen, Framo, and others. This work is required reading for those interested in the role of object relations in psychopathology.
Finkelstein, L. (1987). Toward an object relations approach in psychoanalytic marital therapy. *Journal of Marital and Family Therapy, 13*(3), 287–298.
   This book describes the features that distinguish psychoanalytic marital therapy from other forms of marital therapy, as well as how object relations theories can be applied to psychoanalytic marital therapy. The author also indicates certain directions for further study.
Scharff, D. E., & Scharff, J. S. (1987). *Object relations family therapy.* Northvale, NJ: Jason Aronson.
   This book represents the Scharffs' efforts to develop a psychoanalytic object relations approach to families and family therapy. The Scharffs demonstrate that object relations theory provides the theoretical framework for understanding and the language for working with the dynamics of both the individual and the family system.
Silverstein, J. L. (1994). Power and sexuality: Influence of early object relations. *Psychoanalytic Psychology, 11,* 33–46.

This article challenges traditional concepts of masculine and feminine roles with the emergence of new realities that defy gender specification.

Slipp, S. (1988). *The technique and practice of object relations family therapy.* Northvale, NJ: Jason Aronson. This book extends the clinical application of object relations family therapy that Slipp began in an earlier book. He further develops the application of his family typology to the treatment process with specific attention to techniques and process.

References

Applegate, J. S. (1990). Theory, culture and behavior: Object relations in context. *Child and Adolescent Social Work Journal, 7*(2), 85–100.

Baliant, M. (1952). *Primary love and psychoanalytic technique.* London: Hogarth.

Baliant, M. (1968). *The basic fault: Therapeutic aspects of regression.* London: Tavistock.

Berenstein, I. (2004). *Psychoanalysis of families.* Paper presented at the International Psychoanalytic Congress, New Orleans, LA.

Bion, W. (1962a). *Learning from experience.* London: Heinemann.

Bion, W. (1962b). A theory of thinking. *International Journal of Psychoanalysis, 43,* 110–119.

Bion, W. (1963). *Elements of psychoanalysis.* New York: Basic Books.

Blanck, G., & Blanck, R. (1972). Toward a psychoanalytic developmental psychology. *Journal of the American Psychoanalytic Association, 20,* 668–710.

Blanck, G., & Blanck, R. (1987). Developmental object relations theory. *Clinical Social Work Journal, 15,* 318–327.

Blazina, C. (2001). Part objects, infantile fantasies, and intrapsychic boundaries: An object relations perspective on male difficulties with intimacy. *Journal of Men's Studies, 10.*

Boszormenyi-Nagy, I. (1967). Relational modes and meaning. In G. H. Zuk & I. Boszormenyi-Nagy (Eds.), *Family therapy and disturbed families.* Palo Alto, CA: Science and Behavior Books.

Boszormenyi-Nagy, I., & Spark, G. (1973). *Invisible loyalties.* New York: Harper & Row.

Bowen, M. (1965). Family psychotherapy with schizophrenia in the hospital and in private practice. *Comprehensive Psychiatry, 7,* 345–374.

Bowen, M. (1978). *Family theory in clinical practice.* New York: Jason Aronson.

Bowlby, J. (1953). *Child care and the growth of love.* Harmondsworth, UK: Penguin.

Bowlby, J. (1969). *Attachment and loss. Vol. I: Attachment.* London: Hogarth.

Bowlby, J. (1973). *Attachment and loss. Vol. II: Separation: Anxiety and anger.* London: Hogarth.

Bowlby, J. (1980). *Attachment and loss. Vol. III: Loss: Sadness and depression.* London: Hogarth.

Buber, M. (1958). *I and thou.* New York: Scribner.

Dicks, H. V. (1963). Object relations theory and marital studies. *British Journal of Medical Psychology, 36,* 125–129.

Dicks, H. V. (1967). *Marital tensions.* New York: Basic Books.

Fairbairn, R. (1952). *Psychoanalytic studies of the personality.* London: Routledge and Kegan Paul.

Finkelstein, L. (1987). Toward an object-relations approach in psychoanalytic marital therapy. *Journal of Marital and Family Therapy, 13*(3), 287–298.

Fonagy, P., Gergely, G., Jurist, E., & Target, M. (2002). *Affect regulation, mentalization and the development of the self.* New York: Other Press.

Fonagy, P., & Target, M. (1996a). Playing with reality I: Theory of mind and the normal development of psychic reality. *International Journal of Psychoanalysis, 77,* 217–233.

Fonagy, P., & Target, M. (1996b). Playing with reality III: The persistence of dual psychic reality in borderline patients. *International Journal of Psychoanalysis, 81*(5), 853–874.

Framo, J. L. (1970). Symptoms from a family transactional viewpoint. In N. W. Ackerman (Ed.), *Family therapy in transition.* Boston: Little, Brown.

Framo, J. L. (1972). Symptoms from a family transactional viewpoint. In N. W. Ackerman, N. Lielg, & J. Pearce (Eds.), *Family therapy in transition.* New York: Springer.

Freud, S. (1905). *Fragment of an analysis of a case of hysteria: Collected papers.* New York: Basic Books.

Freud, S. (1915). *Instincts and their vicissitudes. Collected Works: Vol. 7.*

Freud, S. (1917). *Mourning and melancholia. Collected Works: Vol. 14.*

Freud, S. (1940a). An outline of psychoanalysis. *Standard Edition, 23,* 139–171.

Freud, S. (1940b). *Splitting of the ego in the mechanism of defense. Collected Works: Vol. 23.*

Gomez, L. (1997). *An introduction to object relations.* New York: New York University Press.

Grinberg, L., Sor, D., & Tabak de Bianchedi, E. (1977). *Introduction to the work of Bion.* New York: Jason Aronson.

Grotstein, J. S. (1981). *Splitting and projective identification.* New York: Jason Aronson.

Guntrip, H. (1968). *Schizoid phenomena, object relations and the self.* London: Hogarth.

Hamilton, G. N. (1989). A critical review of object relations theory. *American Journal of Psychiatry, 146*(12), 1552–1560.

Juni, S., & Grimm, D. W. (1994). Sex roles as factors in defense mechanisms and object relations. *Journal of Genetic Psychology, 155,* 99–106.

Kernberg, O. F. (1972). Early ego integration and object relations. *Annals of the New York Academy of Science, 193,* 233–247.

Klee,T. (2007). *Object relations theory and psychotherapy.* Accessed April 30, 2008, at www.objectrelations .org/orkey.htm and stages.htm.

Klein, M. (1935). A contribution to the psychogenesis of manic-depressive states. In *Love, guilt and reparation.* London, England: Hogarth.

Klein, M. (1936). Weaning. In *Love, guilt and reparation.* London: Hogarth.

Klein, M. (1937). Love, guilt and reparation. In *Love, guilt and reparation.* London: Hogarth.

Klein, M. (1940). Mourning and its relations to manic-depressive states. In *Love, guilt and reparation.* London: Hogarth.

Klein, M. (1946). Notes on some schizoid mechanisms. *International Journal of Psychoanalysis, 27,* 99–110.

Langs, R. (1982). *Psychotherapy: A basic text.* New York: Jason Aronson.

Mahler, M. S. (1952). *Psychoanalytic study of the child: Vol. 7. On child psychosis and schizophrenia: Autistic and symbiotic infantile psychoses.* New York: International Universities Press.

Nichols, M. (1984). *Family therapy: Concepts and methods.* New York: Gardner Press.

Ogden, T. H. (1982). *Projective identification and psychotherapeutic technique.* London: H. Karnac.

Ogden, T. H. (1997). *Reverie and interpretation, sensing something human.* Northvale, NJ: Jason Aronson.

Parker, G. (1996). Personal communication with A. Kilpatrick.

Piercy, F. P., Sprenkle, D. H., Wetchler, J. L., and Associates. (1986). *Family therapy sourcebook.* New York: Guilford Press.

Sampson, H., & Weiss, J. (1977, March). Research on the psychoanalytic process: An overview. *Psychotherapy Research Group* (Bulletin no. 2). San Francisco: Mt. Zion Hospital and Medical Center, Department of Psychiatry.

Scharff, D. E. (1982). *The sexual relationship: An object relations view of sex and the family.* London, England: Routledge & Kegan Paul.

Scharff, D. E., & Scharff, J. S. (1987). *Object relations family therapy.* Northvale, NJ: Jason Aronson.

Scharff, J. S. (Ed.). (1989). *Foundations of object relations family therapy.* Northvale, NJ: Jason Aronson.

Schore, A. N. (1994). *Affect regulation and the origin of the self: The neurobiology of emotional development.* Mahwah, NJ: Erlbaum.

Schore, A. N. (2000). Attachment and the regulation of the right brain. *Attachment and Human Development, 2,* 23–47.

Silverstein, J. L. (1994). Power and sexuality: Influence of early object relations. *Psychoanalytic Psychology, 11,* 33–46.

Slipp, S. (1984). *Object relations: A dynamic bridge between individual and family treatment.* New York: Jason Aronson.

Slipp, S. (1988). *The technique and practice of object relations family therapy.* Northvale, NJ: Jason Aronson.

Stewart, R. H., Peters, T. C., Marsh, S., & Peters, M. J. (1975). An object-relations approach to psychotherapy with marital couples, families and children. *Family Process, 14*(2), 161–178.

Stierlin, H. (1976). The dynamics of owning and disowning: Psychoanalytic and family perspectives. *Family Process, 15*(3), 277–288.

Vogel, E. F., & Bell, N. W. (1960). The emotionally disturbed as the family scapegoat. In N. W. Bell & E. F. Vogel (Eds.), *The family.* Glencoe, IL: Free Press.

Winnicott, D. W. (1958). *Collected papers: Through pediatrics to psychoanalysis.* London: Hogarth.

Winnicott, D. (1965). *The maturational processes and the facilitating environment.* London: Hogarth.

Wynne, L. C. (1965). Some indications and contraindications for exploratory family therapy. In I. Boszormenyi-Nagy & J. L. Franco (Eds.), *Intensive family therapy.* New York: Hoeber.

Young-Eisendrath, P., & Miller, M. (Eds.). (2000). *The psychology of mature spirituality, integrity, wisdom, transcendence.* London: Routledge.

Part VI

The Family in the Community: Ecosystem Implications

Throughout this book, we have been working within the overall metatheories of ecological systems and social constructionism as the philosophical and theoretical base for working with families on four levels of family need. Each type of family intervention for each level of need includes ecological and system implications. As discussed in Chapter 2, the ecological system includes the microsystem, mesosystem, exosystem, and macrosystem.

Many of these levels of ecosystems are included in the interventions in the various chapters. However, this concluding section serves to bring them all together with a focus on the community and the total sociocultural environment within which the family functions and has their needs met—or not met. This concluding section integrates the theoretical and philosophical underpinnings from Part One and the microsystem level interventions from Parts Two through Five with the ecosystem implications of working with families at the macrosystem level. It helps the practitioner to see the larger contextual issues when working with individual families.

In Chapter 13, Vonk and Yoo focus on the role of the community in the health and well-being of families. They broaden the family practitioner's focus by including community and societal structures that affect the lives of individuals and families. They also present the roles and skills needed for assessment and intervention at the community level. They then discuss ways to address obstacles that may block work at the community level and identify the process of community development in three different approaches.

13

The Family in the Community

**M. Elizabeth Vonk, M.S.W., Ph.D.,
and Sun Young Yoo, M.S.W.**

This chapter will focus on the role of community in the health and well-being of families. Guided by ecosystems theory, family practitioners have a responsibility to direct attention to every systemic level, from micro to macro. As discussed in Chapter 2 of this book, the micro- and mesosystems involve the individual, family, and small groups as they interact on a day-to-day basis. Assessment and interventions at the micro- and mesolevels have been the primary focus of this text up to this point. This chapter, however, extends the view of practice with families to include consideration of the exo- and macrosystem levels.

The exosystem broadens the family practitioner's focus by including community and societal structures that affect the lives of individuals and families. For example, the availability of resources that support families is often considered to be an exosystem factor. The macrosystem further broadens the perspective through inclusion of cultural values and societal power structures that affect individuals, families, and communities and the interactions among them. Institutionalized racism, culturally based gender stereotypes, and inequitable distribution of wealth and health care are examples of macrosystem-level factors. In short, exo- and macrosystem factors largely determine the community context in which families are situated and with which families interact. This makes it very important for family practitioners to develop the knowledge and skills necessary to address problems in the community.

This chapter will begin to address community assessment and intervention by defining *community* and describing how community factors relate to families' needs. Next, a case study will be provided that illustrates the interconnectedness of families and communities. Finally, the chapter will examine ways in which family practitioners can begin to meet families' needs at the community level, including a look at community assessment, resources, and development.

The Relationship of Community and Families' Needs

Communities have been defined as complex social systems that share a number of characteristics. Groups of people who share institutions, values, social interactions, and a sense of belonging over time are communities (Johnson & Yanca, 2007). Some communities of people share common interests but are not connected by living in a particular locale. For example, some families may be connected by faith, such as belonging to the Jewish community. Others may be connected by racial or ethnic identity, such as belonging to the Korean American community. Most often, however, a community is identified with a specific geographic area and provides a variety of functions for the people who live there, including the following (Johnson & Yanca, 2007; Sheafor & Horejsi, 2006):

- production, distribution, and consumption of goods and services, such as utilities, food, housing, health care, and recreation
- employment opportunities that are accessible to community members
- socialization and sense of belonging
- mutual support, such as assistance beyond that provided by the family
- social control, including laws, regulations, and their enforcement
- opportunity for participation in community decision making

Communities overlap with one another, and families are members of many geopolitical communities at the same time, including the neighborhood, the town or city, the county and state, a geographic region, and the nation. The neighborhood surrounds the family at the most intimate level.

Ideally, neighborhoods would fulfill community functions well, providing a nurturing environment in which all families would be safe, have access to necessary goods and services, receive extra support from social programs when needed, feel included in the political process that affects local issues, and develop a sense of belonging with their neighbors. A drive through any city or county, however, will show the reality that communities meet families' needs variously, not just from neighborhood to neighborhood but within neighborhoods from one group of families to another.

Examples of differences are numerous. For instance, families in one neighborhood may have easy access to a variety of recreational opportunities, while families in another neighborhood may be unable to find any safe space where children can play due to violence and crime. Similarly, suburban neighborhoods may have fire protection close by, while such protection in poor, rural communities may be available only at a much greater distance. Within neighborhoods, families of a specific socioeconomic class or racial/ethnic identity may easily develop a sense of belonging, while those of lesser means or minority identity may find themselves isolated. In the same way, families with employer-provided health insurance may have ample access to medical and psychological health care, while those without employment or in low-paying jobs will not.

Clearly, conditions in some communities provide support and nurturance for families, while others place families at high risk for dysfunction. Thus, the community provides the context in which families fall apart, survive, or thrive and as such should be part of the focus in family intervention.

A Case Study

The following case illustrates the interconnectedness of communities and families. As you read about this family, consider the following questions:

1. What is needed to improve the family's functioning?
2. What are some of the objectives that could be addressed at the family level?
3. What are some of the objectives that could be addressed at the community level?

Mrs. C

Mrs. C, a 49-year-old married woman and mother of two children, called the Asian community center asking for help with her husband and children. With reluctance, she explained that her husband has been hitting her "when he is tired and frustrated." With encouragement from the worker at the community center, Mrs. C filled in the details of her situation.

Seven years ago, Mrs. C's family immigrated to the United States with the hope of obtaining greater financial opportunity and education for their children. In their home country, Mr. C worked in a large company and she was a homemaker. Since coming to the United States, however, Mr. C has been working in a low-paying job and has had no success in realizing his dream of starting his own business. Recently, Mrs. C also has had to work part time to keep up with increasing rent and food costs. In addition, her children, now in high school, have become increasingly disrespectful of their parents and "too American." The children's grades have deteriorated, but due to her minimal knowledge of English, Mrs. C does not feel comfortable talking to their teachers to find out more about the school situation. Mr. C is angry that his wife cannot manage their children.

While frustrations in the family have mounted, Mrs. C and her husband have experienced increasing conflict. About three years ago, Mr. C began to occasionally throw things at Mrs. C when they were arguing. At first, she thought her husband's violent behavior would stop, but this has not been the case. As her husband's violence has gradually become more serious and more frequent, Mrs. C has begun to feel desperate about her situation. She feels isolated without having family and close friends with whom to share her difficulties. Further, she does not know what kinds of services are available for her, and she does not know how to access them. She is also very ashamed of being "the kind of wife who is beaten by my husband" and who needs help from "outside my family."

Although Mrs. C knows she could call the police when her husband is violent, she does not because she fears being deported. In addition, her family still depends primarily on her husband's income, and she does not have the financial resources to support herself and her children on her own. Mrs. C decided to call the community center for help after an incident in which she was so badly bruised that she was unable to go to work for three days. She reports that she "cannot continue to endure this situation" and "wants to get help in any way."

Meeting Families' Needs through Practice in the Community

The preceding case study illustrates the need for family practitioners to think about intervention from both the family and community perspectives. Earlier chapters of this text have described a variety of interventions that might improve family functioning. For example, structural family interventions (Chapter 7) may help Mr. and Mrs. C to reassume responsibilities of the parental role. Social learning interventions (Chapter 8) may assist Mr. C to manage his frustration and anger in a nonviolent way. As with family interventions, community interventions are numerous and vary in their focus. The next sections of this chapter will examine community interventions in terms of assessment, resources, and development.

Community Needs Assessment

In the community, as in all practice, sound intervention begins with a thorough assessment. A *needs assessment* is the process of gathering and analyzing information to produce a report on the extent and scope of a community problem. In addition, a needs assessment evaluates potential resources, obstacles, and solutions available to address the problem (Kirst-Ashman & Hull, 2009; Rubin & Rubin, 2008).

An *empowerment approach* includes community members in every step of the process, the first of which is to identify the issue to be studied. Questions may arise from many sources, including practitioners, consumers, and even the media. For example, a family practitioner may notice that food banks are no longer able to help families for whom they have previously provided. Why is this? Are there more families in the community who need help? Have volunteers stopped supplying the food banks? Has unemployment increased? Have rising costs outstripped wage increases? Are the community's demographics changing? What can be done differently to meet the level of need?

To answer such questions, data must be gathered. There are a number of ways to collect relevant data in and about the community, including the following (Kirst-Ashman & Hull, 2009; Rubin & Rubin, 2008):

- *Use existing information.* Much information about social indicators and utilization of government-based services in communities, including Temporary Assistance to Needy Families (TANF) and Medicaid, can be found in government documents such as the report of the U.S. Census. The assessor must have the knowledge and skills to access and interpret the data.
- *Develop and implement a survey.* A survey provides information that enables the assessor to quantify answers to questions such as How many? and What kinds? The assessor must have research skills related to survey development and sampling.
- *Interview key informants.* Persons in the community, including professionals and laypersons who have in-depth knowledge about the issue, may be able to provide valuable insights and opinions. This requires knowledge of the community and good interviewing skills.

- *Conduct a focus group.* Focus groups bring together community members who have an interest in an issue for a moderated group discussion. Group facilitation skills are useful for focus groups.
- *Hold a community forum.* By gathering a large group of community members, the assessor can gain a wider perspective on an issue or problem from the general public. Networking skills, as well as knowledge of large group dynamics and facilitation, are needed to hold a successful community meeting.

After data have been gathered, the next step is to analyze and present the results. Data can provide powerful evidence of need in a community. While numbers provide evidence of the scope of a problem, qualitative data tell the story of the problem. In the food bank example, analysis might show that the number of people requesting food has doubled, while contributions have decreased by 20 percent. These numbers take on a human perspective by reporting this statement from Mrs. Smith: "My husband lost his job six months ago. Since then, I've been working as many extra hours as they can give me at the store, but food and gas just keep going up, and by the time we pay rent, we don't have much left. The food bank used to help us get by, but the last time I went there, they told me they had nothing left. I can tell you, it hurts to put your kids to bed hungry."

A number of decisions need to be made about the presentation of results. First, to whom will the results be reported? Whatever the answer to this question, it must include community members, as well as other persons who have the formal and informal power to respond to the identified need. Next, in what form will the results be presented? Priority should be placed on providing the information in a form that will be easily understood by the audience, such as using charts, graphs, and pictures (Rubin & Rubin, 2008). Finally, how will the report be presented in a way that suggests solutions? It is important to include discoveries about resources and strengths with which to address the problem.

Community Resources

Once needs have been identified in a community, practitioners look toward resources to meet them. Community resources may target needs at any of the four levels described in Chapter 1 and throughout this text.

Services aimed at meeting the needs of families who struggle with issues related to basic survival (Level I) include unemployment compensation, food stamps, TANF, homeless shelters, and Medicaid. Strengthening and empowering families (Level II) is the target of programs such as job training and placement, public housing assistance, after-school programs, and family preservation. Prevention of family dysfunction, strengthening resilience, and self-realization (Levels III and IV) are targeted by services such as psychotherapy, parent education, and youth mentorship programs.

There are several ways practitioners can attend to resource issues for families at any level of need. First, even when resources are available, families may require help to access them, due to the following potential barriers (Boyle, Hull, Mather, Smith, & Farley, 2006):

1. physical difficulties, such as lack of equal access for those with disabilities or lack of transportation
2. policies that restrict access for particular groups of people, such as legislation that prohibits undocumented persons from receiving public assistance
3. psychosocial issues, such as personal shame and public humiliation related to help seeking
4. cultural issues, such as unequal treatment of African Americans by physical and mental health facilities
5. informational deficits, the most common of which is being unaware of available resources

By providing brokering services, family practitioners can help their clients push past these barriers to locate and utilize available resources. A broker does not stop with educating a client about available resources, however, but also works to help actualize the connection. Kirst-Ashman and Hull (2009) have defined an effective broker as a professional who knows the resources in terms of what is available, what eligibility criteria must be met, what scope of services is provided, and what persons should be contacted. In addition, in the role of broker, the family practitioner must sometimes negotiate, mediate, and advocate on behalf of a family when referrals break down. For example, a family member may need assistance with transportation to get from a hospital that will soon discharge her to an interview for placement at a halfway house. In another case, a mother from a low-income family may need emotional support to go to a first appointment with a child's school counselor. Following referral, the family practitioner should always follow up to evaluate with the family whether their needs were met and to make adjustments accordingly (Kirst-Ashman & Hull, 2009).

Another way practitioners can assist with resources is through coordinating services. Families often need resources that are supplied by many separate agencies. Services are funded and delivered by a maze of agencies that includes federal and state governments, private nonprofits, and faith-based institutions, among others. Moreover, these agencies are rarely linked in ways that allow families to move seamlessly from survival to empowerment to self-realization goals.

For families to be served effectively, two types of coordination among the agencies are needed. One involves providers working together toward the common goal of serving a particular need in the community (Johnson & Yanca, 2008). For example, administrators of organizations that serve the elderly may form a council with the goal of helping all members of the community age in place.

A second type of coordination involves networking among agencies to help mend fragmentation of services among the four levels of need. This would involve establishing communitywide policies that link agencies through information systems and goal setting with clients. Ideally, each program would be designed to demonstrate families' achievement at one level, their readiness to go to the next level, and agencies' preparation to receive families from previous levels (Kilpatrick, Turner, & MacNair, 2006). Thus, a family with basic survival needs (Level I) would be able to see the possibility of moving past mere survival to working on the development of strengths and resiliency (Level IV).

Finally, the resources needed by families are not always available in the community. In this case, program development is required to develop specific programs that meet the needs going unfulfilled. For example, suppose a practitioner in an agency that serves families in a low-income neighborhood has noticed that many clients are struggling to provide care for elderly parents with varying degrees of cognitive deficits. In some cases, one adult in the family has had to stop working to care for the aging parent. A senior day care facility is needed to support these families. The worker begins to document the problem and talks about it with various members of the community, including church pastors. In time, a task group of community leaders forms with the goal of developing an adult day care program at a local church. The task group asks the practitioner to provide them with information about the problem. In addition, they ask the practitioner to describe a few programs that have been successful in other communities.

Community Development

To meet families' needs, it is sometimes necessary to bring about change in the organizations or communities in which family practitioners work. Within organizations, there may be policies, rules, procedures, regulations, and management practices that obstruct meeting families' needs. In such cases, practitioners should try to remove the barriers that prevent the organization from becoming more responsive to the needs of families (Johnson & Yanca, 2007).

For example, a practitioner working with immigrant families may discover that the organization's practices or policies prevent adequate service delivery due to inattention to cultural aspects of the families' lives. In such circumstances, practitioners could suggest various remedies to the decision makers within the organization, such as hiring diverse staff and conducting cultural sensitivity training for practitioners. In this example, practitioners' efforts to produce organizational change could also provide immigrant families with more effective, culturally competent services.

In addition to creating organizational change, family practitioners may be called on to help create changes within communities when societal policies and procedures are needed to support the well-being of families. The practice of changing communities has been interchangeably referred to as *community development, community organization, community practice, social planning,* and *advocacy.* In this chapter, the term *community development* will be used. Community development focuses on change within broad social systems, including political, legal, economic, educational, cultural, and social service delivery systems. The purpose of community development is to empower families that may be considered vulnerable or oppressed by challenging inequalities and promoting social justice.

Practitioners who work directly with families are best able to understand the need for and impact of community change on families. In addition, although practice that focuses directly on family functioning may be effective, it is often difficult to bring about substantive change until inequalities and injustices of the larger social structures or systems have been addressed. For these reasons, it is important for family practitioners to recognize the importance of community change and to participate in the process of community development.

Three approaches for community development have been described (Johnson & Yanca, 2007; Kirst-Ashman & Hull, 2009):

1. influencing the political process (social reform)
2. organizing oppressed peoples (social action)
3. representing families or a cause (advocacy)

These three approaches overlap and often are used together.

Social reform attempts to influence the political process through legislative action. Public social policy is an outcome of these efforts. To influence the political process, practitioners must have knowledge of local, state, and federal political processes, as well as information about the relevant issues and their effects on families. In addition, practitioners should acquire the skills necessary to utilize government publications, documents, and official statistical materials; to establish working relationships with key political figures; and to provide political leaders with facts and information regarding the impact of policies on families.

Social action attempts to influence existing power structures to enhance the social status of groups that are oppressed or targeted by discrimination. This is accomplished through organizing and involving people in actions that take aim at issues that negatively affect their lives. Social action has the potential of empowering members of vulnerable or oppressed groups. Empowered individuals feel confident that they are able to collectively bring about positive change and also learn that by helping others, they help themselves (Rubin & Rubin, 2008).

Finally, *advocacy* requires practitioners to speak and act on behalf of vulnerable groups of families who do not have adequate environmental and personal resources. In addition, advocacy is required on behalf of oppressed populations who are victimized by social stigma and exclusion (Freddolino, Moxley, & Hyduk, 2004). The purpose of advocacy is to represent the interests of such families and to help them obtain fundamental rights and entitlements. To be effective advocates, practitioners must understand families' needs and rights, the characteristics of the opposition, the process of appealing decisions that deny fulfillment of families' rights, and the availability of resources to support their cause.

To engage in any form of community development, the practitioner must be aware of the necessary steps and potential risks. The process of community development has been described as follows (Johnson & Yanca, 2007; Kirst-Ashman & Hull, 2009):

1. identification of problems
2. assessment of potential resources and resistance to change
3. formulation of the targeted goal
4. planning of actions
5. implementation of actions
6. evaluation

Any of these stages may be met with resistance for a number of reasons but primarily because it involves shifting power from those who hold more to those who hold less. Accordingly, practitioners should carefully assess the potential backlash and negative effects on the families or on the social system itself. In addition, the organizational context in which practitioners work may constrain the worker from action. For this reason, when considering community interventions, practitioners should take into account their role as an employee of an organization and the risk involved, such as potential job loss or strained working relationships.

As an example of community development, consider the case of Mrs. C, described earlier in this chapter. The practitioner at the community center in Mrs. C's neighborhood may become aware of a number of financial, cultural, and legal barriers that prevent battered immigrant women from seeking help. In this case, the practitioner would first need to conduct research to assess the scope and nature of the problem. The practitioner may then decide to address the problem by influencing the political system. He or she could provide information to legislators about ways that current policies restrict access to service or how supporting legislation would increase funding at community centers serving immigrants.

Another possibility is social action, in which the practitioner would help to organize and empower women in the community to take action against family violence, such as by holding educational workshops at their churches or writing articles for community newspapers. The practitioner could also attempt to speak on behalf of women like Mrs. C to raise awareness of the problem and to advocate for accessible support services for those immigrant women who are affected by family violence. Clearly, there are any number of ways to frame the goals of community intervention and a multitude of choices for action toward those goals.

Summary

Every family lives within the context of community. Their health depends on goodness-of-fit—that is, a balance between stressors and resources. The community can be a source of both stress and resources, thus playing a major role in the goodness-of-fit for families. To help families thrive, practitioners should not forget the importance of the community as part of their overall assessment and intervention.

Despite the importance of community-based interventions, family practitioners often find it difficult to engage in them, for a number of reasons. First, assessment and intervention at the community level require some roles and skills that are different from those typically used in family therapies (see Table 13.1). All of these roles and skills are considered part of generalist social work practice. However, quite often in education as well as in practice, micro and macro interventions are artificially separated from one another. Practitioners who are comfortable in micropractice are often unfamiliar or uncomfortable with assuming new roles and developing new skill sets.

In addition to the new roles and skills associated with macro-level work, there are several other obstacles that may block family practitioners at the community level. These include time constraints, lack of relevant supervision, and lack of agency support for community interventions. None of these obstacles is insurmountable, but to address them, support from administrators and funding sources will be necessary.

The purpose of this chapter has been to show the importance of overturning the obstacles in the way of community interventions on behalf of families. Future family practitioners should be encouraged to expand their perspective on family practice to include community involvement on behalf of their families.

TABLE 13.1   *Focus, Roles, and Skills Necessary for Community Interventions*

Focus	Required Role	Required Knowledge and Skills
Needs assessment	Evaluator	Data collection Data analysis Presentation of findings
	Group facilitator	Group dynamics Group interviewing
Connecting families to resources	Broker	Community resources Referral Problem solving
	Networker	Maintenance of relationships Linkage
Program development	Planner	Documenting Educating Initiating
Community development	Social reformer	Political processes Influencing decision makers
	Social activist	Empowerment/educating Bargaining Confronting Public speaking
	Advocate	Persuading Negotiating Mediating

Discussion Questions

1. Is it important for family practitioners to develop knowledge and skills with which to intervene in the community? Why or why not?

2. Why is it sometimes difficult for family practitioners to intervene in the community on behalf of their clients? What steps would need to be taken where you practice to get more involved in community practice?

3. What steps would you take if you wanted to conduct a needs assessment in Mrs. C's neighborhood?

4. What are the most important resource-related problems for Mrs. C? How would you begin to address them?

5. If an assessment of Mrs. C's community indicated a widespread problem with family violence among immigrant families, what community development goals and corresponding actions would you recommend?

Internet Resources

www.census.gov/main/www/cen2000.html
www.commbuild.org/index.html
www.comm-dev.org

Suggested Readings

Ezell, M. (2001). *Advocacy in the human services.* Pacific Grove, CA: Brooks/Cole.
 The author contends that the advocacy practice is an integral component of all human service practice. This book deals with general issues of advocacy, the ethics of advocacy, and essential strategies of practice in agency, legislative, legal, and community advocacy. It also discusses dilemmas and challenges of advocacy.

Hardcastle, D. A., Powers, P. R., & Wenocur, S. (2004). *Community practice: Theories and skills for social workers* (2nd ed.). New York: Oxford University Press.
 This book explains how to practice effectively in complex systems and diverse communities. It provides an integrated overview of the community practice theories and skills, introduces contemporary experiments, and analyzes classic modes of community practice and change.

Rubin, H. J., & Rubin, I. (2008). *Community organizing and development* (4th ed.). Boston: Pearson/Allyn & Bacon.
 This book examines the infrastructure of social change that enables it to be successfully accomplished. The book deals with empowering individuals, building community, establishing social change organizations, social mobilization, and community economic development.

Weil, M., & Reisch, M. (2005). *The handbook of community practice.* Thousand Oaks, CA: Sage Publications.
 This book encompasses community development, organizing, planning, and social change. It examines practice, theory, and research methods on community practice and introduces various intervention methods used in community practice.

References

Boyle, S. W., Hull, G. H., Mather, J. G., Smith, L. L., & Farley, O. W. (2006). *Direct practice in social work.* Boston: Allyn & Bacon.

Freddolino, P. P., Moxley, D. P., & Hyduk, C. A. (2004). A differential model of advocacy in social work practice. *Families in Society, 85*(1), 119–128.

Johnson, L. C., & Yanca, S. J. (2007). *Social work practice: A generalist approach* (9th ed.). Boston: Allyn & Bacon.

Kilpatrick, A. C., Turner, J. B., & MacNair, R. H. (2006). The family in community. In A. C. Kilpatrick & T. P. Holland (Eds.), *Working with families* (pp. 244–254). Boston: Allyn & Bacon.

Kirst-Ashman, K. K., & Hull, G. H. (2009). *Understanding generalist practice* (5th ed.). Belmont, CA: Brooks/Cole.

Rubin, H. J., & Rubin, I. S. (2008). *Community organizing and development* (4th ed.). Boston: Allyn & Bacon.

Sheafor, B. W., & Horejsi, C. R. (2006). *Techniques and guidelines for social work practice* (7th ed.). Boston: Allyn & Bacon.

Appendix

Ethics Cases and Commentaries

The ethics cases and commentaries in this appendix are taken from a publication by the National Association of Social Workers (NASW), *Current Controversies in Social Work Ethics: Case Examples* (1998). Each example first lists the primary relevant citation of a standard of the NASW *Code of Ethics* (1996). Other applicable standards are listed in numerical order and are not ranked.

Case 1

An undocumented Mexican woman lives in southern California with her husband and two school-age children. Her husband is frequently physically and verbally abusive to her. She cannot drive and has little facility with English. She is completely dependent on her husband for transportation and assistance with English. She loves her husband and wishes he would not abuse her but fears he may abuse the children if she is not at home. Because she feels she has few options, she rarely seeks medical help. A friend insisted she seek help from the local shelter for battered women, and when she went there, she met with a social worker, who is feeling caught between the shelter's philosophy of encouraging women to leave abusive homes and her client's desire to return home. The social worker understands that through occasional stays at the shelter, her client may become more self-determining and assertive and eventually find safe alternatives for herself and her children. The shelter's board of directors is considering a policy that women must leave abusive situations to receive ongoing services.

NASW Code of Ethics: 1.01; 1.02; 1.05; 1.15; 2.06a; 3.09b

Commentary

Surely, the social worker's understanding of cultural factors in this situation is essential to inform her work with and understand the behavior of this client. It is her responsibility to help the client identify and clarify her goals and perhaps develop their priority. The social worker may need to develop a long-range strategy that ensures some continuity of service, despite the interruptions. If the shelter can offer counseling services to clients who are not residing in the shelter, she could work with the client toward strengthening her resolve to change factors in her life and toward obtaining help for the husband.

The social worker should initiate a legitimate study of clients' real needs in the context of agency resources and guide the policy and program development of the agency accordingly. If there is not a resolution of the conflicting factors, the social worker should explore other community resources that could better serve the client on an ongoing basis.

Case 2

A child protective services worker must present recommendations to the court regarding placement for the 10- and 12-year-old daughters of a recently deceased lesbian mother. Since their separation five years ago, the mother's former lesbian partner has paid monthly child support and all medical and dental costs for the girls. She has also maintained positive relationships with the girls and their mother, visiting regularly and taking the children on vacations. She and the mother had an unwritten understanding that the former partner would become the guardian for the children should something happen to the mother. The biological father maintains only occasional contact with the girls and has arranged for a few visits to his mother and sisters. The father and mother were never married. The social worker favors placing the girls with their father because of her religious convictions in which homosexuality is considered immoral.

NASW Code of Ethics: 1.02; 1.01; 1.03c; 1.05b,c; 1.14; 4.02; 4.06a; 5.01b; 6.01

Commentary

Although the children are not of an age to make a final decision regarding with whom they will reside, their preferences still must be sought and weighed. Limitations in their self-determination should not relate to a social worker's preferences for heterosexual environments, a value she may hold as a private individual but that should be distinguished from her professional position. The girls have grown up with lesbian parental figures, and the social worker's competence should encompass an understanding of such.

Social justice issues are inherent in the development of a plan for these youngsters and an optimal environment for them. The social worker's recommendation to the judge is likely to be a significant factor in the outcome for the young clients.

Case 3

A first-year MSW student has a field placement at a city psychiatric hospital. Her first unsupervised intake interview is with the wife of a well-known physician, who has published many articles. During the intake, the student learns that the client has been treated over many years at various mental health facilities. Believing that all other possible forms of treatment have been exhausted without lasting success, the client's husband has recommended hospitalization, and the client has agreed. During the intake interview, the client reveals that her husband has been involved in romantic affairs with other women. The social work student completes the interview, makes a provisional diagnosis, and decides against recording specific assertions made by the woman.

NASW Code of Ethics: 1.07a; 2.05a,c; 3.04a,c

Commentary

This is the MSW student's first unsupervised intake interview, which may mean it is the first interview she has conducted alone. She has access to a field instructor, however, and the case should be discussed carefully with him or her. Is there anything to argue that because the client's information has not been verified and the information conveyed relates to a prominent person that extra care should be taken to protect the physician's privacy? The competence of the student to make a decision regarding what should be included in the record and to make a provisional diagnosis is questionable. The field instructor and the agency-based supervisor of the student bear ultimate responsibility for case decisions and should be involved in determining the significance of information.

The *Code of Ethics* states that social workers should not solicit private information from clients unless it is essential to the provision of service. Furthermore, information included in the record should be directly relevant to the care and treatment of the client. At the same time, social workers should keep accurate records and include sufficient information to facilitate delivery of services and ensure continuity of services. Is the wife's perception of her husband's behavior based on fact? Is her perception significant to her condition?

The student should discuss the case carefully with the field instructor and consult with the agency supervisor to determine the recording procedure that is required and the usual information that is recorded. Every effort should be made to protect the rights of the client, the privacy of her husband, and the policies of the hospital.

Case 4

A clinical social worker meets weekly for therapy with a 15-year-old female client. During a session, the client reports that she is dealing drugs and has begun seeing a boyfriend who just completed a six-month jail sentence for selling drugs. The client's parents have forbidden contact between their daughter and her boyfriend and have asked the social worker to inform them if their daughter reported that she is seeing the boy again. The social worker believes that her client trusted her not to pass on this information to anyone else and that disclosure might permanently impair the trust in their relationship. However, the social worker told her client when they first began their sessions that she could not promise to keep confidential any statements that indicate a threat to harm self or others. The social worker is concerned for her client's safety with the boyfriend but also is far more concerned about her illegal involvement in the sale of drugs and the dangers she may face from the drug trade.

NASW Code of Ethics: 1.07a,c,d; 1.01; 1.02; 1.03a

Commentary

The social worker must struggle among obligations to her primary client, a minor; to her parents, who are inevitably part of the client system; and to society, whose laws are intended to protect. She can seek to work with the client toward the goal of achieving consent to bring the parents into active work as a family unit. The social worker would endeavor to support the client and work toward accomplishing consent to reveal the relationship but with the goal of establishing a growing alliance with her parents. Or she can weigh the dangers to the client of the renewed relationship with her boyfriend plus the betrayal of the collateral clients' (the parents) expectations for the protection of their daughter and decide that revealing the information to them constitutes a compelling exception to confidentiality. If she decides on the latter course of action, the primary client (the daughter) must be informed in advance of the disclosure.

Case 5

Social workers regularly discuss client progress and receive supervision at a community mental health center's weekly case review. In the case review, a social worker reports that her client has recently discovered that he is HIV positive, and she requests help in considering changes in his treatment plan in light of this information. Another social worker, who is treating the wife of the recently diagnosed HIV positive client, learns of her client's husband's HIV status because she attends the same case review. She knows that the couple is having unprotected sex and that the wife is unaware of her husband's HIV status.

NASW Code of Ethics: 1.07c,d,q; 2.05a

Commentary

The value of confidentiality is frequently challenged in providing services to clients. Although social workers should protect the confidentiality of a client, there are limitations, and the possibility of an exception should be addressed with the male client. The social workers participating in the case review are obligated to keep confidential all cases discussed, yet there may exist sufficient compelling reason to breach a client's confidence. The exception that requires a disclosure to prevent serious, foreseeable, and imminent harm to the client's wife must be considered as a basis of the social worker's decision making. The client's wife is at high risk of becoming HIV positive, thus providing a compelling reason to breach confidentiality. In working with the husband, the social worker needs to provide information, incentive, and details about her obligation to breach his confidentiality if the client takes no steps to inform and protect his wife.

Case 6

A social worker who specializes in marriage and family counseling sometimes works with couples who decide to divorce. In one such case, the social worker receives a subpoena to provide testimony regarding his sessions with the divorcing couple. The husband's lawyer has recommended that the social worker be asked to give a deposition, and the wife and her attorney have agreed; both have provided signed consents for release of information. In his sessions with the husband, the social worker learned that the husband had had an affair that his attorney is unaware of. Although the social worker does not believe it is in the husband's interest that he testify, he considers that he is being ordered "by a court of law or other legally authorized body" to disclose "confidential or privileged information."

NASW Code of Ethics: 1.07d,e,f,g,j; 1.06d

Commentary

It is not unusual for social workers to be subpoenaed to testify about their contact with clients. As in this case, social workers may be subpoenaed in conjunction with divorce proceedings. As a general rule, social workers should not disclose confidential information without their clients' consent or unless they have been ordered to do so by a court of law. If a court of law or other legally authorized body orders social workers to disclose confidential or privileged information without a client's consent and such disclosure could cause harm to the client, social workers should request that the court withdraw or limit the order.

In this particular case, the social worker should have discussed with the husband the possibility that his or her knowledge of the husband's affair, if disclosed during the deposition, could be harmful to the husband's legal interests. The social worker should have given the husband an opportunity to consider this possible consequence when he or she obtained the husband's informed consent for the social worker to testify. The requirement to inform clients of the limitations of confidentiality applies whether social workers disclose confidential information on the basis of a legal requirement or with client consent. In addition, social workers who provide services to two or more people who have a relationship with each other, such as couples, should clarify with all parties which individuals will be considered clients and the possibility of conflicts of interest among them.

Case 7

A social worker employed in a well-respected sectarian mental health agency met with his supervisor to discuss treatment of an HIV-positive adolescent client's disclosure that he has anonymous sex with men. The following week the social worker's supervisor, espousing agency policy—whether formal or informal—advised him that his client's case must be closed because he poses a safety risk to the other adolescents in the program and because the agency's reputation could be tarnished for serving gay boys with AIDS.

NASW Code of Ethics: 1.16b; 3.07d; 3.09c,d; 4.02; 6.04b

Commentary

The central conflict is the client's right to treatment regardless of sexual orientation and the social worker's obligation to the agency. A sectarian agency has a legal right to develop policies according to its religious beliefs. However, the social worker has a professional obligation not to discriminate against a client based on sexual orientation. In terms of the mission of a mental health agency that employs social workers and other mental health professionals, how the agency could morally justify discrimination by refusing services to this client should be questioned. The manner in which it is doing so amounts to a requirement that the social worker abandon the client.

This has both ethical and legal implications. The sectarian organization, by the nature of its mission grounded both in social work values and religious values, should be helped to recognize its moral responsibility to this client. The Code of Ethics requires that social workers, as a part of their commitment to employers, inform them of their ethical obligation as prescribed by the Code. Moreover, the social worker has the responsibility to help administrators create a work environment that helps their employees carry out their ethical responsibilities.

In situations such as these, the social worker may have to consider whether he or she can continue employment with an agency where there is a conflict between one's professional values and an agency's prerogatives. Religious agencies should make their policies based on religious values and how these are expected to be carried out in practice clear at the time of contracting with an employee. All of the relevant facts are needed to determine one's ethical action; the situation suggests the need for consultation.

References

National Association of Social Workers (NASW). (1996). *Code of ethics.* Washington, DC: Author.
National Association of Social Workers (NASW). (1998). *Current controversies in social work ethics: Case examples.* Washington, DC: Author.

Glossary

accommodation The process of adjustment of family members to each other to coordinate their functioning, or a therapeutic tactic used by practitioners, especially in structural family interventions, to adapt to the family style in order to create a therapeutic alliance.

alignment Who is with or against the other in the transaction generating the problem.

amplification Used by a solution-focused therapist when a client mentions positive changes. The therapist asks numerous questions to help the client expound on these changes.

attachment theory Concepts about the stages that children go through in developing social relationships and the influence of this development on relationships in later life.

behavior rehearsal A technique used in social learning family interventions in which the practitioner suggests desired behavior and then encourages the person or family to behave similarly through demonstrations, role-plays, or descriptions.

boundary What defines who is in or out of a family relationship vis-à-vis the focal issue, as well as what their roles are in this interaction.

brief family therapy Short-term interventions that are usually goal oriented, active, and focused. They emphasize resolving the presenting problem rather than seeing it as a symptom of underlying dysfunction.

brokerage A function of case managers to identify, locate, and obtain needed community resources for individuals and families.

case management A procedure for planning, securing, and monitoring services on behalf of a person or family from a variety of relevant agencies and resources.

circular causality The recursive nature of interactions of the family and other systems where the behavior of one component affects the behavior of all others.

circular question Used by a solution-focused therapist to assist family members in understanding the motivation for their behaviors—namely, "What do you think she thinks?"

coaching In Bowen's family theory, the practitioner's role is to be both a role model for individual family members in the differentiation of self-process and a facilitator or coach as they explore their families of origin.

cognitive restructuring Procedures that attempt to modify or restructure disruptive or maladaptive thought patterns that may result in maladaptive behaviors by changing feelings and actions.

collusion An integral part of projective identification in object relations theory, where the recipient of the split-off part of the partner does not disown the projection but acts on the conscious or unconscious message.

confidentiality A principle of ethics where the family practitioner or other professional may not disclose any information about the individual or family without that person's or family's consent. This includes identity, content of verbalizations, or opinions.

consulting break A break taken by a solution-focused therapist to consult with or without a team regarding recommendations to make to a client following a session.

coping question Used by a solution-focused therapist to switch the client from problem-talk to solution-talk—namely, "Given all of these problems, how do you cope?"

cultural pluralism The coexistence and mutual respect for differences and strengths of cultures and groups other than one's own.

customer The person in solution-focused therapy who is the most motivated to effect change.

detriangulate In Bowen's family theory, this intervention consists of pointing out the triangulation process in order to withdraw a person from the buffer or go-between role, usually with parents so as not to be drawn into alliances with one against the other. This is often more helpful than dealing with the presenting issues.

developmental transitions The movement of persons or families from one life stage to another. This is a time of greater stresses, problems, and conflicts, as tasks from the previous stage are consolidated and progress toward the tasks of the next stage is begun.

differentiation In family systems theory, this is the psychological separation of intellect and emotion in the differentiation of self and also the ability of family members to separate their identities, emotions, and thoughts from those of other family members in terms of autonomy and independence. This is the opposite of fusion or enmeshment.

eclecticism The use of many theories together or in sequence or selected parts of them used in combination. Caution is urged in the selection of theories to use together.

ecological systems perspective A metatheory that shows the systemic relatedness of family variables and the environment and allows for multiple intervention methods and practitioner roles.

ecology A science that studies the relationships that exist between organisms and their environment. In human ecology, it relates to how humans adapt or achieve goodness of fit with the environment.

ecomap A diagram used to show reciprocal influences between a family and their environment. It would include extended family members, relevant social institutions, and environmental influences.

ecosystem A concept pertaining to the physical, biological, and social environments of family members and the interaction between every relevant component contained therein.

effectiveness Producing a definite or desired result. Research into the effectiveness of different theories can help determine their validity; however, because many theories are not prescriptions for actions but are about ideas and interpretations, the research findings do not give all the answers about usefulness.

empowerment The process of helping a person or family increase their influence and strength over their own lives and circumstances.

enactment Where a family lives out its focal struggle in a therapy session that approximates its experience at home.

encopresis The inability to control one's bowel functions; an elimination disorder.

enmeshment In structural family theory, this is where boundaries are blurred between family members, so that there is little autonomy or independent functioning.

environment The conditions, circumstances, and influences of ecological or situational forces that affect the development and behavior of individuals or groups in a particular setting.

equifinality The premise that the same result may be reached from different beginning points.

Eriksonian theory Erik Erikson's conceptualization of human psychosocial development through eight stages of life. Each stage has a task to be accomplished before the next stage can be reached. There are conflicts or danger at each stage that could interfere with development.

ethnic competence The ability to behave in a manner that is congruent with expectations of various ethnic groups, thus demonstrating respect for the family's cultural integrity.

ethnocentrism The belief that one's own culture or ethnic group is superior to others.

ethnographic interviewing Learning about specific cultures or groups by going into their natural settings, as is done when family preservation workers go into a family's home and community to provide services.

exceptions to the rule   Instances where a problem behavior did not exist or was successfully overcome; used in solution-focused therapy.

exosystem   This system represents the social structures, both formal and informal, that influence, limit, or constrain what happens there. Exosystem practice focuses on community-level factors that have an impact on the way people function.

externalizing problems   A technique in the narrative approach of getting families to view problems as external to them, thus motivating them to strengthen exceptions to the problems and control them.

family preservation   Intensive services based on family strengths that are provided to families whose children are at imminent risk of out-of-home placement.

family structure   The pattern of organization underlying family interactions.

fictive kin   Friends and neighbors who often share child care tasks, give advice about child care, and give emotional support, or may contribute financially.

first-order change   In systems theory, this is a temporary and superficial change in the family system and the way it functions that leaves the basic structure and functioning of the system unchanged.

formula tasks   Very general tasks that are scripted by the solution-focused therapist for use with any client regardless of the presenting problem.

fusion   Occurs when blurred intellectual and emotional functioning within an individual parallels the degree to which that person loses autonomy and differentiation with other family members.

generic   Relating to more basic universal characteristics or patterns like those commonly found in all families, such as boundaries and authority.

genogram   A graphic presentation of a multigenerational relationship system where recurring behavior patterns within the family system can be traced.

grounded theory   A concept from qualitative research methods that refers to developing a theory inductively through identifying common themes across a number of qualitative case studies or the results of such efforts (as contrasted with more deductive reasoning from grand theory to explanations for more specific circumstances).

habitat   The place where a person or family lives, including the physical and social setting within cultural contexts.

hedging words   Words used by a solution-focused therapist to suggest to a client movement or change in a positive direction (e.g., *might, seems, could*).

holistic   An individual or family is seen as more than the sum of all its parts, and problems are more than specific symptoms. Physical, social, psychological, spiritual, and cultural influences are integrated.

homeostasis   A dynamic balance or equilibrium in a family or other system where one or more variables are very stable.

hypnotic situations   Nontrance-induced situations developed by the solution-focused therapist that result in the client becoming more susceptible to a therapeutic suggestion.

idiographic research   The study of an individual, couple, or family where baselines are established and repeated measures are used to determine results of interventions. The results may be replicated with other individuals, couples, or groups.

idiosyncratic   Characteristics that are unique to a particular family with their own expectations, meanings, interactions, and behaviors that would not be representative of other families.

indigenous workers   Members of a community who work with helping professionals in providing services such as those used in family preservation.

introjection   In object relations theory, a primitive form of identification involving a process where an individual takes in the characteristics of other people, which then become part of the individual's own self-image.

joining A process whereby the practitioner enters the family system and relates to all members individually and to subsystems, thus developing a therapeutic alliance so that treatment goals may be reached.

levels of need Used specifically in this book to refer to families' specific needs, where lower-level needs must be met before higher-level needs are addressed.

life stage theory The idea that every period of life, including that of an individual, couple, or family, has certain goals and dangers inherent in it that serve to modify behavior and order priorities. Each higher stage builds on the accomplishments of the previous stage or may be hampered by unfinished tasks.

macrosystem The larger system that includes the overall broader context and culture. Macrosystem practice works toward improvements in the general society through such means as political action and community organization.

maintenance An accommodation technique that is supportive of a family's structure as it is. The practitioner may relate to other family members through this structure, as, for example, a parent as the central figure.

Mental Research Institute (MRI) The original developer of so-called brief therapy, this institute is in Palo Alto, California, and the model is based on the work of Gregory Bateson. MRI involves a cybernetic systems approach to working with families that focuses on observable behavioral interactions and the interventions that alter the system.

mesosystem The system that incorporates the interactions of individuals, families, and groups within the person's microsystem. Mesosystem practice focuses on interpersonal relationships within these systems.

metaphor A figure of speech containing an implied comparison, where a word or phrase ordinarily used for one thing is applied to another to express feelings, imagination, or objective reality.

metatheory A comprehensive system of thought that covers a wide area of practice and that would accept the inclusion of other perspectives and methods.

microsystem This system represents the individual in family and group settings that incorporate the day-to-day environment. Microsystem practice focuses on interventions on a case-by-case basis to deal with the problems faced by individuals and families.

mimesis A therapeutic tactic used especially by structural family practitioners as an accommodation technique, where the practitioner imitates or mirrors a family's style and communication and behavioral patterns in order to gain acceptance and accomplish goals.

miracle question A future reality co-constructed between the solution-focused therapist and client, in which the present problems do not exist—namely, "If a miracle happened and your problems no longer existed, what would you be doing differently?"

modeling Used in social learning theory to encourage the imitation and acquisition of behaviors observed in others that have led to more desirable outcomes.

multiculturalism Understanding, appreciating, and valuing cultures other than one's own with their own uniquenesses and strengths.

narrative A story created by a person or family where objective and subjective experiences are selectively arranged and serve to organize and give meaning to the person or family.

niche The particular role or status of an individual or family in its community and environment resulting from accommodation to this environment.

normalizing A therapeutic technique that depathologizes problems in a way that changes perceptions of the situation, gives relief to the family, and deemphasizes the problem.

object relations theory An interactional systems theory that views the basic human motivation as the search for satisfying interpersonal relationships. It is based on early parent–child interpersonal relationships, which the child internalizes and which become the model for later interpersonal relations in the family of origin, mate selection, family of procreation, and other intimate relationships.

oppression   When a group, institution, or government places severe restrictions on or withholds power from other groups or institutions.

power   The relative or comparative influence of the participants on one another in the interactions that create the problem.

Premack principle   A social learning principle that requires the completion of a desired activity or low-probability behavior before doing a preferred activity or high-probability behavior; also known as "Grandma's law."

prescription   Recommendation made to a family by a solution-focused therapist following a consulting break with or without a team. It generally consists of compliments, reframes, and a task.

presuppositional questioning   In solution-focused interventions, a family is led to believe that a solution will be achieved by implying the occurrence of a specific event or selecting a specific verb tense—for example, saying "What good things happened since last session?" instead of "Did anything good happen since last session?"

projective identification   An unconscious defense mechanism and interactional style of families where unwanted aspects of the self are attributed to another person, thus inducing that person to act according to these projected feelings and attitudes in an act of collusion.

relabeling   A therapeutic intervention that involves reframing a problem in more positive terms so that it is perceived differently and so that the person or family can respond to it differently and in a healthier way.

resilience   The ability to withstand and rebound from crises and adversities.

restructuring   The process of producing change in a family system through changing its structure—for example, strengthening the boundaries around the spousal subsystem.

scaling question   Used by the solution-focused therapist to gauge the severity of a problem—namely, "On a scale from 1 to 10, with 1 being terrible and 10 being good, how would you rate your problem?"

second-order change   In systems theory, this is a basic and lasting change in the structure and functioning of a family.

self-help organizations   These are formally structured groups, such as Parents Without Partners and Alcoholics Anonymous, that provide mutual assistance for group participants who have a common problem with which some of the members have coped successfully.

service networks   The linking of formal or informal persons, agencies, or organizations on behalf of a person or family to make the services available, accessible, and need satisfying.

shaping   A procedure used especially in behavioral therapy where an area of competence or desired behavior is acknowledged and reinforced.

social constructionism   A metatheory where behaviors and relationships are seen in terms of organized efforts to create meaning out of personal experiences. Reality is seen as constructed by the person or family, family functioning is based on shared meanings, and the family practitioner becomes a coauthor of a living story with them.

social learning theory   This theory focuses on reciprocal relationships and uses principles from social and developmental psychology and learning theory for understanding and treating behavior.

solution-focused intervention   A style of intervention that emphasizes solutions or exceptions that families have already developed for their problems rather than the problems themselves.

spiritual genogram   A multigenerational map of family members' religious and spiritual affiliations, events, and conflicts that enables families to make sense of their religious/spiritual heritage and to explore ways their experiences impact present couple or family issues.

spirituality   The dimension of life that contains the meaning people give to their lives, their standards of morality, and their definition of the social context within which they practice their beliefs.

splitting In object relations theory, a primitive defense process where a person separates the good from the bad in an external object and then internalizes this split perception. These splits can then be projected upon other people.

strategic family interventions A therapeutic approach where the practitioner designs interventions to resolve specific problems that will, at the same time, require the family system to modify other interactions. The focus is on second-order change and breaking the recursive sequence that seems to be maintaining the problem.

structural family therapy A model of therapy that works through immediate experience to solve present-day key issues by altering the underlying structure of people's relationships.

symbiosis An intense emotional attachment where the boundaries between individuals become indistinct and they react as one as in an undifferentiated ego mass.

Tarasoff decision A 1976 ruling by the Supreme Court of California in the case of *Tarasoff* v. *Regents of the University of California,* stating that, under certain circumstances, psychotherapists whose clients tell them that they intend to harm someone are obliged to warn the intended victim.

therapeutic alliance The capacity of the practitioner and family systems to mutually invest in and work together toward their goals.

therapeutic contract The agreement that the family and the practitioner have worked out together concerning what the problem is and how they will work on it. Goals, methods, mutual obligations, and timetables may be a part of the formal or informal agreement.

triangle In family systems theory, this is a three-person system that results when a dyad under stress pulls in a third person to dilute the stress and maintain the system. The triangle is considered to be the smallest stable emotional system.

triangulation In family systems theory, it can refer to any triangle where the conflict of two persons pulls in a third person and immobilizes this third person in a loyalty conflict. Most commonly it involves two parents and a child.

underorganization Family structures that have not achieved the constancy, differentiation, and flexibility they need to meet the demands of family functioning.

yes-set A hypnotic situation developed by the solution-focused therapist, in which the therapist manages to elicit affirmative responses from the client generally during the delivery of the prescription. This yes-set is meant to make the client more susceptible to a therapeutic suggestion.

Name Index

Note: A page number followed by an *f* indicates a figure; one followed by a *t* indicates a table.

Subject Index

AAMFT. *See* American Association for Marriage and Family Therapy
Abuse, in families, 51, 215
Adaptations, and ecological perspective, 17, 19
Advocacy, by case managers/practitioners, 103, 105, 107–108, 255, 256. *See also* Case management
African Americans
  child care among, 85
  fathers' involvement among, 97
  single parenthood among, 44
Alcohol use. *See* Substance abuse
Alignment, as structural dimension of family, 118
American Association for Marriage and Family Therapy (AAMFT), 51, 52, 58
American Indians, and narrative family interventions, 215
American Psychiatric Association (APA), 202
Amplification, in solution-focused family interventions, 153–154
Anorexia nervosa, 118, 203
Anxiety, and family systems theory, 173–174, 182–183
APA. *See* American Psychiatric Association
Assessment
  in case management approach, 97–99, 106
  of children, 79

of community problems, 252–253
in family systems interventions, 171–177
of Level I families, 78–84, 97–99
of Level II families, 118–120, 132–134
of Level III families, 149–150, 171–177
of Level IV families, 204–205, 227–231
in narrative family interventions, 204–205
of neglectful families, 78–84
in object relations family interventions, 227–231, 237, 238*t*
of parents, 79–81
in social learning family interventions, 132–134
in solution-focused family interventions, 149–150
sources of information for, 78–79
spiritually sensitive practice and, 61–63 (62*t*)
in structural family interventions, 118–120
Audiotapes, in narrative family interventions, 213

Baylor University Religion Survey, 59
Beavers Family Competence Scale, 5, 8

Behavioral/interactional choice for inventions, 10
Boundaries, as structural dimension of family, 118
Brokerage, by case managers/practitioners, 103, 254. *See also* Case management

Case management, 96–109
  application of, 104–105
  assessment in, 97–99, 106
  case study about, 98–99
  definition of, 96
  demand for, 109
  ecosystems perspective and, 104
  ethical challenges in, 109
  evaluation in, 108
  family development and, 97
  goals of, 96, 99–100, 108
  interventions in, 105–108
  key features of, 100–103 (102*t*), 104
  with Levels III and IV families, 109
  models of, 100
  plan for, 106–107
  roles of case worker, 105–106
  social systems and, 100, 101*f*
  timeframe for, 108
Case management team, 100. *See also* Case management
Case plans, 106–107
Case studies
  case management approach, 98–99

Note: A page number followed by an *f* indicates a figure; one followed by a *t* indicates a table.